Frommer's

SECOND EDITION

NYC
Free &
dirt cheap

by Ethan Wolff

BICENTENNIAL
1807
WILEY
2007
BICENTENNIAL

Wiley Publishing, Inc.

ISBN-13: 978-0-470-03720-1
ISBN-10: 0-470-03720-2

Editor: Cate Latting
Production Editor: Ian Skinnari
Cartographer: Guy Ruggerio
Production by Wiley Indianapolis Composition Services
Interior design by Melissa Auciello-Brogan
Anniversary Logo Design: Richard Pacifico
Photos on p. 4, p. 16, p. 144, p. 186, p. 226, p. 284, and p. 320 by John Vorwald
Photos on p. xii and p. 106 by Ethan Wolff

CONTENTS

5 Shopping — 187

6 Exploring New York — 227

LIST OF MAPS

About the Author

Ethan Wolff is a native New Yorker (born and raised in Virginia, but that was a geographic anomaly). He lives in the heart of the Bargain District, on the Lower East Side. His other books include *Frommer's Irreverent Guide to Manhattan* and *Frommer's Memorable Walks in New York*.

Acknowledgments

Thanks to John Vorwald, who came up with the idea for this book and shepherded it through development; to Cate Latting for her stellar editing; and to Evelyn Grollman and Anna Sandler for all their hard work. Thanks also to Elroy Wolff and Jenny Bauer, and to anyone who has had to put up with my cheapness over the years. It was all just research.

—Ethan Wolff

An Invitation to the Reader

In researching this book, we discovered many wonderful places—hotels, restaurants, shops, and more. We're sure you'll find others. Please tell us about them, so we can share the information with your fellow travelers in upcoming editions. If you were disappointed with a recommendation, we'd love to know that, too. Please write to:

Frommer's NYC Free & Dirt Cheap, 2nd Edition
Wiley Publishing, Inc. • 111 River St. • Hoboken, NJ 07030-5774

An Additional Note

Please be advised that travel information is subject to change at any time— and this is especially true of prices. We therefore suggest that you write or call ahead for confirmation when making your travel plans. The authors, editors, and publisher cannot be held responsible for the experiences of readers while traveling. Your safety is important to us, however, so we encourage you to stay alert and be aware of your surroundings. Keep a close eye on cameras, purses, and wallets, all favorite targets of thieves and pickpockets.

Other Great Guides for Your Trip:

Frommer's New York City

Frommer's Portable New York City

Frommer's Memorable Walks in New York City

Frommer's Irreverent Guide to Manhattan

Pauline Frommer's New York City

The Unofficial Guide to Manhattan

Frommer's Great Escapes from NYC without Wheels

Frommer's New York City Day by Day

Free & Dirt Cheap Icons & Abbreviations

We also use **four feature icons** that point you to the great deals, in-the-know advice, and unique experiences that separate urban adventurers from tourists. Throughout the book, look for:

FREE Events, attractions, or experiences that cost no more than your time and a swipe of your Metrocard.

FINE PRINT The unspoken conditions or necessary preparations to experience certain free and dirt cheap events.

 The best free and dirt cheap events, dining, shopping, living, and exploring in the city.

Special events worth marking in your calendar.

Frommers.com

Now that you have the guidebook to a great trip, visit our website at **www.frommers.com** for travel information on more than 3,000 destinations. With features updated regularly, we give you instant access to the most current trip-planning information available. At Frommers.com, you'll also find the best prices on airfares, accommodations, and car rentals—and you can even book travel online through our travel booking partners. At Frommers.com, you'll also find the following:

- Online updates to our most popular guidebooks
- Vacation sweepstakes and contest giveaways
- Newsletter highlighting the hottest travel trends
- Online travel message boards with featured travel discussions

Priceless views of the Manhattan skyline and New York Harbor are yours for the taking, courtesy of the Governors Island ferry. See p. 254 for more information.

THE BEST THINGS IN LIFE ARE FREE

t's no secret that NYC costs are out of control. Even so, the last year has witnessed enough pricing chutzpah to make a Park Avenue plutocrat wince. Interested in renting a four-bedroom condo off Columbus Circle? There was one just on the market for $50,000. Per month. And that's almost reasonable when compared to the $10,000 martini. The Algonquin Hotel serves up a version with vermouth. And a diamond. If you stop by the bar, order carefully. Drink carefully, too. That's a novelty item, of course, but on a regular night at the World Bar you can find yourself out $50 for a tipple. The World Cocktail comes with a mix of Remy XO, Veuve Clicquot, and

23-carat liquid gold. Still got too much money on your hands? NYC will also sell you a $255 white T-shirt (courtesy of Marc Jacobs), a $41 hamburger and a $19 hot dog (thank the Old Homestead restaurant), and a $1,000 lobster and caviar omelet (Norma's at the Parker Meridian will hook you up).

Publicity-stunt extremes aside, prices are up all across the city. The subway went to $2 and, following the established economic model, most pizza slices followed. The bagel jumped 30%, on top of the extra 26% we were already paying for our semi-monthly cab rides. Apartment prices have hit yet another all-time high. One-point-three million is the latest figure. And that's the average. So, in a town with $41 hamburgers and $1,000 plates of eggs, where an apartment that would make a convict feel claustrophobic costs well over a million, a book on living on the cheap must be a pretty slim volume, right?

Wrong.

New York takes a lot of pride in being the cultural capital of the world, and to maintain that reputation we let a lot of the goods go for free. Art, music, dance, drama, and history can all be found for simply the price of showing up. Many of our top-tier museums set aside several hours a week where you pay what you wish to enter. The best work of the world's emerging artists hangs in our galleries, which never charge a fee. TV shows tape all over Midtown and with a little planning you can join the audience for free. New York's libraries circulate thousands of books, videos, and albums, in addition to offering us free films, classes, and lectures.

Attending a big free New York event also entitles you to complementary camaraderie. There's no better feeling than knowing you're in on something amazing, like a band playing its heart out in front of the sunset on the Hudson, or a night spent soaking up the group spirit at a Bryant Park film, or wending your way through Central Park with fellow theatergoers after a world-class Shakespearean production. Our legendary festivals and parades kindle that same energy. Even little everyday moments can be inspiring. How many years has it been since Hollywood made a movie half as entertaining as a couple of hours sitting on the steps of the New York Public Library, or Federal Hall, or the Met?

These experiences are literally priceless. They're gifts bestowed by the city, enough to make parsimony feel like one of humanity's crowning virtues. Whether you've checked this book out of the library or picked it up from the bargain bin, you should revel in your cheapness. What's better than beating the system?

In the post-9/11 era we all appreciate the city in new ways, but it's easy enough to forget that New York is not an inevitability. It's a rare phenomenon. Taking advantage of all the amazing resources here is practically a civic duty. You don't have to be a millionaire to get the most out of the Big Apple. When you walk across the Brooklyn Bridge on a sunny afternoon, or park yourself by the waters of the Temple of Dendur, or cruise through New York Harbor, you own them as much as anyone else does. The city's great charm is that it's available to anybody, at any time. This book will show you the hundreds of ways to get the most for the least in New York City.

After all, the best things in life are free.

Not NYC's most famous freebie, but with a jaw-dropping view and great flicks, the *Brooklyn Bridge Movies With a View Film Series* is one of the city's treasures. See p. 12.

BEST OF THE FREE & DIRT CHEAP APPLE

A lot of great bargains in this world don't withstand close scrutiny. Anyone who's ever "won" a free weekend at a North Carolina timeshare can attest to that. New Yorkers are lucky, however, in having a menu of freebies and cheapies that aren't just discards or traps. From Shakespeare in the Park to car-less drive-in movies to kayaking along the Hudson, there's a host of remarkable activities here that can't be had in other cities for any price. In the dirt cheap realm, the Big Apple's big volume creates bargain opportunities left and right. From cheap ethnic food to cheap avant-garde theater, an urban adventurer can go far on very little. What follows is the best of the best.

1 Best Entertainment Bets

● **Best Manhattan Parade:** New Yorkers are pros at assembling en masse. My favorite pageant is one of the city's most inclusive, the **Greenwich Village Halloween Parade,** at which elaborate costumes and a healthy dose of gallows humor make the festive spirit infectious. See p. 25.

● **Best Outer-Borough Parade:** As New York events become more and more commercialized, it's nice to have one occasion that's defiantly do-it-yourself. Coney Island's **Mermaid Parade** brings low-budget finery to the Atlantic shore. Classic cars serve as the chariots for a procession of mermaids and Neptunes who will never be accused of being overdressed. See p. 22.

● **Best Festival: Harlem Week** began as a single day 30 years ago and now stretches across the entire month of August. Film, jazz, and food festivals are among the highlights to be found along lovely brownstone blocks Uptown. See p. 23.

● **Best DIY Rock Show:** Why trek out to the Nassau Coliseum to watch some aging monsters of rock, when the Lower East Side offers up the same three chords

for free? **Arlene's Grocery** (95 Stanton St.; ✆ **212/358-1633**) is the tri-state's best place to play rock star, with a real-live rock band standing in for soulless laser discs. See p. 29.

● **Best Cultural Center with Beer: Pete's Candy Store** (709 Lorimer St.; (✆ **718/302-3770**) does its part to keep Williamsburg elevated and enlightened, bringing in a bushel of live music and readings. Backgammon, quiz, spelling, and Scrabble nights round out a full schedule of free diversions. See p. 31.

● **Best New-York-Studio-Sized Music Venue:** The stage is tiny and the seats are few, but the back room of **The Lakeside Lounge** (162 Ave. B; ✆ **212/ 529-8463**) brings in improbably big acts. Rock and rock tributaries can be found on most nights and there's never a cover. See p. 30.

● **Best Jazzy Venue:** Upper West Siders can enjoy cover-free jazz on the weeknights at **Smoke** (2751 Broadway; ✆ **212/864-6662**). Retro and nouveau bebop, Hammond B-3 organs, and even a little funk fill out the diverse schedule. Drink minimums apply, but they're not too onerous, especially midweek. See p. 33.

- **Best Concerts for Skipping Out on the Office:** The worker bees of the Financial District have long taken advantage of the great classical performances heard during the **"Concerts at One"** series at **Trinity Church** (74 Trinity Place; ✆ **212/602-0747**) and **St. Paul's Chapel** (Broadway and Fulton St.). St. Paul's hosts lunchtime Mondays, and Trinity handles Thursdays. The acoustics are great in both churches and the $2 suggested donation doesn't begin to reflect the caliber of talent. See p. 37.

- **Best Summer Music Festival:** Every year **SummerStage** (Central Park; ✆ **212/360-2777**) seems to get even better organized, efficiently channeling music fans into a stage area just off the Rumsey Playfield in the middle of Central Park. Though several shows a year are benefit performances with steep ticket prices, the calendar is still littered with huge names playing for free. See p. 46.

- **Best Summer Music Festival That's Not SummerStage:** The massive **Lincoln Center Out of Doors** (70 Lincoln Center Plaza; ✆ **212/546-2656**) festival presents hundreds of acts every August. The range is staggering, covering jazz and dance and opera and everything in between. See p. 43.

- **Best Movie Screenings with a Roof:** Every Sunday night guest curators put together intriguing mini–film festivals for **Ocularis at Galapagos** (70 N. 6th St., Williamsburg, Brooklyn; ✆ **718/388-8713**). The films are usually shorts and a long way away from anything you'll find in a multiplex. See p. 50.

- **Best Movie Screenings without a Roof:** Forty-second Street welcomes movie fans with an eclectic selection of classics during the **HBO/Bryant Park Summer Film Festival** (✆ **212/512-5700**). The lawn crowds up quickly, but that only enhances the festive atmosphere. See p. 53.

- **Best Movie Date Night: Friday nights the **Rubin Museum of Art** (150 W. 17th St.; ✆ **212/620-5000**) throws open its doors. You can tour intriguing Himalayan art for free, and for $7 you can treat yourself to a drink and a movie. The **Cabaret Cinema** series brings an eclectic selection of films, along with the occasional related celebrity, thrown in with the price of a tipple or a snack at the bar. See p. 47.

● **Best Outdoor Summer Theater:** Forsooth, New York's greatest summer asset is no secret. **Shakespeare in the Park** (✆ 212/539-8750) hooks up tens of thousands of bard hounds with the best in Elizabethan drama (using some of today's best actors and directors). The Delacorte Theater's site in the middle of Central Park is well nigh enchanted. See p. 63.

● **Best Outdoor Summer Theater That Isn't Shakespeare in the Park:** Energetic performances substitute for big names and big budgets in downtown's alternative **Shakespeare in the Park(ing) Lot** (✆ 212/253-1813). The setting couldn't be less formal, but somehow the troupe manages to cast its spell. See p. 64.

● **Best Free Dance:** Modern and experimental dance has a home during **Movement Research at the Judson Church** (55 Washington Sq. S.; ✆ 212/539-2611). Dancers and choreographers vary from week to week, but the talent level stays consistently high. The series only seems to be getting better, especially now that the Judson Church has installed its lovely new dance floor. See p. 76.

● **Best Comedy Troupe:** The founders of **The Upright Citizens Brigade** (307 W. 26th St.; ✆ 212/366-9176) have gone on to movie and television fortune and fame, but the institution's classes continue to crank out rapier wits. Improv nights here are cheap when they're not free, and the legendary ASSSCAT 3000 is not to be missed. See p. 80.

● **Best Readings:** The great writerly look of **KGB Bar** (85 E. 4th St.; ✆ 212/505-3360) is well matched by the great writers who come through here almost every night of the week. Enough quality words have been spilled beneath the Soviet-kitsch furnishings to justify the publishing of KGB anthologies in addition to a monthly journal. See p. 93.

● **Best Readings in a Bookstore:** New York has many great literary events at its mom and pop shops, but the little players don't have quite the juice to bring in huge names every time. The **Union Square branch of Barnes & Noble** (33 E. 17th St.; ✆ 212/253-0810) has no difficulty booking the literati glitterati—check out their calendar for a steady stream of famous scribes. See p. 88.

2 Best Cheap Eats

● **Best Investment of 75¢ (Bagel):**
New York exported the bagel to
the four corners of America, but
after the indignities that have
been performed (piña colada
bagels?) we should ask for them
back. Fortunately, New York
still has the best, and 75¢ will
let you sample one at **Kossar's
Bialys** (367 Grand St.; ✆ **212/
473-4810**). With flavor and texture honed to perfection, you
can't make a better carb investment. See p. 126.

● **Best   Investment   of $1
(Dumplings):** Purveyors of
super-cheap dumplings can be
found across Chinatown, but
Eldridge Street Dumpling House
(118a Eldridge St.; ✆ **212/625-
8008**) beats them all hands
down. The flavorful dumplings
here are handmade and cooked
fresh right before your eyes.
Most amazingly, a single green-
back can be exchanged for five
of them. See p. 108.

● **Best Investment of $1.50 (Pizza
Bread):** The pizza bianca at the
Sullivan St. Bakery (73 Sullivan
St.; ✆ **212/334-9435**) is closer
to a piece of bread than a Noo
Yawk slice, but it's long on
old-world charm. Subtly flavored with rosemary and olive
oil (no tomato or cheese), the

dough manages to be simultaneously fluffy and chewy. A
mere $1.50 nails a nine-inch
piece. See p. 127.

● **Best Investment of $2 (Tacos):**
Served in a huge corn tortilla
and garnished with fresh pico
de gallo and guacamole, the
tacos at **Tulcingo Del Valle
Restaurant** (655 Tenth Ave.;
✆ **212/262-5510**) burst with
flavor. Starting at $2 for stand-
outs like chicken and carne
asada, they're the cheapest way
to pay a visit south of the border without leaving NYC. See
p. 310.

● **Best Investment of $2.50 (New
York Slice):** First-time visitors to
Sal's & Carmine's Pizza (2671
Broadway; ✆ **212/663-7651**),
spurred to spontaneous com-
pliments by the spectacular
pies, can expect to hear back
from the eponymous proprietors "Well, where the Hell
you been this whole time?"
One taste of the crispy crust
and character-full sauce and
you'll be asking yourself the
same question. See p. 127.

● **Best Investment of $3 (Falafel):**
I wouldn't put any New York
falafel over **Rainbow Falafel &
Shawarma** (26 E. 17th St.;
✆ **212/691-8641**). A big fresh

pita holds marinated onions and crisp, flavorful falafel balls. The rest of the Syrian menu here isn't too shabby, either. See p. 114.

● **Best Investment of $3.75 (Hot Dogs & a Drink):** The best dogs in the East Village are impounded at **Crif Dog** (113 St. Marks Place; ℂ **212/614-2728**). The house special gets you a pair with a soda kicker. Protein cravings are accommodated well into the wee hours—4am on the weekends. See p. 120.

● **Best Dirt Cheap Sit-Down Meal with Atmosphere:** Cheap Asian too often means over-lit, dingy cafeteria settings. Not so at **Galanga** (149 W. 4th St.; ℂ **212/228-4267**), where a stylish, modern interior makes for a perfect date spot. With such great atmosphere, food that is spicy, fresh, and original almost seems like a lagniappe. See p. 123.

● **Best Burger:** New Yorkers have voted with their palates by keeping the **Corner Bistro** (331 W. 4th St.; ℂ **212/242-9502**) busy at every hour. With the succulent, unpretentious $5.50 burgers here, it's no wonder. The city's expense-account $15 rivals at the fancy-shmancy places don't even come close. See p. 123.

3 Best Living Bets

● **Best Free School:** With college tuitions spiking endlessly upward, **Cooper Union** (Cooper Sq.; ℂ **212/353-4120**) is a definite anomaly: The 1,000 students here get their education for exactly $0 and 0¢. The rest of us are invited in for exhibitions, readings, and a great series of lectures. See p. 147.

● **Best Free Smarts:** The **Graduate Center at the City University of New York (CUNY)** (365 Fifth Ave.; ℂ **212/817-8215**) keeps adults educated with a terrific selection of lectures, seminars, and panel discussions. Fees are reasonable and big chunks of the program are on the house. See p. 148.

● **Best Cheap Bed:** Who needs a mint on his pillow and a bill for $250, when **Big Apple Hostel** (119 W. 45th St.; ℂ **212/302-2603**) can provide a good night's sleep for under $40? You'll get a high-rent location, too: right in the heart of the Theater District. See p. 161.

- **Best Gyms:** Stay thin without a fat wallet. For less than 14¢ a day, 36 gyms and rec centers can belong to you. The facilities of the **Department of Parks and Recreation** (© **212/360-8222**) include tracks, weight rooms, dance studios, and boxing rings. For $75 a year ($25 more), you get access to the swimming pools, too. See p. 171.

- **Best Grooming:** Style-conscious New Yorkers flock to Bumble and bumble salon for the latest looks. Savvier souls sign up for the model calls at their school, **Bumble and bumble.University**

(415 W. 13th St.; © **866/ 7-BUMBLE**). If you're selected for the stylist training program, you'll get a free cut, a head full of styling products, and an invitation to call back in 8 to 10 weeks to do it all over again. See p. 165.

- **Best Boat Ride:** Transform yourself into river traffic through the programs at the **Downtown Boathouse** (Pier 40, Pier 96, and at 72nd St.; © **646/613-0375**). They'll loan you a kayak and let you paddle around their west side piers. If you get your strength up, you'll be eligible for a longer ride into New York Harbor. See p. 176.

4 Best Shopping Bets

- **Best Thrift Shopping: Housing Works Thrift Shop** (143 W. 17th St.; © **212/366-0820,** plus other locations) brings the prices of fashionable clothes and furniture down to levels real people can afford. The inventory is lightly used and quick to turn over, and the money you spend goes to support a great cause (housing, services, and advocacy for people living with HIV and AIDS). See p. 192.

- **Best Department Store: Century 21** (22 Cortlandt St.;

© **212/227-9092**) is the Shakespeare in the Park of shopping—everybody knows about it, it's in great demand, and despite New Yorkers' high expectations it rarely comes up short. Amazing selection and equally amazing prices draw in the crowds 7 days a week. See p. 202.

- **Best Gourmet Food Shop for Tightwads:** Tracking down fancy fromage is not a difficult task in NYC, but to actually purchase a wedge without emptying your purse is another issue. Thank

New York's Top-Five Best-Kept Free Secrets

❶ As far as New York vistas go, it's hard to beat the Brooklyn Bridge at night with the Manhattan skyline twinkling in the background. The **Brooklyn Bridge Movies With a View Film Series** (☎ 718/802-0603) does its best to enhance the view by projecting Brooklyn-angled fare against the epic scenery. Compared to its Manhattan competitors, this event is much more under control. The friendly, low-key crowd is perfect for watching a flick with. See p. 54.

❷ Though the **National Museum of the American Indian** (1 Bowling Green; ☎ 212/514-3700) has seen the bulk of its collection moved to the Mall in D.C., the three gallery spaces here still put on great exhibits of contemporary and historic Native American art. The building itself, a magnificent Beaux Arts customs house, is worthy of a visit of its own. See p. 235.

❸ In addition to free Internet, 5,000 videos, 8,500 films, and 35,000 CDs, the **Donnell Library Center** (20 W. 53rd St.; ☎ 212/621-0618) is also the place Winnie-the-Pooh calls home. The original Winnie and his pals Piglet, Eeyore, Kanga, and Tigger have lived in Manhattan for 50 years now, most recently in a glass case in the Central Children's Room at the Donnell. Oh yeah, they've got some books here, too. See p. 253.

❹ The **New York Earth Room** (141 Wooster St.; ☎ 212/989-5566) is just that: 140 tons of soil hidden away in a SoHo loft. Even after multiple visits it's a completely unexpected sight, and a few whiffs of the earthy scent can be oddly rejuvenating. See p. 260.

❺ Malcolm Forbes' affection for his idiosyncratic collections is obvious from the well-crafted displays at the **Forbes Magazine Galleries** (62 Fifth Ave.; ☎ 212/206-5548). As you wind through model boats, toy soldiers, Monopoly boards, and trophies, you just may find Forbes' enthusiasm rubbing off on you. See p. 232.

the cheese gods then for the **East Village Cheese Store** (40 Third Ave.; ⓒ **212/477-2601**), which has a gigantic selection

at humble prices. This is the ideal place for cocktail party hosts and hostesses to fortify themselves. See p. 207.

5 Best Exploring Bets

● **Best Exhibits:** The main branch of the public library, formally known as the **Humanities and Social Sciences Library** (Fifth Ave. and 42nd St.; ⓒ **212/869-8089**), puts on terrific shows in the hushed interiors behind the lions. Rare editions and manuscripts are often on display, accompanied by thoughtful captions that make equally illuminating reading. See p. 254.

● **Best Tour:** The mayor and the city council still have their offices in graceful old **City Hall** (Broadway, at Murray St.; ⓒ **212/788-2170**). This underpublicized free tour allows you to catch glimpses of NYC politico celebs, while admiring gorgeous portraiture and architecture. As an added bonus, you'll get to see the Board of Ed in inaction, right next door at the opulent Tweed Courthouse. See p. 267.

● **Best Use of a Former Factory Space in Queens**: The perfunctory design of MoMA QNS couldn't touch Long Island City's **SculptureCenter** (44-19

Purves St.; ⓒ **718/361-1750**). Maya Lin left a lot of rough edges, but the overall effect is reminiscent of a cathedral, complete with a catacomblike basement. The intriguing sculptures and installation art shown here further justify the trip to Queens. See p. 237.

● **Best Art Museum:** The **P.S. 1 Contemporary Art Center** (22-25 Jackson Ave.; ⓒ **718/ 784-2084**) puts on great art shows just a stop away from Manhattan in Long Island City. The museum is a beautiful conversion of a Renaissance Revival public school, and the interior spaces have been inventively redone to complement the cutting-edge art displayed here. Entrance is by suggested donation. See p. 250.

● **Best Dirt Cheap Date Night: First Saturdays** at the **Brooklyn Museum of Art** (200 Eastern Pkwy.; ⓒ **718/638-5000**) are among the best parties of the year. You can generate conversation fodder at exhibits, films, and lectures. You'll also find plenty of live music, should all that talk lead to a little dancing. See p. 242.

● **Best Natural Oasis:** Visions of rhododendron valleys, waterfalls, and wetlands conjure up only one place in New York: the Bronx. If you've never seen the **New York Botanical Garden** (200th St. and Southern Blvd.; ✆ **718/817-8700**), you'll be amazed at the biological diversity here. It's arguably the country's greatest public garden. See p. 270.

● **Best Elephant Procession:** Forget Republican conventions—the best **elephant show** occurs when the circus (Ringling Brothers; ✆ **212/465-6741**) comes to town. Once a year, around midnight, the elephants (sometimes accompanied by their zebra and camel comrades) stroll through the Queens–Midtown Tunnel and across town to Madison Square Garden. As far as New York wildlife goes, this spectacle is hard to beat. See p. 275.

Every summer, the Joseph Papp Public Theater hands out tickets to Shakespeare in the Park, one of New York's best free events. See p. 63 for a full review.

ENTERTAINMENT

2

For a little while in the boom years, it looked like dot.com zillionaires would be the only folks able to afford New York entertainment. Taverns upped cover charges, cigar and champagne bars came into fashion, and Broadway ticket prices went through the roof. But that was a whole different city. With youth pouring into the area, entertainment for the people has made a major comeback. It's easy to find top-tier dance, drama, film, and comedy for no more than the price of showing up. Shakespeare in the Park, the Metropolitan Opera, and the Upright Citizens Brigade are among the New York legends that give it up for free. Big-time wits can be found at TV-show

tapings, and big-name scribes make themselves accessible at complimentary literary readings. Meanwhile, music seeps up from the subway platforms and fills our parks and bars. Everything from jazz to
classical to country to rock can be heard in NYC, and a surprising
amount of it comes without cost. For those attractions that do charge,
discerning patrons can easily keep the cost down in the $5 range.
New York is a magnet for talent and even the performances on the
cheap end of the entertainment spectrum can be spectacular. In short,
money is no longer the barrier to experiencing great New York entertainment. Now it's an issue of time management.

FREE & DIRT CHEAP CALENDAR OF EVENTS

New York knows how to throw a
party. Throughout the year, you can
find massive celebrations of ancient
tribal affiliations, sexual orienta-
tions, and pagan holidays. Money
isn't an object, either, as most of
these celebrations are free. Of
course, event quality is in direct proportion to audience size. The Big
Apple's big events draw huge
crowds, and if you want a decent
view, you'll have to stake out your
spot hours early. Lesser events may
be more spur-of-the-moment accessible, but four or five listless floats
later you may find yourself fully
sated with the rites of Zemblan
Independence Day.

In addition to the numbers listed
below, **NYC Visit,** the city's convention and visitor's bureau, has the
lowdown on most events (© **212/
484-1222;** www.nycvisit.com).

JANUARY

Midnight Run in Central Park `FREE`   Times Square is hellish
enough on a Sunday afternoon, but it's an absolute nightmare on New
Year's Eve. For a saner first night out, one option is to hook up with the
New York Road Runner's Club. Their annual 4-mile Midnight Run takes
racers from 72nd Street to the Central Park East Drive, north to 102nd,
and back around. The registration fee will set you back between $25
and $35, but if you don't feel an absolute need to get winded in the
small hours, you can enjoy the prerun dancing, costume show, and
fireworks display for free. Dancing begins at 10pm and the parade
starts an hour later. Gather near the Central Park Bandshell, just south
of the 72nd Street Transverse. © **212/860-4455.** www.nyrr.org. Subway: B/C to 72nd St.; 6 to 68th St. Midnight December 31 (January 1).

Idiotarod   Late January and Brooklyn's brains turn to mushing. It's
hard to believe that a committee of structural engineers came up with

this idea, sober. The plan: to replace lovable blue-eyed sled dogs with teams of liquored-up bipeds, and have them drag shopping carts instead of sleds. The result is more *Cannonball Run* than athletic exposition, complete with dastardly competitors dropping marbles and banana peels along the route. The terrain covers Fulton Ferry Pier in Brooklyn to Tompkins Square Park in Manhattan (where the awards ceremony takes place), but expect last-minute scene shifting in order to stay one step ahead of Johnny Law. There is a $5 registration fee per person to participate, but it goes toward cash prizes, and it's free to watch. www.precisionaccidents.com. Subway: F to York St.; A/C to High St. Last Saturday in January.

FEBRUARY

Chinese New Year `FREE`   Come February Chinatown will be partying like it's 4704, in honor of the lunar new year. The omnipresent firecrackers of Chinese new years past have been taken out of the public's hands and entrusted to professionals at a central viewing area along Mott and Bayard, but there's still plenty of noise and chaos to go around. The annual parade sees dragon and lion dancers winding down Mott, across East Broadway, and back up along the Bowery. For a newer New York New Year's tradition, check out the flower market inside Columbus Park (Mulberry St., between Bayard and Worth sts.). The Museum of Chinese in the Americas supplements supple blossoms with live performances. ✆ **212/966-0100.** www.betterchinatown.com. Subway: J/M/N/Q/R/W/Z/6 to Canal St. Late January or early February.

MARCH

Saint Patrick's Day Parade `FREE`   The free entertainment on St. Patrick's Day starts on the subway ride. In years past I've ridden in cars that local teens have magically transformed into mini–Irish pubs, complete with energetic gossip, Guinness cans rattling down the aisles, and clouds of cigarette smoke. And then there's the parade. The green wave gathers momentum through Midtown and converges on Fifth Avenue, where 150,000 marchers (and at least that many spectators) celebrate Ireland's patron saint. Much of the crowd arrives well before the 11am start time. The entertainment continues with live music and drunken shenanigans at New York's thousand-plus Irish pubs. Wear green or risk pinchery. The parade runs from 86th to 44th streets, right past Patrick's own cathedral. ✆ **212/484-1222.** www.saintpatricksdayparade.com. Subway: N/R/W or E/V to Fifth Ave. March 17.

Easter Parade FREE   With the return of spring nature is reborn from the small deaths of winter, and what better way to symbolize new life than by showing off your new threads? That's been the thinking behind New York's Easter Parade for almost a century and a half. More an informal procession than a parade, people join and leave as they please. Expect amazing hats and plenty of pastels. The stroll runs from 10am until 3 or 4pm, along Fifth Avenue between 48th and 57th streets. ✆ **212/484-1222.** Subway: E/V to Fifth Ave.; B/D/F/V to 47th–50th sts.–Rockefeller Center. Easter Sunday.

APRIL

Dachshund Friendship Festival FREE   Twice a year New York's dachshunds gather with their humans in Washington Square Park to mix, mingle, and wear diabolically adorable little wiener outfits. Watch dachshund brides samba with dachshund cowboys before the whole herd runs in circles around the center of the park. The festival ends with a chorus of "The Dachs Song." With the hounds lifted overhead and the spring air filled with the refrain of "Dachsie, meine dachsie," there's nary a dry eye to be found. Washington Square Park is bounded by Waverly Place, 4th Street, University Place, and Mac-Dougal Street. ✆ **212/475-5512.** www.dachshundfriendshipclub. com. Subway: A/B/C/D/E/F/V to W. 4th St.–Washington Sq. Noon, the last Saturday in April, and again the first Saturday in October. Rain date Sunday.

Pieces of April 1st   FREE

The press releases for Fifth Avenue's April Fool's Day Parade promise elaborate floats with budgets in the billions and throngs of costumed celebrities, but the most action you can hope to see at this event is the occasional irritated news crew standing around watching the traffic flow. Fox News and CNN have showed up for the parade in years past only to discover that they've been played for April fools. www.joeyskaggs.com.

MAY

Ninth Avenue International Food Festival FREE   If some human in an obscure corner of the globe will shove it in his mouth and call it a comestible, odds are you can find it at this festival. Come mid-May, street fair standbys like Italian sausages and pad Thai mingle with offerings from Ninth Avenue's indigenous roster. Do not miss the hot-from-the-oven Greek pastries from Poseidon Bakery, between 44th and 45th streets. Prices start at around $1.75 for an empanada and top out at around $6 for most plates. Free live music adds to an already festive scene. Ninth Avenue, from West 37th to 57th streets. ☎ **212/581-7217.** Subway: A/C/E or 7 to 42nd St. From 9am until 7pm, Saturday and Sunday in mid-May.

Fleet Week `FREE`   For 1 week, New Yorkers get nostalgic at the sight of thousands of sailors on the make in the port of Manhattan. Squint and pretend it's VE Day. Along the west side piers you can get a closer look. Navy, Coast Guard, and Marine reps will let you tour some of the floating behemoths you spent all those tax dollars on. ☎ **212/245-0072.** www.fleetweek.navy.mil or www.intrepidmuseum.org. Last week in May.

JUNE

Museum Mile Festival `FREE`
The classiest fair in New York sees Fifth Avenue closed to car traffic so 50,000 culture vultures can take in Manhattan's Gold Coast to the sounds of string quartets. Kids get live performances and special arts and crafts opportunities. Nine of the museums that give the mile its moniker offer free admissions. This is one street fair where low-rent commerce doesn't predominate: No vendors are allowed. Fifth Avenue, from 82nd to 104th streets. ☎ **212/606-2296.** www.museummilefestival.org. Subway: 4/5/6 to 86th St.; 6 to 77th, 96th, or 103rd sts. From 6pm to 9pm, usually the second Tuesday in June.

The Street Fair Sham

It takes less than a New York minute for a newcomer's excitement about "street fairs" and "block parties" to fizzle into the reality of another traffic-clogged exercise in low-end commerce. Each fair has the exact same CDs, massage stands, and three-for-a-buck socks (whose multitudinous apertures are more reminiscent of Swiss cheese than footwear). The deep-fried corn can be tasty if you're in a certain mood, and occasionally a band will play live, but generally it's hard to fill more than a couple of minutes at one of these affairs.

Lesbian and Gay Pride Week and March `FREE`   The city bursts with Pride every June in a week that begins with rallies and protests and ends in a dance, fireworks, and a parade. Pride commemorates the

June 27, 1969, Stonewall Rebellion, where gay men first stood against police harassment outside the Stonewall Inn in the West Village. Thirty-five-plus years later seeing Fifth Avenue overtaken by rainbows is a heartening sight, as the Sunday Gay Pride March wends its way from 52nd Street down into the Village. Just standing on a street corner downtown can be almost as entertaining as the parade, especially the spectacle of drag queens teetering on high heels as they rush across multiple lanes of traffic. ℂ **212/807-7433.** www.hopinc.org. Mid- to late June.

Puerto Rico Day Parade `FREE` Fifth Avenue's staid character goes into remission for the Puerto Rico Day parade. There's salsa music and festive floats and millions of spectators lining the way. The parade has been running annually since 1958, and despite some ugly incidents, it remains a quality spectacle. Fifth Avenue, from 44th to 86th streets. ℂ **718/401-0404.** www. www.nationalpuertoricandayparade. org. From 11am to 6pm, the second Sunday in June.

☆ **Mermaid Parade** `FREE` Old-time New Yorkers had one destination for the best in tattoos, sideshows, and amusement parks. In its '20s heyday, Coney Island saw over a million visitors a day. Now only a lone roller coaster remains, but some continuity with the glorious, tawdry past remains, especially during the eclectic freak show that is the Mermaid Parade. With body paint and beads—plus a few strategic scraps of fabric to keep things legal—the avatars of New York's retro-culture scene transform themselves into mermaids and Neptunes. Classic cars join the procession as the parade works its way up Surf Avenue, dispersing when the participants dash down the beach to the ageless Atlantic. In the evening, live bands can be heard at the **Mermaid Parade Ball** (check **www.mermaidparadeball.com** for the exact location), where the $10 ticket will get you a free Rheingold, plus the chance to buy many more Rheingolds for just a buck each. Surf Avenue, from West 15th to West 10th streets. ℂ **718/372-5159.** www.coneyisland.com/mermaid.shtml. Subway: D/F/N/Q to Coney Island/Stillwell Ave., then walk toward the Atlantic. First Saturday after the summer solstice, 2 to 6pm.

JULY

Battery Park 4th of July Concert `FREE` New York puts the free back in freedom with an outdoor concert in Battery Park. Past performers have ranged from legend Emmylou Harris to Ryan Adams.

Either way, there's a festive, laid-back vibe, with blankets spread on the grass and New York Harbor in the background. Gates open at 2pm and the show starts around 3:30 pm. Lines get long, so show up early if you want to get in and claim a patch of grass. ℂ **212/835-2789.** www. downtownny.com. Subway: R/W to Whitehall St.; 1 to S. Ferry. July 4.

Fourth of July Fireworks `FREE`   In New York's previous incarnation, you knew July 4th was coming because starting mid-June your sleep was interrupted by nightly amateur firework shows. With quality-of-life crackdowns, however, firepower is hard to come by and The Man has a monopoly on the summer eye-candy. Fortunately, The Man does a nice job of blowing up stuff for our entertainment. Locations can shift, but generally Macy's explodes 80,000 shells into the air over the East River in the 20s and 30s. At 7:30pm the FDR closes to traffic between 14th and 42nd streets and folks start to grab seats on the guardrails. If you're not totally Manhattancentric, the other side of the river has decent views. Try Hunter's Point in Long Island City, Queens, and Greenpoint in Brooklyn. ℂ **212/494-2922.** www.macys.com. July 4.

August

☆ **Harlem Week** `FREE`   Harlem Day was first celebrated in 1975, and over the subsequent 3 decades it has grown from a day to a week to an entire month of cultural celebration. Harlem Week now includes the Black Film Festival, the Harlem Jazz and Music Festival, and the Taste of Harlem Food Festival. The two biggest days come in the middle of the month, with Uptown Saturday Nite taking over West 135th Street between Malcolm X Boulevard and St. Nicholas Avenue. Sunday is Harlem Day, from 10am to 9pm. West 135th, between Fifth and St. Nicholas avenues. ℂ **212/862-8477.** www.harlemdiscover.com. Subway: B/C to 135th St.; 1 to 137th St. From noon to 9pm, the month of August.

Howl! Festival of East Village Arts `FREE`   Though the East Village's legendary artistic past is increasingly obscured by layers of gentrifying paint, 1 week in late August brings back the old contrarian spirit. The Howl! Festival serves up theater, live music, and art. Although there's an admission charge for many events (usually reasonable, in the $7 range), the Allen Ginsberg Poetry Festival in Tompkins Square Park is free. Also free is the legendary Wigstock (www.wigstock.nu). This premier drag fest outgrew its humble Tompkins roots to reach mass acclaim on the Hudson piers. After peaking there, the show has come back home, with a performance usually late Saturday afternoon. Avenue A, between 7th and 10th streets. ✆ **212/502-1225.** www.howlfestival. com. Subway: L to 1st Ave.; 6 to Astor Place; N/R/W to 8th St. Third or fourth week in August.

SEPTEMBER

Tugboat Festival `FREE` One day a year New York's attention-starved tugs get some play at the Intrepid Museum's annual Tugboat Festival. The rites begin with a tug parade down the Hudson, continue with nose-to-nose tug-pushing-tug contests, races, and line-throwing competitions, and conclude with prizes for best crew and best tattoo. Pier 86. Twelfth Avenue, at 46th Street. ✆ **212/245-0072.** www.intrepid museum.org. Subway: N/Q/R/Q/1/2/3/7 to Times Square; A/C/E to 42nd St./Port Authority. From 12:30 to 4pm, the Sunday before Labor Day.

West Indian–American Day Parade `FREE` New York's biggest parade takes place a long way from Fifth Avenue, along Eastern Parkway in Brooklyn. Two million revelers (yup, *2,000,000*) come together on Labor Day for the West Indian–American Day Parade. The Caribbean rhythms are infectious and the costumes out of control, and the food's not a bad t'ing either. Jerk chicken ($6), oxtail ($5–$8), and veggie roti ($4) are among the delicacies that make the trip worthwhile. The route varies, but generally follows Eastern Parkway at Utica Avenue in Crown Heights down to the arch at Grand Army Plaza in Prospect Heights. ✆ **718/625-1515.** www.wiadca.com. Subway: 2/3 to Grand Army Plaza. From 11am to 6pm, Labor Day.

September Concert `FREE` In any other circumstances, a day bringing hundreds of performers to dozens of venues across all five boroughs would be cause for upbeat excitement, but the context of the September Concert is a somber one. To commemorate the World Trade Center attacks, the city fills with the healing sounds of music. Through-out the day, find the free sounds in the city's cafes, bars, libraries, squares, and parks. It's a perfect excuse for people to be together. ✆ **212/333-3399.** www.septemberconcert.org. Multiple venues, check the website. From noon to 10pm, September 11.

The Feast of San Gennaro `FREE` This is New York's oldest and biggest street fair—11 days of *zeppoles,* pork *braciole,* and deep-fried Oreos in honor of the patron saint of Naples. Little Italy main drag Mulberry Street becomes an extremely narrow small-town carnival. There are rides for the kids, cannoli-eating contests for the adults, and an abusive clown in a dunking booth that's discomfiting for everybody. With the heavy emphasis on commerce and the beer-addled crowds, the fair gets old fairly quickly. Mulberry Street, between Canal and Houston, with runoff on Hester and Grand. ⓒ **212/226-6427.** www. sangennaro.org. Subway: N/R to Prince St.; 6 to Spring St. or Canal. Starts the second Thursday in September, from 11:30am to 11:30pm, midnight on Friday and Saturday.

OCTOBER

New York's Great Halloween Party `FREE`   The hobgoblins of little minds can be found in haunted sites across 40 of the city's back acres come Halloween. Central Park fills with excitable costumed children, looking for the perfect pumpkin among the 7,500 scattered throughout the straw at the Bethesda Fountain. Once the little demons have made their incisions they take the resulting jack-o'-lanterns north, to the Charles A. Dana Discovery Center, midpark at 110th Street. A parade is followed by an annual pumpkin sail, where the jack-o'-lanterns glow on the Harlem Meer as they gently float away. ⓒ **212/ 860-1370.** www.centralparknyc.org. Subway: 6 to 68th or 77th sts.; 1/2/3/B/C to 72nd St. Generally from 3:30 to 6:30pm. Saturday, a few days before Halloween (date varies).

☆ **Greenwich Village Halloween Parade** `FREE`   For many New Yorkers, every day feels like Halloween. Come late October, the last thing we need to wade through is another crowd of costumed freaks. Fight this instinct, however, and you will enjoy New York's most underrated holiday. The central event is the annual Halloween parade. Running up Sixth Avenue from Spring to 23rd, the parade shows off New Yorkers' legendary gallows humor. If you're feeling restless, the neighborhood's surrealistic collisions—javelin-toting African warriors kibitzing with drag-queen astronauts—are entertainment enough. Note: This parade is one of New York's most participatory events; no one will think any less of you for not being covered in body paint or latex, but you run the risk of feeling like you're in a wet-blanket minority. Village Voice Parade hot line: ⓒ **212/475-3333,** ext. 4044. www.halloween-nyc. com. Subway: C/E to Spring St.; A/B/C/D/E/F/V to W. 4th St.–Washington Sq.; F/V/L to 14th St. October 31, with the coming of night.

NOVEMBER

The New York Marathon   As much fun as it looks to completely deplete your body while forming manhole-sized blisters from pounding

26.2 miles of hard pavement, I'm happy to leave the marathoning to the pros. There is five boroughs' worth of prime viewing territory, and the steady stream of runners, with their varied looks of determination and exhaustion, has an unexpected poetry. The race ends in Central Park near Tavern on the Green, where you can watch the survivors, adorned in the glory of heat-retaining silver blankets, as they walk it off. The race begins in the morning, with the elite runners getting off around 11am. ✆ **212/423-2249** or 212/860-4455. www.ingnycmarathon.org. Subway (to Central Park): B/C to 72nd St. First Sunday in November.

Macy's Thanksgiving Day Parade `FREE`   New York's favorite excuse for dragging bloated floating cartoon characters down the west side of the city comes with the Macy's Thanksgiving Day Parade. Rocky, Bullwinkle, and Garfield join slightly less-inflated celebrities to march down Central Park West from 77th Street to Columbus Circle, where they turn onto Broadway and head straight for the Mothership (Macy's in Herald Square). The wee ones love this event and crowds are thick, with a lot of prime viewing territory reserved for VIP's, so arrive well before the scheduled start time. Tip: Balloon fanatics can get a head start on the action the night before, when the balloons get their helium fixes on the broad sidewalks around the Natural History Museum. ✆ **212/ 494-2922.** www.macysparade.com. Subway: B/C to 72nd St.; A/B/C/D/1 to Columbus Circle. From 9am to noon, Thanksgiving morning.

DECEMBER

Alternatives to the Rockefeller Tree Lighting `FREE`   It's not like Rock Center has the only Christmas tree in New York City. The Tuesday after Thanksgiving sees 100,000 lights softly glowing in the Winter Garden at the World Financial Center. On the same day on the Upper West Side, Lincoln Center hosts its own Christmas celebration. A tree lighting supplements crafts booths and live music along Broadway and Columbus from 61st to 68th streets. You'll find plenty for the kids and the crowds are a fraction of Rock Center's. **World Financial Center:** ✆ **212/945-0505.** www.worldfinancialcenter.com. Subway: 1/2/3/A/C to Chambers St. **Lincoln Center BID:** ✆ **212/581-3774.** www. lincolnbid.org. Subway: 1 to 66th St./Lincoln Center. The Tuesday after Thanksgiving.

Lighting of the Christmas Tree at Rockefeller Center `FREE` The week after Thanksgiving marks the first major "Gridlock Alert" of the holiday shopping season. Traffic comes to a near stop on the blocks around Rockefeller Center. Down on the rink professional ice-skaters make graceful turns, live music plays, and Hizzoner throws the switch on 30,000 bulbs strung along 5 miles of wire. Rock Center's overflow crowd, many of whom have been waiting in the cold for 4 or 5 hours, cheer with relief. Even for grinches like myself, watching the tree come alive is a pretty cool moment, but they'd have to make the spruce levitate while spouting a fountain of $50 bills for me to want to weather that crowd twice. Better to come back at a more mellow time, especially if you can visit at dusk, when the tree is at its most quietly dramatic. ✆ **212/332-6868.** www.rockefellercenter.com. B/D/F/V to 47th–50th sts.– Rockefeller Center. At 9pm, the Wednesday after Thanksgiving.

Festival of Lights `FREE` If you want to celebrate the other half of the Judeo–Christian cultural tradition, you can attend the lighting of Midtown's menorah. This skyscraping candle-holder (at 32 ft., it's the world's largest) shines at sunset on the first night of Hanukkah, gaining another light on each of the following 7 days. Grand Army Plaza on Fifth Avenue, at 59th Street. Subway: N/R/Q/W to Fifth Ave.; F to 57th St. During Hanukkah.

The Station at Citigroup Center `FREE` Most New Yorkers don't have the surplus square footage for obsessive train sets, but fortunately the Citigroup Center does. Goggle-eyed urchins revel in a massive whirring creation that portrays all the regions and seasons of New York State. Thirty-two rail and trolley lines ply the byways for the holiday month between Thanksgiving and New Year's. Visiting is free, but the show is popular, so expect plenty of company. Citigroup

Free Radical Theater `FREE`

New York supplements its famous parades with other festive mass gatherings: protest marches and rallies. Whether you're standing up to be counted or just on the sidelines digging the spectacle, you won't find yourself shorted on stimuli. New Yorkers have sharp senses of humor and the creative placards alone are worth a look. The confluence of political relevance and cutting cultural commentary recurs often, as in this gem: BEN AFFLECK IS A TERRIBLE ACTOR. NO WAR IN IRAQ.

There's no arguing with at least one of those points.

Center, 153 East 53rd Street. at Lexington Avenue. ✆ **212/559-1747.** www.dunhamstudios.com/cititour.htm. Subway: E/V to Lexington; 6 to 51st St. Mon–Sat 10am–6pm, Sun noon–5pm.

A Brooklyn Christmas `FREE` The big department stores offer the sidewalks plenty of entertainment with elaborate window displays, but for my money, New York's best free Christmas show is in Brooklyn. Homeowners from Bay Ridge to Bensonhurst run up the Keyspan bills to bring bulb envy to their neighbors. Dyker Heights is "Christmas Central," with 100,000 tourists drawn every year to the blocks around 83rd and 84th streets, between Tenth and Thirteenth avenues. Choruses of mechanical Santas and snowmen compete to prove the lights are always brighter on the other side of the fence. Take the D/M to 79th Street or the R to 86th Street and walk toward the lines of wide-eyed-munchkin-packed minivans. Between Thanksgiving and New Year's.

New Year's Concert for Peace at the Cathedral of St. John the Divine `FREE` Leonard Bernstein inaugurated this event, and in the subsequent decades, it's become a beautifully honed candlelit legend. St. John's is the largest Gothic cathedral in the world and can seat 6,000, though the best spots are reserved and come with steep price tags. Except for those seats the concert is free. General seating is open to all comers, who sit in wide rows in the back of the church. Cathedral of St. John the Divine. 1047 Amsterdam Ave., at 112th St. ✆ **212/316-7540.** www.stjohndivine.org. Subway: 1 or B/C to Cathedral Parkway/110th St. December 31.

Brooklyn New Year's Prospect `FREE` There's no borough envy in Brooklyn as rival pyrotechnics welcome the new year above Prospect Park. Enjoy the fresh air as the embers cascade above the Grand Army Plaza at the stroke of midnight. Prime viewing areas include West Drive and along Prospect Park West, between Grand Army Plaza and 9th Street. ✆ **718/965-8999.** www.prospectpark.org. Subway: 2/3 to Grand Army Plaza; B/Q to 7th Ave. December 31.

1 Music Uncovered

New York is in the midst of yet another great rock-'n'-roll scare. A slew of young bands have rediscovered the jittery energy of New York's '70s and '80s heyday, and they're threatening to become a movement. The jury is still out on how much of this is hype (and how much of the sound is anything more than derivative), but in the immediate a surplus of live music bangs away across the city. It's not just rock, either. Classical performances, acoustic acts, salsa bands, jazz quartets, even alt-country make a stand in Yankee confines. The only fly in this ointment is capitalism; the bars have to pay rent. Most places try to keep the booze flowing, although with a few exceptions New York is not super uptight about enforcing its drink minimums. The musicians certainly don't care—most of the time they're just happy you're there to listen. You'll find free music waiting 7 nights a week. You might as well embrace the cacophony because Lord knows it's hard to find a quiet hour in New York City.

> **FREE** **Free & E-Zeens**
>
> With a city in endless flux and so much stuff going on, it's hard to stay abreast of the best in free and cheap events. My favorite means of keeping up is via electronic newsletters, conveniently e-mailed right to my inbox. Of the e-lists, **Nonsense-nyc's** (www.nonsensenyc.com) is my favorite, specializing in the cheap and offbeat, and providing a comprehensive rundown of the city's many hipster events. A few other newsletters worth reading can be found at **www.dailycandy.com, www.flavorpill.net,** and **www.manhattanusersguide.com.**

FOR THOSE ABOUT TO ROCK

☆ **Arlene's Grocery**   From the outside, this popular music hall still resembles the humble bodega it replaced. Inside the bands are polished, but a little too obviously courting major label attention. Their confidence won't dim as long as no one minds that they all sound exactly the same. Cover charges vary, generally $7 or so. Some of the best nights are free (see "Sing, Sing: Karaoke," on p. 76).

95 Stanton St., between Orchard and Ludlow sts. ℂ 212/358-1633. www.arlenes grocery.net. Subway: F/V to Second Ave.; J/M/Z to Essex St.

The Baggot Inn   Nestled in a cozy basement beneath street level, the Baggot Inn brings in a mix of rock and old-timey music. Wednesday nights feature a Bluegrass and Good Times Jam, where the folks on stage have the most fun. The sound is good and generally there's no cover Sunday through Wednesday nights. FINE PRINT A two-drink minimum applies.

82 W. 3rd St., between Thompson and Sullivan sts. Ⓒ **212/477-0622.** www.the
baggotinn.com. Subway: A/B/C/D/E/F/ V to W. 4th St.-Washington Sq.

Continental Proximity to St. Marks Place assures a young, semi-
punk demographic at the Continental. Bands tend to err on the side
of loudness and aggression, although the talent level is fairly high.
Classic rock tribute bands fill out the rest of the schedule. Most weeknights are free. FINE PRINT If there's a cover it'll be $5, or maybe $10
on Saturday night.

25 Third Ave., between St. Marks Place and 9th St. Ⓒ **212/529-6924.** www.
continentalnyc.com. Subway: 6 to Astor Place; N/R to 8th St.

☆ **The Lakeside Lounge** FREE The Lakeside may lack in lake
views, but it has no shortage of great music. Steve Earle, Amy Allison,
and Freedy Johnson have all played here. The back room that holds
the stage is tiny, so you're guaranteed an intimate experience. If you
arrive late, there's extra standing room off to the side. Never a cover,
or a minimum, and during set breaks you can buy yourself a souvenir
from the notorious black-and-white photo booth.

162 Ave. B, between 10th and 11th sts. Ⓒ **212/529-8463.** www.lakeside
lounge.com. Subway: L to First Ave.

The Living Room A mellow music mecca, The Living Room hosts
a slate of live performances every night, biased toward acoustic and
otherwise low-key up-and-comers. The musical taste here is good, if
at times a tad bland (how many over-earnest singer-songwriters does
one society really need?). Rarely a cover, though they do pass the hat
and suggest a $5 contribution. The one-drink minimum per set is
casually enforced.

154 Ludlow St., between Stanton and Rivington sts. Ⓒ **212/533-7235.** www.
livingroomny.com. Subway: F/V to Second Ave.; J/M/Z to Essex St.

Paddy Reilly's Here's an odd innovation: an Irish pub with live
music. Most nights you can find someone strumming or picking in
here, whether it's bluegrass, folk, or a traditional Irish session. With
regular Joes from the street invited to sit in, earnestness often trumps
professionalism, but the results are no less enjoyable. Weekend covers tend to be reasonable ($7 and less), and other nights are usually
free.

519 Second Ave., at 29th St. Ⓒ **212/686-1210.** www.paddyreillys.com. Subway: 6
to 28th St.

Parkside Lounge   Nestled between projects and East Village tenements, this former brothel brings in an eclectic crowd. Being too far east for most trendroids helps, too. The back room brings in rock shows and electric Friday-night salsa. Comedy and improv also appear on the calendar. FINE PRINT If there's a cover it'll be $5 for the band, and there's often a loosely enforced two-drink minimum in the back room.

317 E. Houston St., at Attorney St. ℂ 212/673-6270. www.parksidelounge. com. Subway: F/V to Second Ave.

☆ **Pete's Candy Store** FREE So much good music comes through this Brooklyn gem that you'll feel like a kid in a great music venue. Housed in a friendly former fountain shop on a quiet Williamsburg block, the small stage area brings in surprisingly big acts. There's also a rotating selection of nonmusical entertainment, from readings to Scrabble to quiz night (check out "Game Night" and "Word Up: Readings," on p. 82 and 88, respectively). No cover or drink minimum, but the staff encourages contributions to the musicians' tip jar.

709 Lorimer St., between Frost and Richardson sts., Williamsburg, Brooklyn. ℂ 718/302-3770. www.petes candystore.com. Subway: L to Lorimer St.; G to Metropolitan Ave.

Avoid the "Rock Bars" Around NYU

Close to NYU in the West Village sit a cluster of "rock bars" that purport to offer "no cover" entertainment. This is as pure a tourist trap as New York offers, as the various clubs try to cash in on their West Village cache. Although the joints may boast Bleecker or Macdougal addresses, there is little of the neighborhood's old rock-'n'-roll spirit here. The patrons are almost exclusively bridge and tunnel burbsters, drinks are overpriced, and the best you can hope for music-wise is an earnest cover band. If you want to hear at least one original thought per set, better to avoid this zone altogether.

Rodeo Bar FREE   This is as country as Manhattan gets, which isn't saying much. The sprawling space doesn't have the feel of an intimate honky-tonk, but the stage area is segregated and more or less self-contained. The cream of the local crop rounds up here, as do a host of great national acts. Mostly Americana and alt-country (whatever that is). There's no cover and no minimum.

375 Third Ave., at 27th St. ℰ **212/683-6500.** www.rodeobar.com. Subway: 6 to 28th St.

Sidewalk Café Having outlived the other live-music spots on Avenue A, the Sidewalk Café maintains a loyal following. The Café serves as a home base for East Village singer-songwriters, and a little comedy gets thrown in as well. Each night sees a big bunch of acts. FINE PRINT No cover, but a two-drink minimum during performances.

94 Ave. A, at the corner of 6th St. ℰ **212/473-7373.** www.antifolk.net/sidewalk. html. Subway: F/V to Second Ave.

JAZZ IT UP

Arthur's Tavern A West Village relic, Arthur's would be eligible for Social Security if it were a person and not an amiable, low-rent jazz joint. The music runs the Dixieland-to-trio gamut and the quality can be spotty, but something's on stage 7 nights a week. FINE PRINT No cover, but a one-drink per set minimum.

57 Grove St., between Bleeker and W. 4th sts. ℰ **212/675-6879.** www.arthurs tavernnyc.com. Subway: 1 to Christopher St.

Cleopatra's Needle Organ trios and quartets highlight the calendar at this Upper West Side neighborhood club. In the wee hours, the floor belongs to jam sessions. On Wednesday evenings and Sunday afternoons things get even more neighborhoody with open mics. Never a cover, though there is a $10 minimum per set. A decent Mediterranean menu provides an alternative to boozing the night away. Shows start at 8pm.

2485 Broadway, between 92nd and 93rd sts. ℰ **212/769-6969.** www.cleopatras needleny.com. Subway: 1/2/3 to 96th St.

55 Bar Still not entirely recovered from its Prohibition days, 55 Bar has been entertaining the Village on the sly since 1919. The cluttered room brings in top-shelf acts. The cover charges reflect it on some nights (they can run as high as $15), but generally you can slip in for a pittance (say, $3). Tuesday and Sunday nights are your best bets for inexpensive jazz. You'll find other no-cover nights, and the early shows are often free. FINE PRINT Officially, there's a two-drink minimum, but the laid-back staff enforces it loosely.

55 Christopher St., between Seventh Ave. and Waverly Place. ℰ **212/929-9883.** www.55bar.com. Subway: 1 to Christopher St.

Jazz Detour   Jazz Detour waylays music fans with a full schedule of no-cover acts. Trios and quartets make up the majority of the acts, although Wednesday provides an intriguing departure. "The Intimate Room" is a torch-song evening, with the likes of Bacharach and Gershwin providing the tunage, and a different singer every week to provide the mellow vibe. (The dimmed lights don't hurt either.) Sunday through Thursday features free live music from 9:30pm to 12:30am; Friday and Saturday have $5 covers and music plays from 10pm to 1:30am. FINE PRINT There's a two-drink minimum, and patrons are asked to tip the musicians.

349 E. 13th St., between First and Second aves. ℂ 212/533-6212. www.jazzat detour.com. Subway: L to First Ave.

☆ **Smoke**   A quintessential old-fashioned jazz classic except for the Bloomberg-era pristine air, Smoke offers cover-free music on the weeknights. There's bebop of both the retro and nouveau varieties, funk on Wednesdays, and Latin jazz on Sundays. Tuesday nights vibrate with Hammond B-3 Organ Grooves. Best of all, your eyes aren't red and burning when you leave. FINE PRINT Covers are enforced on the weekends, but weeknights are free with a $10 drink minimum (Tues–Thurs it's only a one-drink minimum).

2751 Broadway, between 105th and 106th sts. ℂ 212/864-6662. www.smoke jazz.com. Subway: 1 to 103rd St.

CLASSICAL ACTS

Gotham's classical pedigree is indisputable, boasting the nation's oldest orchestra (the New York Philharmonic), on top of a couple of venues whose renown just might extend beyond New York Harbor (Carnegie Hall and Lincoln Center leap to mind). The future of music can also be found here, with the nation's most prominent conservatories (think Juilliard) settled on Manhattan schist. Although high prices can accompany the high notes, you aren't obligated to pay through the nose for auditory ecstasy. Schools present a bevy of free shows, big-name venues offer obstructed-view cheap seats, and the Philharmonic and the Metropolitan Opera both gig for free in the summer (see "High Culture for Free," in the Outdoor Summer Concerts section below). So weigh your musical options before settling for that Quiet Riot tribute band on Bleecker Street.

FREE The Underground Scene

In this modern world it's hard to find a spontaneous public expression that can't be codified and regulated. Even street performers in New York get caught up in bureaucracy's net (the MTA's underground music Web address is a good indicator of the situation: www.mta.nyc.ny.us/mta/aft/muny.htm). The New York Metropolitan Transit Authority's program is called "Music Under New York," and it allows preselected performers to legally play at preselected stations. Illegally stationed musicians are often more melodically challenged—the quality level varies wildly beneath the streets. Times Square, Penn Station, Union Square, and Columbus Circle are the most heavily trafficked in the system, and it takes very little to draw an audience. In addition to the ubiquitous pan-flute Andean bands and tumbling demonstrations, you can hear amplified funk bands, jazz quartets, weird Chinese bow work, Brazilian drumming, blues, gospel, Calypso, and rock. The quality often competes with the music played aboveground on gel-lit stages. Not bad for the price of a swipe.

Bargemusic FREE Of all the world's barges dedicated to chamber music, this one is my favorite. Docked just off the Fulton Ferry landing in Brooklyn Heights, the recital room here hosts over a hundred concerts a year. Tickets are generally $35, but at least once a month one concert is given away. It's "potluck," so you won't know the program until showtime, but it'll be classical and the performance will be intimate. (There are only 130 seats.) No reservations are taken, so show up before the doors open, which is an hour before showtime.

26 New Dock St., at Water St., at the East River. ✆ **718/624-2083.** www.barge music.org. Subway: 2/3 to Clark St.; A/C to High St.

Carnegie Hall If you don't mind part of a support column affecting your sightlines, you can waltz right into Carnegie Hall for a mere Hamilton. The first-come, first-served partial-view seats become available at the box office at noon on the day of the show (limit two per person). If a show is presented by Carnegie Hall and it's taking place in the Isaac Stern Auditorium, it's eligible for the cheap treatment.

(The exceptions are gala events and Carnegie Hall Family Concerts, but the latter are a bargain in their own right. Targeted to the wee ones, tickets are only $8. To further soften the blow, that $8 will also get you into a screening at the nearby Museum of Television & Radio. Simply present your program from the Family Concert and you'll be treated to related kid-friendly television programming.) Carnegie Hall also takes its show on the road. The Neighborhood Concert Series fans out across all five boroughs, bringing everything from classical to jazz to folk. Some 80 shows a year are performed for free—check the website for details.

154 W. 57th St., at Seventh Ave. ℂ 212/247-7800. www.carnegiehall.org. Subway: A/B/C/D/1 to 59th St.-Columbus Circle; N/Q/R/W to 57th St.-Seventh Ave.

City Opera   Since its 1944 inception, City Opera has strived to be an accessible alternative to the Met. With innovative programming, at times the upstart can even eclipse its rival. Though premium tickets top out over $100, on the day of the show you can get in the standing room only section for $16. Tickets go on sale at the box office, Monday to Saturday at 10am, and Sundays at 11:30am. Or save that $16 by attending the VOX: Showcasing American Composers program, which comes around every spring. Some dozen young composers get a chance to air their work, and the public gets to preview the future of opera for free. Look also for the "On the Edge" free reading series that same weekend. Both are usually performed at NYU's Skirball Center downtown.

City Opera, New York State Theater, 20 Lincoln Center. ℂ 212/870-5570. www. nycopera.com. Subway: 1 to 66th St./Lincoln Center.

Free for All at Town Hall FREE   One of the city's newer classical programs, the 2006 Free for All put on five free performances at gracious Town Hall. From solo piano to string quartets, the shows bring serious music to knowledgeable fans. Tickets are distributed at the box office, two per person, at noon on the day of the show. Usually on Sundays in late spring.

123 W. 43rd St., between Sixth Ave. and Broadway. ℂ 212/707-8787. www.free forallattownhall.org. Subway: B/D/F/V to 42nd St.; 1/2/3/7/N/Q/R/S/W to 42nd St./Times Square.

The Juilliard School FREE   Juilliard's reputation couldn't be much more burnished, with luminaries like Philip Glass, Yo-Yo Ma, and Itzhak Perlman among its alums. Since its current students are nominally

FREE Quarter Pounding the Keys

McDonald's and classical music go together like a Big Mac and fries. Er, maybe not. Sunday afternoons see a bizarre cultural collision at the McDonald's nearest Ground Zero. Classical pianist Andrew Shapiro, and his occasional guests, layer additional atmosphere onto the scents of seared meat with lovely sessions of new-agey music. Tourists wander in with only an occasional perplexed glance at the grand piano in the window of the second floor balcony. For music fans, this is probably the calmest it's possible to feel inside a McDonald's.

160 Broadway, between Liberty and Cortlandt sts. ✆ 212/385-2063. www.andrewshapiro.com. Sundays, sets beginning at noon, 1pm, 2pm, and 3pm.

amateurs, the Lincoln Center school presents most of its concerts for free. Soloists play Morse and Paul Hall, and you can catch the entire orchestra at Alice Tully Hall. Though there is no charge, tickets are required, available from the box office up to two weeks prior to the show. The Downtown workforce can enjoy the Juilliard via the artist series at 180 Maiden Lane, Tuesdays at 12:30pm, in an office atrium. Admission is ticketless and free (p. 314 in "Free & Dirt Cheap Days").

60 Lincoln Center Plaza. ✆ 212/769-7406. www.juilliard.edu. Subway: 1 to 66th St./Lincoln Center.

Manhattan School of Music FREE With an Art Deco auditorium and four performing halls (plus two more under construction in the dorm across the street), there are plenty of places to listen here. Classical music performances are joined by jazz, which snuck into the curriculum after its founding 80 years ago. Many performances are free to the public, as are a series of master classes. (They'll even throw in snacks and drinks if you trek to Harlem for jazz combos on Tuesday nights.) Most events take place during the school year.

601 W. 122nd St., at Broadway. ✆ 917/493-4428. www.msmnyc.edu. Subway: 1 to 125th St.

Mannes College of Music FREE During the school year, this ninety-year-old institution presents some 400 free concerts. Student groups include baroque chamber, guitar, brass, and opera ensembles. Two concert halls at the college's headquarters host the free shows.

There are also remote performances in Lincoln Center, Carnegie Hall, and Symphony Space. Many of these are free as well, although some require tickets, which can be picked up from the security desk. Check the calendar for the full listings.

150 W. 85th St., between Amsterdam and Columbus aves. ⓒ 212/496-8524. www.mannes.edu. Subway: B/C to 86th St.

Metropolitan Opera The Met is the biggest (240 shows a year, each with seating for 4,000) and the best, with elaborate productions and unrivalled star power. Seats start around $26 and soar from there to over $300. In addition to the free summer shows (see below), standing-room-only tickets can be found. Prices tend to be $20 for orchestra and $15 for family circle, on sale at the box office on Saturday mornings at 10am for the next week's performances (i.e., Saturday through Friday performances). FINE PRINT It's cash only and one ticket per person, and by 10am the line is already at least an hour old.

Metropolitan Opera at Lincoln Center, between W. 62nd and 65th sts. and Columbus and Amsterdam aves. ⓒ 212/ 362-6000. www.metoperafamily.org. Subway: 1 to 66th St./Lincoln Center.

New York Grand Opera FREE
Conductor Vincent La Selva has spent the last 30 years performing the quixotic—or Sisyphean— task of mounting fully staged grand operas for no charge. He's pulled it off, too, with compelling performances that shine despite the occasional lack of polish. A few years of bad rain timing have afflicted the Naumberg Band Shell

FREE **Divine Inspiration: Concerts at the Churches**

Even heathens can find entertainment under the city's steeples. Choirs are only the beginning, as recitals and operas also take the altars, often for free. Worker bees downtown love the **"Concerts at One"** series at St. Paul's Chapel and Trinity Church. My personal faves are the performances by the **New York Repertory Orchestra**. Though this all-volunteer group has many amateurs in its ranks, the renditions of Brahms, Mahler, and Stravinsky are all professional. Programming is adventurous and the shows are free. Usually Saturday nights at 8pm, Good Shepherd Presbyterian Church, 152 W. 66th St., between Broadway and Amsterdam Ave. ⓒ 212/662-8383. www.nyro.org. Subway: 1 to 66th St./Lincoln Center.

shows in the summer, but winter church performances go on rain or shine. Check the website for the scheduling of various Verdis and Puccinis.

Naumberg Band Shell, Central Park, midpark, just below 72nd St. ℂ **212/245-8837.** www.newyorkgrandopera.org. Subway: B/C to 72nd St.; 6 to 68th St./ Hunter College. Other location: Church of Saint Paul and Saint Andrew, W. 86th St. and West End Ave. Subway: 1 to 86th St.

New York Philharmonic   The Philharmonic has been satisfying New Yorkers since 1842. The symphony's international fame translates into pricey tickets (usually it's over $100 to sit in the orchestra), but pikers needn't despair. In addition to free summer shindigs in the parks (see below), the Philharmonic also performs the odd show around town, including periodic visits to St. John the Divine. There are also low-priced kid-friendly shows, and series like "Hear & Now," which presents guided tours through new composers' work, usually with the composer sitting in. Half the house sells for $10 for the latter program. You can also save money with the Open Rehearsal program. Watching a piece take shape under a conductor's molding is a fascinating process and it's only $15 to sit in.

Avery Fisher Hall, 10 Lincoln Center Plaza. ℂ **212/875-5900.** www.nyphil.org. Subway: 1 to 66th St./Lincoln Center.

Peoples' Symphony Concerts   A good bet on IBM stock in 1923 is the basis for the endowment of these popular populist concerts. Three separate groupings, the Festival, Chambers, and Artists' Series, present world-class ensembles. Festival shows are held at Town Hall, and the others are at Washington Irving High School (with a 1,500-seat capacity and good acoustics, this is not your high school's auditorium). Most single tickets are $9 ($11 and $18 are the top-end prices), but if you invest in a series subscription, the per-show price dips below $5.

Washington Irving High School, 16th St., at Irving Place. ℂ **212/586-4680.** www.pscny.org. Subway: L/N/Q/R/W/4/5/6 to 14th St./Union Sq. Other location: Town Hall, 123 W. 43rd St., between Sixth Ave. and Broadway. Subway: B/D/F/V to 42nd St.; 1/2/3/7/N/Q/R/S/W to 42nd St./Times Square.

OUTDOOR SUMMER CONCERTS

The high season for free music is summer, when cool sounds seem to be coming from every corner. You would think that with so many events the crowds would spread thin, but concerts tend to be

Free Outdoor Summer Concerts

Monday	Tuesday	Wednesday	Thursday	Saturday	Sunday
Martin Luther King Jr. Concert Series, 7:30pm	Naumburg Orchestral Concerts, 7:30pm	Madison Square Park, 7pm	BAM Rhythm & Blues Festival at MetroTech, noon	East River Park Amphitheater, 1pm	Harlem Meer Performance Festival, 4pm
	Washington Square Music Festival, 8pm	Rockefeller Park, 7pm	Castle Clinton, 7pm		Summer-Garden at the MoMA, 8pm
	World Financial Center, 7pm		Seaside Summer Concert Series, Coney Island, 7pm		
			Summer Soul Nights, Battery Park, 7pm		

consistently well attended. If you're going primarily to see the band, better allow at least an hour to carve out some space. For particularly big names you'll have to get there even earlier. If the scene is more interesting than the sound, however, New York concerts are laid back enough that you can just wander in and out as the mood strikes you. With concerts at so many spectacular sites, a sunset on the Hudson or late afternoon light on the Brooklyn skyline often comes with your metaphorical price of admission (pretty much everything is free).

BAM Rhythm & Blues Festival at MetroTech `FREE`   MetroTech Commons is as close to a municipal center as Brooklyn gets, and in the summer it's the site of a free lunchtime concert series. As the name suggests, R&B is the focus, though the definition stretches to include blues, reggae, and funk as well. Surprisingly big names like the Neville Brothers and Ohio Players come through. Ten shows are held in all, Thursdays from noon to 2pm, mid-June to mid-August.

MetroTech Commons, at Flatbush and Myrtle aves. ✆ **718/636-4100.** www.bam. org. Subway: 2/3 to Hoyt St.; M/R to Lawrence St.; A/C/F to Jay St./Borough Hall.

Battery Park `FREE`   Battery Park has the city's most spectacular gardens and shoreline, but its corner-pocket location causes it to be overlooked. Come quitting time, much of the working crowd rushes off to subway cars and ferries, leaving the rest of us more space to enjoy the cultural resources. The River to River festival cosponsors several summer concerts down here, many of which are underattended by New York standards. There's no better way to watch dusk settle over the island. My favorite spot is **Robert F. Wagner, Jr. Park,** at the south end of the park. Boat traffic in New York Harbor and the Statue of Liberty provide the backdrop. A little ways north is the **World Financial Center Plaza.** Nestled between the Winter Garden and the North Cove Yacht Harbor, the space rings into life on Tuesday nights in summer when live bands play. Recent booking has brought in some solid indie rockers like Fountains of Wayne. Shows also begin at 7pm. Wednesday nights the place to be is **Rockefeller Park,** on the northernmost end of Battery Park, for another series of 7 o'clock concerts. Indie rock and alt-country are favored here, with bigish names like the Old 97's making the scene. Check www.rivertorivernyc.org for full schedules.

Robert F. Wagner, Jr. Park, between Battery Place and New York Harbor. ✆ 212/ 267-9700. www.bpcparks.org. Subway: 1 to Rector St. or South Ferry; 4/5 to Bowling Green.; World Financial Center Plaza, due east of the North Cove Yacht Harbor. ✆ 212/528-2733. www.worldfinancialcenter.com. Subway: E to World Trade Center; R/W to Cortlandt St.; Rockefeller Park, at the west end of Chambers and Warren sts. ✆ 212/528-2733. www.batteryparkcity.org. Subway: 1/2/3 or A/C to Chambers St.

Bryant Park `FREE`   Every year, Bryant Park seems to pack its live music schedule a little tighter. There's a big range of genres and the park's central location makes it a convenient place to catch some sounds. Broadway's brightest croon on selected summer afternoons (p. 67), while the Good Morning America Summer Concert Series (p. 84) brings out beats at 7am. On a less-elaborate note, you can also hear pianists every weekday in summer. The songs are old-timey, popularized by the likes of Fats Waller, Scott Joplin, and the Gershwins. Piano in the Park can be heard Mondays and Fridays from noon to 2:30pm, and Tuesdays through Thursdays from 3:30pm to 6pm.

Bryant Park, between W. 40th and 42nd sts., along Sixth Ave. www.bryantpark. org. Subway: B/D/F/V to 42nd St.; 7 to Fifth Ave.

Castle Clinton `FREE`   This old defensive battery took a turn as a fashionable concert hall in the first half of the 1800s, and it recalls those former duties on Thursday nights in summer. Indie favorites like Cat Power, The Magnetic Fields, and Del McCoury have done the honors in the past. The series kicks off with a July 4th show in Battery Park. All shows are free, although you need to pick up tickets for

Thursday nights. Distribution begins at Castle Clinton at 5pm, but people start lining up a good couple of hours before.

Battery Park, on the west side at New York Harbor. ✆ **212/566-6700.** www.down townny.com. **Subway: 1 to South Ferry; 4/5 Bowling Green.**

Celebrate Brooklyn!   The Prospect Park Bandshell is a perfect place for a concert, with a festive and friendly crowd. The audio selections are as eclectic as Brooklyn, with acts like Rufus Wainwright, the Spanish Harlem Orchestra, and the Brooklyn Philharmonic. Shows are generally well attended, so show up early if you want a decent view. Check the website for schedules. A $3 donation is suggested.

The Prospect Park Bandshell, Park Slope, Brooklyn. ✆ **718/855-7882.** www. celebratebrooklyn.org. **Subway: F to Seventh Ave.; B/Q to Seventh Ave.; 2/3 to Grand Army Plaza. Enter at Prospect Park West and 9th St.**

City Parks Foundation `FREE`   This group is a major player in New York's free music scene, putting on some 900 performances every year. Shows take place in parks across the boroughs; check online to see what's playing and when. One event to keep an eye out for is late August's **Charlie Parker Jazz Festival.** Bird gets honored with shows in two of his home neighborhoods, Harlem and the East Village. The Harlem show is Saturday afternoon in Marcus Garvey Park. Tompkins Square Park takes over on Sunday.

Marcus Garvey Park, 18 Mount Morris Park West, at Fifth Ave. ✆ **212/860-1373.** www.cityparksfoundation.org. **Subway: 2/3 or 4/5/6 to 125th St. Tompkins Sq., between 7th and 10th sts. and aves. A and B; 6 to Astor Place; F/V to Second Ave.**

East River Park Amphitheater `FREE`   This newly renovated spot on the East River, with beautiful Brooklyn and bridge views, hosts free music programs on summer Saturdays. Proximity to the Lower East Side and East Village ensure that the hipness readings are off the charts; artists such as Cat Power and Ted Leo perform. You can usually hear four acts over the afternoon. The amphitheater's capacity is around 1,000, so you may be able to wander in late and still snag a seat.

600 Grand St., at the East River. www.eastrivermusicproject.com. **Subway: F to Delancey St.; J/M/Z to Essex St. Walk along the south side of the Williamsburg Bridge and take the pedestrian bridge over the FDR. Turn left and follow the river down to the amphitheater.**

High Culture for Free

New York Philharmonic Concerts in the Parks `FREE`
The New York Philharmonic, one of the world's premier sym-
phonies, gives away a week's worth of shows every summer. The
covered composers range from Mendelssohn to Strauss to Ives.
While the atmosphere is more hackey sack than Harnancourt—
background for a group picnic rather than an event for the serious
music lover—the performances by guest conductors and musicians
are often inspired. If the classical music doesn't lure you in, you
might stop by just for the free fireworks show afterwards. Performance locations vary, but generally all five boroughs and Long
Island are included. Check the website (**www.newyorkphilharmonic.
org**) for exact locations. Shows start at 8pm, no tickets required.
© **212/875-5709.**

Met in the Parks `FREE`   Critics may sniff that the Metropolitan Opera rests on its laurels, but this institution maintains
extremely high standards. Tickets can exceed $300 for shows at
the Opera House, but for 2 weeks every summer the fat lady sings
for free. Shows are held in parks in all five boroughs, with a couple
of Jersey visits thrown in as well. Two different operas are performed, usually six performances of each. Check the website for
exact locations and times; no tickets are required. © **212/362-
6000. www. metoperafamily.org.**

   The classic summer Met and Phil shows are performed on the
Great Lawn in Central Park (midpark, just below 86th St.; Subway:
B/C or 4/5/6 to 86th St.). There are two different programs for
each institution each year, and they're wildly popular, with the picnic blankets spread out hours before the music begins. The leafy
setting is ideal, but if you want a closer view and a shorter waiting
time, I recommend checking out the less-crowded shows in Queens
and the Bronx.

Harlem Meer Performance Festival `FREE`   Latino and African
sounds predominate at this meer-front festival. The scene is as upbeat
as the music, which is usually very danceable. Blankets and picnics

are encouraged. Concerts are Sunday afternoons from 4 to 6pm, Memorial Day weekend through late August, near the Charles A. Dana Discovery Center. The same site also hosts "Dancing on the Plaza," on Thursday evenings in summer. There are lessons from 6 to 6:45pm, and then live music until 8:30pm. Disco and soul are among the offerings.

Central Park, at 110th St., between Fifth and Lenox aves. © **212/860-1370.** www.centralparknyc.org. Subway: 2/3 to Central Park N.

☆ **Lincoln Center Out of Doors** FREE   Lincoln Center is a veritable city of performing arts, and every summer for over 30 years now, the great public square has been home to a diverse series of shows. The breadth is breathtaking, from Chinese opera to Greek dance to cutting-edge jazz to children's story time. Incredibly, it's all free. Check online for exact schedules, covering 4 weeks in August. *Note:* Look for several shows that take place in the nearby Damrosch Park Bandshell, at West 62nd Street and Amsterdam Avenue.

70 Lincoln Center Plaza, at Broadway and 64th St. © **212/546-2656.** www.lincoln center.org. 1 to 66th St./Lincoln Center.

Madison Square Music FREE   Madison Square's refurbished park has joined the summer music scrum. Radio thrift shop proprietress Laura Cantrell and jazz axeman Charlie Hunter have been heard here. Taste buds more than cochleae are what make this concert special, however. The legendary **Shake Shack** (© **212/889-6600;** www. shakeshacknyc.com), with its $3.23 burgers, makes for the perfect accompanying picnic. (*Note:* If planning on eating from the Shake Shack, allow an extra 8 to 10 hours to get through the line, which in nice weather stretches to Brooklyn.)

Madison Square Park, Fifth Ave. at 23rd St. © **212/538-4071.** www.madison squarepark.org. Jun–Aug Wed 7pm. Subway: N/R/W or 6 to 23rd St.

Martin Luther King, Jr. Concert Series FREE   Jazz, soul, gospel, and old school are some of the genres that can be heard on the Monday night program here. Seating is limited, so you might want to bring your own chair. In case of rain, concerts are postponed to Tuesday.

Wingate Field, Winthrop St., between Brooklyn and Kingston aves., Brooklyn. © **718/ 469-1912.** www.brooklynconcerts.com. Subway: 2/5 to Winthrop St.

Naumburg Orchestral Concerts FREE   The Naumburg Bandshell in Central Park hosts this concert series, which varies from classical orchestral presentations to brass to flamenco. The series is one of the oldest in the country, with over a century's worth of experience in entertaining New Yorkers. Shows are Tuesday nights at 7:30pm, with no rain dates.

Midpark, Central Park, just below 72nd St. www.naumburgconcerts.org. Subway: B/C to 72nd St.; 6 to 68th St./Hunter College.

RiverRocks FREE I love the festive atmosphere of this concert series. The crowd is friendly, and sunset over the Hudson and the Jersey skyline is inspiring. Roomy Pier 54 does the hosting. If you show up late you won't get very close to the band, but you will find plenty of space for hanging out, or even dancing. Music varies, from up-and-comers, to groups in slow decline. Check the website for time and dates, and also check for other concerts on the same pier.

Pier 54 on the Hudson, at 13th St. ⓒ 212/533-PARK. www.hudsonriverpark.org. Subway: A/C/E to 14th St.; L to Eighth Ave.

Seaport Music Festival FREE The South Street Seaport isn't much more than a glorified mall, which is cause enough for most locals to give it a wide berth. In the summer, however, Pier 17 is loaded with great free music. Selections are diverse, from salsa to zydeco, with recent visits from Clap Your Hands Say Yeah and Jay Farrar. Events are held just about every Wednesday through Friday night from 6 to 9pm. The festival runs late June through August.

Pier 17, between Beekman and Fulton sts., just east of South St. ⓒ 212/ SEAPORT. www.seaportmusicfestival.com. Subway: A/C/J/M/Z/2/3/4/5 to Fulton St./Broadway Nassau.

Seaside Summer Concert Series FREE This free series attracts Coney Island locals, who settle into Asser Levy Park for convivial evenings. The booking for this event is borderline scary, with both Michael Bolton and Liza Minnelli making the list in 2005. Concerts begin at 7:30pm on Thursday nights from mid-July to mid-August.

W. 5th St. and Surf Ave., Coney Island, across from the aquarium. ⓒ 718/469-1912. www.brooklynconcerts.com. Subway: F/Q to W. 8th St./NY Aquarium.

Siren Music Festival FREE The best in below-the-radar rock can be found at the *Village Voice*'s annual Siren Music Festival. Over a hundred thousand fans assemble near the Coney Island boardwalk for music on two stages. The bands tend to be high-quality performers, on the cusp of breakthroughs, or not too far removed from indie-rock triumphs. See p. 291 in chapter 7 for more information.

Main stage: 10th St., at the boardwalk. Second stage: Stillwell Ave., at the board-walk. ℂ 212/475-3333. www.villagevoice.com/siren. Saturday in mid-July noon–9pm. Subway: D/F/Q/W to Still-well Avenue/Coney Island.

SummerGarden FREE The MoMA beats to a soundtrack three parts classical to one part jazz, and that's approximately the proportion of music in this summer concert series. The Abby Aldrich **Rockefeller Sculpture Garden** plays host, so if your mind wanders from the music you have Philip Johnson's elegant layout to study. Julliard students can often be found doing the classical honors, while jazz is performed by innovators like Henry Threadgill. The free tickets get distributed at 5:30pm on the day of the show outside the garden gate on 54th between Fifth and Sixth avenues. In case of rain, the concerts move indoors to The Agnes Gund Garden Lobby.

11 W. 53rd St., between Fifth and Sixth aves. ℂ 212/708-9400. www.moma. org. July–Aug Sun 8pm. Subway: E/V to Fifth Ave.

Summer Nights at El Museo del Barrio FREE Latin flavors are on the bill on summer Thurs-days at this Harlem institution. Shows are performed outdoors in the courtyard, with music rang-ing from Cuban son to modern Latino rock. In case of rain,

FREE **Wall Street Rising**

Not outside and not in summer, the Music Downtown series is a New York free-music anomaly. Sponsored by Financial District boosters, the site is the lovely Tribeca Performing Arts Center on the campus of the Borough of Manhattan Community Col-lege (BMCC). Booking is excel-lent, with Jeff Tweedy, Aimee Mann, and the Blind Boys of Alabama on the inaugural sea-son's bill. Tickets are distrib-uted on a weekday morning at the Downtown Information Center (25 Broad St., www.down towninfocenter.org), with two seats for two different shows available per person. Ticket-holders have to show up by 8:15 on the night of the show or they forfeit their seats, mean-ing there's some additional space available for ticketless standbys needing a miracle.

BMCC Tribeca Performing Arts Center, 199 Chambers St., between Greenwich St. and the West Side Highway. ℂ 212/ 509-0300. www.musicdown town.org. Subway: 1/2/3 or A/C to Chambers St.

shows move indoors. Select Thursday nights from 6 to 9pm, In July and August.

1230 Fifth Ave., at 104th St. ℂ 212/831-7272. www.elmuseo.org. Subway: 6 to 103rd St.

⭐ **SummerStage** FREE   Words like summer and music and free conjure an idyllic picture, especially in the context of Central Park. SummerStage is a crack outfit that brings big-name performers to a stage just off the Rumsey Playfield. To get a seat in the bleachers, better show up a couple of hours before start time. If you're not that patient, you can just wander in at any time, and you should be able to find a spot to stand and/or dance. Since no tickets are required, it's easy to come and go freely unless it's a super-popular show. Acts as varied as James Brown, Sonic Youth, and Hugh Masekela have played here. Every summer it seems more and more of the concerts are pricey benefit shows, with tickets going for about $40. To further support the series, donations are solicited as you enter. (No contribution is required.)

Central Park, at the Rumsey Playfield, near E. 72nd St. ℂ 212-360-2777 or 212/360-2756. www.summerstage.org. Subway: 6 to 68th or 77th sts.; B/C to 72nd St. Enter the park at 69th St. and Fifth Ave.

Washington Square Music Festival FREE   One of the city's oldest festivals brings classical music (and a little jazz) to the heart of the Village. Three pieces, connected by an overall theme, are played Tuesday nights in July and early August from 8 to 10pm. The last Tuesday of the month is often set aside for jazz, salsa, or swing. The festival is held in the southeast corner of Washington Square Park. Limited seating is available.

Near the intersection of Washington Sq. S. and Washington Sq. E. ℂ 212/252-3621. www.washingtonsquaremusicfestival.org. Subway: A/B/C/D/E/F/V to W. 4th St.-Washington Sq.

2 The Reel Cheap World

The movies love New York. Blithely ignoring our existing congestion, productions flock to the city to steal our parking spaces and tie up our sidewalks. Gotham-themed films line the video store shelves. Is it because we're a convenient symbol of urban glamour? Or is it simply because New York is the greatest city in the history of the world? Either way, NYC has a lot of cinematic pride, which allows New Yorkers to be extorted with $10.75 movie tickets, a dearth of cheap afternoon matinees, and new releases sold out by 4pm even on gorgeous sunny days. Fortunately in New York there are always alternatives. Our libraries are stocked with videos, our bars screen in their backrooms, and in the summer we get spectacular film alfresco. Most events are on the house, and those that aren't won't break the bank.

INDIES, CULTS, CLASSICS & MORE

Arlene's Grocery Picture Show `FREE`   Even at $10 a ticket or more, it's tough to get into a show at most of the city's slick corporate-sponsored film fests. One exception remains, on the Lower East Side, of course, where Arlene's Grocery puts on an annual Picture Show. The fest is growing exponentially, with over 500 shorts now. The submission fee is a democratic $5, and all the showings are free, including the awards ceremony ("The Groceries," with mounted cans of pigeon peas instead of Oscars). The series takes place across four spring weekends.

95 Stanton St., between Orchard and Ludlow sts. © 212/358-1633. www.arlenes grocery.net. Subway: F/V to Second Ave.; J/M/Z to Essex St. Other screenings at additional neighborhood venues.

Barbès `FREE`   In the international spirit of its namesake Parisian neighborhood, Barbès presents Traveling Cinéma, a film series that veers from *Nosferatu* to *Bringing Up Baby*. The back room hosts on Mondays at 7pm, all films in 16mm and free as the air.

376 9th St., at Sixth Ave. Park Slope, Brooklyn. © 718/965-9177. www.barbes brooklyn.com. Subway: F to Seventh Ave. Take the southwest exit and make a U-turn when you get out, walking downhill on 9th St. toward Sixth Ave.

☆ **Cabaret Cinema**   Beneath the Rubin Museum of Art's sparkling new galleries is an intimate screening room. Friday evenings see projections of a terrific lineup of films. When the "Holy Madness," exhibit was up, the museum screened related reels that ranged from *Siddhartha* to *Monty Python's Life of Brian*. Some shows come with related commentary, like Wallace Shawn answering questions about *My Dinner with Andre*. The movies roll at 9:30pm. There's a $7 bar minimum, but no other charge.

150 W. 17th St., between Sixth and Seventh aves. © 212/620-5000. www.rma nyc.org. Subway: 1/2/3/F/L to 14th St.

Membership Has Its Privileges

Does Hollywood still make movies that aren't just flimsy remakes of second-rate television shows? Just when we're ready to give up forever on the medium, the marquee of the **Film Forum** draws us in with some irresistible nugget and we're hooked again. Three screens rotate between revivals, retrospectives, and indies that can't be found elsewhere. The crowd is just as interesting, with big-shot actors and directors often in the house, upping their avant-garde cinematic cred. A 1-year membership to Film Forum is one of the city's best steals. Sixty-five bucks buys you half-price movie tickets for all three screens 365 days a year. That's $5 instead of $10. The next membership level up is an even sweeter deal: $95 entitles you to two half-price tickets for every show. Imagine: cheap date opportunities every single day. Membership is good for 1 year from the date of purchase. But wait, there's more. It's also 100% tax deductible. Now if only they could make the seats a little more comfortable. 209 W. Houston St. between Sixth Ave., at Varick. ✆ **212/727-8110**. www.filmforum.com. Subway: 1 to Houston St.

Flick fans in the County of Queens have a steal of their own. The **Museum of the Moving Image** shows up to four films a day. The screenings are thematically connected (a Robert Altman retrospective, for example), usually repertory. For the regular admission price

Coney Island Museum   On Saturday nights in summer, the museum drags its carny relics to the side and lays in rows of chairs so it can show off Coney Island's sideshow heritage, or at least movies made in the same spirit. In addition to explorations of burlesque, expect uplifting cinematic triumphs with the words bikini or bandit in the title. The low-budget productions beget budget prices: just $5. And the popcorn's free! Saturdays at 8:30pm.

1208 Surf Ave., 2nd floor. ✆ **718/372-5159**. www.indiefilmpage.com. Subway: D/F/N/Q to Coney Island/Stillwell Ave.

Freddy's Bar `FREE`   The much ballyhooed Brooklyn Nets development intends to displace beloved local dive Freddy's. While you can, of $10, you can see as many of the daily films as you like. Watch four Kubricks in succession, and you're only paying $2.50 a pop. For an option that'll cause less eye strain, consider the museum's membership. A $65 individual plan will get you unlimited access to the exhibitions and regular screenings. The $100 plan covers you and a guest (plus your own kids, where applicable). There's hundreds of films to choose from annually; see six of them and your individual membership pays for itself. (Like Film Forum's, it's also 100% tax deductible.) 35th Ave. at 36th St., Astoria, Queens. ℂ **718/784-0077.** www.movingimage.us. Subway: G/R/V to Steinway St.

For just $20 a year you can pick up a membership at the East Village's **Pioneer Theater.** Regular tickets will only cost you $6.50, compared to the $9 nonmembers price, for a savings of $2.50 a shot. Your membership will pay for itself in eight screenings. The Pioneer is only a uniplex so the options are limited, but the programming is every bit as intriguing as the institutions above. Between docs, indies, classics, and mini-festivals, you'll find plenty of reasons to blow off your TiVo at the Pioneer. 155 E. 3rd St., at Ave. A. ℂ **212/254-3300.** www.twoboots.com/pioneer. Subway: F/V to Second Ave.

enjoy the scene before Freddy's is dead. There's never a cover or minimum for the back-room acts, which include music, quiz nights, spelling bees, and arts and crafts nights. For movies, every first and last Sunday at 4pm sees the materialization of "The Alpha-Omega Science-Fiction Filmfest." *Torpedo of Doom* and other instructive fare flicker in living 16mm. Stimuli freaks should check out Rev-99, a collective that makes live audio and video mixes on every other Wednesday night. Call it jazz channel-surfing, clips of the mixes can be watched nightly on the front-room monitors. At least until Bruce Ratner gets his claws around them.

485 Dean St., at Sixth Ave., Brooklyn. ℂ **718/622-7035.** www.freddysbackroom.com. Subway: 2/3 to Bergen St.

Manhattan Short Film Festival `FREE`   As media over-saturation contracts our attention spans ever further, short films become increasingly useful. Union Square brings little flicks from around the world to the Manhattan Short Film Festival every September. Though repeating the arc of beginnings, middles, and endings twelve times in a row can be tiresome, the quality of film here is very high, with the best of the festival represented. The screenings are free, as is the music that kicks off the show around 5pm.

Union Square Park Center Lawn. Ⓒ **212/529-8640.** www.msfilmfest.com. Subway: L/N/Q/R/W/4/5/6 to 14th St./Union Sq.

Millennium Film   Despite the Y2K-sounding name, Millennium Film has been providing a home for experimental and cutting-edge film since 1966. The regular calendar of movies often highlights unfairly forgotten flicks and directors. Open film nights come around on Fridays, with filmmakers allowed to contribute anything they want as long as it's finished and not more than 20 minutes—first come, first served. Most shows are $8; open films and selected other nights are admission by contribution.

66 E. 4th St., between Second Ave. and Bowery. Ⓒ **212/673-0090.** www.millenniumfilm.org. Subway: F/V to Second Ave.

☆ **Ocularis at Galapagos**   Ocularis ("of eyes" in Latin) began its Brooklyn run with rooftop screenings, before finding a permanent home at Galapagos, the Williamsburg mayonnaise factory turned cultural center. Ocularis presents some of the most exciting cinema in the city every Monday at 8pm, with a mix of themed shorts and amazing discoveries in lost avant-garde film. Tickets are $6.

70 N. 6th St., Williamsburg, Brooklyn. Ⓒ **718/388-8713.** www.ocularis.net or www.galapagosartspace.com. Subway: L to Bedford Ave., walk west on 6th St., toward the East River.

Rififi/Cinema Classics   This shabby-chic bar put itself on the East Village cultural map with weekly screenings of *The Wizard of Oz*, creepily synched to Pink Floyd's "The Dark Side of the Moon." Burlesque and comedy nights have been added to the mix, the former for $5, the latter mostly free with one-drink minimums. Monday night is Metropol's screening night, with 10pm projections of the best in splatter and horror. Shows are free with a one drink minimum. Check the website for the full calendar of events.

332 E. 11th St., between First and Second aves. ℂ 212/677-1027. www.cinema classics.com. Subway: L to First Ave.; N/Q/R/W/4/5/6 to 14th St./Union Sq.

Rooftop Films   Rooftops. Brooklyn's got 'em in spades. Rooftop Films has a lovely one on top of the American Can Factory. This sprawling industrial compound dates back at least as far as the Civil War. On Friday nights in summer, God dims the overheads and indie shorts play. Despite perennially low budgets, Rooftop Films does a good filtering job and quality is surprisingly high. Film themes run along the lines of "Home Movies" or "Scenes from Texas." Screenings cost around $7, a bargain if you value films made by actual human beings and not Hollywood-studio automatons. Other venues, including the lawn at the Automotive High School in Williamsburg, have recently been added. Check the website for exact ticket prices and times. Movies start after sunset (9pm usually), with live music beforehand.

232 3rd St., Bldg. B, between Third and Fourth aves., Brooklyn. ℂ 718/417-7362. www.rooftopfilms.com. Subway: F/G to Carroll Gardens; N/R to Union St./Fourth Ave. When it rains, screenings are held indoors at the same location.

Thursdays at Chelsea   Chelsea's Clearview 9 Cinema keeps the natives from getting too restless over a diet of mainstream Hollywood fare by hosting this popular weekly reduced-rate night. Drag darling Hedda Lettuce warms up the room before camp classics get projected. Expect Joan Crawford and Bette Davis to be comprehensively represented. Thursdays at 7pm, only $6.

260 W. 23rd St., between Seventh and Eighth aves. ℂ 212/777-FILM. www.clear viewcinemas.com. Subway: 1 or C/E to 23rd St.

Sony Wonder Technology Lab FREE   Sony goes to bat for high-def technology by hosting sporadic free films in its 73-seat theater. The flicks tend to be well-known Hollywood products of recent vintage. Sprinkled throughout the year are additional screenings for the kiddies. Adults get select weekend days at 2pm; the kids get select Thursdays at 2pm, sometimes at noon as well. Reservations recommended; call on Monday morning when a screening is scheduled for later in the week.

550 Madison Ave., at 56th St. ℂ 212/833-7858. www.sonywondertechlab.com. Subway: 4/5/6 to 59th St.; N/R/W to Lexington Ave./59th St.

Telephone Bar & Grill FREE   Cinephiles and the people who love them gather at Gene's Backroom Cinema Club for flicks on a big

Current Releases for Little Currency

"That $3 theater" became "that $4 theater" and then closed altogether. The uptown bargain-matinee place got torn down to make
way for million-dollar condos. It's becoming harder and harder to
find a current release for anything less than the usurious $10.75
charged for prime-time viewing. If you're in the right neighborhood,
though, there are still a couple of options left.

Cobble Hill Cinema   Monday through Friday all shows before
5pm are only $6, as are the first shows of the day on the weekend
(as long as they start before 2pm). If matinees don't do it for you,
there are also two bargain days, Tuesdays and Thursdays, when all
seats for all shows all day and all night are a humble $6. The only
exceptions are special engagements and holidays. 265 Court St., at
Butler, Boerum Hill, Brooklyn. ✆ **718/596-9113.** Subway: F/G to
Bergen St.

Kew Gardens Cinemas   First-run films play here, with several
bargain showtimes. Monday, Wednesday, and Friday, all seats are
$6 until 5pm, as are seats for the first show before 2pm on Satur-
days and Sundays. Tuesdays and Thursdays are bargain days, with
all shows day and night going for $6. Holidays and special engage-
ments are excepted for the cheap seats. ✆ **718/441-9835.** 81-05
Lefferts Blvd., at Austin St., Kew Gardens, Queens. Subway: E/F to
Kew Gardens/Union Turnpike.

MJ Harlem 9   Magic Johnson offers matinees (shows before
6pm) at a discounted rate of $7.50. On the weekdays the same deal
goes for any show before 2pm. 2309 Frederick Douglass Blvd., at
124th St. ✆ **212/665-6923.** www.enjoytheshow.com. Subway:
A/B/C/D to 125th St.

UA Kaufman Astoria 14   Right across the street from the
legendary Kaufman Astoria Studios, this Queens megaplex has
bargain matinees on the weekdays. Every show before 6pm is only
$7. 35-30 38th St., off Steinway, Astoria, Queens. ✆ **718/786-
2020.** Subway: G/R/V to Steinway St.

(LCD) screen. Free films are shown every week, conforming to monthly themes that shift from Oscar winners to foreign faves. Tuesdays at 8pm. (Also check the calendar for free or cheap music, poetry, comedy, and play readings.)

149 Second Ave., between 9th and 10th sts. ℂ 212/529-5000. www.telebar.com. Subway: 6 to Astor Place; L to Third Ave.

NYC'S DRIVE-IN: OUTDOOR SUMMER SCREENINGS

We may be too cheap for insurance, garages, tickets, tolls, and all the other joys of car ownership, but New Yorkers do know how to enjoy their very own brand of drive-in movie. Come summer, the parks roll out the big screens and the locals trundle in with blankets and picnic dinners. Each festival has its own identity, with movies ranging across the decades and the genres, assuring something for every cineaste's taste. As dusk settles over the city, around 8 or 8:30pm, the crowd hushes and the reels spin. Lie back and be transported by the magic of the movies under the starry skies. Well, skies.

Central Park Film Festival `FREE`   Central Park has been lending atmosphere to films since 1908 (a silent version of *Romeo and Juliet* was the first movie shot here). The Park celebrates its long starring career with this late-summer fest, which screens several of the more than 200 movies that have had major scenes here. *Breakfast at Tiffany's* and *Tootsie* are among past players. Admission is free, at the Rumsey Playfield, usually over five nights leading up to Labor Day.

Central Park, at the Rumsey Playfield, near E. 72nd St. ℂ 212-310-6600. www.centralparknyc.org. Subway: 6 to 68th or 77th sts.; B/C to 72nd St. Enter the park at 69th St. and Fifth Ave.

Crotona Park Hip Hop Film Festival `FREE`   The Bronx celebrates hip-hop culture with free movies, dancing, and, of course, a surfeit of spinning DJs. The jam runs from 7 to 8:30pm and then gives way to the films, which vary from hip-hop docs to camp classics like Krush Groove. Usually Wednesdays in July.

Crotona Park E. and Charlotte St. ℂ 718/378-2061. Subway: 2/5 to 174th St. Walk south on Boston Rd. to Suburban Place, take a right on Crotona Park E. and then a left onto Charlotte St., where you'll see Indian Lake and the festival.

☆ **HBO Bryant Park Summer Film Festival** `FREE`   Bryant Park is the most famous and most popular of New York's outdoor talkies. A

Free Outdoor Summer Movies

Note: All movies begin at dusk.

Monday	Wednesday	Thursday	Friday
HBO Bryant Park Summer Film Festival	Crotona Park Hip Hop Film Festival	Brooklyn Bridge Movies With a View	RiverFlicks- Pier 25
	Outdoor Cinema Program at Socrates Sculpture Park		
	Summer on the Hudson: Movies Under the Stars		
	RiverFlicks-Pier 54		

huge screen goes up along Sixth Avenue across from the library, and the lawn fills with friendly movie fanatics. Film selections run from kitsch like *Jailhouse Rock* to classics like *The Philadelphia Story* to tripped-out wonders like *2001: A Space Odyssey*. Watching the latter from the grass brings a creepy resonance: Bryant Park was once a potter's field. The gates open for blanket spreading at 5pm, and if you want a decent view you should be on-site by then. Bring a crossword puzzle and a picnic dinner and pretend you're just sitting in the park and not waiting for a show. Latecomers have to watch from way back or the wings. It's not untenable, it's just not as much fun as dancing through the HBO trailer from the heart of the crowd. If you time things right, and the director's done his work, this event is totally worth its logistical impositions. Monday nights June through August.

W. 40th to 41st, on the Sixth Ave. side of Bryant Park. ✆ **212/512-5700.** www.bryantpark.org. Rain date Tues. Subway: B/D/F/V to 42nd St.; 7 to Fifth Ave.

☆ **Movies With a View** FREE What could be better than the spectacular sight of downtown lights shimmering behind the Gothic span of the Brooklyn Bridge? A free movie flickering in front, that's what. Every summer, Brooklyn Bridge Park, a DUMBO oasis on the former site of the Fulton Ferry Landing, shows a themed series of flicks. This program is the anti–Bryant Park—it's low key, with no hassles, and you don't have to be überorganized to carve out a decent spot to watch. Thursday nights at dusk, in July and August.

Empire-Fulton Ferry Park, just west of Water St. ✆ **718/802-0603.** www.bbpc. net. Subway: F to York St.; A/C to High St.; Water Taxi to Fulton Ferry Landing.

The New Committee: The *Voice*'s Ticket Giveaways

Before the Internet ruled our lives, the **Village Voice** sponsored weekly movie ticket giveaways. You'd queue up somewhere near the NYU campus with a great crowd of fellow-scroungers known as "The Committee." Anything the city offered up for free would attract them. If you showed up early enough at the location, you'd be guaranteed a ticket for you and a guest. With the Internet's ascendance, however, promoters have a more direct way of getting your butts in the seats. Scroll down the left side of the *Voice*'s homepage (www.villagevoice.com) and you'll see a selection of giveaways that almost always includes a movie premiere or two. **Time Out New York** (www.timeoutny.com) has contests and give-aways, too, though usually it's for theater, and they only offer a couple of seats, making for some long odds. In these new lottery systems, they get your name, address, e-mail, and other invasive disclosures, which the old Committee members wouldn't have given up for anything less than a T-shirt. Oh well—at least it's still free.

Outdoor Cinema Program at Socrates Sculpture Park `FREE`
Queens is the most culturally diverse spot on the planet, so it makes sense that a Queens film festival would show off movies from around the world. You'll even find culture-appropriate food vendors, so you can eat Italian during *The Bicycle Thief* or Indian while *Monsoon Wedding* plays. The movies flicker at Socrates Sculpture Park in Long Island City, a former dump site resuscitated as an artistic gem along the East River. There are great skyline sightlines, along with slightly less uplifting Costco parking lot views. Music, dancing, and food at 7pm, movies at dusk. Wednesday nights in July and August.

32-01 Vernon Blvd., at Broadway, Astoria, Queens. ✆ **718/784-4520**. www.socrates sculpturepark.org. Subway: N/W to Broadway. Walk 8 blocks along Broadway toward the East River. Rain site is the American Museum of the Moving Image, 8pm. ✆ **718/784-0077**. www.movingimage.us. Subway: G/R/V to Steinway St.

Prospect Park Film Series Celebrate Brooklyn! FREE   Celebrate Brooklyn! earns superfluous exclamation points with an amazing program of music and film. At times the two are combined, like a showing of *The Creature from the Black Lagoon*! in 3-D! with a live performance from The Jazz Passengers. The series runs from June to August; check the website for exact dates. A $3 donation is suggested.

The Prospect Park Bandshell, enter at Prospect Park W. and 9th St. Park Slope, Brooklyn. ✆ 718/855-7882. www.celebratebrooklyn.org. Subway: F to Seventh Ave.; B/Q to Seventh Ave.; 2/3 to Grand Army Plaza.

RiverFlicks FREE   The waters of the Hudson and the Jersey skyline provide the backdrop for RiverFlicks. It's a viewer-friendly scene, with chairs laid out on the pier, free popcorn, and films that tend toward crowd-pleasing recent hits. *Legally Blonde, 8 Mile,* and *Gladiator* have all made the cut. If you're too late to garner a seat, there's space aplenty for blanket spreading. Pier 54 hosts Wednesday nights and Pier 25 takes Fridays in July and August.

Pier 25, at North Moore and the Hudson. ✆ 212/533-7275. www.hudsonriver park.org. Subway: 1 to Franklin St.; A/C to Chambers St. Walk toward the river. Pier 54, at W. 13th St. and the river. Subway: A/C/E to 14th St./Eighth Ave. Walk toward the river.

Solar-Powered Film Festival FREE   Solar One is New York's first freestanding building to get all of its power not from recycled dinosaurs, but from Helios himself. Every summer to celebrate this achievement (and to raise awareness about the inevitable need to live greener in NYC), the building hosts a film festival. Over two August weekends projectors running on sun power alone project hipster fare like *Grey Gardens* and *Screen Door Jesus*. Look also for the dance series, with stage lights that run on solar power.

Stuyvesant Cove Park, 23rd St. and the FDR. ✆ 212/505-6050. www.solar1.org. Subway 6 to 23rd St.; L to First Ave.

Summer on the Hudson: Movies Under the Stars FREE   With Trump residential structures inflating into place seemingly over night, lower Riverside Park is sure to have a higher profile with a few thousand newly minted West Siders. For their—and our—entertainment, the park's brand-new acreage is opening itself up to culture. In addition to acoustic music Sundays and other concerts, there's a thus-far underrated movie series at 8:30pm on summer Wednesdays. Curating is thematic, with "On the Hudson River Waterfront" the mouthful title to '06's version (*Showboat* and *The African Queen* made the cut). Picnics encouraged; at the end of Pier I.

Pier I, the Hudson at 70th St. ☎ 311. www.nyc.gov/parks. Subway: 1/2/3 to 72nd St.

Tribeca Drive-In `FREE`   The North Cove of the World Financial Center shows off the big-budget capabilities of the Tribeca Film Festival. A huge screen and sweet sound make the most of crowd pleasers like *Saturday Night Fever* and *Mad Hot Ballroom*. `FINE PRINT` The event is free (two or three films per year), but required tickets are a bit of a chore to score, at the end of a long line at the Festival Box Office (13-17 B Laight St., between Varick St. and Sixth Ave.). Late April, check the website for details.

North Cove, enter through the Winter Garden off the West Side Highway, just south of Vesey St. ☎ 212/941-2400. www.tribecafilmfestival.org. Subway: 1/R/W to Rector St.

SCREENINGS AT THE NEW YORK PUBLIC LIBRARY

New York's book repositories bear no hard feelings for the many indignities the movies have imposed over the years. Our libraries are so forgiving, in fact, that dozens of branches offer free film screenings every week. Check the NYPL website (**www.nypl.org**) for showings besides the ones listed below. The offerings are all over the map, from classics to avant-garde to recent Hollywood hits. There's even a few adaptations mixed in.

IN MANHATTAN

Donnell Library Center   Movies for adults at various times, generally Wednesday and Thursday at 2:30pm, again on Thursday at 6pm, and select Saturdays at 11am and 2pm. 20 W. 53rd St., between Fifth and Sixth aves. ☎ 212/621-0618. Subway: E/V to 53rd St.; F to 57th St.

58th Street Library   Films for adults, Fridays at 2pm. 127 E. 58th St., between Lexington and Park aves. ☎ 212/759-7358. Subway: N/R/W or 4/5/6 to 59th St.

Yorkville Branch   The Yorkville Film Festival features classic films, generally every other Friday at 3pm. 222 East 79th St., between Second and Third aves. ☎ 212/744-5824. Subway: 6 to 77th St.

For Real Culture Vultures

Our allies across the globe maintain cultural outposts throughout the city. With the support of universities and embassies, these organizations are able to offer a swath of free readings, lectures, and films. Though the material can be esoteric if you're not from the nation in question, pick the right events and you'll find plenty of accessible entertainment.

Austrian Cultural Forum `FREE` See "Donau, Dunak, Duna, Dunav, Dunarea" along with the rest of your favorite new Austrian flicks. Generally two showings, 6 and 8pm, day of the week varies. Admission is free; no reservations necessary. 11 E. 52nd St., between Fifth and Madison aves. ℂ **212/319-5300.** www.acfny.org. Subway: E/V to 53rd St.

Czech Center `FREE` The only Czech center outside of Europe, our Czech mates offer Video Thursdays. Screenings are generally at 7pm, but not every Thursday, and other days of the week have films as well. Check the Czech Center schedule. Look also for art exhibits in this space. 1109 Madison Ave., at 83rd St. ℂ **212/288-0830.** www.czechcenter.com. Subway: 4/5/6 to 86th St.

Deutsches Haus `FREE` This NYU-related institution bridges old and new worlds. Regular screenings of German-language films. Check the website for a calendar of events. 42 Washington Mews, between Fifth Ave. and University Place. ℂ **212/958-8660.** www.nyu.edu/deutscheshaus. Subway: N/R/W to 8th St.; 6 to Astor Place.

French Institute Fans of freedom flicks (French film) enjoy screenings of contemporaries and classics every Tuesday at the Florence Gould Hall. English subtitles come at no additional charge. Other film nights can be found scattered through the schedule. 55 E. 59th St., between Madison and Park aves. ℂ **212/355-6160.** www.fiaf.org. Regular tickets are $9, but admission is free to French Institute members. Membership costs $90 per year. Subway: N/R/W or 4/5/6 to 59th St.

The Early Childhood Resource and Information Center (ECRIC) Wednesdays at 11am is Baby Lap Time, for babies and toddlers up to 18 months. Thursdays at 3:30pm is Picture Book Time for kids ages 18 months to 4 years. On the second floor of the Hudson Park Branch Library. 66 Leroy St., off Seventh Ave. ⓒ 212/929-0815. Subway: 1 to Houston St.

Fort Washington Branch Toddler Time for kids ages 18 to 36 months, Wednesdays at 11am. ⓒ 212/927-3533. 535 W. 179th St., between St. Nicholas and Audubon aves. Subway: 1 to 181st St.; A to 175th St.

Jefferson Market Library Picture Book Time for kids ages 4 to 8 on Tuesdays at 4pm. 425 Sixth Ave., at 10th St. ⓒ 212/243-4334. Subway: F/V to 14th St.; L to Sixth Ave.; A/B/C/D/E to W. 4th St.–Washington Sq.

St. Agnes Library Picture Book Time for kids ages 3 to 8,

> **FREE** **Let's Go to the Videotape**
>
> New York's libraries have extensive video collections. They're like Blockbuster, only less censorship and you don't have to pay for anything. The **Donnell Library Center** has some 3,000 popular movies, on top of 2,200 unpopular arty movies. Plus, if you still haven't gotten around to upgrading to DVD, they've got 8,500 16mm films. The collection is predominantly circulating. (While you're there, you can skip a trip to Tower Records by checking out their 35,000 CDs, too.) 20 W. 53rd St., between Fifth and Sixth aves. ⓒ 212/621-0609. www.nypl.org. Subway: E/V to 53rd St.; F to 57th St.

Tuesdays at 4pm. Thursdays at 4pm, films for kids ages 3 to 8. Films for adults on select Wednesdays, 2pm. 444 Amsterdam Ave., between 80th and 81st sts. ⓒ 212/877-4380. Subway: 1 to 79th St.; B/C to 81st St.

Yorkville Films for adults Fridays at 3pm. Wednesday at 4pm for kids 3 to 5. 222 E. 79th St., between Second and Third aves. ⓒ 212/744-5824. Subway: 6 to 77th St.

IN THE BRONX

Baychester Library Films Fridays at 3:30pm, for kids ages 5 to 12. 2049 Asch Loop N., north of Bartow Ave. ⓒ 718/379-6700. Subway: B/D to Bedford Park Blvd., or BX26 bus to Aldrich St.

Castle Hill Branch Kid Picture Book Time on some Mondays, 4pm, for ages 5 and up. 947 Castle Hill Ave., at Bruckner Blvd. ✆ **718/ 824-3838.** Subway: 6 to Castle Hill Ave.

Fordham Library Center Branch Wednesday at 3:30pm, for kids ages 5 to 12. 2556 Bainbridge Ave., near Fordham Rd. ✆ **718/ 579-4244.** Subway: B/D to Fordham Rd.

Grand Concourse Branch Fridays at 4pm, for kids ages 5 to 12. 155 E. 173rd St., east of the Grand Concourse. ✆ **718/583-6611.** Subway: B/D to 174th–175th St.; 4 to Mt. Eden.

Hunt's Point Regional Branch Mondays at 4pm, for kids 5 to 12. 877 Southern Blvd., at Tiffany St. ✆ **718/617-0338.** Subway: 6 to Longwood Ave.; 2/5 to Simpson St.

Melrose Mondays at 4pm, for kids ages 4 to 12. 910 Morris Ave., at E. 162nd. ✆ **718/588-0110.** Subway: B/D/4 to 161st.

Morrisania Branch Tuesdays at 3:30pm, for kids ages 6 to 8. 610 E. 169th St., at Franklin Ave. ✆ **718/ 589-9268.** Subway: 2/5 to 149th St. then BX55 bus to 169th St.; B/D/4 to 167th St. then BX35 bus to 169th St.

Box: Bank Withdrawals

In yet another step in the inevitable Blade Runnerization of the city, video stores have gone automated. **MovieBankUSA** has set up some dozen video rental kiosks and storefronts around the city, with more on the way. Basically ATMs for films (and video games), charges go as low as 99¢. If you want longer than a 6-hour rental, it's $2.49. Membership is free. Browse through the friendly computer screen, make your selection, and 30 seconds later the DVD pops out of the slot. Best of all is the security of knowing the product is never touched by human hands. ✆ **877/586-6060.** www.moviebankusa.com.

Pelham Bay Branch Wednesdays at 3:30pm, for kids ages 3 to 6. 3060 Middletown Rd., north of Crosby Ave. ✆ **718/792-6744.** Subway: 6 to Buhre Ave.

Riverdale Branch Videos on some Thursdays at 4pm, for kids ages 3 to 12. Picture Book Time Tuesdays at 4pm, for kids 5 and older. 5540 Mosholu Ave., at W. 256th St. ✆ **718/549-1212.** Subway: 1 to 231st St., then BX7 bus to Riverdale Ave. and W. 256th; A to 207th, then BX7 bus to Riverdale Ave. and W. 256th.

Westchester Square Branch   Picture Book Time Thursdays at 4pm. 2521 Glebe Ave., at St. Peters Ave. ℭ **718/863-0436.** Subway: 6 to Westchester Sq.

IN BROOKLYN

Brooklyn Public Library   Film selections here often correspond to monthly themes. Screenings for adults on Fridays at 6pm. Look also for silent film and Brooklyn docs, and shows for kids on Saturdays at 11am. Grand Army Plaza, 2nd Floor Auditorium. ℭ **718/230-2100.** www.brooklynpubliclibrary.org. Subway: 2/3 to Grand Army Plaza.

3 The Theatah

Just as models and those who look like them often make their way to California for its surfeit of Beach Girl #4 roles, dramatic actors are drawn to New York City. They're not just waiting on our tables, either. In NYC you can find great performances on every level of theater, from big-time Broadway (with its $100-plus orchestra seats) to $10 Off-Broadway to raw productions in the basements of bars, performed for whatever can be garnered by passing the hat. Cost is not necessarily a barometer of quality. You can drop a few Jacksons to discover the cast of a Broadway blockbuster is just phoning it in, while across town some hungry young talent is drawing tears at a free production of Shakespeare. Other free productions are offered up by schools, institutions, and work-in-progress programs. If you need something more polished than that, try downtown, where dirt-cheap theaters will get you the dramatic goods for $10 or less.

FREE THEATER

FREE WILLIE: SHAKESPEARE ALFRESCO

The Earl of Oxford would probably be gratified to know that all these centuries later his little plays dominate the summer theater scene in the world's capital. Sure, the plays are published under the name of an actor from Stratford, but the passions and conflicts resound just as the Earl wrote them. Troupes love to try their hand at the Bard, and free Shakespeare abounds in the Big Apple. Join your fellow mortals and enjoy the midsummer night dreams.

FREE Rise of the House Ushers

If you have the ability to pass out Playbills, point to seats, and enunciate the phrase "enjoy the show," then you're qualified to see free plays. Many smaller theater companies save money on the cost of ushers by trading your sweat equity for a complimentary seat. Each house has a different set of rules, and the number of volunteers needed varies from one to eight per night. Popular productions can have a backlog of a few weeks. The best plan of attack is to find a play you want to see and call the front office to see what their deal is. It may take some tenacious dialing and a measure of persistence, but it'll be easily worth it when you settle back in your seat without a penny spent. The venues listed below are just a starting point; dozens of stages in the city will let you usher your way to free entertainment.

Blue Man Group Performance art meets the masses via drums, food, and a lot of blue body paint during this long-running favorite. The services of four volunteer ushers are required for each show. You can schedule 1 to 2 weeks in advance. Help cleaning up may be required for a few minutes after the show. Astor Place Theatre, 434 Lafayette St., between E. 4th and E. 8th sts. ℂ **212/387-9415,** ext. 220. www.blueman.com. Subway: N/R/W to 8th St.; 6 to Astor Place.

New York Theatre Workshop This small downtown theater doesn't shy from experimentation, including occasional hip-hop fare. Five ushers are used per show. Call ℂ **212/780-7037** during regular business hours to synch your schedule with theirs. 79 E. 4th St., between Second Ave. and Bowery. www.nytw.org. Subway: 6 to Astor Place.

Second Stage Theatre This organization specializes in giving contemporary playwrights second chances to find audiences. The new 296-seat theatre is nicely designed and a comfortable place to usher. Call to see when your available dates match their needs. 307 W. 43rd St., at Eighth Ave. ℂ **212/787-8302,** ext. 216. www.secondstagetheatre.com. Subway: A/C/E/7 to 42nd St./Port Authority.

☆ **Shakespeare in the Park** FREE   Shh! Top secret! No one else knows about this amazing cultural giveaway. Every summer a William Shakespeare play is performed in a gorgeous open-air theater in the center of enchanted Central Park. Just show up a couple of minutes before showtime and whisper the password "Birnham Woods." Oh, were it that easy. Some 90,000 people attend the Public Theater's productions every summer, and it's the worst-kept free secret in the city. It takes a lot to justify an hours-long Soviet-style wait for a lousy two-ticket ration, but Joseph Papp's Public Theater rarely disappoints. Design, direction, and acting (often featuring A-list stars) are all world class. The productions vary from faithful classical interpretations to avant-garde reimaginings. In summer, 1,800-plus seats are given out at the Delacorte in Central Park, and outside the Public Theater Downtown. The downtown location gives out fewer tickets, but the line is more under control. You'll need some determination for your free will, as people start lining up 2 or 3 hours early for the 1pm giveaways. For a hot show, you'll find bodies outside the Delacorte before 8am. In extreme cases—say Meryl Streep and Christopher Walken doing Checkhov—the line can start the night before.

Sources

Fledgling shows that are having trouble filling seats often go trolling for audiences on craigslist. Check under "free" on **www.craigslist.org** and you might spy a free night of drama. A sharp eye can also reward a person with preview seats. Check *Time Out* and the *Village Voice* for advertisements of newly opening productions. In addition to specials on tickets for the first few weeks, sometimes you'll spot an offering for a preview. You'll get something halfway between a dress rehearsal and the final polished show, but it won't cost a cent.

Just treat the ticket queue, with its natural camaraderie, as part of the experience. The outer boroughs also have their own ticket locations for selected performances, in addition to special arts education programs. Check the "Shakespeare in the Boroughs" page on the Public Theater website for more information.

The season runs June through August and features one or two Shakespeare plays, and often a play that's completely unrelated to the Bard.

Public Theater, 425 Lafayette St., just below Astor Place. ℭ **212/539-8750.** www.publictheater.org. Subway: 6 to Astor Place; N/R/W to 8th St.; Delecorte Theater, Belvedere Castle, near 79th St. and West Dr. ℭ **212/539-8750.** Subway: B/C to 81st St.

☆ **Shakespeare in the Park(ing) Lot** FREE Central Park is classy and well groomed, with lush grass and trees softening the hard edges of the city. The municipal parking lot on Ludlow Street has none of these graces, but the graffiti-slathered asphalt patch does compete in the realm of Tudor drama. The troupe Drilling CompaNY puts on Shakespeare every summer, with a wealth of energy and wit to make up for the lack of big-name casts and big-budget backdrops. It's a wonderfully surreal scene, with sword fights and intrigue in the foreground while befuddled neighbors cut through the parking spaces in back. FINE PRINT Seating is first-come, first-served, or bring your own (though padding is a must, as that pavement gets hard when you've been parked for a while).

Ludlow St., between Broome and Delancey sts. ℭ **212/414-7717.** www.drilling company.org. July–Aug Thurs–Sat 8pm. Subway: F to Delancey; J/M/Z to Essex St.

Inwood Shakespeare Festival FREE Inwood Hill Park, with its Bald Eagles and huge natural forest, is as un-Manhattan as Manhattan gets. The verdant hills here are the backdrop for the Moose Hall Theatre Company's annual takes on the Bard. They also branch out to other classic material, like *The Three Musketeers* or *The Hunchback of Notre Dame*. Shows are casual, with a tailgating feel, as local families kick back on blankets. Families also enjoy the annual children's' concert. The plays run about a dozen times each, Wednesdays through Saturdays at 7:30pm.

Inwood Hill Park Peninsula, Isham St. at Seaman Ave. ℭ **917/918-0394.** www. moosehallisf.org. Subway: A to 207th St.; 1 to 215th St.

MORE ALFRESCO THEATER

Boomerang Theatre FREE Boomerang comes back each year with performances of Shakespearean plays in parks around New York. Riverside, Central, and Prospect have all served as stages, with shows starting at 2pm. Boomerang has also been known to give away a Eugene O'Neill performance or two. See The Drama Book Shop (p. 90) for the free First Flight play reading series. The website has show schedules and locations.

ℭ **212/501-4069.** www.boomerangtheatre.org.

Circus Amok `FREE`   Amok rakes muck as it entertains, combining activist sentiments with traditional circus arts. Acrobats, jugglers, and a bearded woman are among the draws. The Circus Amok band often trolls through neighborhoods, gathering an audience for shows performed in local parks. Look for some two dozen shows spread out across the month of September.

© 718/486-7432, ext. 1. www.circusamok.org.

New York Classical Theatre `FREE`   NYCT takes advantage of the natural contours of Central Park to stage its summer Shakespeare productions. Plays begin around 103rd Street and Central Park West, but NYCT's innovation is to not cast its performers' feet in cement. As scenes shift, the location does as well, furthering the sense of an unfolding story. When Shakespeare isn't on the bill, look for other classics like Moliere.

Central Park. © 212/252-4531. www.newyorkclassical.org. Usually 2 plays per summer, no tickets or reservations required. June–Aug Thurs–Sun 7pm. Subway: B/C to 103rd St.

Theatreworks USA `FREE`   Every summer, this organization puts up a production aimed at rug rat edification (or at least amusement). The group concentrates on one play per season, usually a modern musical. The venue changes from year to year, but you'll get dozens of opportunities to catch a show. Weekday afternoons are often filled up by camp groups, but if you go on the weekends or evenings, you shouldn't have trouble grabbing free seats.

© 212/647-1100. www.theatreworksusa.org.

Tobacco Warehouse in Empire-Fulton Ferry State Park `FREE`
The ancient brick walls of this Athensesque ruin are the site of one of the city's newest alfresco theater traditions. The Illyria Theatre Company put on a modern version of Euripides's *Andromache* in 2006. Look for dance among other cultural events here as the space evolves.

Empire-Fulton Ferry Park, just west of Water St. © 718/802-0603. www.bbpc. net. Subway: F to York St.; A/C to High St.; Water Taxi to Fulton Ferry Landing.

THEATER WITH CLASS

In the working and reworking of new plays, feedback devices are essential. An audience of warm bodies makes a great barometer for figuring out which lines are killing and which scenes need trimming. With so much untested drama in NYC, it's easy to find showcases,

FREE Tune In

Give our regards to theatrical greatest-hits packages. The casts of the Great White Way leave the confines of their stages to flog their shows in Midtown, usually in musical form. Huge stars wander down from nearby dressing rooms, making these very popular events. And you thought Times Square was crowded already.

Broadway on Broadway   A special stage in Times Square hosts this massive concert on a Sunday in mid-September. At least a baker's dozen of shows make an appearance, including heavy hitters like *The Lion King, Avenue Q,* and *Mamma Mia!* For the finale, enough confetti rains down to give onlookers flashbacks to New Year's Eve. Times Square. ✆ **212/768-1560.** www.broadwayonbroadway.com. Usually around 11:30am. Subway: 1/2/3/7 or N/Q/R/S/W to Times Square.

Broadway's Stars in the Alley   On the Wednesday before the Tonys, Shubert Alley brings out representatives from some two dozen shows to prance about for your amusement. Though appearances are brief, wattage is high, with the likes of Leslie Uggams, Lynn Redgrave, and Harvey Fierstein. Shubert Alley, access from 45th St., just west of Seventh Ave. ✆ **212/764-1122.** www.starsin

workshops, and readings that are eager for your presence. You'll often be sharing the room with a parcel of pros: agents, producers, and casting directors on the prowl for the next big things. If you don't mind putting up with some unsanded edges, it's a great way to catch a night of free theater.

Cap21 FREE   The Collaborative Arts Project dedicates itself to fostering innovative new productions. Part of the process involves developing new audiences, which are invited in for the free **Barbara Wolff Monday Night Reading Series.** The series presents plays and musicals still seeking their footing.

18 West 18th St., 6th floor, between Fifth and Sixth aves. ✆ **866/811-4111.** www.cap21.org. Mon 7pm (not every week, check the website). Subway: L/N/Q/R/W/4/5/6 to 14th St./Union Sq.

Jean Cocteau Repertory Theater FREE   Now in its 35th year, this Bowery institution remains committed to keeping the classics alive.

thealley.com. Usually 11am, around June 1st. Subway: 1/2/3/7 or N/Q/R/S/W to Times Square.

Broadway in Bryant Park   Every summer Broadway teases fans with a quick sampler on the Bryant Park stage. *Rent, Chicago,* and *Wicked* are among the standbys that perform excerpts for a crowded lawn. In addition to those afternoon gigs, look for **Broadway Under the Stars,** now entering its sixth year. This spectacle comes on a Monday night in mid-June and kicks off the summer outdoor concert season. The **Rockettes** make the short commute from Radio City to join Broadway bigs in the singing and dancing shmaltz-o-rama. (*Note:* This event sometimes takes place in Central Park. Please call to confirm the site before setting out.) Behind the Public Library, between 40th and 42nd sts. and Fifth and Sixth aves. ⓒ **212/768-4242.** www.bryantpark.org. www.www.nycvisit. com/broadwayunderthestars. Broadway in Bryant Park, Thurs 12:30–1:45pm, 4 musicals per afternoon. Broadway Under the Stars, 8:30pm. Subway: F/V/B/D to 42nd St./Bryant Park; 7 to Fifth Ave.

Although regular tickets here hover around $50, great free programs can be found on Monday nights at 7pm. The New Classics Reading Series puts on professional readings of untested material. You'll find re-interpreted classics along with fresh adaptations and translations. Look also for the Instant Shakespeare Company's readings. The actors don't rehearse, but the productions come off surprisingly smoothly thanks to Shakespeare's own cues, preserved in original First Folio and Quarto versions.

330 Bowery, at Bond St. ⓒ **212/677-0060.** www.jeancocteaurep.org. Subway: B/D/F/V to Broadway/Lafayette; 6 to Bleecker St.

The Juilliard School   The fourth-year students of Juilliard's Drama Division mount full-scale productions to catch the eyes of agents, casting directors, and the press. The general public is invited in as well, although to get an invitation you'll need to sign up for Juilliard's Drama Division mailing list. The plays are free during their fall and winter run, and then come back tweaked and enhanced for $15 in the spring. Free tickets go fast. You'll have to wait at the box office the first day they become available, although sometimes you can snag same-day standbys.

Broadway, at 65th St. ✆ 212/769-7406. www.juilliard.edu. 1 to 66th St./Lincoln Center.

The New School for Drama `FREE`   The New School integrates the arts of acting, directing, and playwrighting. The fruits of these syner-gies can be found during two spring festivals. The Random Acts! One-Act Play Festival presents thesis projects in the form of 30 different shows. Those that weren't written in-house range from classics to con-temporaries. The season runs February through April, Thursday through Saturday at 8pm, and a Saturday matinee at 3pm. Five plays are grouped together each night. Shows are free, but it's best to reserve a seat in advance (✆ **212/279-4200**). Newly-minted plays get treated to readings during the Final Draft series, which shows on a Monday, Tuesday, and Wednesday at 5 and 7pm in mid-May. Six showcased works fill the bill, with professional direction to sweeten the plots. Again, free, but call ahead for a reservation (✆ **212/229-5859,** ext. 2631).

The New School for Drama Theater at the Westbeth, 151 Bank St., 3rd floor, between Washington St. and the West Side Hwy. www.newschool.edu/academic/drama. Subway: A/C/E/L to 14th St./Eighth Ave.; 1/2/3 to 14th St.

NYU Graduate Acting Program   NYU's Tisch School of the Arts is justly famous for the high-profile directors, actors, and dramatic writ-ers it has produced. You can get a glimpse of burgeoning talents at several free shows. Most are put on by second years (by third year they can get away with charging), in various theaters on and around the NYU campus. The tickets for charged shows tend to be reason-able, $12 and less. Check the website or the Grad Acting box office.

Tisch Main Building, 721 Broadway, between Waverly and Washington places (just south of 8th St.). ✆ 212/998-1921. www.gradacting.tisch.nyu.edu. Subway: 6 to Astor Place; N/R/W to 8th St.; A/B/C/D/E/V to W. 4th St.-Washington Sq.

The Public Theater `FREE`   Shakespeare in the Park is only the beginning for the Public Theater, which churns out amazing produc-tions all year long. Look for the **New Work Now!** series, which high-lights all-new material, and "Conversations With . . . ." Both are free;

check the website for exact scheduling, as programs vary from year to year.

425 Lafayette St., just below Astor Place. ✆ **212/260-2400. www.publictheater. org. Subway: 6 to Astor Place; N/R/W to 8th St.**

Rattlestick Playwrights Theater   The Rattlestick targets upcoming playwrights and new plays. They nurture projects from creation and development all the way to production. For 3 or 4 weeks every spring they put on the **Exposure Festival,** with new plays and works in progress. Performances are free, though they'd be delighted to have a $5 donation for readings and $10 for blackbox productions. Check the website for other free readings and events during the rest of the year.

234 Waverly Place, just west of Seventh Ave., between Perry and W. 11th St. ✆ **212/627-2556. www.rattlestick.org. Subway: 1 to Christopher St.**

Women's Project Theatre `FREE`   Women playwrights are the exclusive focus of the Women's Project. New plays, often by new authors, get exercised in the Women's Work series. The festival takes place in early November, with plays on multiple nights.

Julia Miles Theater, 424 W. 55th St., between Ninth and Tenth aves. ✆ **212/765-2105. www.womensproject.org. Subway: 1/A/B/C/D to 59th St./Columbus Circle.**

The York Theatre Company `FREE`   Inside the tasteful modern confines of St. Peter's Church, the York Theatre trots out new musicals for free performances. The **Developmental Reading Series** is often on Tuesday nights at 7:30pm, with other nights and matinee performances also in the mix. Polished performances here come in around $50. `FINE PRINT` Developmental Reading Series shows are free but do sometimes "sell out," so reserve early.

619 Lexington Ave., at 54th St. ✆ **212/935-5824, ext. 24. www.yorktheatre.org. Subway: E/V to Lexington; 6 to 51st St.**

DIRT CHEAP THEATER
ALL ABOUT LA MAMA: BIG DRAMA IN SMALL SPACES

Small theater groups are notorious for their shoestring budgets, which means most don't have the luxury of permanent stages. All it takes to make a theater is some matte-black paint, a few gelled lights, and a bunch of folding chairs, and walk-up lofts in Midtown are constantly

NYC's Best Theater Discount Strategies

TKTS   TKTS has been dispensing same-day half-price seats for some 3 decades now. As far as bargains go, this is probably better for the tourists, who are more excited about spending "only" $40 to see some hoary musical. It's also worth remembering that the things they're selling tickets to are shows the producers are having trouble moving anyway. That said, the seats themselves tend to be good, and the selection is pretty broad. At any given time, you can probably select from 25 different Off-Broadway shows. TKTS is open 3 to 8pm for evening performances, 10am to 2pm for Wednesday and Saturday matinees, and from 11am until 3pm for Sunday matinees, and then until showtime for Sunday night performances. *Note:* Until the end of '06, TKTS will be in a temporary spot in front of the Marriott Marquis, 1535 Broadway between 45th and 46th streets. As of '07, it should be back in its usual home at Father Duffy Square, 1 block north between 46th and 47th streets.

A second TKTS location can be found downtown at John and Front streets in the South Street Seaport area. The lines are much shorter and matinee tickets are sold for the following day only, if you're the type that plans ahead (11am–6pm Mon–Fri; until 7pm Sat; 11am–3pm Sun for Sun night performances only). Show availability is posted on a digital bulletin board that's updated as ticket supplies dwindle. Remember, TKTS accepts only cash or traveler's checks, no credit cards, no personal checks. Discounts are generally 50%, with a few shows at a 25% reduction. ✆ **212/221-0013.** www.tdf.org.

TDF Vouchers   The Theatre Development Fund also brings us an Off-Off-Broadway equivalent to the TKTS booth. For $28 you get four vouchers that can be used for a host of shows, crossing the disciplines of drama, dance, and light opera. At $7 a pop, it's a good way to get into the cutting edge. ✆ **212/221-0013.** www.tdf.org.

Evening Rush   For those of the serendipitous bent, there's always last-minute rush ticket specials. Broadway, Off-Broadway, and even a few mega-hits set aside seats for students (sometimes seniors are included, too). The seats are made available between 30 minutes and an hour before curtain. Make sure to bring plenty of ID.

Another option is SRO seats, but do not attempt standing room only if you're not in comfortable shoes. The seats for either program are usually $20 and up, which on the surface is no great bargain, but is actually pretty respectable when you consider that a full-price ticket would probably run three times as much. A great place for the rundown on the permutations of the individual theaters is www.talk inbroadway.com/boards.

Academic Advantages   If you've got an in with a library or a school, you may have an in for discount coupons through the **School Theater Ticket Program.** Librarians, teachers, students, and their families are all eligible. Musicals, Broadway on and off, and opera and ballet at Lincoln Center, are among the offerings. Check out the website, www.schooltix.com. Offices at 1560 Broadway, Suite 1113, open Monday to Friday 11am to 5pm. ℃ **212/354-4722.**

Other Discounts   Several online sites will hook you up with discount codes for half-price tickets. Some require you to join to play, but the only tax they levy is the occasional piece of spam; otherwise, they're free. (And if you're not a spamphobe, you can get regular e-mail newsletters trumpeting the latest specials.) **Playbill Online** (www.playbill.com) has the best range of Broadway and Off-Broadway shows. **Best of Broadway** (℃ **212/398-8383;** www.best ofbroadway.com) has coupons and puts together group discount packages. The **Hit Show Club** (℃ **212/581-4211;** www.hitshow club.com) is good for tourists. They have several packages that combine restaurants and attractions with well-known Broadway hits.

For Teens: High 5 Tickets to the Arts   High 5 doesn't shy away from the controversial notion that the children are our future. To uplift the level of cultural literacy of today's teens, High 5 makes a bushel of $5 theater and museum programs available. Adults can compartmentalize their jealousy, as mentors, parents, and friends can also cash in. They can accompany a teen for the same measly $5. Check the website for ticket details; there's also a listing of free and nearly free events. ℃ **212/HI5-TKTS.** www.highfivetix.org.

taking form as Off-Off-Broadway bastions. Downtown, especially the area around East 4th Street, is a locus with more staying power. Several companies work out of the area and most shows have East Village–friendly prices of $15 or less.

Dixon Place Experimentation is the norm at Dixon Place, which bills itself as an "artistic lab with an audience." Since performances are in varied stages of evolution, ticket prices are on the low side, usually $5 to $15. There are also intermittent "7 Minutes" free open performance nights, where anyone is welcome and anything goes except stand-up comedy.

258 Bowery, 2nd floor, between Houston and Prince, but slated to move to a more permanent home at nearby 161 Chrystie St. ✆ **212/219-0736.** www.dixon place.org. Subway: F/V to Second Ave.

Emerging Artists Theatre For over a dozen years, EAT has been nurturing new playwrights. New York debuts are frequent here, part of a collaborative process that involves company actors and associated directors. Labs and festivals fill the calendar, including the EAT Developmental Series. Three separate programs ("One Woman Standing", "Double Double Decker", and "Notes From a Page") are each performed for only a $10 suggested donation. Though the plays can be a little rough in spots, the company's level of commitment is impressive.

311 W. 43rd St., between Eighth and Ninth aves. ✆ **212/247-2429.** www.eatheatre. org. Subway: A/C/E to 42nd St.-Port Authority.

Galapagos Art Space This Brooklyn bar first became known for the moat at its entryway, which creates a soothing mini–Temple of Dendur effect. A couple of expansions later, the bar's renown is as a Williamsburg cultural headquarters. Comedy, theater, music, and film (p. 50) all make their way here, and cover charges rarely reach double digits. One day a week there's arty smut in the form of **Monday Evening Burlesque.** It starts at 9:30pm, and it's absolutely free.

70 N. 6th St. Williamsburg, Brooklyn. ✆ **718/782-5188.** www.galapagosartspace. com. Subway: L to Bedford Ave.

La Mama This venerable avatar of the avant-garde is fully established in the East Village, where it remains dedicated to artistic experimentation. Productions are high quality and the ticket prices reflect it—shows can run from $5 to $30. One notable exception is the **Experiments** readings series, performed in La Mama's club theatre space. Experiments features in-progress plays read with the writers in attendance, to provide instant-gratification feedback. Check the website for exact days and times; admission is free, with tickets distributed on the night of the show.

74 E. 4th St., between Second Ave. and Bowery. ℂ 212/475-7710. www.lamama. org. Subway: F/V to Second Ave.; 6 to Bleecker St.

The Slipper Room   The stage in this Lower East Side bar sees all manner of risqué business. Comedy and drama make the scene, but the best night is Saturday, when New York's longest-running burlesque holds court. **Mr. Choad's Upstairs/Downstairs** allows vaudeville acts and go-go girls to split time under the lights.

167 Orchard St., at Stanton. ℂ 212/253-7246. www.slipperroom.com. Cover usually $5; other shows $5-$15. Subway: F/V to Second Ave.

Spaghetti Dinner   For almost two decades, **Great Small Works** hosted monthly dinners at P.S. 122. As of 2006, the show has gone on the road, trying out various local spaces before it chooses its next long-term home. Audience members/diners are treated to performance of every stripe—from puppetry to dance to drama to film—along with a fine vegetarian spaghetti meal. Don't be surprised to find left-wing polemic in the mix as well. Tickets hover around $10, a price that wouldn't have seemed unreasonable when the series started in 1978. Call for info about their current performance space.

Great Small Works, ℂ 718/840-2823. www.greatsmallworks.org.

The Tank   This up-and-coming theater group saw its Midtown space fall to the wrecking ball, but they have a new home inside the confines of downtown stalwart **Collective: Unconscious.** Comedy, film, music, and poetry supplement theater. Though shows can run as high as $15, much of the calendar comes in at $5. The Tank also hosts the **Bent** circuit-bending festival (www.bentfestival.org), dedicated to an art form that repurposes electronic toys into musical instruments. If you've ever wanted to hear a Speak & Spell employed as a jazz instrument, this is your fest. Performances take place over multiple days, with tickets ranging from free to $10. (The event, like several of The Tank's nights, takes place away from the Collective: Unconscious space.)

The Tank at Collective: Unconscious, 279 Church St., between Franklin and White sts. ℂ 212/563-6269. www.thetanknyc.com. Subway: 1 to Franklin St.

Theater at the Edge: Fringe NYC

In late August a chunk of the city goes on vacation and the **Fringe Festival** comes rushing in to maintain Gotham's equilibrium. This annual theatrical explosion brings hundreds of acts to Lower East Side theaters, schools, storefronts, and streets. The troupes hail from around the world and range from the baldly amateurish to the highly polished. Tickets aren't super-cheap, but at $15 they're cheaper than a trip to the Guggenheim or the MoMA. Free previews, with 7-minute teasers of upcoming shows, are given on several afternoons in Washington Square Park. Look also for a free full-length Shakespearian production as part of the **FringeAL FRESCO** program. Less organized shows spill out onto the streets of down-town. We've seen actors project their lines over neighbors' repeated calls to "Shut the f--- up!" Whether appreciated by the full general public or not, the Fringe is a feast of theater, comedy, music, and performance art, and well worth a visit. ⓒ **212/279-4488** or 888/ FRINGE-NYC. www.fringenyc.org. Various locations.

The Theater for the New City   This alternative theater is known for giving breaks to unknown playwrights. Productions are consis-tently high quality, though ticket prices are usually only $15, with some shows as low as $5. Over Memorial Day you can sample the dramatics for free during the Lower East Side Festival of the Arts. Thea-ter is only the beginning, as spoken word, cabaret, film, video, and dance performances take over East 10th Street, between 1st and 2nd avenues. Events run until after midnight and everything is free. 155 First Ave., between 9th and 10th sts. ⓒ 212/254-1109. www.theaterforthe newcity.net. Subway: 6 to Astor Place.

4 Let's Dance

Giuliani-era enforcement of cabaret laws hit most New Yorkers by sur-prise. Laws regulating public dance had been on the books forever, but it had been many years since anyone had thought to enforce them. Innocuous tremors and inadvertent hip shakes were suddenly categorized as unlicensed dance expressions. Fortunately, dance in

New York has never been limited to the clubs and bars. In the parks, on stages, and even in sanctuaries of the city, dance of all levels can be found, and often for free.

Dance Conversations `FREE` Choreographers present works in progress at this monthly program. Each evening presents four different choreographers. It's a discussion series as well, so expect jawing to following the dancing. Usually on Tuesday mid-month at 7pm. Check the calendar online, as Dance Conversations will sometimes flee to a different location.

Flea Theater, 41 White St., between Broadway and Church. ✆ 212/226-0051. www.theflea.org. Subway: 1 to Franklin St.

Dancing in the Streets `FREE` This arts organization brings site-specific performances to spots across the city. The integration of cityscape and moving bodies is a great way of seeing familiar spaces in a new way. The big show is the annual dance and demonstration at Dag Hammarskjöld Plaza, highlighting international moves beneath the windows of the UN. Check the website for complete performance dates and locations.

Dag Hammarskjöld Plaza, E. 47th St., between First and Second aves. ✆ 212/ 625-3505. www.dancinginthestreets.org. Subway: E/V to Lexington; 6 to 51st St. Other sites, including Red Hook and Brooklyn, vary.

Evening Stars `FREE` The **Joyce Theater** has been at the forefront of NYC's modern dance since 1982. Every September they help sponsor the best of American dance with free performances as part of downtown's River to River Festival. Programs pivot from the music of Sinatra to the Sugar Hill Gang to the Grateful Dead. Generally there are four evening shows at 7:30pm (Wednesday through Saturday), with an additional Saturday matinee. There's a large stage, but if you want to be up close, you can spread your blanket up to two hours earlier, when the park opens. (That blanket is all but obligatory, as no seating is provided.)

Co-sponsored by the Lower Manhattan Cultural Council and the Joyce Theater at Battery Park, on State St. at Pearl St. ✆ 212/219-9401, ext. 304. www.lmcc.net. Subway: 4/5 to Bowling Green; R/W to Whitehall; 1 to South Ferry.

MoonDance `FREE` July and August bring marvelous nights for this dance on Pier 25. Sunday evenings begin with a lesson at 6:30pm and cede to dancing half an hour later, when you're a full-fledged expert.

Dance varieties run from swing to salsa to R&B. Live music from crack bands enhances the lovely riverside setting.

Pier 25. ✆ **212/533-PARK.** www.hudsonriverpark.org. Subway: 1 to Franklin St., walk west to the river.

☆ **Movement Research at the Judson Church** `FREE` The Judson Memorial Church has been an anchor of the West Village since 1890. The aging church has recently been renovated (a lovely new dance floor has been installed), and is again hosting the popular Movement Research dance program. The dancers and choreographers vary from week to week, but the emphasis on pushing boundaries remains consistent. Performances reflect experimentation and emerging ideas but the quality tends to be consistently high. No reservations are required but the event is popular, so arrive early. Mondays at 8pm, doors open at 7:45pm.

Judson Church, 55 Washington Sq. South, between Thompson and Sullivan sts. ✆ **212/539-2611.** www.movementresearch.org. Subway: A/B/C/D/E/F/V to West 4th St./Washington Sq.

Tap City, the New York City Tap Festival `FREE` New York's tap tradition began with the cross-pollination of African and Irish dances in the Five Points slum of the 1840s. Once a year, tap still marks the spot, with Tap City's "Four Shows at Five Points." An afternoon of performances keeps the clomping and clogging going. Tap City also presents tap jams and sand dances at venues from Chelsea to Harlem. Though the main program is at the end of June, events like Jam it Up at Capezio Dance Theatre Shop run on three Sundays in late spring. Check the website for exact scheduling, which includes a mix of ticketed shows and free events.

Four Shows at Five Points, Foley Square, Worth St. between Lafayette and Centre sts. ✆ **646/230-9564.** www.atdf.org. Subway: J/M/Z to Chambers St.; 4/5/6 to Brooklyn Bridge/City Hall; R/W to City Hall.

5 Sing, Sing: Karaoke

Maybe it's a side effect of our new blog culture, but it seems the old gatekeeping editorial controls have fallen by the wayside. Local music is no exception, with a profusion of live-band karaoke nights allowing amateur lungs to step up to the mic and perform frontsperson duties. Join the caterwauling carousel and do your part to reaffirm the inherent dignity of the human race by drinking way too much tequila and then letting loose on a heartfelt version of "Feel Like Making Love." The traditional canned-music and bouncing ball karaoke can also be found citywide. The venues below don't enforce drink minimums, and often karaoke nights are too crowded for anyone to notice if you're not tippling. Then again, doesn't sobriety kind of go against the very spirit of karaoke?

Arlene's Grocery `FREE` If you've ever wondered where the tri-state has been hiding its best Ozzy and David Lee imitators, you've been missing out on the live music karaoke at Arlene's Grocery. The house band has changed, but the emphasis on hard-rocking good times has not. With an elaborate opening ceremony, the Monday night shows are as entertaining as before, filling 3 hours with the soul-uplifting sounds of '70s classic rock and '80s hair metal. Before you start practicing in empty elevators, check out the set list at www.arlenesgrocery.net. If you do sign up and ascend the stage, you'll find the crowd enthusiastic, and nothing beats the thrill of belting out "Black Dog" or "Paradise City" over an ass-kicking band. It's worth a visit just to check out the regulars. Many of them have come all the way from Jersey to show off how well they can work a club full of rabid fans with fingers spread in devil's horns. Best of all: There's no cover for these covers.

95 Stanton St., between Ludlow and Orchard sts. ℂ 212/358-1633. www.arlenesgrocery.net. Karaoke Mon 10pm–2am. Subway: F/V to 2nd Ave.; J/M/Z to Essex St.

Hank's Saloon `FREE` The painted flames on Hank's wall identify the place as prime rockabilly territory. Live music plays most nights, with a little alt-country thrown in with the '50s stylings. It's all no cover, no minimum, and ordinary Joe's and Josephina's get the chance to lead the parade during Live Band Kuntry Karaoke, with Rob Ryan and the Brooklyn Country All-Stars. Every other Monday or so, let that tear in your beer inspire your best Johnny, Patsy, or Dolly. While you're at it, have some barbeque, on the house (p. 130). Show starts at 9pm.

46 Third Ave., at Atlantic Ave., Brooklyn. ℂ 718/625-8003. www.exitfive.com/hankssaloon. Karaoke every other Monday at 9pm. Subway: 2/3/4/5/Q to Atlantic Ave.; M/N/R/W to Pacific St.

Iggy's `FREE` Drink specials help lubricate the slippery slope that leads to late-night karaoke cacophony at Iggy's. There's no live band, but from noon to 10pm, shots and Bud, Bud Light, and Yuengling drafts are only $2. These specials in turn fuel the karaoke action, which can be found 7 nights a week.

1452 Second Ave., between 75th and 76th sts. ℂ 212/327-3043. www.iggysnew york.com. Karaoke nightly. Subway: 6 to 77th St.

The Lucky Cat FREE   Monday nights in Brooklyn find Loser's Lounge keyboardist Joe McGinty tinkling the keys for the pleasure of your pipes. His website (www.joemcginty.typepad.com) delineates the song list, which hops from Boz Skaggs to Bette Midler, though there's usually a monthly thematic focus (say, the best of Abba). The show is free at 10pm, in the recently renovated confines of Billyburg's Lucky Cat.

245 Grand St., between Driggs and Roebling sts., Williamsburg, Brooklyn. ℂ 718/ 782-0437. www.theluckycat.com. Karaoke Mondays at 10pm. Subway: L to Bed-ford Ave.; G to Lorimer-Metropolitan.

Magnetic Field FREE   Things on the Brooklyn side of town are always a little more laid back, and if it's fronting live band karaoke you crave, you'll have a better chance of getting to the top of the list out here. Bunnie England & The New Originals bust their tails to bring a full selection of metal, punk, pop, and rock, to the good burghers of BoCoCa. "Brandy," by Brooklyn-connected '70s sensations Looking Glass, is on the set list—what more can we ask of life?

97 Atlantic Ave., between Hicks and Henry sts., Brooklyn Heights, Brooklyn. ℂ 718/834-0069. www.magneticbrooklyn.com. Karaoke every other Thursday 8-11pm. Subway: M/N/R/2/3/4/5 to Borough Hall; F to Bergen St.

Rothko FREE   We all know the extraordinary levels of talent required to make it in the rap world (just look at Kid Rock), but that doesn't mean the unpolished among us can't entertain. "Hip Hop Karaoke" is quickly becoming a phenomenon, with packed monthly shows letting little Biggies rhyme away for a forgiving crowd. (And no one will think less of you if you're reading off a crib sheet.)

116 Suffolk St., at Rivington St. ℂ 212/475-7088. www.rothkonyc.com. Karaoke first Friday of the month at 11pm (sign up at 10pm). Subway: F to Delancey St.; J/M/Z to Essex St.

Second on Second FREE   This low-lit Japanese lounge keeps the drink specials coming to accompany the karaoke machine. Monday night from 10 to 11pm you'll find a $5 open bar for well drinks, and happy hours see $3 beers. The open mic karaoke action starts up

FREE Movieoke at Den of Cin

Unwilling to sing but still eager to make an ass of yourself? Thank God for "movieoke," which promises to do for armchair actors what karaoke did for shower singers. Rehearse a scene at home, bring in some ringers, or steel yourself to go it alone, and ask your hostess to hop upstairs to the video store. She'll come back with the appropriate DVD, and you'll stand before the big projection screen and show off your chops. Silly? Um, yeah. But somebody made a nice living selling karaoke machines—maybe movieoke is the next big thing. Catch the wave at the Den of Cin, beneath Two Boots Pizza and Video, 44 Ave. A, at E. 3rd St. *©* **212/254-0800.** www.movie oke.net. Subway: F/V to Second Ave.

around 9pm. A limited menu provides Thai and Japanese snacks, so you can show off those golden tonsils and enhance someone's dining experience at the same time.

27 Second Ave., at 2nd St. *©* **212/473-2922.** www.2ndon2nd.com. Karaoke nightly, around 9pm. Subway: F/V to Second Ave.

Winnie's Hipsters and Chinatown locals just never have enough opportunity to chill together, which is where Winnie's comes in handy. The place is an ungentrifiable dive, but the savings get passed on to the crooning customer: It's only a buck a song to play along with the hit machine.

104 Bayard St. *©* **212/732-2384.** Karaoke daily 8pm-4am. Subway: J/M/N/Q/R/ W/Z/6 to Canal St.

6 Humor Us: Comedy

There's no shortage of frustrating and surreal experiences in New York, ensuring plenty of fodder for the comedians in our midst. The city is currently stacked with young comic talent, which means amateur nights are more common than headliner-thick extravaganzas. Alas, amateur nights can also be express trips to the nether regions of stand-up hell. Somehow bad comedy is infinitely more painful than bad tragedy. I advise stepping carefully through the city's improv, open mic, and stand-up minefield. Fortunately, plenty of quick wits can be found in this town. Small investments can lead to big laughs if you hit the right nights. For all the side-splitting and beer-spewed-through-nose details, see below.

SHOWCASES, IMPROV & OTHER COMEDY ANTICS

☆ **The Upright Citizens Brigade**   The UCB brings Chicago-style long-form improv comedy to the Big Apple. With founders that can be found on SNL and in the movies, the talent level is high, which is crucial in the hit-or-miss medium of improvisation. Plus, the complete lack of scripts saves you money. Sunday night sees two performances of ASSSCAT 3000. The extra S? For savings: The 7:30pm show is $8, but the 9:30pm version is absolutely free. Tickets are distributed at 8:15, but it's popular so try to get there at least 45 minutes early. Shows from Monday to Wednesday at 11pm are also free, as are midnight shows on Fridays. The rest of the schedule runs between $5 and $8, which is still a steal. The Harold Night's two $5 shows (Tuesday at 8 and 9:30pm) are especially noteworthy, with some rapier wits putting the old Harold technique through its paces.

Upright Citizens Brigade Theatre, 307 W. 26th St., between Eighth and Ninth aves. ℂ **212/366-9176.** www.ucbtheatre.com. Subway: C/E to 23rd St.

The Pit   This upstart has yet to reach the UCB's level of improv evolution, but it's headed in the right direction. The People's Improv Theater's primary mission is as a school, with an ex-SNL writer and Second City alum among the faculty. Many shows involve student performers and are priced accordingly. Monday through Saturday averages four shows a night, with one more on Sunday. Tickets for nuggets like the improv version of *Law & Order* run between $5 and $8. Wednesday night is the night not to miss. The Faculty + Big Black Car show brings out the heights of the Pit, and it's totally free.

154 W. 29th St., between Sixth and Seventh aves. ℂ **212/563-7488.** www.thepit-nyc.com. Subway: 1 or N/R/W to 28th St.

Manhattan Comedy Collective   In bringing affordability to comedy, it helps to have a volunteer army. This collective pools talents to put on nights of stand-up, improv, plays, solo shows, and even short film. With much of the staff working for love not money, the ticket prices are usually $5. At the Gene Frankel Underground theater.

Will Work for Stage Time

No one ever perfected his comic timing in the bathroom mirror. Comedians learn from audiences, but most clubs are justifiably reluctant to put green talent up on stage. Fortunately for the aspiring, many clubs are equally reluctant to lay out cold cash for busboys, telemarketers, and barkers. The stars of tomorrow can exchange elbow grease for free stage minutes, assuming management sees a glimmer of talent there. At **Ha!,** barking and other glamorous tasks can be exchanged for face time with audiences (✆ **212/977-3884;** www.hacomedynyc.com). **New York Comedy Club** funny folks can double as bussers or telemarketers. The club will also trade time for ringers—if you bring in five audience members, you'll get 5 minutes on stage. It's exactly what families were made for. See the review below for contact information.

24 Bond St., between Lafayette St. and the Bowery. ✆ **917/450-6659.** www.manhattancomedycollective.com. Subway: 6 to Bleecker St.; B/D/F/V to Broadway/Lafayette.

New York Comedy Club FREE Monday night's open mic night is the only affordable slot on the schedule here. It's the longest-running open mic in New York, there's no drink minimum, and although it's statistically unlikely, it's possible to see an overlooked talent just breaking in. Open mic on Mondays, 5 to 7:30pm. For aspiring comedians, it's $3 for 5 minutes on stage.

241 E. 24th St., between Second and Third aves. ✆ **212/696-LAFF.** www.newyorkcomedyclub.com. Subway: N/R/W or 6 to 23rd St.

Otto's Shrunken Head Otto's was quick to fill a Polynesian void in the city's heart. With thatch galore, this exotic locale hosts live music and plenty of comedy. Stand-up and sketch both appear, with Tuesdays, Wednesdays, and Fridays the usual nights. Despite the joint's name, expect no psychiatric benefits.

Otto's Shrunken Head, 538 E. 14th St., between aves. A and B. ✆ **212/228-2240.** www.ottosshrunkenhead.com. Subway: L to First Ave.

Underground Lounge   Musical acts provide respite between comedy routines during this open mic night. The room is supportive, heavy on Columbia students with a few Manhattan Valley locals thrown in. Popular open mic shows are Mondays at 8pm and again at 10:30pm. Look for other comedy nights through the week, with sketch work on Tuesdays. [FINE PRINT] There's a two-item minimum for performances in the back room.

955 West End Ave., at 107th St. ℭ 212/531-4759. www.theundergroundnyc.com. Subway: 1 to 103rd St.

7 Game Night

Bars across the city offer trivia nights, an excuse to meet new people and show off the fruits of all those wasted hours learning to differentiate between Arnold Snarb and Arnold Strong. Too damn smart? Gather up some compatriots, or join a team of fellow-stragglers, and convert that synaptic alacrity into free bar tabs.

The Baggot Inn   Tuesday night brings the brains to the Baggot. Teams are quizzed in five-question rounds, with winners getting free drinks. The extraordinary trivia geeks who end up the night's overall winners get $10 and $25 bar tab credits—you know, a person can work up a mean thirst answering questions about Liza Minelli's personal life. Games happen from around 7 to 10pm. [FINE PRINT] No cover, but there is a two-drink minimum.

82 W. 3rd St., between Thompson and Sullivan. ℭ 212/477-0622. www.thebaggot inn.com. Subway: A/C/E/F/S/V to W. 4th St.-Washington Sq.

Pete's Candy Store   At Pete's Wednesday Quizz-Off, categories range from general knowledge to music to top 10s, with prizes for the top three finishers. The action starts at 7:30pm. Alternatively, wordsmiths hammer at their tile forges during Scrabble Saturdays. Bring a partner and try your luck at doubles on Saturdays from 5 to 8pm. Tuesday nights from 7 to 9pm, Pete's feels even more small-town than usual when bingo scorecards fill the bar. Old and young show off their number/letter cognitive prowess for gag prizes. Not all gamed-out yet? How about revisiting ancient humiliations with a spelling bee? Every other Monday trip over words like "roriferous" and "keratic." Or is it kerratic? That's why the Williamsburg Spelling Bee operates on a three-strike basis. Every other Monday 7 to 9pm. Events are free, though there's a loosely enforced two-drink minimum.

709 Lorimer St., between Frost and Richardson, Williamsburg, Brooklyn. © **718/ 302-3770.** www.petescandystore.com. Subway: L to Lorimer St.; G to Metropolitan Ave.

Pub Quiz @ Last Exit   This quiz night isn't free, but the $5 cover can be considered an investment. The cash goes into a pot for the eventual winner. Teams of four compete, and if you show up shorthanded, they'll make a team for you. Warm up: Who wrote *Last Exit to Brooklyn*? First and third Monday, from 9 to 11pm. Register around 8:30pm. (Answer: Hubert Selby, Jr.)

136 Atlantic Ave., between Clinton and Henry. Brooklyn Heights, Brooklyn. © **718/222-9198.** www.lastexitbar.com. Subway: M/N/R/2/3/4/5 to Borough Hall; F to Bergen St.

Rocky Sullivan's FREE   You can show off those muscular brain cells at Rocky's, where teams of trivia hounds compete at the prodding of a congenial host every Thursday night at 9pm. Victorious founts of knowledge are rewarded with fermented hops. Quiz show night has no cover or minimum.

129 Lexington Ave., between 28th and 29th sts. © **212/725-3871.** www.rocky sullivans.com. Subway: 6 to 28th St.

8 Talk It Up: TV Tapings

Why saddle yourself with those endless cable, satellite, and electric bills, when you could be watching TV for free? New York is home to a bunch of the top-flight shows, many of which rely on live in-studio audiences to keep the energy levels high. In exchange for your enthusiasm (and patience), you'll get a great peek behind the curtain. Fans are always amazed at just how small the sets—and stars—really are. To make it even more worth your while, most shows employ MCs to get the crowd in a good mood, and often you can pick up some swag, in the form of T-shirts or tickets to the MC's upcoming show.

TALKING POINTS

New York's most famous shows are incredibly popular, with waits of 6 months or longer commonplace. Often you'll have to send in a postcard with your relevant info and preferred dates (tickets to a taping make a great cheap birthday present). For those who arrive without tickets, it is possible to get standbys on the morning of the show. They'll only give one ticket per standee, so everyone in the party has to be there waiting at the crack of dawn. Even then it's no guarantee, since standby status only kicks in if there are enough no-shows among the regular ticket holders. Of course, if you're not choosey about what you want to see, plenty of shows in New York are unpopular enough to get you in without delay. The NYCVB has more details on tapings (www.nycvb.com; © **212/484-1222**).

The Colbert Report FREE   Stephen Colbert's nightly "news" program is rapidly approaching the cult status of *The Daily Show,* which spun it off in the fall of '05. Colbert's studio is *The Daily Show*'s cramped former home, meaning that there aren't many seats to go around. Comedy Central has suspended ticket giveaways for the unconnected, though it does promise to develop an online ticket request system soon. For standby seating, you could hope for a no-show by going to the studio door. Tapings are Mondays through Fridays at 7pm, but to have a shot for a standby you should get there a couple of hours earlier. You'll increase your chances if there isn't a big-name guest on the docket. Audience members must be 18 or over.

513 West 54th St., between 10th and 11th aves. © **212/767-8600.** www.comedy central.com. Subway: A/B/C/D/1 to 59th St./Columbus Circle.

The Daily Show with Jon Stewart FREE   There's been no drought of mockable material in the news recently, which helps Jon Stewart's satirical news/talk show continue to be a water-cooler conversation staple. In addition to biting analysis of current events, if you attend a taping you'll be treated to a few minutes of personable conversation with Jon himself. Though the show is more popular than ever, it's filmed in a new and larger studio, so tickets aren't impossible to come by. Tapings are Monday through Thursday with doors open at 5pm, though they want you there an hour early. An online request system is in the works, but for now the best bet is to request via email (requesttickets@thedailyshow.com); see the Comedy Central website for complete details. You can also check for last-minute tickets for the upcoming week; call on Fridays between 11 and 11:30am. You must be at least 18.

733 11th Ave., between 51st and 52nd sts. © **212/586-2477.** www.comedy central.com. Subway: A/B/C/D/1 to 59th St./Columbus Circle.

Good Morning America FREE   If seeing the face of Diane Sawyer first thing in the morning is actually an enticing prospect for you, join the live audience in ABC's studio right on Broadway. Tickets for the 7 to 9am broadcast can be wrangled by filling out the online request or by calling during business hours. If you do get tickets, plan on arriving at 6am. Sans tickets you can still join the throng outside the Broadway and 44th Street studio window. *Note:* In the summers, big-name performers come to Bryant Park for the **Good Morning America Summer Concert Series.** The shows are free and require no tickets, running from 7 to 9am (but get there by 7am at the latest).

ABC Studios, 7 Times Square, at 43rd St. ℂ 212/580-5176. www.abcnews.go. com/sections/GMA. Subway: N/Q/R/S/W/1/2/3/7 to Times Sq./42nd St.

Late Night with Conan O'Brien FREE   Though still in Letterman's shadow, Conan's show has matured and solidified, making it another tough New York ticket to nail down. The guests are A-listers and the sketches are some of the funniest on television. Tapings run Tuesday through Friday at 5:30pm, though they ask you to be there 45 minutes early. You can call or apply online to try and reserve up to four tickets. NBC hands out standbys on the day of taping, starting at 9am outside 30 Rockefeller Plaza (under the NBC Studios awning on the 49th Street side). You must be 16 or older to attend.

NBC Studio, 30 Rockefeller Plaza, 49th St., between Fifth and Sixth aves. ℂ 212/664-3056. www.nbc.com. Subway: B/D/F/V to 47th-50th sts.-Rockefeller Center; N/R/W to 49th St.

The Late Show with David Letterman FREE   And the number-one hottest New York TV taping ticket is . . . yeah, it's still Letterman. Though it's not what it was in the '80s, the show has really picked it up in the last year, with our favorite Hoosier squeezing the most out of his regulars, and Paul and the band keeping things energetic. Tapings are Monday through Thursday at 5:30pm, sometimes with a second taping Thursday at 8pm. You can request tickets online (it's a lottery, and usually a six-month wait) or you can stop by the theater in person. The lobby handles walk-ins on weekdays from 9:30am to 12:30pm, and weekends from 10am to 6pm. If you're feeling lucky, you can also try calling in for a same-day standby seat. The phone line opens at 11am. Be patient and use your redial button liberally. Also bone up on your Letterman trivia because you may need to pass a test to get the tickets (which aren't actually tickets, but are spots on the standby line, should anything open up and should you have correctly identified Biff Henderson's real first name as James). You must arrive an hour and a quarter before tape time, be 18 or older to attend, and be ready to show some ID.

Ed Sullivan Theater, 1697 Broadway, between 53rd and 54th sts. ℂ 212/247-6497. www.cbs.com/latenight/lateshow (click on "Get Tickets"). Subway: B/D/E to Seventh Ave.

Live! with Regis and Kelly FREE   If you don't have any plans for a year from now, why not go see Kelly and Rege? To join the absurdly long waiting list, send a postcard with your data to "Live with Regis and Kelly" Tickets, Ansonia Station, P.O. Box 230-777, New York, NY 10023-0777. You can request up to four tickets at a time. To line jump, you can try for a standby ticket. Show up at the studio by 7am at the latest on a taping day. Tapings are Monday through Friday at 9am at the ABC Studios in Lincoln Square on the Upper West Side. You must be 10 or older to attend (anyone under 18 must be accompanied by a parent).

7 Lincoln Sq., at Columbus Ave. and W. 67th St. ℂ 212/456-3054. http://tvplex. go.com/buenavista/regisandkelly/showinfo/tickets.html. Subway: 1 to 66th St./ Lincoln Center.

The Montel Williams Show FREE   Montel has hit his 15-year anniversary of service to the housebound and underemployed, with a continuing run of titillating topics designed to make Jerry Springer throw around chairs in envy. Tapings are on Wednesday and Thursday at 10am, 1pm, and 4pm. Montel and co. usually take July and most of August off. You can apply online, or call the number listed below between 9am and 5pm.

433 W. 53rd St., between Ninth and Tenth aves. ℂ 212/989-8101. www.montel show.com. Subway: C/E to 50th St.

Saturday Night Live FREE   SNL's steady devolution hasn't made getting in to see the show any easier. There's a lottery (around August usually; submit your name via email) for the upcoming season; otherwise, your only shot is trying for standbys on the date of the taping. One ticket per person may be available at 7am at 30 Rockefeller Plaza, on the 49th Street side of the building, though even a standby ticket is no guarantee you'll get in. Tapings are Saturday at 11:30pm from fall to late spring, with a dress rehearsal at 8pm (arrival time 7pm). You must be 16 or older to attend.

NBC Studio, 30 Rockefeller Plaza, 49th St., between Fifth and Sixth aves. ℂ **212/ 664-3056.** www.nbc.com. Subway: B/D/F/V to 47th-50th sts.-Rockefeller Center; N/R/W to 49th St.

The Today Show **FREE**   Watching NBC's morning mainstay is free and easy; just show up outside Today's glass-walled studio at Rockefeller Center, on the southwest corner of 49th Street and Rockefeller Plaza. Tapings are Monday through Friday from 7 to 10am, but if you want to be up front, 7am is way too late to be rushing over with your goofy hat and hand-painted sign. In the summer, Today holds a series of concerts in Rockefeller Center, generally Friday mornings at 7am. It's always big names playing, and they attract commensurate huge crowds.

Southwest corner of 49th St. and Rockefeller Plaza. ℂ **212/664-3056.** www. msnbc.msn.com. Subway: B/D/F/V to 47th-50th sts.-Rockefeller Center; N/R/W to 49th St.

Total Request Live **FREE**   Carson Daly's countdown show continues to entrance Generation XL, which gathers below MTV's glass studio at 44th Street and Broadway in Times Square before the 3:30pm tapings. Reservations can sometimes be made by calling the TRL Ticket Reservation Hot Line at ℂ **212/398-8549.** Failing that, show up by 2pm at the latest and watch for a TRL producer to come through the crowd. Standby tickets are exchanged for the correct answers to trivia questions. The MTV Store on the corner of 44th and Broadway usually has flyers for additional tapings and events next to the register. To get inside to the studio you must be at least 16 and look no older than 24.

1515 Broadway, at 44th St. ℂ **212/398-8549.** www.mtv.com. Subway: N/Q/R/S/W/1/2/3/7 to Times Sq./42nd St.

The View **FREE**   Barbara and crew chat away about cellulite, diets, calories, weight issues, and the other matters of substance every Monday through Friday at 11am. You can request online or by sending a postcard to Tickets, The View, 320 W. 66th St., New York, NY 10023. Ticket holders are expected 1½ hours before showtime. The ticket backlog runs about 12 months, but you can try to nab a standby from a View Audience Associate at the studio entrance. Starting at 8:30am they'll give seats away. You must be at least 18 (bring ID).

320 W. 66th St., off West End Ave. ℂ **212/465-0900.** www.abc.go.com/theview. Subway: 1 to 66th St./Lincoln Center.

Who Wants to be a Millionaire `FREE`   Millionaires miss out on all the fun listed in this book, but you can look on with condescending pity should anyone run the table against Meredith Vieira (or Regis). Tapings are Monday through Thursday at 4pm, with an additional 12:30pm Wednesday show. Note that they'll want you there 2 hours early and the show can take 2 hours or longer to tape, so make sure you're fed and watered before you go in (and be warned that as posh as the set looks on televisions, those benches are hard). For tickets, write 2 months in advance to New York TV Show Tickets, Inc., Who Wants to be a Millionaire?, Columbia University Station, PO Box 250225, New York, NY 10025.

Taping address: ABC at 30 West 67th St., between Columbus Ave. and Central Park West. ✆ 212/838-5901. www.abc.com. Subway: 1 to 66th St./Lincoln Center.

9 Word Up: Readings

New York has always been a city of writers, and modern Gotham has no shortage of literary lights. Undiscovered hopefuls, midlist strivers, and the huge names with cultlike followings all find their way to lecterns across the city. Bars, galleries, libraries, book stores, and schools do the hosting. With eight million other stories unfolding in the Naked City, most people don't take the time to be read to, and I usually find literary events are pleasantly underattended. There are exceptions—voices of the moment and package nights that bring in a bunch of big names at once—but generally you have a better chance to see a big-time writer than you'll get with any actress, athlete, or musician. And almost always you'll get to do it for free.

AT BOOKSTORES

Bookshops are good spots for getting a hit of that sweet, sweet literature, and getting it for free. Some stores offer regular readings, and some just signings, although on a quiet night you'll have the chance to talk up a favorite author.

☆ **Barnes & Noble** `FREE`   The Union Square location gets the biggest names and most frequent readings. Literary stars like David Sedaris, Helen Fielding, and Michael Cunningham come through to read from their works or participate in conferences and discussions. For kids, Sundays at 2:30pm is storytime. The seating area is large and comfortable, but you should show up early for the best-sellers because it does get crowded. A close second is the Lincoln Center location, with its steady big-shot parade.

33 E. 17th St., between Broadway and Park Ave. S. ℰ **212/253-0810.** www. bn.com. Subway: L/N/Q/R/W/4/5/6 to 14th St./Union Sq. Other location: *Lincoln Center*, 1972 Broadway, at 66th St. ℰ **212/595-6859.** Subway: 1 to 66th St./Lincoln Center.

Black Orchid Bookshop FREE This mystery novel shop has regular author signings. It's a friendly scene, complete with complimentary wine and snacks.

303 E. 81st St., between First and Second aves. ℰ **212/734-5980.** www. ageneralstore.com. Subway: 4/5/6 to 86th St.

Bluestockings FREE DIY ethos is in full effect at this newly expanded communal bookstore. Frequent readings of a feminist and lesbian bent intersperse with seminars and meetings. The read-

FREE **The Chain Gang**

With so many interesting mom and pop book stores in NYC, it would be tempting to ignore the corporate giants, if they weren't so ubiquitous. Despite the lack of indie cred, both Barnes & Noble (www.bn.com) and Borders (www.borders stores.com) are actually solid centers for free entertainment. With the square footage to pack in listeners by the bushel, and the juice to draw top names, some of the best readings in the city take place at Barnes & Noble (my favorite selection comes from the Union Sq. store; p. 88). Check the store windows or the website for the latest heavy-hitter to come shilling New York way.

ings and many lectures/discussions are free; other events can ask for suggested donations of $5 to $10. The **Dyke Knitting Circle** (ℰ **212/ 714-8375**) meets the third Sunday of every month from 4 to 6pm. It's open to all levels of knitting skill, with a $1 to $5 suggested donation.

172 Allen St., between Rivington and Stanton sts. ℰ **212/777-6028.** www.blue stockings.com. Subway: F/V to Second Ave.; J/M/Z to Essex St.

BookCourt FREE For over 2 decades now, this Cobble Hill favorite has been a clean and well-lit place for literary fans. The local authors section is comprehensive, which is impressive considering how many writers are calling the area home. In-store readings and signings bring in the hip new voices.

163 Court St., between Dean and Pacific sts., Cobble Hill, Brooklyn. ℰ **718/875-3677.** www.bookcourt.org. Subway: F/G to Bergen, M/N/R/W to Court St.; 2/3/4/5 to Borough Hall.

Books of Wonder `FREE`   The agenda here is books for the kiddies. Storytime comes every Sunday at noon, with a dramatically inclined staff member doing the honors. Additional readings and events, including the occasional publication party, are scattered through the calendar.

18 W. 18th St., between Fifth and Sixth aves. ℭ 212/989-3270. www.booksof wonder.net. Subway: L/N/Q/R/W/4/5/6 to 14th St./Union Sq.

Bowery Poetry Club   Poetry is just the beginning here, with music, theater, and beer adding to the enticements. A ramshackle vibe pervades, with exposed brick on the walls and a communal attitude. The calendar overflows with burlesque, book parties, slams, and plenty of poesy. Covers average around $6, but many free events can be found.

308 Bowery, between E. 1st and Bleecker sts. ℭ 212/614-0505. www.bowery poetry.com. F/V to Second Ave. 6 to Bleecker St.

Coliseum Books `FREE`   Midtown readers lamented when Coliseum Books' old location disappeared into the same Time Warner oblivion that claimed the Columbus Circle Coliseum itself. Coliseum has been reborn a few blocks away, in a spiffy new space near Times Square. The store now has more room for maneuvering, and the Coliseum's procession of quality writers earns universal thumbs-ups.

11 W. 42nd St., between Fifth and Sixth aves. ℭ 212/803-5890. www.coliseum books.com. Subway: B/D/F/V to 42nd St.; 7 to Fifth Ave.

Drama Book Shop   When this venerable performing-arts bookstore relocated a couple of years ago, they added a performing-arts space to the mix. The **Arthur Seelen Theatre** hosts a resident theater company in addition to regular discussions, readings, and workshops. They've even started showing film shorts. Look for The Boomerang Theatre's First Flight play readings program, and African-American women playwrights in the Potpourri! staged reading series. Check online for the calendar; events can run as much as $20, but a lot are offered for free.

250 W. 40th St., between Seventh and Eighth aves. ℭ 212/944-0595. www. dramabookshop.com. Subway: A/C/E or 1/2/3/7 or N/R/Q/S/W to 42nd St.

McNally Robinson NYC `FREE`   As every last retail inch of SoHo and NoLita seems primed to become a trendy restaurant or bar, the last newcomer one might expect would be a big, sophisticated bookstore. McNally Robinson is thriving, however, with an independent spirit and a knowledgeable staff. A full slate of readings, discussions, and signings can be found here.

50 Prince St., between Lafayette and Mulberry sts. ✆ 212/274-1160. www.mcnallyrobinsonnyc.com. Subway: 6 to Spring St., N/R/W to Prince St.

192 Books `FREE` This lovely new shop brings in authors for 7pm readings. Night of the week varies, and seating is limited so call ahead for reservations. Mary Gaitskill and A.M. Homes have graced this intimate space. Check the website for schedule.

192 Tenth Ave., at 21st. ✆ 212/255-4022. www.192books.com. Subway: C/E to 23rd St.

Printed Matter `FREE` "Artwork for the page" is the niche cornered by this organization, which specializes in affordable artists' publications. Book signings, launches, and exhibitions all can be found in their space in the heart of the Chelsea galleries.

195 Tenth Ave., between 21st and 22nd sts. ✆ 212/925-0325. www.printed matter.org. Subway: C/E to 23rd St.

Revolution Books `FREE` The revolution will be televised, and it will also make its way into print. Alternative viewpoints are aired during in-store readings here. No website yet, so you'll have to call or visit for a schedule of events.

9 W. 19th St., between Fifth and Sixth aves. ✆ 212/691-3345. Subway: 4/5/6/L/ N/Q/R/W to 14th St./Union Sq.

The Scholastic Store `FREE` The retail outlet for the children's publisher Scholastic has books and toys and a full schedule of in-store events. Book signings and story readings are free, as are the craft workshops on Saturdays. The Scholastic Auditorium hosts more free events, although you have to call in and get a reservation first. Check online or call for the latest schedule.

557 Broadway, between Prince and Spring sts. ✆ 212/343-6166. www.scholastic. com/sohostore. Subway: N/R/W to Prince St

Three Lives & Company `FREE` Just browsing in this low-key West Village legend can make a person feel smart and sophisticated. Pressed-tin ceilings and exposed brick complement a classy selection. Though space is tight here, the readings and signings are worth checking out.

154 W. 10th St., at Waverly Place. ✆ 212/741-2069. www.threelives.com. Subway: 1 to Christopher St.

AT BARS & CAFES

What better way to advertise the intelligent conversation your coffee shop or booze hall induces than by associating yourself with articulate new voices? Reading series have cropped up in bars and cafes across the city, and the informal settings encourage more showmanship than a bookshop lectern. With extreme readings the latest trend, these venues are the most likely spots to be entertained while listening to an author intone.

Ear Inn `FREE`   The structure housing this TriBeCa tavern was condemned as unfit for habitation in 1906. Somehow it's still upright, and still putting on one of the city's best reading series. Poetry, and occasional prose, can be heard at the Ear every Saturday at 3pm.

326 Spring St., west of Greenwich St. © **212/226-9060.** www.mbroder.com/ear_inn. Subway: C/E to Spring St.; 1 to Canal.

The Half King `FREE`   *The Perfect Storm* author Sebastian Junger is a co-owner of this bustling Chelsea bar and cafe. He's also an occasional contributor to their weekly reading series, which presents poets and prose writers every Monday night. One Monday a month is set aside for the overlooked category of magazine writing. Readings Mondays at 7pm.

505 W. 23rd St., near Tenth Ave. © **212/462-4300.** www.thehalfking.com. Subway: C/E to 23rd St.

Happy Ending `FREE`   This Chinatown lounge, whose name advertises a salient detail about the services of the former tenant (a massage parlor), is home to the city's most ambitious reading series. Monthly "In the Flesh" nights bring echoes of the space's past as writers strut their smut. "Varsity Letters" is New York's only sports-writing series, and every other Wednesday is reserved for the "Music and Reading" night, which requires participants to take at least one public risk. That risk might be a cooking demonstration and it might be the public airing of a credit card number; it'll definitely be more than somebody with a nose in a book mumbling into a lectern. Wednesdays at 8pm.

302 Broome St., at Forsythe St. © **212/334-9676.** www.happyendinglounge. com. Subway: B/D to Grand St.; F/J/M/Z to Essex/Delancey St.

Housing Works Used Book Café `FREE`   In addition to a great selection of used books, Housing Works attracts an impressive lineup of writers. Readings are free, but if you drop some money on cafe items it'll end up in a good place; Housing Works is a charity that donates proceeds to help support people living with AIDS. Times and days of the week vary; check the website for the schedule.

126 Crosby St., between Houston and Prince sts. ✆ **212/334-3324.** www.housing works.org. **Subway: B/D/F/V to Broadway/Lafayette; 6 to Bleecker St.**

☆ **KGB Bar** `FREE`   Hidden away in a former speakeasy on the second floor of an East Village tenement, KGB has the most comprehensive reading series in the city. Sunday night brings fiction, Monday poetry, Tuesday nonfiction, and some Wednesdays feature the fantastic, in the form of sci-fi authors. Drunken! Careening! Writers! is a great monthly night, with at least one big laugh guaranteed. Additional readers on the balance of evenings make it almost impossible to find a wordless night, though there are free films on the schedule, too. The bar was once the clubhouse of the Ukrainian Labor Home, and the commie kitsch adorning the walls perfects the literary atmosphere. Most readings start at 7pm.

85 E. 4th St., at Second Ave. ✆ **212/505-3360.** www.kgbbar.com. **Subway: B/D/F/V to Broadway/Lafayette; 6 to Bleecker St.**

One Story at Pianos `FREE`   *One Story* is a literary magazine with a self-explanatory philosophy. Once a month (the third Friday at 7pm) at Pianos, the magazine trots out a singular writer for a short, free reading and a happy hour, with a spotlight on One Drink chosen by the author. Check the Pianos website (www.pianosnyc.com) for other free music and karaoke nights.

158 Ludlow St., at Stanton St. ✆ **212/505-3733.** www.one-story.com. **Subway: F/V to Second Ave.; J/M/Z to Essex St.**

Pete's Candy Store `FREE`   Not content with a mere single literary evening, Pete's brings in the ink-slingers on Thursdays and Fridays. Alternating Thursdays focus on local writers, favoring fiction, with Jonathan Ames and Ben Greenman making recent appearances. Alternating Fridays are reserved for those of the poesy persuasion. Jams succeed the orating (check "For Those About to Rock"; p. 29). Readings start at 7pm.

709 Lorimer St., between Frost and Richardson sts., Williamsburg, Brooklyn. ✆ **718/302-3770.** www.petescandystore.com. **Subway: L to Lorimer St.; G to Metropolitan Ave.**

Reading Between A and B at 11th Street Bar FREE This series specializes in emerging poets, with occasional fiction and nonfiction sprinkled into the mix. The neighborhood bar that hosts couldn't be more congenial. Every other Monday at 7:30pm.

510 E. 11th St., between aves. A and B. ℂ 212/982-3929. www.readab.com. Subway: L to First Ave.

AT THE LIBRARIES

The sharks running New York's libraries have cooked up a scheme for self-perpetuation. Free readings, that's how they hook you. You like what the writer has to say, you can't resist the urge to learn more, and before you know it you're checking out books left and right. Diabolical.

The following libraries are the best for frequent readings. Check in at **www.nypl.org** for full schedules and other branches.

Brooklyn Public Library Grand Army Plaza. ℂ **718/230-2100.** www.brooklynpubliclibrary.org. Subway: 2/3 to Grand Army Plaza.

Langston Hughes Community Library and Cultural Center 100-01 Northern Blvd., between 102nd and 103rd sts., Corona, Queens. ℂ **718/651-1100.** Subway: 7 to 103rd St./Corona Plaza.

New York Public Library Schomburg Center for Research in Black Culture. 515 Malcolm X Blvd. (Lenox Blvd.), at 135th St. ℂ **212/ 491-2200.** Subway: 2/3 to 135th St.

New York Public Library Fort Washington Branch 535 W. 179th St., between Audubon and St. Nicholas aves. ℂ **212/927-3533.** Subway: A/1 to 181st St.

New York Public Library Humanities and Social Sciences Library Fifth Ave., at 42nd. ℂ **212/869-8089.** Subway: 7 to Fifth Ave.; 4/5/6 to Grand Central; B/D/F/V to 42nd St.

New York Public Library for the Performing Arts Donald and Mary Oenslager Gallery. 40 Lincoln Center Plaza, between 64th and 65th sts. ℂ **212/870-1630.** Subway: 1 to 66th St./Lincoln Center.

10 Big Leagues, Little Prices

It's said that it's now cheaper to be an opera fan than to follow a major league sports team, and with ticket prices racing well ahead of inflation it's easy to believe. A seat in the mezzanine of Giants Stadium to

Playing the Horses

Horse racing has seen its bottom line repeatedly gouged by the dumb luck of state lotteries. Every year fewer and fewer fans trek out to the track, which means Belmont and the Big A will be happy to see you when you go. So happy, in fact, that they'll let you in for only a nominal charge. While it's possible to lose some real money on the ponies, I have a system. Always pick the first horse off the rail that's wearing red, or any horse whose name begins with B. You can't miss.

Aqueduct Racetrack   Thoroughbred racing runs from late October or early November to early May. 110th St. and Rockaway Blvd., Rockaway Beach, Queens. ☏ **718/641-4700**. www.nyra.com/aqueduct. Tickets $1-$3 (grandstand is free Jan-early March). Closed Mon-Tues. Subway: A to North Conduit.

Belmont Park   Whenever the horses don't run at Aqueduct (see above), they're racing here. Season is May to mid-July and late August, or early September to October. Hempstead Ave., Belmont, Long Island. ☏ **718/641-4700**. www.nyra.com/belmont. Tickets $2-$5. Closed Mon-Tues. Train: LIRR Belmont Express from Penn Station or Flatbush Ave.

watch Big Blue will set you back $85, and you can't get to the field level in Yankee Stadium for less than $100. Premium Knicks seats? Prices hit $330. This for a team that went 23-59 last year? Even the New York Rangers don't do us any favors—their cheapest hockey ticket is $27. However, if you have no fear of heights, there are a few inexpensive ways of getting into the big games.

The Amazing Mets   It's hard to believe that mostly charmless, modern Shea Stadium is the sixth-oldest stadium in the majors. For approximately 15 games a year, the Mets roll back the prices for cheapskate fans. The seats in question (parts of the upper, loge, and mezzanine) all have one thing in common: They're in the back rows and many miles from the action on the field. Also, they're not available for "Gold" tier games (Yankees, Cubs, and so on), but only for

"Value" tier (a late-Aug series with the Brewers, say). Still, at a paltry $5, it's a cheap way to see a big league team in action.

Shea Stadium, 126th St., at Roosevelt Ave., Flushing, Queens. ℂ **718/507-8499.** www.mets.com. Subway: 7 to Willets Point/Shea Stadium.

Damn Yankees   Even though the Boss has broken the bank to buy up just about every player in Major League Baseball, there are still dirt cheap ways to get into the cozy nest of our beloved Evil Empire. Tier box, tier reserved, and bleacher seats at Yankee Stadium are a mere $5 a pop during 11 Fujifilm games a year (they're midweek games, but against decent opponents). Bleacher seats are otherwise $12. Before you enter the bleacher zone, it's worth noting that the phrase "bleacher creatures" wasn't coined solely for its rhyming qualities. It's not exactly kid-friendly territory, unless your kids are thuggish drunks.

Yankee Stadium, 161st St. and River Ave., the Bronx. ℂ **718/293-6000.** www. yankees.com. Subway: B/D/4 to 161st St./Yankee Stadium.

Knicks & Cut-Rate Seats   Ten-dollar Knick seats are about as elusive as Knick playoff victories. They do exist, but they're nosebleeds and they tend to sell out quickly. If you don't pick them up in September when they first go on sale, your best bet is to check the "Stub Hub" on the Knick website, where season-ticket holders unload their spares at list.

Madison Square Garden, 4 Pennsylvania Plaza, Seventh Ave., at 34th St. ℂ **212/ 465-6741.** www.nba.com/knicks. Subway: A/C/E or 1/2/3 to Penn Station.

Sweet Land of Liberty   The Liberty offer more cheap ways to get into Madison Square Garden than their male counterparts. They also play harder. Though prices go as high as $229.50, you can find a fair amount of upper-row seating for $10.

Madison Square Garden, 4 Pennsylvania Plaza, Seventh Ave., at 34th St. ℂ **212/ 465-6075.** www.wnba.com/liberty. Subway: A/C/E or 1/2/3 to Penn Station.

Baby Bombers   The **Staten Island Yankees** have a lovely new waterfront stadium just a few steps from the ferry terminal. Running from $9 to $11, tickets are easier to come by than the Cyclones', although they're scarce when the two rivals play. For '06, new seats have been added down the first- and third-base lines. Called the "Cheap Seats," they're only $5 each.

Richmond County Bank Ballpark, Staten Island. *©* **718/720-9200.** www.siyanks.com. Subway: R/W to Whitehall St.; 1 to South Ferry, take the ferry to Staten Island and follow the signs.

Mini Mets   No one confuses the **Brooklyn Cyclones** for dem bums of old, but the new stadium near the Atlantic Ocean and the Coney Island boardwalk has fast become a borough fave. Box seats are $11 or $13 on the weekdays, and $12 or $14 on the weekends. General admission seats will only set you back $6 weekdays, $7 weekends. Though some of the sheen is off the new stadium, tickets still go quickly here.

Keyspan Park, 1904 Surf Ave., at W. 19th St., Coney Island, Brooklyn. *©* **718/449-8497.** www.brooklyncyclones.com. Subway: D/F/N/Q to Coney Island/Stillwell Ave.

ENTERTAINMENT DOWNTOWN

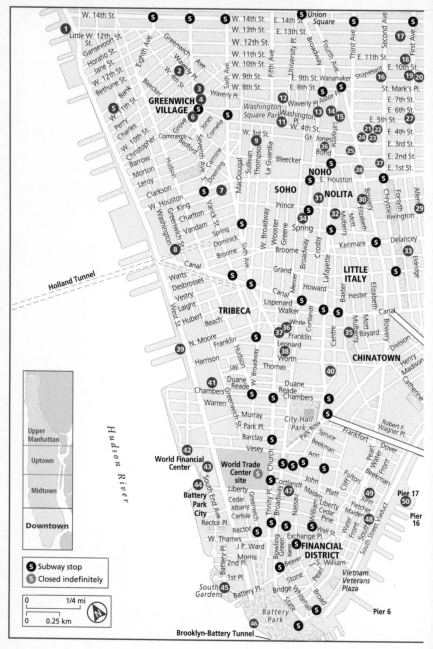

ENTERTAINMENT MIDTOWN

ENTERTAINMENT UPTOWN

Barnes & Noble Lincoln Center **9**
Black Orchid Bookshop **20**
Cleopatra's Needle **4**
Czech Center **19**
Delacorte Theater **14**
El Museo del Barrio **21**
Ethical Culture Society **13**
Florence Gould Hall **17**
Good Shepherd Presbyterian Church **10**
Harlem Meer/Dana Discovery Center **22**
Iggy's **18**
The Juilliard School **12**
Live! with Regis and Kelly **8**
Mannes College of Music **5**
Metropolitan Opera (Lincoln Center) **12**
Naumburg Bandshell **15**
New York City Opera (Lincoln Center) **12**
New York Philharmonic
    (Lincoln Center) **12**
New York Public Library for the
    Performing Arts **12**
Pier I **6**
Smoke **3**
St. John the Divine **1**
SummerStage at Rumsey Playfield **16**
Underground Lounge **2**
The View **11**
Who Wants to be a Millionaire
    at ABC Studios **7**

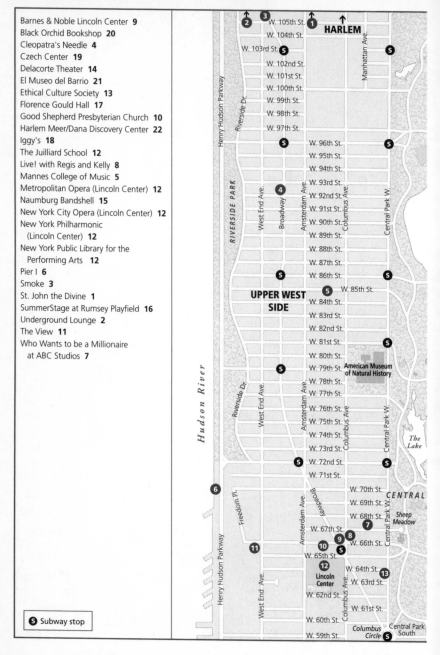

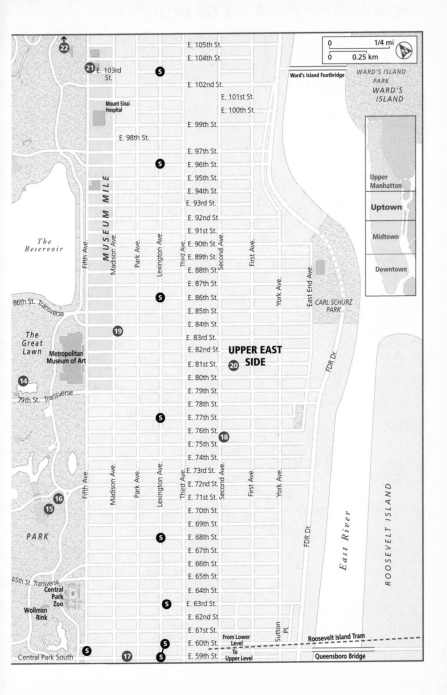

ENTERTAINMENT IN BROOKLYN

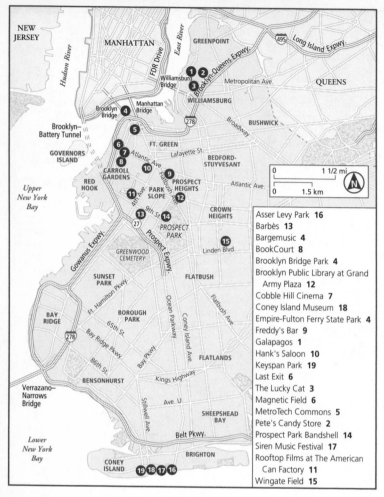

Asser Levy Park **16**
Barbès **13**
Bargemusic **4**
BookCourt **8**
Brooklyn Bridge Park **4**
Brooklyn Public Library at Grand
   Army Plaza **12**
Cobble Hill Cinema **7**
Coney Island Museum **18**
Empire-Fulton Ferry State Park **4**
Freddy's Bar **9**
Galapagos **1**
Hank's Saloon **10**
Keyspan Park **19**
Last Exit **6**
The Lucky Cat **3**
Magnetic Field **6**
MetroTech Commons **5**
Pete's Candy Store **2**
Prospect Park Bandshell **14**
Siren Music Festival **17**
Rooftop Films at The American
   Can Factory **11**
Wingate Field **15**

ENTERTAINMENT IN QUEENS

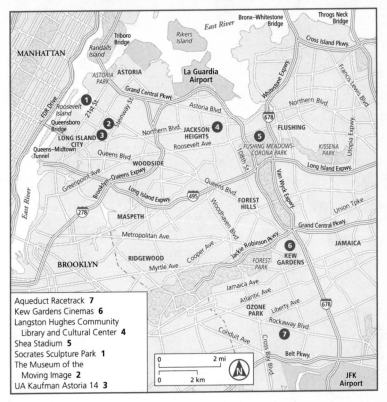

Aqueduct Racetrack **7**
Kew Gardens Cinemas **6**
Langston Hughes Community
  Library and Cultural Center **4**
Shea Stadium **5**
Socrates Sculpture Park **1**
The Museum of the
  Moving Image **2**
UA Kaufman Astoria 14 **3**

Selective diners can find cheap eats all over Gotham; the Lower East Side's Tiengarden serves sit-down lunches at takeout prices. See p. 115 for a review.

EATING & DRINKING

ew Yorkers speak over 100 languages, and we eat at least that many different cuisines. Many of the ethnic superstars are hidden away in low-rent corners of the boroughs, but plenty of spectacular cheap eats can be found in even the high-rent districts of Manhattan. Being selective about price doesn't necessarily mean sacrificing quality. Some of my favorite cooking just happens to be some of the city's cheapest. The island tilts toward downtown when it comes to budget grazing—Chinatown and the Lower East Side dominate. Across the rest of the city, Asian eateries offer the most for the least. Culinary trends have been favoring the low end of late. New purveyors of cheap burgers, hot dogs, fried chicken, and pizza have spread across the city. Lunch specials are a great way to sample the city's harvest with a minimal investment, but for all meals I'm constantly surprised by how far $5 can take me in NYC. Leave the Jacksons in the wallet and bon appétit.

1 Fine Chinese

New York's headquarters for cheap eating is Chinatown. Between the foreign language and the strange sights and smells, it's easy to feel like you've wandered into another country—a country where the local currency is weak and the dollar is strong. Don't bother recalculating the exchange rate, however. The check really is that low.

Congee Village *CHINESE* LOWER EAST SIDE   Though the Chinese–Disney–acid trip decor here doesn't scream authenticity, the food and the clientele are the real thing. The house specialty is congee, a hearty rice porridge that starts at $2 and comes in multiple combinations. My favorite is squid with ginger, for $2.50. For sharing, try the house special chicken, a banquet plate of garlicky delight at $9.95 for a half. Lunch specials, served over rice, average $3.50.

100 Allen St., between Delancey and Broome sts. ℂ **212/941-1818.** Daily 10:30am–2am. Subway: F to Delancey St.; J/M/Z to Essex St.

☆ **Eldridge Street Dumpling House** *CHINESE/DUMPLINGS* LOWER EAST SIDE   If they tripled their prices, this little take-away stand on the Lower East Side end of Chinatown would still be laughably cheap. They offer an amazing sandwich. For $1.50 you get a big wedge of sesame pancake with beef in a fresh cilantro and carrot dressing. All that flavor disguises a little toughness of the beef. Dumplings make a great side, five for $1 and cooked in a tasty thick wrapping. Soups are $3 and under, and steamed buns range from 50¢ to 75¢. FINE PRINT There's limited counter space to eat in.

118a Eldridge St., between Broome and Grand sts. ℂ **212/625-8008.** Daily 8am–10pm. Subway: B/D to Grand St.

Grand Sichuan International *CHINESE* CHELSEA   Don't be fooled by the average decor or below average prices—this place serves the best Chinese food in the city. The menu is phone book thick, but it's hard to make a bad pick here. Orange beef, string beans, and General Tso's chicken are three normal-sounding dishes that get reworked into Szechuan gems. You can splurge on more expensive items like the spectacular $15.95 smoked tea duck, but if you limit your ordering to $8.95-and-under entrees you won't be disappointed. The soup dumplings ($5.25–$6.25) are legendary. Lunches are not heavily attended, despite the $5.25 specials. At dinner time arrive early or arrive patient.

229 Ninth Ave., at 24th St. ✆ 212/620-5200. www.thegrandsichuan.com. Daily 11:30am–11pm. Subway: C/E to 23rd St. Other locations: *Midtown*, 745 Ninth Ave., between 50th and 51st sts. ✆ 212/582-2288. Subway: C/E to 50th St. *Chinatown*, 125 Canal St., at Chrystie St. ✆ 212/625-9212. Subway: B/D to Grand St. *East Village*, 19-23 St. Marks Place, between Second and Third aves. ✆ 212/529-4800. Subway: 6 to Astor Place; N/R/W to 8th St.

Joe's Ginger Restaurant *CHINESE* CHINATOWN   Joe's Shanghai is an ill-kept Chinatown secret, with lines as legendary as the food. Most folks haven't caught on to the offshoots, however, which have Joe's same great cooking with slightly lower prices and significantly less waiting. The homemade noodles are delicious, especially in soup form. A big bowl averages $4.25 and comes with a choice of four different noodles. Most veggie dishes are $6.95, most pork $7.95, and beef are $8.95. Ambience is minimal, but the staff is friendly by Chinatown standards.

113 Mott St., between Canal and Hester sts. ✆ 212/966-6613. www.joesginger. com. Sun–Thur 11am–10:30pm; Fri–Sat 11am–11:30pm. Subway: J/M/N/R/Q/W/Z/6 to Canal St. Other location: 25 Pell St., between Doyers and Mott sts. ✆ 212/285-0333. Sun–Thur 11am–10:30pm; Fri–Sat 11am–11pm. Joe's Shanghai: *Chinatown*, 9 Pell St., between Bowery and Doyers St. ✆ 212/233-8888. Subway: J/M/N/R/Q/W/Z/6 to Canal St. Other location: *Midtown*, 24 W. 56th St., between Fifth and Sixth aves. ✆ 212/333-3868. Subway: N/R/Q/W or F to 57th St.

2 Pots and Pan-Asians/ Cheaps From the East

There's no excuse for ever getting bored with New York cuisine. When you've had your share of Chinese, check out the Pan-Asian possibilities, which offer the best in New York's cheap ethnic alternatives.

Bennie's Thai Café *THAI* FINANCIAL DISTRICT   This unprepossessing basement spot serves authentic Thai food that bursts with flavor. Worker bees stream in for the $4.75 lunch specials, served over rice on weekdays from 11am to 3pm. Red, yellow, and green curries are the highlights. The dishes are pork, chicken, and beef, so vegetarians have to order off the regular menu. Helpfully, vegetarian entrees, including an awesome pad thai, are under $7.

88 Fulton St., at Gold St. ⓒ 212/587-8930. Daily 11am–9pm. Subway: A/C/J/M/ Z/2/3/4/5 to Fulton St./Broadway Nassau.

Café Himalaya *TIBETAN* EAST VILLAGE   This little mom and pop restaurant serves tasty Tibetan/Nepali meals. There's a slight resemblance to Indian and Chinese dishes, as you might imagine, but the flavoring is its own thing—soy, carrot, and ginger are major players. Veggie dinner entrees run from $5.99 to $6.99, and sautéed noodle and meat dishes are $6.75. Things get even cheaper at lunch, where you can get a curry or dumplings or noodles for only $4.99. Lunch specials run weekdays from 11:30am to 4pm. The seating is limited, and for cheap date purposes it's BYOB.

78 E. 1st St., between Ave. A and First Ave. ⓒ 212/358-0160. Tues–Sat noon– 11pm; Sun noon–10pm. Subway: F/V to Second Ave.

Kofoo *KOREAN* CHELSEA   Where students congregate, cheap food cannot be far away. An F.I.T. clientele flocks to nearby Kofoo, for a wide selection of Korean delights. *Kim bop*, Korean sushi, comes in ten varieties, each $4.50. Korean rice classics are also served, including sliced-beef *bulgogi* and *bibim bop* for $6.50 each. Fresh, crisp kimchi on the side stands out, too. FINE PRINT There are just a couple of seats; most business is takeout.

334 Eighth Ave., between 26th and 27th sts. ⓒ 212/675-5277. Mon–Sat 10:30am–10pm. Subway: C/E to 23rd St.

Pho Viet Huong *VIETNAMESE* CHINATOWN   This is the best Vietnamese food in the city, and it's just a little added bonus that it's also among the cheapest. Huge bowls of *pho* (beef noodle soup) are only $4 and both vermicelli noodle and rice dishes come in under $5. The daily specials are usually under $10 and are routinely delicious. Keep an eye out for the beef stuffed with onions.

73 Mulberry St., between Bayard and Canal sts. ⓒ 212/233-8988. Daily 10am–10pm. Subway: J/M/N/Q/R/W/Z/6 to Canal St.

Saigon Grill *VIETNAMESE* UPPER EAST SIDE   Saigon Grill, on the Upper East Side, misses nothing in its pursuit of fresh, flavorful Vietnamese food. My favorites are the noodle dishes. The "bun" ranges from $6.95 to $9.95 and comes with a huge plate of lettuce, vermicelli noodles, and the meat or vegetable of your choice. Veggie entrees, including the delectable basil vegetables, are $7.50. Several weekday lunch specials are offered, too, in the $5.50 range.

1700 Second Ave., at 88th St. © **212/996-4600.** www.saigongrill.com. Daily 11:30am–11:30pm. Subway: 4/5/6 to 86th St. Other location: *Upper West Side,* 620 Amsterdam Ave., at 90th St. © **212/875-9072.** Daily 11am–midnight. Subway: 1 to 86th St.

Woorijip *KOREAN* MIDTOWN   Korean delis are ubiquitous in New York, but most serve up bland, mainstream cafeteria fare. To find real Korean dishes the natural destination is 32nd Street in Midtown, where a delicious by-the-pound deli is hidden among pricier Korean restaurants. Bulgogi, squid, tofu, jellyfish, Korean pancakes, and, of course, kimchi, can be found on the serve-yourself buffet line. It costs $5.49 per pound, and you can also get pre-made snacks and meals from $1 to $6.

12 W. 32nd St., between Broadway and Fifth Ave. © **212/244-1115.** Daily 24 hr. Subway: B/D/F/N/Q/R/V/W to 34th St.

3 Fast Food Alternatives

NYC is unkind to huge restaurant chains. The cost of labor here favors family-run enterprises, and New Yorkers' finely honed tastebuds run counter to the lowest common denominator flavors of the hinterland. Thankfully, for low-cost fast food, small franchises and one-off shops provide excellent alternatives to the golden arches and their ilk.

Carl's Steaks *CHEESESTEAKS* FINANCIAL DISTRICT   City of Brotherly Love transplants have long looked down their noses at New York's feeble attempts at the cheesesteak. A slew of hopefuls have stepped up, but only Carl's delivers a sandwich able to hold its own in South Philly. The shaved sirloin melts on the tongue, while taut rolls make the meal substantial. Fromage on offer includes American and provolone, but connoisseurs know Cheese Whiz is the only way to go. A steak sandwich alone is $5.50, with cheese $6; $2 for a side of fries.

79 Chambers St., between Broadway and Church St. © **212/566-2828.** www.carlssteaks.com. Mon–Sat 11am–11pm; Sun noon–10pm. Subway: A/C or 1/2/3 to Chambers St.; R/W to City Hall. Other location: *Midtown,* 507 Third Ave., at 34th St. © **212/696-5336.** Subway: 6 to 33rd St.

L & L Hawaiian Barbecue *HAWAIIAN* FINANCIAL DISTRICT   For most New Yorkers, the *katsus, loco mocos,* and *lau lau* combs here will be unfamiliar. The tangy Asian-inflected flavors make quick converts, however. Plates come with creamy macaroni salad and scooped rice. Short ribs in black pepper sauce is $5.49; a mixed barbecue combo that could feed a family for a week is $7.99. Manhattan is blessed with the only two versions of this franchise east of Colorado.

64 Fulton St., between Cliff and Gold sts. ℂ 212/577-8888. www.hawaiian barbecue.com. Mon-Fri 10:30am-11pm; Sat-Sun 11am-11pm. Subway: A/C/J/M/Z/2/ 3/4/5 to Fulton St./Broadway Nassau.

Otafuku *JAPANESE* EAST VILLAGE   Ideal drunk food can be found at this tiny takeout in the East Village. The dishes are hot, flavorful, filling, and slightly odd. The mainstay is *okonomiyaki,* a pizza-shaped pancake fried up with shredded cabbage, bonito flakes, and a choice of meat. At $7, it's large enough to be shared. *Yakisoba* (fried noodles with seafood) is only $6. FINE PRINT Aside from a bench in front, there's no seating.

236 E. 9th St., between Second and Third aves. ℂ 212/353-8503. Daily 1-10pm. Subway: 6 to Astor Place; N/R/W to 8th St.

Tebaya *JAPANESE* CHELSEA   All the way from Nagoya, Japan, comes this recipe for extraordinary chicken wings. No dowdy breading here: Wings are double fried to burn off the fat and then basted in a savory garlic sauce. I had no idea chicken wings could taste this good. City of Buffalo, hang your head in shame. Eight pieces are $5.50. For your next Super Bowl party, volume discounts bring the price of each wing as low as 65¢. Japanese fast food items like teriyaki chicken sandwiches and fried potato cakes fill out the rest of the offerings. FINE PRINT Seating is limited.

144 W. 19th St., between Sixth and Seventh aves. ℂ 212/924-3335. www.goo japan.com/tebaya/index.htm. Mon-Fri 11:30am-11:30pm; Sat noon-11pm; Sun noon-9pm. Subway: 1 to 19th St.

Tuck Shop *AUSTRALIAN* EAST VILLAGE   Tuck shop is Australian for "canteen," and this neat mess hall specializes in quick and casual pies. Savory, flaky crusts hold veggies, beef, or a chicken version with leeks and diced ham. At $5, they're not huge, but hearty and filling all the same. The $3 vegetarian sausage roll is a mash of chickpea and mushrooms with an addictive sour taste.

68 E. 1st St., between First and Second aves. ℂ 212/979-5200. www.tuckshopnyc. com. Mon-Wed 8am-midnight; Thur-Fri 8am-2am; Sat 10am-2am; Sun 10am-10pm.

Subway: F/V to Second Ave. Other location: *Midtown,* 250 West 49th St., between Eighth Ave. and Broadway. ℂ **212/757-8481.** Subway: C/E or 1 to 50th St.

Yonah Schimmel *KNISHES* LOWER EAST SIDE   The knish is a New York classic and can be found everywhere from delis to hot dog stands, but for the best in gut bombs you have to go to the source, the Lower East Side. Yonah Schimmel offers up flavors traditional (potato, mushroom, kasha) and sacrilegious (pizza), cooked with a generations-old recipe. For $2.50, it's hard to get more filled up. The rich cheese versions are less cost conscious ($3), but equally delicious.

137 E. Houston St., between First and Second aves. ℂ **212/477-2858.** www.yonah schimmel.com. Subway: F/V to Second Ave.

4 Falafel Good

I've never understood how a little shredded chickpea can come out tasting so meaty and delicious. Somehow falafel satisfies in a way no vegetable can match. The deep-frying probably doesn't hurt any. As far as blessings to count in New York City, falafel availability is right up there with the Met and Central Park.

Bereket Turkish Kebob House *TURKISH/FALAFEL* LOWER EAST SIDE   The guys working here clearly never got the memo that fast food doesn't require four-star taste. The $3.50 falafel is crispy, served up in a flavorful pita with farm-fresh tomatoes and lettuce. As good as the falafel is, the rest of the menu might be even better. Both chicken sandwiches, the shish, and the kebab, are steals for $6.

187 E. Houston St., at Orchard St. ℂ **212/475-7700.** Open 24 hr. Subway: F/V to Second Ave.

Mamoun's *MIDDLE EASTERN/FALAFEL* WEST VILLAGE   This NYU favorite opened in 1971 and they've been so busy serving up Middle Eastern delicacies that they haven't had the chance to revise their prices. At $2, the falafel sandwich here is one of the city's best buys. The balls are small, dense, and packed with flavor. Other veggie pitas, like the baba ghanouj, are also $2. The chicken kabob is a highlight of the $4 meat sandwiches. Several competitors have hung their shingles on the block, but Mamoun's is still the best. Seating is limited; in nice weather Washington Square Park serves as Mamoun's back garden.

119 Macdougal St., between Minetta Lane and W. 3rd St. ℂ **212/674-8685.** www. mamounsfalafel.com. Daily 10am-5am. Subway: A/B/C/D/E/F/V to W. 4th St.

☆ **Rainbow Falafel & Shawarma** *SYRIAN/FALAFEL* UNION SQUARE   Rainbow has the best tasting falafel in the city. Marinated onions liven up the already-flavorful falafel balls. The other Syrian specialties here—shawarmas and kebabs, in particular—are just as good. FINE PRINT It's all take-away, but nearby Union Square's benches and tables invite picnicking.

26 E. 17th St., between Broadway and Fifth Ave. ℂ 212/691-8641. Mon-Fri 11am-6pm. Subway: L/N/Q/R/W/4/5/6 to 14th St./Union Sq.

Taim *ISRAELI/FALAFEL* WEST VILLAGE   Though Taim takes a gourmet approach to its Middle Eastern cooking, it's barely reflected in the prices. Falafel is the specialty here, balled into small and taut bites. The options are varied: green, with mint, parsley, and cilantro; roasted red pepper; and *harissa,* a Tunisian version spiced up with paprika and garlic. A sandwich is $4.50 and comes dressed with tahini and homemade hummus. Everything is made fresh daily, more than justifying this carryout's name (Hebrew for "delicious"). FINE PRINT Seating is limited.

222 Waverly Place, between Perry and W. 11th sts. ℂ 212/691-1287. Daily noon-10pm. Subway: 1/2/3 to 14th St.

5 Vegetarian

For years, frequenters of NYC's vegetarian restaurants could be forgiven for thinking they might as well all be named "Food Haters" for their bland and limited cuisine. The next generation of meatless purveyors has put a stop to all that, however. Vegetarians can achieve culinary satisfaction just as easily as their carnivorous brethren, and they don't have to pay through the nose to do it.

Chennai Garden *INDIAN* MURRAY HILL   I am a fascist about Downtown being better at all things, but when it comes to Indian, Curry Hill is way ahead of the East Village's Curry Row. Chennai Garden may be the city's best, with an extensive menu of Southern Indian delights. Vegetarians can relax, as the long list of *dosai, utthappam,* and curries doesn't contain a scrap of meat. Entrees are under $10, and portions are substantial. The weekday lunch buffet is a steal at $5.95.

129 E. 27th St., between Park and Lexington aves. ℂ 212/689-1999. Mon-Fri buffet 11:30am-3pm, dinner 5pm-10pm; Sat-Sun noon-10pm.

Hummus Place *MIDDLE EASTERN* WEST VILLAGE   New York is known for diner menus packed with just about every dish and combination imagined by humanity. There's something nice, however, about a place that only does one thing, especially when they do it so damn well. Imported white tahini is the key ingredient to the rich hummus served here. For only $4.95 you can have your choice of three versions, plain, with fava bean stew and egg, or with whole chickpeas. Hummus haters are limited to *shakshuka*, a hearty Israeli tomato stew, for $5.95.

99 MacDougal St., between Carmine and Bleecker sts. ✆ **212/533-3089.** Sun-Thurs 11am-midnight; Fri-Sat 11am-2am. Subway: A/B/C/D/E/F/V to W. 4th St.; 1 to Houston St. Other location: *East Village*, 109 St. Marks Place, between First Ave. and Ave. A. ✆ **212/529-9198.** Subway: L to First Ave.

Pukk *THAI* EAST VILLAGE   Don't be intimidated by the over-designed interior of this narrow restaurant. The food here transcends the trends to deliver inventive soups, curries, and tofus. Among the fake meats, the duck is the standout. Entrees and noodle dishes start at $7 (the spicy eggplant tofu comes in a huge, delicious portion), and two-course lunches are $6.

71 First Ave., between 4th and 5th sts. ✆ **212/253-2741.** www.pukknyc.com. Sun-Thu 11:30am-11pm; Fri-Sat 11:30am-midnight. Subway: F/V to Second Ave.

Punjabi *INDIAN* EAST VILLAGE   Local hipsters have discovered this Punjabi taxi stand, which serves both its constituencies with equal cordiality. Choose from six daily veggie entries, which are then microwaved and served over rice. Have one on a small plate for $2, or splurge for three over a big plate for $4. The food is fresh and tasty, and you can throw in two samosas for only $1.50 more.

114 E. 1st St., between First Ave. and Ave. A. ✆ **212/533-9048.** Subway: F/V to Second Ave.

Tiengarden *VEGETARIAN* LOWER EAST SIDE   A mix of pencil-thin model types and local hard-core vegans frequent this quirky little storefront for some of the healthiest food around. The Chinese-inspired menu is prepared without dairy, onion, or garlic, but somehow manages to be packed with flavor. Noodle dishes start at $6.50 and soups at $5.95, and most every entree is under $10. I could eat the Spicy Eggplant or Seitan Innovation every day of the week and not get bored. The $4.95 weekday lunch special runs until 4pm. See if you're not filled with a subtle sense of well-being when you leave.

Box: Best Food Inside A Jewelry Shop (Tie)

Bánh Mì Saigon Bakery *VIETNAMESE* CHINATOWN   One of New York's best sandwiches is also one of its cheapest. Vietnamese bánh mì layers cilantro, carrot, cucumber, and a light dressing onto a crusty baguette. Beyond the bread, French influence can also be found in the thinly-sliced pâté that accompanies crumbled pork sausage in the classic version. This purveyor's tiny counter in the back of a jewelry shop reinforces a sensation that anything this delicious must be illegal. 138-01 Mott St., between Grand and Hesters sts. ✆ **212/941-1541.** Subway: B/D to Grand St.; J/M/Z to Bowery. Other location: 88 E. Broadway, Unit #108, along Market St., near the Chinatown busses. Subway: F to East Broadway.

Taam-Tov *BUKHARAN* MIDTOWN   To reach the elevator to this unmarked Diamond District legend, you have to pass through a series of jewelers' stalls. The upstairs lunchroom is packed with Jewish expats chatting over the comfort food of Bukhara, Uzbekistan. Skewered kebabs are $2.99 each, a perfect match for thick-cut French fries. House specialties run a little more; the green-tinted bakhsh, a hearty cilantro pilaf, comes in at $5.99. 46 W. 47th St., Fourth floor, between Fifth and Sixth aves. ✆ **212/768-8001.** www.nytaamtov.com. Mon-Thur 10am-5pm; Fri 10am-two hours before shabbos. Subway: B/D/F/V to 47th-50th sts.-Rockefeller Center.

170 Allen St., between Stanton and Rivington sts. ✆ **212/388-1364.** Mon-Sat noon-10pm. Subway: F/V to Second Ave.; J/M/Z to Essex St.

6 Healthy

When $1.50 hot dogs beckon, it can be hard for dirt cheap eaters to remember to show their bodies a little occasional respect. If organic groceries were any example, it would seem that healthy eating is plain out of reach for the little guy. Luckily, NYC has a couple of spots that will add years to your life without draining your wallet.

Dojo *HEALTH/JAPANESE* WEST VILLAGE   As any NYU student will tell you, the cheapest sit-down meals can be found at Dojo. The menu is Japanese inspired, but the restaurant serves a full array of healthy-ish food for almost token fees. A soy burger goes for $2.75, salads for $3.50 to $5.25, and a big plate of veggie don noodles is $5.25.

14 W. 4th St., between Broadway and Mercer St. ℂ 212/505-8934. Mon-Thurs 11am-1am; Fri-Sat 11am-2am; Sun 11am-1am. Subway: B/D/F/V to Broadway/ Lafayette; 6 to Bleecker St. Other location: *East Village*, 24-26 St. Marks Place, between Second and Third aves. ℂ 212/674-9821. Subway: 6 to Astor Place; N/R/W to 8th St.

The Pump Energy Food *HEALTH* MIDTOWN WEST   A Garment District find, Pump cooks everything to order and they eschew salt, butter, frying, preservatives, and other body-unfriendly shortcuts to taste. The result of this effort is fresh and healthy food. For $5.75 you can get a grilled lemon chicken or turkey burger stuffed in a pita. A delicious baked falafel salad, served over crisp lettuce, with tomato and cukes, is only $6. And when you're done you won't feel all logy.

112 W. 38th St., between Sixth Ave. and Broadway. ℂ 212/764-2100. www.the pumpenergyfood.com. Mon-Thurs 7:30am-8:30pm; Fri 7:30am-7pm; Sat-Sun 11:30am-5:30pm. Subway: B/D/F/N/Q/R/V/W to 34th St. Other locations: *Midtown*, 40 W. 55th St., between Fifth and Sixth aves. ℂ 212/246-6844. Subway: E/V to Fifth Ave./53rd St.; F to 57th St.; 113 E. 31st St., between Park and Lexington aves. ℂ 212/213/5733. Subway: 6 to 33rd St.; 31 E. 21st St., between Park Ave. and Broadway. ℂ 212/253-7676. Subway: N/R/W or 6 to 23rd St.; 805 Third Ave., at 50th St. ℂ 212/421-3055. Subway: 6 to 51st St.; E/V to Lexington Ave./53rd St.

7 Loved Latinos

After Asian, the best bet for cheap eating is Latino food. Our Spanish-speaking neighbors to the south (and east, when you count the Caribbean) have a surprisingly varied cuisine, and some great examples of it can be found here in El Norte.

Caracas Arepa Bar *VENEZUELAN* EAST VILLAGE   An *arepa* is a Venezuelan improvement on bread, with flavorful corn standing in for wheat flour. The small arepa sandwiches at this East Village shop start at $3.75 with plain white cheese and top out around $6. The selection is varied for such a small place, with ingredients changing with the seasons.

Grand Prix Fixe

NYC's restaurant weeks are one way New Yorkers on budgets can graze on grub they normally couldn't afford. A couple of times a year, participating chuck wagons set up special multi-course menus. At $25 for lunch and $35 for dinner, they're hardly charitable give-aways, however. Prix Fixe is French for fixed price, and it's our year-round version of restaurant week. Much of the Theater District will offer limited-option, three-course meals in the $20-$25 range, so long as you order ahead of the local curtain calls. (They'd call these "early bird specials," if not for the connotations of Florida retire-ment communities.) Again, they're not super-cheap, but they do reflect discount pricing. On the plus side, New York is not without a couple of fixed-price steals.

Dallas *BARBEQUE* CHELSEA   This local chain won't win any prizes for authenticity, but they do a mean take on comfort food. Ribs, pulled pork, and beef brisket highlight the menu. The early bird special is not to be missed—two full meals for $8.99. You'll get double soups, double servings of rotisserie chicken, cornbread, and a choice of potatoes or rice. It's as filling as New York gets for less than $4.50. FINE PRINT Available weekdays from 11am-noon, and again from 2pm-5:30pm; weekends 11am-4pm. Dine-in only.

91 E. 7th St., between First and Second aves. ☏ **212/228-5062.** www.caracas arepabar.com. Tues-Sat noon-11pm; Sun noon-10pm. Subway: F/V to Second Ave.

Cubana Café *CUBAN* SOHO   In its quick trip to becoming New York's outdoor answer to the Mall of America, SoHo has managed to squeeze out most of its low-rent neighbors. At this quaint Cuban bou-tique restaurant, however, most every entree comes in under $9. Spicy huevos rancheros are only $6 and are served all day, along with a host of other breakfast items. A hearty Cuban sandwich is $7.50. Strong flavors help to compensate for portions that are on the small side.

110 Thompson St., between Prince and Spring sts. ☏ **212/966-5366.** www.cubanacafeelchulo.com. Daily 11:30am-11pm. Subway: C/E to Spring St.

261 Eighth Ave., at 23rd St. ℂ **212/462-0001**. www.dallasbbq.com. Sun-Thurs 11am-midnight; Fri-Sat 11am-1am. Subway: C/E to 23rd St. Other locations: *Upper East Side*, 1265 Third Ave., between 73rd and 74th sts. ℂ **212/772-9393**. Subway: 6 to 77th St.; *Upper West Side*, 27 W. 72nd St., near Central Park W. ℂ **212/873-2004**. Subway: B/C to 72nd St.; *Washington Heights*, 3956 Broadway, at 166th St. ℂ **212/568-3700**. Subway: A/C/1 to 168th St.; *East Village*, 132 Second Ave., at St. Marks Place. ℂ **212/777-5574**. Subway: 6 to Astor Place.

Primitivo Osteria *ITALIAN* CHELSEA   Harking back to Italian *osterias*, or taverns, this sociable neighborhood joint is conscientious about making all its meals affordable. Prix-fixe lunches start at $8, offering a choice of three different pastas on top of soup or salad and a drink. Weekend brunches, with double bloody marys, screwdrivers, or all-you-can-drink mimosas, start at just $11. Despite the rock bottom pricing, the Southern Italian cuisine here is fresh and well prepared. 202 W. 14th St., between Seventh and Eighth aves. ℂ **212/255-2060**. www.primitivorestaurant.com. Daily, 11:30am-midnight. Subway: 1/2/3 to 14th St.; A/E/C/L to 14th St.-Eighth Ave.

Empanada Mama *LATINO* CLINTON   This Queens transplant is a patty pro, offering up over two dozen takes on this humble Latin pocket. I prefer the tried and true to exotics like the Polish (keilbasa and sauerkraut) or the Elvis (peanut butter and bananas.) Wheat-wrapped rascals average $2.50, and triangular corn flour versions are a cheaper $1.75. Beef in the latter form is a can't miss. A pleasant, colorful shop rounds out the eating experience.

763 Ninth Ave., between 51st and 52nd sts. ℂ **212/698-9008**. Daily 9am-midnight. Subway: C/E to 50th St.

Noche Mexicana *MEXICAN* UPPER WEST SIDE   Authentic Mexican food has long been lacking in the New York gastronomic scene, but places like this are starting to raise standards. You can take your choice of savory red or green mole atop enchilada platters ($7.50), triple orders of tamales ($6), or corn-tortilla chicken chilaquiles ($7.50). Tacos are excellent and a mere $2 each. A glass of wine on the side is but $4 more.

852 Amsterdam Ave., between 101st and 102nd sts. ✆ **212/662-6900.** Sun–Thurs 10am–11pm; Fri–Sat 10am–midnight. Subway: 1 to 103rd St.

La Taza de Oro *PUERTO RICAN* CHELSEA   The daily specials at this classic make it easy to get filled up for under $7.75. My favorites are *bacaloa* (stewed codfish), *ropa vieja* ("old clothes"—a stew made with shredded beef), and roast chicken, which come in around $7.50 each, including knock-out rice and beans.

96 Eighth Ave., between 14th and 15th sts. ✆ **212/243-9946.** Mon–Sat 6am–10:30pm. Subway: A/C/E to 14th St.; L to Eighth Ave.

8 Hot Dog Days

Papayas and hot dogs aren't an intuitive combination, but the city is the site of a heated rivalry over the best fruit and meat combos. Skeptics may argue that the difference between any two tube steaks is academic, but connoisseurs can parse the subtle distinctions in density, skin, texture, and taste. For cheap protein and quick bursts of patriotic fervor, New York's dogs can't be beat.

☆ **Crif Dog** *HOT DOGS* EAST VILLAGE   Night owls flock to this friendly dog house, and it's no wonder given how good the hot dogs are and how far a few bucks will take you. No more than $3.75 is required for dinner and a drink: two New Yorker dogs and a soda. The smoked Crif Dog is 25¢ more ($1.75 each) than the New Yorker and even tastier. For $5.50 you get two dogs and a beer. The high end is represented by the Tsunami—a bacon-wrapped, deep-fried Crif Dog with teriyaki sauce, pineapple, and scallions. I'd lay short odds that whoever came up with that delicious combo wasn't sober.

113 St. Marks Place, between First Ave. and Ave. A. ✆ **212/614-2728.** Daily noon–midnight, till 2am Thurs, till 4am Fri–Sat. Subway: 6 to Astor Place.

Gray's Papaya *HOT DOGS* UPPER WEST SIDE   Long live the recession—as long as Gray's continues to offer two hot dogs and a drink for $2.45. The dogs are tasty, as attested by the quickly moving queues that form every day for the best lunch deal in town. Be warned, though: The dogs are a little on the greasy side, so don't be a hero and go for three. Standing room only to eat here.

2090 Broadway, at 72nd St. ℂ 212/799-0243. Daily 24 hr. (all locations). Subway: 1/2/3 to 72nd St. Other locations: *West Village*, 402 Sixth Ave., at 8th St. ℂ 212/260-3532. Subway: A/B/C/D/E/F/V to W. 4th St.; *Midtown*, 539 Eighth Ave., at 37th St. ℂ 212/904-1588. Subway: A/C/E to 34th St.

Papaya King *HOT DOGS* UPPER EAST SIDE   The self-anointed Papaya King has some 75 years experience in the frankfurter field, going back to when this part of Uptown was a German neighborhood. Gray's has the lead in both taste and price, but the King isn't too far behind. A pair of dogs with kraut and a big tropical drink is only $3.99. An all-beef spicy smoked sausage with obligatory grilled peppers and onions will only set you back $1.99. Standing room only to eat here.

179 E. 86th St., corner of Third Ave. ℂ 212/369-0648. www.papayaking.com. Sun–Thurs 8am–1am; Fri–Sat 8am–3am. Subway: 4/5/6 to 86th St. Other locations: *Harlem*, 121 West 125th St., between Lenox Ave. and Adam Clayton Powell Blvd. ℂ 212/665-5732. Subway: 2/3 to 125th St.; *West Village/Chelsea*, 200 W. 14th St., at Seventh Ave. ℂ 212/367-8090. Subway: 1/2/3 to 14th St.

9 Eastern European

With the demise of Kiev, Leshko's, and Alice's, New York's Eastern European dining scene is much diminished. A couple of holdovers, however, still serve the hearty delights of the Old World. There's also some new blood bringing in flavors most New Yorkers haven't experienced yet.

Christine's *DINER/POLISH* EAST VILLAGE   The blond-wood interior here isn't exactly distinctive, but the food sure stands out. The American side of the menu covers the usual diner bases, but most folks are here for Polish comfort food. Blintzes, goulash, and brisket are expertly prepared. A combo plate of kielbasa and potato pancakes is only $8. Pierogis come by the order of seven, for under $6. If you can't get filled up here for less than $10, consult your physician.

208 First Ave., between 12th and 13th sts. ℂ 212/979-2810. Daily 6am–11pm. Subway: L to First Ave.

Djerdan Burek *BALKAN* MIDTOWN WEST   Burek slices haven't made much of a dent in pizza's supremacy in New York, but the

Balkan treat is worth seeking out. A *burek* is flaky dough stuffed with meat, cheese, or spinach, and cooked up into a hubcap-sized pie. You can get a huge piece to go for only $4, $4.95 to stay. (The restaurant is newly remodeled and has dispensed with its cafeteria service, but sitdown meals still average less than $11.)

221 W. 38th St., between Seventh and Eighth aves. ℂ **212/921-1183.** Tue-Fri 11am-10pm; Sat noon-10pm; Sun noon-7pm; Mon 11am-7pm. Subway: 1/2/3 or A/C/E to 34th St.

Odessa *DINER/POLISH* EAST VILLAGE   This remodeled stalwart provides a Polish take on diner fare. Orders of pirogies and blintzes are $5.50 and under, and stuffed cabbage is $6.95. The early bird dinner special runs daily from 3 to 9pm. An entree plus potato, salad, desert, coffee, and a glass of wine is only $9.25. Breakfasts are cheap, too—I love the huge fluffy slices of challah bread.

119 Ave. A, between 7th St. and St. Marks Place. ℂ **212/253-1482.** Daily 24 hr. Subway: F/V to Second Ave.

10 Bun Appétit

One of New York's most appealing recent trends is the return of the burger. Ground beef seemed to be an afterthought at all but the most blue collar of taverns. The last couple of years, however, have seen the arrival of fast food spots focused purely on the patty. When the upstarts are added to the long-time classics, New York looks well on its way to being a paradise in cheeseburgers.

Big Nick's Burger Joint/Pizza Joint *AMERICAN/BURGERS* UPPER WEST SIDE   When your menu serves every dish ever thought of, you're bound to have a few items that seem a little overpriced. For the most part, though, this Upper West Side joint has great values on big portions. The options are endless—with burgers alone, there are over three dozen choices. Prices start at $5.75 and go to $8.50 for the heart-unfriendly hollandaise and Canadian bacon Benedict burger. A profusion of blue-plate lunch specials are available for $7.25.

2175 Broadway, at 77th St. ℂ **212/362-9238.** www.bignicksnyc.com. Daily 24 hr. Subway: 1 to 79th St.

the burger joint *AMERICAN/BURGERS* GRAMERCY   Unlike the unrelated Parker Meridian joint, this small shop works the mini end of the burger spectrum. Tasty handmade patties are a mere $1.25 each, served on a potato bun, or $1.50 for the cheese version. Double your pleasure with a $2.60 double cheeseburger. Big orders of fries are $1.75. One taste and you'll know why Matthew Broderick, Sarah Jessica Parker, and dozens of police academy cadets are huge fans.

241 Third Ave., between 19th and 20th sts. ⓒ 212/228-1219. Mon-Wed 10am-11pm; Thurs-Sat 10am-2am; Sun 10am-9pm. Subway: 6 to 23rd St.

The Burger Joint at the Parker Meridian *AMERICAN/BURGERS* MIDTOWN WEST   One of the city's best burgers hides behind curtains inside the lobby of a fancy Midtown West hotel. The Burger Joint is as unpretentious and inexpensive as its name, and the burger is a delicious instant classic, juicy and not too greasy. Buy one for $6, or add 50¢ for cheese. Though the entrance is hidden (look for the neon arrow by the check-in desk), the local businessfolk have discovered the place and it's busy at lunch.

118 W. 57th St., between Sixth and Seventh aves. ⓒ 212/245-5000. www.parker meridien.com/burger.htm. Mon-Sat 11:30am-11:30pm. Subway: N/R/Q/W or F to 57th St.

☆ **Corner Bistro** *AMERICAN/BURGERS* WEST VILLAGE   Inside this dark West Village bar you'll find the best burger in the city. The no-frills regular is $5.50, while $6.50 comes with decadent layers of cheese, bacon, and onions. This place is a well-guarded local secret, known only to you and the 10,000 other people waiting beside you at the bar. (Weekday afternoons are the least-crowded times.)

331 W. 4th St., between Jane St. and Eighth Ave. ⓒ 212/242-9502. www.corner bistro.citysearch.com. Mon-Sat 11:30am-4am; Sun noon-4am. Subway: 1/2/3 or A/C/E to 14th St.; L to Eighth Ave.

11 Cheap Dates

A welcome recent trend in Gotham dining is the invasion of the upscalish Asian restaurant. A profusion of new places combine elegant Asian design, friendly staffs, flavorful food, and crazy low prices. Built on small scales, these spots make excellent date destinations. Their locations in otherwise upscale neighborhoods make them accessible. And the food is so good, the person across the table won't notice how little you've spent.

☆ **Galanga** *THAI* WEST VILLAGE   Although this place scores high style points with its refined décor, there's no trade-off in substance.

Witness good-sized portions, exquisite seasoning, and more authenticity than one usually finds this side of distant boroughs. Curries and wok concoctions start at $8.50, and noodles are even less. I have difficulty getting the tangy taste of the charcoal beef salad ($8.95) out of my head. The weekday lunch special comes with soup or salad and starts at $6.50.

149 W. 4th St., between MacDougal St. and Sixth Ave. ℂ 212/228-4267. Mon-Thurs 11:30am-11pm; Fri-Sat 11:30am-11:30pm; Sun 11:30am-10:30pm. Subway: A/B/C/D/E/F/V to W. 4th St.

Kasadela *JAPANESE* EAST VILLAGE　New York has its share of *izakaya,* the Japanese taverns that split the difference between sake bars and restaurants. The ones on St. Marks Place pack the crowds in, but this Alphabet City stop is long on charm and not yet overrun. Exposed-brick walls look down on diners savoring beef skewers, sauteed burdock root, and fried oysters. Though the drinks aren't cheap, the food is very affordable, especially the $3.95 chicken wings.

647 E. 11th St., between aves. B and C. ℂ 212/777-1582. www.kasadela.com. Tues-Thurs, Sun 5:30pm-12:30am; Fri-Sat 5:30pm-1:30am. Subway: L to First Ave.

Land *THAI* UPPER WEST SIDE　Mercer Kitchen alum David Bank presents the flavors of his native Bangkok inside the petite confines of this Uptown newcomer. A brick, tin, and mesh interior provides a romantic backdrop. Seared mains from the wok top out at $11, while noodle dishes hover in the $9–$10 range. The prix-fixe lunch, which includes papaya salad and basil and beef, proffers two courses for $8.

480 Amsterdam Ave., between 81st and 82nd sts. ℂ 212/501-8121. www.land thaikitchen.com. Sun-Thurs noon-10:45pm; Fri-Sat noon-11pm. Subway: 1 to 79th St.; B/C to 81st St./Museum of Natural History.

Lovely Day *JAPANESE/THAI* NOLITA　This little cafe is as hip as affordable gets. The menu features creative takes on Thai and Japanese dishes, with noodles running in the $7.50 to $8.50 range. A plate of meat and pineapple fried rice is only $6.50. The salmon dinner, served with greens and sweet potato mash, is a bargain at $9.50. The seasonings are a little on the sweet side, but the fun, bustling room quickly puts a diner in a forgiving mood.

196 Elizabeth St., between Prince and Spring sts. ℂ 212/925-3310. Daily noon-11pm. Subway: 6 to Spring St.

A SoHo Splurge

Entrees that top out at $10 and $11 push the dirt cheap envelope, but when you're dropping that dough on über-sophisticated, all-organic fine dining, it doesn't feel so bad. **Ivo & Lulu** in SoHo serves French- and Caribbean-inflected food and they're not afraid to experiment. The menu changes seasonally, but gamier meats and unusual flavors can usually be found (recent offerings of duck leg with a spicy mango topping and wild boar sausage with blueberry sauce were both extraordinary). Portions are not huge, but it's all well crafted, and you can BYOB to complete the fine dining experience at a rock-bottom price. Entrees average $10. Gourmands have discovered this place and it only has a few tables, so expect a wait during peak hours. 558 Broome St., between Sixth Ave. and Varick St. ✆ 212/226-4399. Tues–Sat 6–11pm. Subway: 1 to Canal St.

Mooncake *PAN-ASIAN* SOHO   This cheerful little family-run shop serves up fresh food with Asian accents. Portions are decent for such small prices. Six dollars covers a pork chop sandwich with mango chutney, or a steak and pepper sandwich. For $2 more you can get a big salad bowl with lemon grass shrimp and Vietnamese-style vermicelli noodles.

28 Watts St., near Sixth Ave. ✆ 212/219-8888. Mon–Sat 11am–11pm. Subway: A/C/E to Canal St.

Peep *THAI* SOHO   Peep proves that an upscale, modern decor and central location don't require exorbitant prices. Dinners are reasonable ($9 pad thai, $10 meat and tofu entrees, $11 for shrimp), though the real deal comes at lunch. For $7–$8 you get an appetizer and an entree, with a large selection of Thai favorites to pick through. Presentation is as attractive as the crowd. Though the neighborhood's discovered this place, it's usually not so crowded here that you can't get a seat.

177 Prince St., between Sullivan and Thompson sts. ✆ 212/254-PEEP. www.peepsoho.net. Sun–Thurs 11am–midnight; Fri–Sat 11am–1am. Subway: C/E to Spring St.

12 Bagel Hounds

When you're out and about in the city and need some cheap filler, the disc that makes New York is the carb to go to. New York is the only place on Earth that knows how to make a decent firm-on-the-outside, chewy-on-the-inside "real" bagel. Every moment you spend not eating one is a wasted opportunity.

Absolute Bagel UPPER WEST SIDE   The bagels at this Upper West Side shop are absolutely fabulous. They're a little too puffy to be traditional, but the extra air doesn't hinder the taste. For $1.85 you get a bagel loaded with cream cheese. Bagel pudding may sound horrific, but it's actually delicious, syrupy, and enhanced with raisins and cinnamon; $1.50 buys a big block of it.

2708 Broadway, between 107th and 108th sts. ℂ **212/932-2105.** Daily 6am-9pm. Subway: 1 to 110th St.

☆ **Kossar's Bialys** LOWER EAST SIDE   It's no surprise that the best bagel in New York comes from the Lower East Side. Kossar's serves perfect-sized, perfect-textured bagels. The everything version is unparalleled at 75¢, although you're on your own for toppings outside of a handful of schmears in the fridge ($2.25 buys two bagels' worth of whipped kosher cream cheese). The bialys are made with similar dough and flavored with onions, but lack the trademark center hole; 65¢ each. Everything is baked fresh 24/6. No seating available.

367 Grand St., between Essex and Norfolk sts. ℂ **212/473-4810.** www.kossars bialys.com. 24 hr., except closed Fri sunset to Sat sunset and during Jewish holidays. Subway: F to Delancey St.; J/M/Z to Essex St.

David Bagel GRAMERCY   Hot bagels can often be found in the racks of this Gramercy bagelry. For $1.85 get a big, chewy bagel slathered with cream cheese.

228 First Ave., between 13th and 14th sts. ℂ **212/533-8766.** Subway: L to First Ave. Other location: 331 First Ave., between 19th and 20th sts. ℂ **212/780-2308.** Daily 6am-8:30pm. Subway: L to First Ave.

Ess-A-Bagel MIDTOWN & GRAMERCY   The huge bagels here won't win any points with purists, but they make an already good deal even better: 75¢, or $1.85 with a surplus helping of cream cheese. The bustling full-service shop has several tables for your savoring pleasure.

359 First Ave., at 21st St. ℂ **212/260-2252.** www.ess-a-bagel.com. Mon-Fri 6am-around 8:30; Sat-Sun 7am-5pm. Subway: 6 to 23rd St. Other location:

Midtown East, 831 Third Ave., between 50th and 51st sts. ℂ **212/980-1010.** Subway: 6 to 51st St.

13 Slices of Heaven

The most famous pizzas in the city come from restaurants that pride themselves on selling by the pie only. All fine and good, except when you're looking for a quick and inexpensive meal, and you're not about to put seven surplus pieces in the fridge. It's a good thing that by-the-slice 'za can be found just about every ten paces in NYC. And when you tire of the classic slice, there's a bevy of off-kilter alternatives.

Koronet *PIZZA* UPPER WEST SIDE   Extra value is what you get when you buy one of the ludicrously large slices at this Columbia U favorite. For $2.75 you get enough pizza to feed a mid-sized village. The pizza is no more than decent, though it becomes absolutely perfect in the wee, alcohol-shaded hours, as legions of college students will attest.

2848 Broadway, at 111th. ℂ **212/222-1566.** Daily 9am–2am. Subway: 1 to 110th St.

☆ **Sal's & Carmine's Pizza** *PIZZA* UPPER WEST SIDE   At your first taste of the pizza here, you will realize what your previous 10,000 New York slices were supposed to taste like. Creamy mozzarella synchs with a tangy sauce and crispy crust to achieve perfection. Sal or Carmine are usually on hand to ensure quality control, and a curmudgeonly atmosphere. Each pie is a work of art and cannot be expected to endure the indignity of a ride in an insulated plastic carrier: no delivery here. A regular slice is $2.50.

Pizza Frank's Way

In the 70-plus years that the coal oven has been burning at Patsy's in Harlem, the surrounding neighborhood has lost much of its Italian identity. It's not exactly gentrified and it's a haul to get here, but that's the effort required to get the best pizza pie in the city. One taste of the thin and distinctive crust and you'll know why this place was Sinatra's favorite. Inside the restaurant, murky lighting, threadbare furnishings, and a surly staff make the takeout window the more pleasant option. A plain pie is $11. 2287 First Ave., between 117th and 118th sts. ℂ **212/534-9783.** Daily 11:30am–11:30pm. Subway: 6 to 116th St.

2671 Broadway, between 101st and 102nd sts. ✆ **212/663-7651.** Daily 11am–11pm. Subway: 1 to 103rd St.

✰ **Sullivan St. Bakery** *BAKERY* SOHO   One of the best pizzas in town is the bianca at this upscale bakery. The bread is fluffy and lightly seasoned with rosemary, olive oil, and a little salt. It's an Old Country slice—rectangular instead of triangular and lacking red sauce—and it's served at an old economy price. $1.50 gets you a nice big piece.

73 Sullivan St., between Broome and Spring sts. ✆ **212/334-9435.** Daily 7am–7pm. Subway: C/E to Spring St. Other location: *Clinton*, 533 W. 47th St., between Tenth and Eleventh aves. ✆ **212/265-5580.** Mon–Sat 8am–6pm; Sun 8am–4pm. Subway: C/E to 50th St.

Two Boots *PIZZA/SLICES* EAST VILLAGE   This is not a traditional New York slice, nor is it trying to be. Mixing elements of two boot-shaped regions (Italy and Louisiana), the pizzas here are brightly spiced. The crust is thin and crisp, cheese is minimal, and the sauce has lots of oregano. Purists scoff, but I think it's delicious. A regular slice is $2.

42-44 Ave. A, at E. 3rd St. ✆ **212/254-1919.** www.twoboots.com. Sun–Thurs 11:30pm–1am; Fri–Sat 11:30am–2am. Subway: F/V to Second Ave. Other location: *West Village*, 75 Greenwich Ave., between Seventh Ave. and 11th St. ✆ **212/633-9096.** Subway: 1 to Christopher St.-Sheridan Sq. More locations throughout the city.

13 Open Barbeque

Maybe it's a response to relentless urbanity, maybe it's the tail end of the Atkins effect, but whatever the cause, a need for sociability and low carb intake is turning Brooklyn into seared meat central. Even Manhattan has a dog in this race. Sundays tend to be where the grills are. Often you don't even have to put out for these cookouts. A lot of the fests are free, though they may expect you to spring for a drink or two, since they're running bars.

Cattyshack PARK SLOPE, BROOKLYN   Meow Mix took its feline theme across the river, where the sapphic set enjoys open mics, game nights, and drink specials galore. In the warmer months, Sunday afternoons are dedicated to the barbeque arts. Grill masters serve up both meat and veggie options from 2 to 8pm. For $15 it's all you can eat, plus all you can drink Miller Lites. (Teetotalers can substitute soda.)

Sweet Indulgences

Beard Papa Sweets Cafe UPPER WEST SIDE   Cream puffs are the specialty at this Asian import, where the treats are as appetizing as the name is not. Crisp choux pastries hold a cream and custard filling. Everything is fresh baked, and despite a sprinkling of powdered sugar, the treats aren't overly sweet. Specials like green tea or sesame cost $1.55 per puff, and the regular vanilla is only $1.45. 2167 Broadway, between 76th and 77th sts. ⓒ **212/799-3770**. www.muginohousa.com. Daily 10am–8pm. Subway: 1 to 79th St. Other locations: *West Village,* 5 Carmine St., between Bleecker St. and Sixth Ave. ⓒ **212/989-8855**. Subway: A/B/C/D/E/F/V to W. 4th St.; *Astor Place,* 740 Broadway, between Astor and Waverly places. ⓒ **212/358-8888**. Subway: 6 to Astor Place; N/R/W to 8th St.

Dragon Land Bakery CHINATOWN   My favorite sweet cheap stops are in Chinatown. Bakeries litter the landscape here, all of them offering up fresh goods at ridiculous prices. The differences between any two shops are subtle, but Dragon Land does a particularly good job. In addition to baked goods, the mango and green-tea flavored puddings are delicious. Prices range from 75¢ to $4. 125 Walker St., between Centre and Baxter sts. ⓒ **212/219-2012**. Daily 7:30am–8pm. Subway: J/M/N/Q/R/W/Z/6 to Canal St.

249 4th Ave., between President and Carroll sts. ⓒ **718/230-5740**. www.cattyshackbklyn.com. Subway: M/R to Union St.

The Delancey LOWER EAST SIDE   The rooftop of this lowrise bar is an oasis on the Manhattan side of the Williamsburg Bridge. Palms and fountains provide a tropical air. Sundays at 5pm that air fills with burger and dog smoke from the free grill. When you've had your fill of flesh, head downstairs for free live rock.

168 Delancey St., between Clinton and Attorney sts. ⓒ **212/254-9920**. www.thedelancey.com. Subway: F to Delancey St.; J/M/Z to Essex St.

East River Bar WILLIAMSBURG, BROOKLYN   East of the East River is the site of this paint factory turned biker bar turned casual

South Williamsburg hang. Industrial chic corrugated metal adorns the outdoor patio, which holds a real, live barrel drum barbeque pit. That, and three smaller grills, provide the fire for BYOBBQ nights (as in Bring Your Own.) Call ahead to reserve charcoal space. Make it dinner and a movie on Wednesday and Sunday nights, when 16mm classics get projected, rain or shine.

97 S. 6th St., between Bedford and Berry sts. ℂ **718/302-0511**. www.eastriver bar.com. Subway: J/M/Z to Marcy Ave.

Hank's Saloon   Rockabilly and alt-country set the tone for this down-home scene, which peaks on laid-back barbeque Sundays. Delicacies vary, but tend to the hot dog and hamburger side of things, and they're totally free. Honky-tonk masters Sean Kershaw & the New Jack Ramblers provide the soundtrack. Shows start around 9:30pm and run until 1am. Parched gullets can be assuaged with $2 PBRs. Every other Monday, Live Band Kuntry Karaoke (p. 77) comes with the same catered bbq. The cost is the same, too—completely free.

46 Third Ave., at Atlantic Ave. ℂ **718/625-8003**. www.exitfive.com/hankssaloon. Subway: 2/3/4/5/Q to Atlantic Ave.; M/N/R/W to Pacific St.

Laila Lounge WILLIAMSBURG, BROOKLYN   Laila will ease your worried mind with barbecue on the back patio. The party starts around 3 or 4pm every Sunday, when the weather permits. Though the range of food can be limited to just hot dogs, it's hard to complain when the meat comes free. The converted-garage main space often has live music, or at least a DJ.

113 N. 7th St., between Berry and Wythe sts. ℂ **718/486-6791**. www.lailalounge. com. Subway: L to Bedford Ave.

Metropolitan WILLIAMSBURG, BROOKLYN   When the weather turns forgiving, the grill at this gay Williamsburg haunt turns to wings, dogs, and veggie burgers. The patio setting is spectacular, with lots of space beneath the creeping vines. A cheerful crowd gets even friendlier the more they're plied with cheap drinks and free meat (or fake meat, as the case may be). Start time is around 5:30pm on Sunday afternoons.

559 Lorimer St., between Metropolitan Ave. and Devoe St. ℂ **718/599-4444**. Subway: G/L Lorimer St.-Metropolitan Ave.

14 Into the Drink

FREE WINE TASTINGS

The intricacies of wine are endless, which is excuse enough to try as much of the stuff as possible. The tasting experience can be frustrating because you're only getting sips, but if you've come for edification and not to catch a cheap buzz, there's little chance of going away disappointed. Besides, many shops throw in free snacks for your trouble.

Best Cellars New York UPPER EAST SIDE   Tastings can be found 6 days a week at this classy wine shop. Weeknights from 5 to 8pm find wine samples following a weekly theme. On Saturday afternoons from 2 to 4pm, the wine often comes with a free snack provided by a visiting local chef.

1291 Lexington Ave., at 87th St. ✆ 212/426-4200. www.bestcellars.com. Subway: 4/5/6 to 86th St.

Chambers Wines TRIBECA   The tastings at this wine shop are informal and friendly. Free bread and cheese help the wines go down. Check the website for tastings, often scheduled on Saturday afternoons.

160 Chambers St., between W. Broadway and Greenwich. ✆ 212/227-1434. www.chambersstwines.com. Subway: 1/2/3 to Chambers St.

Chelsea Wine Vault CHELSEA   This wine store in the Chelsea Market has an excellent, if somewhat pricey, selection. Wine tastings are held a couple of nights a week. Some of the tastings include free food and are pretty elaborate affairs, so check the website to see if an RSVP is required. The wines in question are sold at 10% discounts during tastings.

75 Ninth Ave., near 15th St. ✆ 212/462-4244. www.chelseawinevault.com. Subway: A/C/E to 14th St.; L to Eighth Ave.

67 Wines and Spirits UPPER WEST SIDE   Rotating hosts walk guests through wine tastings at this shop, highlighting the fruits of a particular country or region. Tastings are on Fridays and Saturdays; check the website for a calendar.

179 Columbus Ave., between 67th and 68th sts. ✆ 212/724-6767. www.67wine.com. Subway: 1 to 66th St.

Union Square Wines UNION SQUARE   Newly relocated to a larger space, this shop still has a friendly vibe. They also still have tastings

When You Want to BYOB

My favorite place to actually buy a bottle of wine is **Astor Wines & Spirits.** The new, humongous space in the basement of the aptly named De Vinne Press Building seems to go on forever. Among the many great values are some very drinkable $5 wines. Everything else is heavily discounted. On Tuesdays, the shop picks a region and sells its wines for 15% off. Free tastings, which often include free food from neighboring restaurants, are held on Thursdays and Fridays from 5 to 8pm, and Saturday afternoons from 3 to 6pm. Look for artisanal champagnes, wines, and sakes among the offerings. During tastings, the wines being poured are discounted 10%. 399 Lafayette St., at E. 4th St. ⓒ **212/674-7500.** www.astorwines. com. Mon-Sat 9am-9pm. Sun noon-5pm. Subway: 6 to Bleecker St.; B/D/F/V to Broadway/Lafayette.

several nights a week. The neighborhood is lousy with great chefs, and food demonstrations (with free tastes) are held here as well.

140 4th Ave., at 13th St. ⓒ **212/675-8100.** www.unionsquarewines.com. Subway: L/N/Q/R/W/4/5/6 to 14th St./Union Sq.

LIQUID ASSETS: DRINK DEALS IN BARS

When Mayor Mike banned smoking inside bars and restaurants, he initiated a brand-new street scene. Now cheap New Yorkers can mix and mingle without even having to buy a drink, simply by hanging around with the smokers in front of the hot spots. Should you venture indoors, you'll find a lot of bars responding to ever-increasing competition with happy hours. Two for ones or $1 off specials are ubiquitous. Some even sweeter deals can be found, too, especially in the cheap drinker's mecca of the East Village.

Bar None EAST VILLAGE   For the longest happy hour in the city the choice is, without exception, Bar None. You have to wait until noon for it to begin, but once it does you get $2 Bud pints and $3 for wells and other drafts. The specials run until 11pm, when the Power Hour begins. Until midnight, take another buck off the well drinks while still enjoying those $2 Buds. The environs are divey, but it's perfectly amiable, and the prices can't be beat.

98 Third Ave., between 12th and 13th sts. © 212/777-6663. www.barnonenyc. com. Daily noon-4am. Subway: L to Third Ave.

B-Side EAST VILLAGE   The vibe here is on the glam-punk side. The bar is no frills, saving you money during happy hour. Late night, enjoy reverse happy hour $2 Rheingold cans, Sunday through Wednesday from 1 to 2am. Afternoon happy hours see prices slashed in half, making Bud bottles and Rheingold cans a mere $1.50. Mini-Bud cans, 8 ounces of joy, are reduced to just 75¢ a pop. And let's face it, outside of office supplies stores it's hard to find any intoxicant for less than a buck. Daily from 3 to 8pm.

204 Ave. B, between 12th and 13th sts. © 212/475-4600. www.b-sidenyc.com. Daily 3pm-4am. Subway: L to First Ave.

Cheap Shots (and Beer) EAST VILLAGE   Cheap Shots is an unreconstructed dive that stays true to its name with rotating drink specials. The aforementioned shots start at $2, and $7 pitchers can be found as well. Tuesdays give you a fifty-fifty shot at half-price drinks: Just call the bartender's coin flip correctly. It makes great practice for football team captains.

140 First Ave., between St. Mark's Place and 9th St. © 212/254-6631. Daily noon-4am. Subway: F/V to Second Ave.; 6 to Bleecker St.

Circus CLINTON   This Rudy's offshoot has yet to acquire the iconic status, following, and embedded filth of its progenitor down the block. It relies on the same formula, however, melding cheap drinks with free food. For the latter expect classic circus fare of peanuts, popcorn, and hot dogs. For the former, look for $3 vodka drinks and domestic beers. In good dive fashion, happy hour begins at 10am and runs for 9 more hours. That's plenty of time to get used to the borderline-creepy three-ring theme.

615 Ninth Ave., between 43rd and 44th sts. © 212/315-4410. Daily 10am-4am. Subway: A/C/E to 42nd St./Port Authority.

Croxley Ales EAST VILLAGE   This pub represents something between the death of a once-proud indie 'hood and a breath of relief in a trendier-than-thou zone. Croxley puts games on its televisions and offers specials at the bar. If you're drinking, you're entitled to 20¢ wings on Sundays. That price goes down to 10¢ on Monday and

Dough Sans Dough

Three sibling bars let boozing New Yorkers soak up some of that hootch with free pizza.

Alligator Lounge WILLIAMSBURG A notch above the Capone's concept, this lounge took over a former pizza joint to exploit an existing wood-burning oven. The result is remarkably good pies, free with the purchase of a drink. Toppings run the same $2/$1 rate as Capone's. The pies roll from 6pm on the weekdays and 3pm on the weekends, and they don't stop until a bleary-eyed 3:30am. 600 Metropolitan Ave., between Leonard and Lorimer sts. Williamsburg, Brooklyn. ℂ **718/599-4440.** Daily 3pm-4am. Subway: G/L Lorimer St.-Metropolitan Ave.

Crocodile Lounge EAST VILLAGE The newest outpost of this mini-chain comes in third for pizza taste, but first for convenience, especially for NYU students. The lure of free pizza (one per drink) attacts a young and hungry crowd. Crocodile kitsch and free Skee-Ball round out the atmosphere. 325 E. 14th St., between Second and First aves. ℂ **212/477-7747.** Daily noon-4am. Subway: L to First Ave.

221 (Capone's) WILLIAMSBURG Al Capone was the namesake and the ancient bar comes from a Chicago joint reputed to be one of the gangster's former hangs, but you don't need to know anybody here to get set up with a free pie. Order a drink at 6pm and you're entitled to a complimentary cheese version; $2 covers the first topping, and $1 each additional after that. It's not the best pizza you've ever had, but it's better than you might expect from a look at the bar's unmarked, unpromising industrial façade. 221 N. 9th St., between Roebling St. and Driggs Ave. Williamsburg, Brooklyn. ℂ **718/599-4044.** Daily 3pm-4am. Subway: L to Bedford Ave.

Wednesday nights. Fridays from 5 to 7pm, take another 10¢ off the price—the wings are free. Weekday happy hours run from 5 to 7pm, with $1 off of most everything.

28 Ave. B, between 2nd and 3rd sts. ℂ **212/253-6140.** www.croxley.com. Sun-Thurs 5pm-1am; Fri-Sat noon-2am. Subway: F/V to Second Ave.

Doc Holliday's EAST VILLAGE   Redneck theme bars would seem to be a tough sell in cosmopolitan Manhattan, but quite a few trashy joints thrive here. Doc Holliday's plies the familiar formula, with attractive bar crews and booze priced to sell. Tuesday nights are all you can drink from 8 to 11pm. It's $7, and the beverage in question is Bud Lite, and the surroundings are less than clean, but after a few trips to the bar who remembers? Buy one get one free happy hours run daily from 5 to 8pm, and canned PBRs are always $2.

141 Ave. A, at 9th St. ℂ **212/979-0312.** www.dochollidaybar.com. Daily noon–4am. Subway: F/V to Second Ave.; 6 to Bleecker St.

Fish WEST VILLAGE   This restaurant is a decent facsimile of a seafood shack, with a lively crowd and walls cluttered with old water-front photos and buoys. Though the sit-down prices aren't cheap, you can net a great deal at the bar. Just $8 covers a half-dozen oysters and a beer or glass of house wine. Available at all hours, 7 days a week, and perfect for date nights.

280 Bleecker St., at Jones St. ℂ **212/727-2879.** Sun–Thurs noon–11pm; Fri–Sat noon–midnight. Subway: 1 to Christopher St.; A/B/C/D/E/F/V to W. 4th St.

Gowanus Yacht Club CARROLL GARDENS   This Brooklyn bar saves money by not bothering to rent a roof. The resulting garden space is restorative, inhabited by locals who do their best to further the small-fishing-town vibe. Beer specials vary, but you can rely on the availability of a $2 can of Pabst. The comestible accompaniments are highlighted by $1 hot dogs and $3.50 burgers. Like any good seaside resort, this one is only open between May and October.

323 Smith St., at President St. ℂ **718/246-1321.** Mon–Fri 4pm–2am; Sat–Sun 2pm–close. Subway: F/G to Carroll St.

Jeremy's Ale House FINANCIAL DISTRICT   When you need to show a tourist real New Yorkers, consider bringing them to über-authentic Jeremy's. A mix of blue and white collars hangs out beneath a burgeoning collection of liberated ties and bras. The house is known for its huge Styrofoam cups, which hold a full *quart* of beer. A Coors is $4.50. Sunday night movie nights feature free popcorn and hot dogs. With the fish market gone from South Street there are fewer tak-ers, but graveyard shifters still avail themselves of "The Eye Opener," $1.75 for a bucket of Coors, available Monday through Friday from 8 to 10am.

What's in a Name?: Free Drinks

If you're one of those people who has a name, you can drink for zero dollars and zero cents at bars **No Idea** and **Antarctica**. There is one small catch: Your name has to synch up with the name of the night. Each bar posts a different monthly list, and although there are some oddball monikers, there are also plenty of occasions to hang out with fellow Meghans, Joshes, and Jessicas. Open tab Name Night runs 5 to 11pm (8pm to 1am at Antarctica on Saturdays) every night but Sunday. Check the websites, www.noideabar.com and www.antarcticabar.com, to see when you're up. FINE PRINT They're not running a charity; the idea is to drag along some friends and let them run up the tab while you hobnob with a roomful of fellow Vartans. If you show up alone they may not let you play along. *No Idea:* 30 E. 20th St., between Park and Broadway. ℂ **212/777-0100.** Subway: 6 or N/R/W to 23rd St. *Antarctica:* 287 Hudson, at Spring St. ℂ 212/352-1666. Subway: C/E to Spring St.

228 Front St., between Peck Slip and Beekman St. ℂ **212/964-3537.** www.jeremy salehouse.com. Mon–Fri 8am–midnight; Sat 10am–midnight; Sun noon–11pm. Subway: A/C/J/M/Z/2/3/4/5 to Fulton St.

Magnetic Field BROOKLYN HEIGHTS AREA   This BoCoCa (that's Brooklyn Heights/Cobble Hill/Carroll Gardens, at least to the local real estate brokers) hang attracts with its low-key neighborhoody feel. During happy hour, select pints or well drinks are only $3 each. Happy hour runs weekdays from 3 to 8pm, except for Tuesdays, where it stretches all the way to closing time (4am). Late-night happy hour starts at the rock star hour of 2am, with more $3 drinks, Sunday through Thursday. Live music, DJs, a reading series, and live band karaoke (p. 78) provide the accompanying entertainment.

97 Atlantic Ave., between Hicks and Henry sts. ℂ **718/834-0069.** www.magnetic brooklyn.com. Daily 3pm–4am. Subway: M/R to Court St.; 2/3/4/5 to Borough Hall.

Slane WEST VILLAGE   Irish conviviality and exposed brick make for a charming atmosphere in the middle of a touristy 'hood. The weekday "Beat the Clock" happy hour ticks down some great deals. From noon to 2pm well drinks are only $1. For the 2pm to 4pm shift, select drafts take over the $1 slot and well drinks go to $2. A series of $3 tipples fill out the afternoon, all the way to 8pm.

102 MacDougal St., between Bleecker and W. 3rd sts. ⓒ 212/505-0079. www.slanenyc.com. Mon–Sat 11am–4am; Sun noon–4am. Subway: A/B/C/D/E/F/V to W. 4th St.

The Slide NOHO   Longtime kitsch fave Marion's has branched out with this next-door gay bar. The basement lounge has a slightly upscale vibe, but happy hour prices couldn't be much more downscale. From 5 to 6pm drinks are only $1. After 6pm, they go two for one until 10pm. Also look for free movie night Mondays, and $10 open bars on Tuesday.

356 Bowery, between Great Jones and 4th sts. ⓒ 212-475-7621. www.theslide bar.com. Daily 5pm–4am. Subway: F/V to Broadway/Lafayette; 6 to Bleecker St.

EATING & DRINKING DOWNTOWN

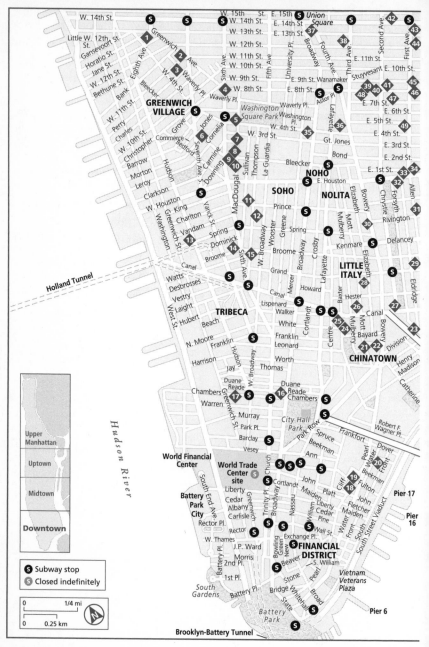

Antarctica Bar **13**
Astor Wines & Spirits **36**
Bánh Mì Saigon Bakery **23, 28**
Bar None **38**
Bennie's Thai Café **18**
Bereket Turkish Kebob House **58**
B-Side **53**
the burger joint **10**
Café Himalaya **34**
Caracas Arepa Bar **47**
Carl's Steaks **16**
Chambers Wines **17**
Cheap Shots (and Beer) **45**
Christine's **44**
Congee Village **60**
Corner Bistro **1**
Crif Dog **50**
Crocodile Lounge **42**
Croxley Ales **56**
Cubana Café **12**
Dallas BBQ **41**
David Bagel **43**
The Delancey **59**
Doc Holliday's **51**
Dojo **35, 48**
Dragon Land Bakery **25**
Eldridge Street Dumpling House **29**
Fish **6**
Galanga **5**
Grand Sichuan International **27, 40**
Gray's Papaya **4**
Hummus Place **8, 46**
Ivo & Lulu **14**
Jeremy's Ale House **20**
Joe's Ginger Restaurant **21, 26**
Joe's Shanghai **22**
Kadadela **54**
Kossar's Bialys **61**
L & L Hawaiian Barbecue **19**
Lovely Day **30**
Mamoun's **7**
Mooncake **15**
Odessa **52**
Otafuku **39**
Peep **11**
Pho Viet Huong **24**
Pukk **49**
Punjabi **57**
Slane **9**
Taim **3**
Tiengarden **31**
Tuck Shop **33**
Two Boots **2, 55**
Union Square Wines **37**
Yonah Schimmel **32**

139

EATING & DRINKING MIDTOWN

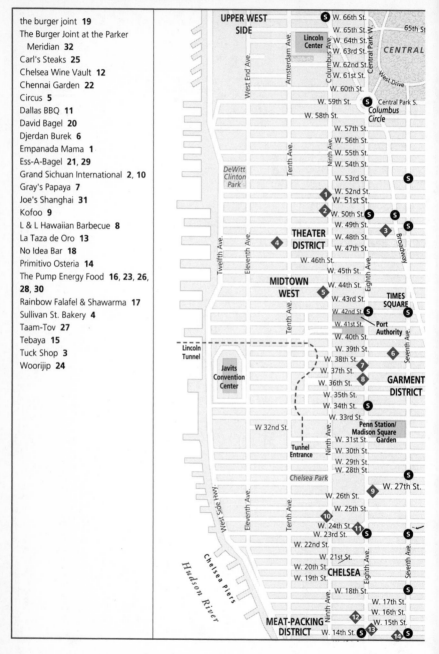

EATING & DRINKING UPTOWN

67 Wines and Spirits **11**
Absolute Bagel **1**
Beard Papa's **8**
Best Cellars New York **14**
Big Nick's Burger Joint/Pizza Joint **7**
Dallas BBQ **9**, **12**
Gray's Papaya **8**
Koronet **2**
Land **6**
Noche Mexicana **4**
Papaya King **13**
Patsy's **16**
Saigon Grill **5**, **15**
Sal's & Carmine's Pizza **3**

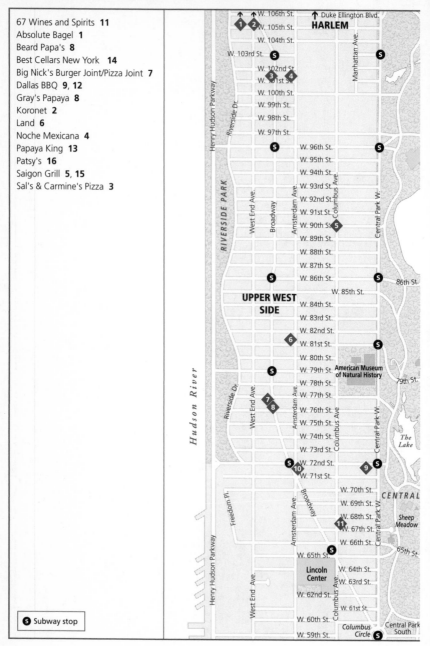

S Subway stop

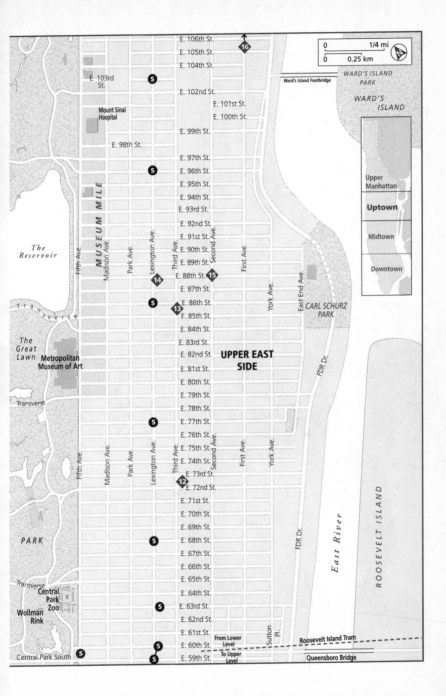

E. 106th St.
E. 105th St.
E. 104th St.
E. 103rd St.
E. 102nd St.
E. 101st St.
E. 100th St.
E. 99th St.
E. 98th St.
E. 97th St.
E. 96th St.
E. 95th St.
E. 94th St.
E. 93rd St.
E. 92nd St.
E. 91st St.
E. 90th St.
E. 89th St.
E. 88th St.
E. 87th St.
E. 86th St.
E. 85th St.
E. 84th St.
E. 83rd St.
E. 82nd St.
E. 81st St.
E. 80th St.
E. 79th St.
E. 78th St.
E. 77th St.
E. 76th St.
E. 75th St.
E. 74th St.
E. 73rd St.
E. 72nd St.
E. 71st St.
E. 70th St.
E. 69th St.
E. 68th St.
E. 67th St.
E. 66th St.
E. 65th St.
E. 64th St.
E. 63rd St.
E. 62nd St.
E. 61st St.
E. 60th St.
E. 59th St.

Mount Sinai Hospital

MUSEUM MILE

The Reservoir

Transverse

The Great Lawn

Metropolitan Museum of Art

Transverse

PARK

Transverse

Central Park Zoo

Wollman Rink

Central Park South

Fifth Ave.
Madison Ave.
Park Ave.
Lexington Ave.
Third Ave.
Second Ave.
First Ave.
York Ave.
East End Ave.

UPPER EAST SIDE

CARL SCHURZ PARK

FDR Dr.

FDR Dr.

Sutton Pl.

East River

ROOSEVELT ISLAND

WARD'S ISLAND PARK

Ward's Island Footbridge

WARD'S ISLAND

Upper Manhattan

Uptown

Midtown

Downtown

From Lower Level
To Upper Level

Roosevelt Island Tram
Queensboro Bridge

0   1/4 mi
0   0.25 km

143

New Yorkers focus their energy before punching the time clock by taking a free morning tai chi class at Bryant Park. See p. 177 for details.

LIVING

4

Anybody who thinks it's easy to live in New York is sitting on an ungodly mountain of cash. You don't have to look any further than the housing market to find trouble. For the privilege of paying $1,500 a month to live in a noisy veal pen, chances are you'll get hit with a 15% broker's fee. Health care, health insurance, health clubs—just about everything can come with an outrageous price tag. And yet eight million of us stay. The experience of being a New Yorker is too exciting and rich for us to complain long or loudly about the costs of living. We'd much rather talk about which neighborhood our apartment is in. Besides, the city presents plenty of free and dirt cheap opportunities to improve your quality of life, from classes and lectures to grooming and recreation. Leases notwithstanding, it is quite possible to live large on small budgets in NYC.

1 Sense for Cents: Education

LECTURES & SEMINARS

Just walking the streets and riding the subways is all too often a learning experience in New York, but most of us have room for further development along less informal lines. A handful of classes and a nearly endless selection of lectures provide New Yorkers with edification opportunities left and right. Cooper Union looks the other way when it comes to tuition, and although other local institutions aren't quite so generous, most have programs open to the public for little or no charge.

Battery Park City `FREE`   In addition to giving us gorgeous open space, landscaping, and music aplenty, Battery Park also helps boost our eye-hand coordination. Three separate drawing classes are offered in the summer. Elements of Nature Drawing (Wednesdays 11:30am to 1:30pm), Drawing in the Park (Saturdays, except in August, 10:30am to noon), and Figure al Fresco (Wednesdays 2:30pm to 4:30 pm), are all led by a bona fide artist. (Alas, the figure in Figure al Fresco, is clothed.) See below for the eye-hand coordination covered by tai chi. See the website for locations.

Battery Park City, along South End Ave., just west of West St. ℂ 212/267-9700. www.bpcparks.org. Subway: 1/2/3 or A/C to Chambers St.; 1 to Rector St. or South Ferry; 4/5 to Bowling Green.

Columbia University `FREE`   New York City's lone envoy to the Ivy League has an impressive events calendar, with talks and colloquiums supplementing literary readings and musical performances. Topics range from esoteric science ("Vitrification and Depletion Phenomena in Soft Colloidal Systems") to less dry material ("The Place of Ozu Within Japanese Film History"). You can also catch free drama department readings of MFA playwrights' thesis projects (www.columbia stages.com/festival.html). Venues vary, although Lerner Hall is a popular location, 2922 Broadway, at 115th Street.

Main Campus, 2690 Broadway, entrance at 116th St. ℂ 212/854-9724. www. columbia.edu. Subway: 1 to 116th St.

☆ **Cooper Union** FREE   Self-made entrepreneur and inventor Peter Cooper founded the Cooper Union for the Advancement of Science and Art in 1857 to allow underprivileged talents to receive free educations. The college's mission hasn't changed, and 1,000 students currently attend without tuition. Admission is based solely on merit, and competition is, as you'd expect, fierce. The public can take advantage of the institution in other ways, however. The Saturday Outreach Program helps high school students further themselves in the arts with free classes (even the materials fee is waived). Student exhibitions can be seen in free galleries, and frequent free lectures are held in the Great Hall. These lectures routinely have inventive and intriguing subjects and the big public room makes a great setting. Check online for an events calendar.

Cooper Sq., 8th St., between Bowery and Third Ave. © 212/353-4120. www.cooper.edu/month.html. Subway: 6 to Astor Place; N/R/W to 8th St.

Downtown Boathouse FREE   Every Wednesday night in summer, the boathouse offers kayaking classes free to the public. Most classes are held in the waters of Clinton Cove Park. Put your new knowledge to work by coming back to borrow a kayak (free, see "Watersports," on p. 175). Classes start at 6pm, during the warmer months (April to October). In the colder months, you can catch a free kayaking skills class, though not in the frigid waters of the Hudson. Weekends from 4 to 6pm, the introductory programs are held in the comfort of an indoor pool at Riverbank State Park.

Clinton Cove Park, Pier 96, West Side Highway at 56th St. © 646/613-0375. www.downtownboathouse.org. Subway: A/B/C/D/1 to Columbus Circle. Riverbank State Park, 679 Riverside Dr., at 145th St. Subway: 1 to 145th St.

Eglise Français du St-Esprit FREE   The French Church of St. Esprit, an Episcopal congregation, performs its services in French. Before services, they offer a series of French classes, one for conversation and a second one for beginners. The classes are free, at 10am every Sunday. Services start at 11:15am.

100 E. 60th St., between Madison and Park aves. © 212/838-5680. ww.stespritnyc.net. Subway: 4/5/6 or N/R/W to 59th St.; F to 63rd St.

The Frick Collection FREE   Inside the Gilded Age confines of this elegant art museum, you can catch regular Wednesday evening lectures. Subjects tend toward painterly subjects like Albrecht Dürer's hands and Goya's black paintings. A series on "Artists, Poets, and Writers," broadens the floor to include in-person luminaries like Frank Stella and analyses of immortals like Henry James. Lectures start at 6pm, with doors opening at 5:30pm. Don't arrive earlier than that, lest they hit you up for the $15 admission fee.

1 E. 70th St., between Madison and Fifth aves. ℂ 212/288-0700. www.frick.org. Subway: 6 to 68th St./Hunter College.

Gotham Writers' Workshop `FREE` The Microsoft of NYC's writing programs, Gotham churns out some 6,000 writers a year. You can sample the goods for free at frequent one-hour workshops. The events are held at the major bookstores around town, on topics like dialogue, travel writing, and Creative Writing 101.

Various locations. ℂ 212-WRITERS. www.writingclasses.com.

☆ **The Graduate Center at the City University of New York** `FREE` Continuing ed lectures, seminars, and panel discussions can be found here, with more possibilities for finding cheap smarts than any other institution in the city. You want range? Titles run from "Jewish Ethics Under Pressure" to "Unzipping the Monster Dick: Deconstructing Ableist Penile Representations in Two Ethnic Homoerotic Magazines." There is a $10 registration fee per season, although not every program requires registration, and the fee is waived for your first attendance of each season. Call to register, or go in person to Suite 8204 during normal business hours.

365 Fifth Ave., between 34th and 35th sts. ℂ 212/817-8215. www.gc.cuny.edu. Subway: B/D/F/N/Q/R/V/W to 34th St./Herald Sq.; 6 to 33rd St.

The Henry George School `FREE` Although Henry George is no longer a household name, in the 19th century his economics texts and lectures made him a major political player. His progressive ideas are still taught today, and in keeping with George's antiprivilege stance, the school that bears his name offers all of its programs for free. Classes are available in English or Spanish, usually in the evenings. Teachings are based on George's championing of shifting tax burdens to landowners. *Note:* Finishing the school's Fundamental Economics course is the prerequisite for most upper-level work. Those interested in samples of the material can attend the Friday Evening Forum, a free lecture series held Fridays at 6:30pm.

121 E. 30th St., between Park and Lexington aves. ℂ 212/889-8020. www.henry georgeschool.org. Subway: 6 to 28th St.

FREE Learning English As a Second Language

If you've read this far, you probably don't need English lessons. Should there be a newly minted American in your circle of acquaintance, however, you can steer him to a couple of great city resources.

The **Riverside Language Program** assimilates people quickly through their intensive 6-week program. Open to permanent residents, classes run from 9:30am to 3:30pm, for levels from beginner to high intermediate. 490 Riverside Dr., at 120th St. and Riverside (enter at 91 Claremont Ave.). ✆ **212/662-3200**. www.riversidelanguage.org. Subway: 1 to 116th St.

For evening-only classes (and for people without permanent resident status), the **New York Public Library** has an extensive English program. Classes are conducted at 20 different branch libraries, and also include civics lessons for prospective citizens. Check www.nypl.org/branches for schedules, or call ✆ **212/340-0918**.

The New School FREE   Though no longer so new (an 85th birthday celebration has come and gone), the New School stays pretty up-to-date, and there's still a progressive edge to its programs. The calendar of free events is cluttered with readings, lectures, panel discussions, student films, and even investing seminars. Events are open to the public, check online for a full calendar.

66 W. 12th St., between Fifth and Sixth aves. ✆ 212/229-5600. www.newschool.edu. Subway: F/V to 14th St.; L/N/Q/R/W/4/5/6 to 14th St./Union Sq.

New York Public Library FREE   It would be easier to list the classes not available for free at New York's public libraries than to mention all of the possibilities. Practical courses predominate, covering topics like writing, crafts, resume updating, job searches, using the Internet, and the ins and outs of genealogical research. You can also attend a self-directed class on how to take maximum advantage of library resources. The best way to get started is to get online and check out the options at your local branch.

For the Bronx, Manhattan, and Staten Island branches, log on to **www.nypl.org/branch**, or call ✆ **212/930-0800.** For the Queens Borough Public Library, check **www.queenslibrary.org**, or call ✆ **718/ 990-0700.** In Brooklyn, log on to **www.brooklynpubliclibrary.org**, or you can call ✆ **718/230-2100.**

The library puts on great readings and lectures, too. One series particularly worth checking out is the NYPL fellows talks. Scholars supported by the library speak on their subjects of interest. The lectures are free, but call in advance to reserve a seat (✆ **212/930-0084**). Humanities and Social Sciences Library, Fifth Ave., at 42nd St. Subway: B/D/F/V to 42nd St.; 7 to Fifth Ave.

Every branch of the New York Public Library offers computers with free Internet, access to electronic databases, and Microsoft Office applications. Many branches also have computers loaded with multimedia CD-ROMs. You can spend free days working on SimCity or Resume Maker, depending on your level of job market optimism.

New York Society for Ethical Culture `FREE`   For over a century and a quarter now, this organization has been providing New Yorkers with humanist alternatives to organized religion. A liberal outlook is usually presented in the free lectures that are held here, as well as at the regular talks on Sunday mornings. A $4 film series, with discussions, comes around every first Friday or so. Expect the films in question to have some ethical grounding (surprisingly, *Showgirls* has yet to play). Log on to the website for exact schedules.

2 W. 64th St., at Central Park W. ✆ 212/874-5210. www.nysec.org. Subway: 1/A/B /C/D/E to 59th St./Columbus Circle.

New York University `FREE`   The streets around Washington Square Park are dominated by NYU architecture and NYU students, but the community has opportunities to take advantage of this private university's immense resources. Lecture programs (the history of the Village, say), talks, and symposia can be found for free here. Other events carry nominal admission charges, in the $2 to $5 range. The new Kimmel Center is a good place to start for free culture.

Kimmel Center, 60 Washington Sq. S., between LaGuardia Place and Thompson St. ✆ 212/998-4900. www.nyu.edu. Subway: A/B/C/D/E/F/V to W. 4th St.-Washington Sq.

Park Slope Food Co-op `FREE`   This Brooklyn cooperative keeps its community informed with lectures, demonstrations, and even a few

FREE Getting Down to Business

The **Brooklyn Business Library** fosters the local small business scene with classes and workshops of an entrepreneurial bent. Everything from start-ups to small investing is covered by talks, and backed up with an excellent book collection. On Wednesday mornings from 10:15 to 11am you can get a free tour of the resources available. 280 Cadman Plaza, between Tech Place and Tillary St. ✆ **718/623-7000.** www.biz.brooklynpubliclibrary.org. Mon, Wed, Fri 10am–6pm; Tues 1–8pm; Thurs 1–6pm; Sat 10am–5pm. Subway: 2/3/4/5 to Borough Hall; M/R to Court St.; A/C/F to Jay St./Borough Hall.

film screenings. Topics here are left-leaning, concerning food, the environment, and timely advice about how not to be killed by eating beef. Don't expect to see Karl Rove on the roster anytime soon. Everything is free, even to non-co-op members, although sometimes a small materials fee is added to food classes. Check online for the latest schedule. Classes and lectures are held on the second floor meeting room unless otherwise noted.

782 Union St., between Sixth and Seventh aves., Park Slope, Brooklyn. ✆ **718/ 622-0560.** www.foodcoop.com. Subway: M/R to Union St.; 2/3 to Grand Army Plaza; B/Q to Seventh Ave.

Poets House FREE   This poetry library keeps a terrific collection of crafted words. For spoken word, poets often read here and lectures can be found as well. Some events have admission charges (usually around $7), but free events turn up frequently. Check the online calendar for details.

72 Spring St., between Lafayette and Crosby sts. ✆ **212/431-7920.** www.poets house.org. Subway: N/R/W to Prince St.; 6 to Spring St.

Teachers and Writers Collaborative   Literary readings and lectures fill the calendar at this long-running nonprofit. For high school students, there's also an excellent after-school program dedicated to the spoken word (www.urbanwordnyc.org). Check the website for upcoming events.

FREE Box: Dancing Days

If you're getting married, or have some other reason to be interested in dance, look into **Dance Manhattan.** Hustle and Carolina Shag are among the offerings. To get your feet wet for free, check out their monthly open houses. At 8pm, there's a lesson, half in ballroom and half in Latin. Lessons are followed by a party, and a performance after that. If you get hooked then and there, you'll be eligible for a discount on regular registration. 39 W. 19th St., 5th Floor, between Fifth and Sixth aves. ℭ **212/807-0802.** www.dance-manhattan.com. Subway: N/R/W or F/V to 23rd St.

If the wedding has already taken place and nature has run its course, you may have children that need entertaining. Battery Park City hosts a series of **Family Dances** on Fridays and Saturdays during the summer. This being New York, expect an international array of steps. West African, Swedish, and Ukrainian highlighted the '06 season. Neither children nor experience with West African, Swedish, or Ukrainian dance moves are required. Battery Park City, along South End Ave., just west of West St. ℭ **212/267-9700.** www.bpcparks.org. Subway: 1/2/3 or A/C to Chambers St.; 1 to Rector St. or South Ferry; 4/5 to Bowling Green.

If Battery Park's locale isn't idyllic enough for you, fox-trot on up to **Riverside Park South** for sunset lessons. Summer Sundays provide the backdrop for a series of salsa and swing dances taught by **Soho Dance Studio.** There's some group steps, too, if you need a couple of bodies to hide behind. Six to 9pm. Pier I, the Hudson at 70th St. ℭ **212/408-0219.** www.nycgovparks.org. Subway: 1/2/3 to 72nd St.

5 Union Sq. West, 7th floor, between 14th and 15th sts. ℭ **212/691-6590.** www.twc.org. Subway: L/N/Q/R/W/4/5/6 to 14th St./Union Sq.

TANGO & NO CASH

Central Park Tango FREE   Under the Bard of Avon's watchful gaze, couples spin away Saturday nights here. Meet up at the south end of The Mall, right next to the Shakespeare statue. Tyros can take advantage of free classes, usually offered at 7pm. In inclement weather, dancers seek the shelter of the nearby Dairy. Otherwise it's al fresco under dusk skies, as they dance their ringlets to the whistling wind.

Central Park, enter around 65th St. www.centralparktango.org. Jun-Sep, Sat 6pm-9pm. Subway: F to Lexington Ave.-63rd St.; 6 to 68th St.-Hunter College; 1 to 66th St./Lincoln Center.

Chelsea Market Milonga `FREE`   Don't cry for New York, not when there's free tango every Saturday afternoon. Beyond the gourmet food and clunky installation art of Chelsea Market you'll find a relaxed scene hosted by the Triangulo. The tangoing happens from 4 to 8pm. Neophytes can take advantage of free beginner's classes at Triangulo's nearby studio; dates vary so check the website.

Chelsea Market, between Ninth and Tenth aves. and 15th and 16th sts.; dancing is just inside the Tenth Ave. entrance. © 212/633-6445. www.tangonyc.com. Subway: A/C/E to 14th St.; L to Eighth Ave.

Tango Porteño `FREE`   Sultry summer nights are made for tangoing. On the Seaport piers, Tango Porteño hosts a weekly dance party with a great atmosphere. The East River rushes gently by and the lights of downtown glitter overhead as couples make their angular dips and spins. A big crew of regulars anchors the scene, and the event is casual and noncompetitive. Instead of a band there's a somewhat tinny sound system, but no one seems to mind. It takes two, but if you arrive alone, just watching can be entertainment enough.

Pier 16 at the South St. Seaport, between the Ambrose and the Peking. In case of rain go to Pier 17, just to the north. www.tangoporteno.org. May-Oct, Sun 7pm-midnight (or later.) Subway: 2/3/4/5/J/M/Z to Fulton St. or A/C to Broadway/Nassau, walk east to the river.

2 Health Sans Wealth

Sadly, far too many New Yorkers get by on a "just don't get sick" health plan. As many as one-fourth of us are uninsured, and medical fees aren't getting any cheaper. Thank goodness, then, for the sliding scale. Several good-hearted community-minded organizations provide care at rates commensurate with an individual's income. If your income is low enough, you may also be eligible for subsidized insurance with an HMO. A good website to check out is that of the **Actors'**

Fund of America (www.actorsfund.org). The fund has comprehensive listings for actors and artists who don't have the kinds of day jobs that throw in insurance and health care. Dentists, shrinks, and acupuncturists can also be tracked down for bodies on budgets.

HEALTH INSURANCE

Folks with cushy jobs can expect to see insurance on their laundry list of benefits. With more and more arts and media freelancers in the marketplace, however, it's easy to find oneself on the wrong side of the feudal walls. The **Freelancers Union** and **Working Today** (📞 718/222-1099; www.workingtoday.org) have combined to garner some of the bulk-rate buying power of a corporation. If you aren't afraid of a high deductible, one plan comes in as low as $113.91 a month. For $185.78 a month you can get a decent deductible and co-pay arrangement. Unfortunately, the program is for artists and media types, leaving out our chef and waitress friends. **Healthy New York** is New York state's program for lower income residents who earn too much for Medicaid. If you work and make less than $25,125 a year (individual) or $33,375 (couple), you may be able to take advantage of this plan. The premiums in Manhattan range from $168 to $253, without drug coverage, depending on which HMO you sign up with. Log on to www.healthyny.com or call 📞 **866/HealthyNY** for more info. And just to keep things simple, stay healthy.

HEALTH CLINICS

New York's clinics tend to target specific constituencies. Though they may specialize in helping the indigent, or the HIV-positive, the clinics make it a policy not to discriminate against anyone. Even if you're uninsured, you can get some attention in places other than the city's emergency rooms.

Callen-Lorde Community Health Center   This primary care center caters to the LGBT (lesbian, gay, bisexual, transgender) community, but makes a point to be open to all. The general medicine and health and wellness programs are charged on a sliding scale.

356 W. 18th St., between Eighth and Ninth aves. 📞 212/271-7200. www.callen-lorde.org. Subway: A/C/E to 14th St. or L to Eighth Ave.; 1 to 18th St.

David Ores, M.D.   Many a Lower East Sider, including your humble correspondent, is grateful to general practitioner Dr. Dave for his attentive care and humane prices. Dr. Dave's tiny clinic serves the neighborhood with a nod to the uninsured. Prices have crept up a little in recent years, but the scale still slides, and Dr. Dave always treats his patients fairly. Call first for an appointment.

15 Clinton St., between E. Houston and Stanton sts. ✆ 212/353-3020. www.davidjoresmd.org. Subway: F/V to Second Ave.; J/M/Z to Essex St.

Gay Men's Health Crisis   Dedicated to slowing the spread of HIV and to helping out those already affected, this great organization offers a host of services for the HIV-positive community. Health care is provided on a sliding scale basis, and there are also workshops, seminars, and even free legal services offered. The well-known GMHC Hotline is open for calls Monday through Friday from 10am to 9pm, and Saturdays from noon until 3pm.

The Tisch Building, 119 W. 24th St., between Sixth and Seventh aves. ✆ 800-AID-SNYC. www.gmhc.org. For other information, the main office line is ✆ 212/367-1000.

New York City Department of Health and Mental Hygiene `FREE` The city operates a dozen clinics in all five boroughs that offer free testing and treatment for STDs and HIV. They also follow up with no-cost counseling. Wait times can be on the long side, so show up before the clinic opens or bring a good book.

303 Ninth Ave., at 28th St. ✆ 311 for hot line, or 212/427-5120. www.nyc.gov/html/doh. Mon-Fri 8:30am-4pm; Sat 8:30am-1pm. Subway: C/E to 23rd St. Check the website for other locations throughout the city.

New York City Free Clinic `FREE`   NYU med students work with a professional at this Saturday morning clinic, where the homeless and the uninsured can get consultations, physicals, and other medical help. Advance appointments are required. First-time patients should call on Monday afternoons between 4 and 5pm. The Free Clinic website serves as an excellent clearing house for sliding scale and no-cost health care, too.

Inside the Sidney Hillman Clinic, 16 E. 16th St., between Union Sq. West and Fifth Ave. ✆ 917/544-0735. www.med.nyu.edu/nycfreeclinic. Sat 9am-noon. Subway: L/N/Q/R/W/4/5/6 to 14th St./Union Sq.

Planned Parenthood `FREE`   Free pregnancy tests are among the many reproductive-oriented services handled by this organization. Brooklyn, the Bronx, and Manhattan each have a clinic that can help out. Other services, including HIV counseling and assistance with STDs, have reasonable fees. Call the main number, ⓒ **212/965-7000,** to schedule an appointment in any one of the clinics.

Margaret Sanger Center: 26 Bleecker St., at Mott St. www.ppnyc.org. Mon–Tues 8am–4:30pm; Wed–Fri 8am–6:30pm; Sat 7:30am–4:30pm. Subway: 6 to Bleecker; B/D/F/V to Broadway-Lafayette. *Borough Hall Center:* 44 Court St., between Remsen and Joralemon sts. (Note that hours may change during renovations at this center.) Tues and Fri 8am–5:30pm; Wed 8am–4:30pm; Thurs 8am–6:30pm; Mon and Sat 8:30am–4:30pm. Subway: 2/3/4/5 to Borough Hall; M/R to Court St.; A/C/F to Jay St./Borough Hall. *Bronx Center:* 349 E. 149th St. at Courtlandt Ave. Mon and Sat 8am–4pm; Tues–Fri 8am–4:30pm. Subway: 4 to 149th Ave.; 2/5 to Third Ave.–149th St.

Ryan Center   The three associated Ryan clinics (on the Upper West Side, the Lower East Side, and in Midtown) provide a huge range of services, from HIV counseling to general medicine to mental health. Prices are set on a sliding scale.

William F. Ryan Community Health Center: Clinic at 110 W. 97th St., between Columbus and Amsterdam aves. ⓒ **212/749-1820.** www.ryancenter.org. Subway: 1/2/3 or B/C to 96th St. HIV and Mental Health Services: 160 W. 100th St., between Columbus and Amsterdam aves. ⓒ **212/316-8367.** Subway: 1/2/3 or B/C to 96th St. *Ryan-NENA Community Health Center:* 279 E. 3rd St. between aves. C and D. ⓒ **212/477-8500.** Subway: F/V to Second Ave. All three clinics above open Mon and Thurs 8:30am–7pm; Tues, Wed, and Fri 8:30am–4:30pm; Sat 9:30am–1pm (except July and August). *Ryan Chelsea-Clinton Community Health Center:* 645 Tenth Ave., between 45th and 46th sts. ⓒ **212/265-4500.** Mon–Tues, Thurs 8:30am–7pm; Wed and Fri 8:30am–4:30pm. Subway: C/E to 50th St.

DIRT CHEAP SHRINKS

National Psychological Association for Psychoanalysis   With a mind to lowering the barriers to psychological treatment, this organization runs a referral service for affordable psychoanalysis and psychotherapy. Potential analysands whose income levels qualify are sent to the Theodore Reik Clinical Center for Psychotherapy. You can get up to three sessions per week for as low as $10 a session. Higher income folks get sent to the Psychological Referral Service, where the fees begin at $40 a session. There's a $30 intake fee, but that's still a small price to pay for sanity.

150 W. 13th St., between Sixth and Seventh aves. ⓒ **212/924-7440.** www.npap. org. Subway: F/V or L or 1/2/3 to 14th St.

ACUPUNCTURE

Pacific College of Oriental Medicine Clinic and Acupuncture Center   Chinese medicine is gathering momentum in New York. More and more people are seeking out Chinese herbs and medicine as an alternative to the escalating costs of Western medicine. This teaching clinic provides relatively inexpensive services, though the best bargains are for going under an intern's needles. A session costs $35, with the eighth one free.

915 Broadway, 3rd floor, between 20th and 21st sts. ℭ **212/982-4600.** www. pacificcollege.edu. Mon-Fri 9am-9pm; Sat 9am-5pm. Subway: N/R/W to 23rd St.

Swedish Institute College of Health Sciences   It's been 10 years since this learning center added acupuncture to its roster, putting it somewhat ahead of the curve in New York. The Yu Wen Acupuncture Clinic lets students gain experience with patients under the watchful eye of licensed instructors. Twelve sessions are $300, but the program is popular so don't expect to get in immediately. You can download an application from the website or have it mailed to you by calling ℭ 212/924-5900 (x130) and leaving your name and address.

226 W. 26th St., between Seventh and Eighth aves. ℭ **212/924-5900.** www. swedishinstitute.edu. Patients seen Mon 6pm-9pm; Tue, Thurs, Fri 1pm-5pm. Subway: 1 to 28th St.

DENTAL

Columbia University College of Dental Medicine   You can get Ivy Leaguers to poke around your mouth for cheap. The students and residents at this popular teaching clinic are well trained and fully supervised. With several eyes on your teeth, the visit will take longer than a trip to a private clinic, but you'll pay a lot less. A first visit, which includes an oral health screening and X-rays, is $75.

Columbia Presbyterian Medical Center, Vanderbilt Clinic, 622 W. 168th St., 7th floor, between Broadway and Fort Washington Ave. ℭ **212/305-6726.** www.dental. columbia.edu. Registration desk Mon-Fri 8:30am-2pm. Subway: 1/A/C to 168th St.-Washington Heights.

New York University College of Dentistry   NYU runs the largest dental college in the country and offers deep discounts on dental care. An initial appointment (which may require two visits) is about $90 and covers a checkup, X-rays, and oral cancer screenings. For further work, the costs here are half of what they would be in a professional office, and for most folks the location is a lot more con-venient than Columbia's.

345 E. 24th St., at First Ave., Clinic 1A. ℂ **212/998-9872.** www.nyu.edu/dental. Mon–Thurs 8am–6:30pm; Fri 8am–3pm. Subway: 6 to 23rd St.

HEARING

League for the Hard of Hearing FREE   Auditory problems aren't just for rock stars, airline mechanics, and people who live beneath NYU students. Most of us haven't followed up on the tests we had in elementary school, but after years of headphone abuse and subway rides, it may be past time for a checkup. This nonprofit offers free hearing screenings on Tuesdays from noon to 2pm and Thursdays from 4 to 6pm. If it turns out you do need services, this group has never turned away anyone due to an inability to pay.

50 Broadway, 6th floor, between Morris St. and Exchange Alley. ℂ **917/305-7700.** www.lhh.org. Subway: 4/5 to Bowling Green; R/W or 1 to Rector St.; J/M/Z to Broad St.

ALEXANDER TECHNIQUE

The American Center for the Alexander Technique FREE Tasmania-born thespian F. Matthias Alexander pioneered this enig-matic science, which seeks to retrain the body out of a lifetime of bad habits. To learn more, check out the free monthly demonstrations at this 40-year-old institution. They're held the first Monday of the month from 7 to 8:30pm. Seating is limited; call in advance to reserve a spot. Should you wish to follow up afterwards, third-year students at the center need volunteers to receive free work. Email volunteer@ acatnyc.org to get involved.

39 W. 14th St., Room 507, between Fifth and Sixth aves. ℂ **212/633-2229.** www. acatnyc.org. Subway: F/V to 14th St.; L to Sixth Ave.; N/Q/R/W/4/5/6 to 14th St./Union Sq.

3 In the Housing

What would New Yorkers have to talk about if we weren't complain-ing about our living arrangements? Or, for a lucky few of us, bragging about them? I, for example, pay $264 a month for my rent-stabilized four bedroom with stunning views of the East River, Paris, and Cairo.

The sad fact is, even as the economy only jogs along, NYC rental rates and housing prices remain firmly in the realm of the absurd. One concept we learn all too well in New York is that of the "relative bargain." For those not easily discouraged, however, a couple of resources can help a home-seeker get ahead.

NO-FEE RENTALS

Broker's fees, the 10% to 15% surcharge slapped on by the Realtor who tours you around a series of spaces that are too small and more than you can afford, are the painful cost of renting in NYC. You can beat the system by contacting real estate firms directly, through their classifieds in the *Voice* and *Times,* and through their websites. It takes some legwork, but if your need for housing isn't urgent, it's the way to go. If you know a specific building you're interested in, try to talk to the super. They'll know what units might be available soon. Another option is **www. apartmentsource.com**. This website is a clearinghouse that lists no-fee apartments (and Realtors often use it to pad their own lists, though their clients will pay for the knowledge with that hefty broker's fee). The database is easily searchable and you can sample it for free, but if you want to get contact information for a building owner, you'll have to pay. You get 1 day's access for $7.95, 45 days for $64.95, and $79.95 covers 3 months. Though not dirt cheap, the rates are cheaper than the competition, and the apartment listings are fairly comprehensive.

FREE **Manhattan Kansas**

If New York real estate really has you down, look no further than depressed Midwestern towns for the ultimate give-away: free land. All across the heartland, places with limited access to drag burlesque nights, human beat box subway train parties, and a decent bagel are giving up their soil for anyone who wants it. There are a couple of little strings attached—you have to build a house or business on the site and then you have to stay there—but the price cannot be beat. Expecially in New York. Visit www.kansasfreeland.com for county-specific details on claiming your free slice of the continent.

MIXED INCOME DIGS

In an effort to keep neighborhoods from becoming entirely mono-lithic, the city offers tax breaks to developers who are willing to set aside a certain number of units for middle- and low-income residents. As with everything else in life, the key is persistence. Waiting lists can be long and your lottery odds can be slim, but every time you make the effort to apply you tilt the playing field in your favor.

Department of Housing Preservation & Development   This city agency connects buyers and sellers. The website lists lotteries for subsidized housing purchases, which will give you the keys at a sub-stantially reduced cost. You'll have to meet income eligibility thresh-olds and you'll have to use the property as your primary residence. Most housing is in lower income neighborhoods, often in outer reaches of the outer boroughs. Right now the pickings are pretty slim, but check the website for future apartment availability. There's also a lottery list for apartments, which are available way below market rates if you're lucky enough to have your application pulled from the hop-per. For information ✆ **311.** For purchases, www.nyc.gov/html/hpd/ html/buyers/lotteries.shtml; rentals www.nyc.gov/html/hpd/html/ apartment/lotteries.shtml.

Mitchell-Lama Housing Companies   This program has been around since 1955, offering housing to New Yorkers with lower-end incomes. You can choose from 132 city-sponsored buildings and 94 state-sponsored. Rents are highly subsidized, but the application process is cumbersome and not every building has an open waiting list. To get a pdf file (readable with Adobe Acrobat) listing buildings with open lists, log on to www.nyc.gov/html/housinginfo/html/ apartments/apt_rental_mitchell-lama.shtml. Each building has to be applied for individually. For general information, call ✆ **212/863-6500** for city units, or ✆ **212/480-7343** for state units.

New York City Housing Development Corporation   The city promotes several mixed-income new developments in the five bor-oughs. The **80/20** program is fairly common. Twenty percent of a building is rented at discount rates to people who earn significantly less than the neighborhood's median income. You have to apply directly to the developer and the process takes a while, but if you get in you'll score a great deal. In many cases, you can move up in income brackets without jeopardizing your cheap rent (or cheap

---

FREE Renters' Assurance

Despite the encrosions of the open market in recent years, there remain some one million regulated apartments in NYC. The **Metropolitan Council on Housing** (www.metcouncil.net) has spent the last 50 years fighting for the rights of renters, and the preservation of affordable housing. It's an uphill battle againt the big-money powers that be, but individuals can arm themselves with knowledge. The Met Council Hotline provides information on tenant rights and dispenses advice. Call ✆ **212/979-0611** on Monday, Wednesday, and Friday afternoons between 1:30 and 5pm for help.

---

purchase). Note that the buildings involved are usually in developing neighborhoods, not in the city's trendiest zip codes. Log on to www. nychdc.org for a full list of HDC-financed sites, or call ✆ **212/227-5500.**

DIRT CHEAP SLEEPS
HOSTELS

Have friends coming to town and in need of a bed? Why not send them over to the Mandarin Oriental, where an executive suite is a mere $1,800 a month. Er, a night. If they're on a budget, you can put them downtown, say a loft suite at The Mercer Hotel for a mere $1,250 per night. New York is the city that never sleeps affordably—even the Super 8 starts at $109 and goes up quickly from there. Savvy travelers (or halves of quarrelling couples who aren't on the lease) can spend the night for $30 or less, however, if they're not hostile to hostel life.

☆ **Big Apple Hostel**   With clean rooms and a primo Midtown location, this is the city's best choice for dirt cheap sleeps. Bunk beds sleep four people per room. A kitchen, a backyard with barbecue, and air-conditioning round out the amenities. Dorm guests should bring their own towels, however.

119 W. 45th St., between Sixth and Seventh aves. ✆ **212/302-2603.** www.big applehostel.com. 112 dorm beds. Tax included, around $37 per night, $45 per night late Dec before New Year's Eve. Subway: 1/2/3/7/N/Q/R/W to Times Sq./ 42nd St.

FREE **Escape from New York**

Artist Colonies   Artists seeking a break from the more merciless elements of urban life can take advantage of rural escapes, several of which offer free stays. The most famous and prestigious of the colonies is **MacDowell,** in Petersborough, New Hampshire. Amazing names have been through the colony, and can still be found there today. It costs $20 to apply for a session and competition is fierce, but if you get through, room and board are covered for up to 8 weeks. Writers, visual artists, filmmakers, composers, and architects all interact during the sessions. www.macdowellcolony.org. ℭ **603/924-3886.** For information on other colonies as well as artist grant programs (free money), the **New York Foundation for the Arts** is a good place to start. Check the website, www.nyfa.org.

Chelsea Center Hostel   This small hostel on two floors of a Chelsea brownstone provides a laid-back alternative to its bustling competitors. A pleasant garden and friendly continental breakfast add to the charms. Accommodations are bunk beds in clean, bright rooms. If you'd rather stay in the East Village, you can request a dorm bed in the center's other location upon booking.

313 W. 29th St., just west of Eighth Ave. ℭ 212/643-0214. www.chelseacenter hostel.com. 20 dorm beds in each location. $33 per night, includes continental breakfast and tax. Cash only. Subway: C/E to 23rd St. Other location: *East Village*, E. 12th St., at First Ave. (Exact address available upon arrival.) Subway: L to First Ave.

Chelsea International Hostel   You can't do much better location-wise than these rooms clustered around a courtyard right in the heart of Chelsea. International travelers love this well-managed place. Your $28–$32 includes taxes, lounge areas, self-service laundry, and free luggage storage. Bring your own towel.

251 W. 20th St., between Seventh and Eighth aves. ℭ 212/647-0010. www. chelseahostel.com. 288 dorm beds. $30 per night. Subway: 1 to 18th St.

Whitehouse Hotel of New York   Not so long ago, a night on the Bowery didn't sound like a very glamorous prospect. With nearby trendy bars and restaurants popping up like post-rain mushrooms, however, this youth-oriented reimagined flophouse is now right at party central. Spaces are tiny and unenclosed at the ceilings, and bathrooms are shared, but what do you expect for around $35 a night? Towels and A/C are included.

340 Bowery, between Second Ave. and Great Jones St. (©) **212/477-5623.** www. whitehousehotelofny.com. 468 beds. $35 per night plus tax. Subway: F/V to Second Ave.; 6 to Bleecker St.

WOMEN'S RESIDENCES

Members of the fairer sex can also take advantage of the cheap accommodations offered by women's residences. These throwbacks to a more genteel era generally don't allow gentleman callers above the parlor levels, nor do they permit boozing (some residences even have curfews). However, rates are lower than New York's multigender hotels, and for newcomers to the city it's a great way to make friends.

Centro Maria   Operated by the Religious Sisters of Mary Immaculate, this Midtown West residence accepts women ages 18 to 27 for both short- and long-terms stays. Rooms are simple singles, doubles, and triples, and some come with private bathrooms. Night owls won't be happy with the curfew (11:30pm on weekdays, midnight on weekends), but what you lack in basic freedom you make up for in money saved; prices include two meals a day on weekdays, and one meal on Saturday. Residents supply their own bed linens and towels. There's an $80 nonrefundable registration fee, and applications must be accompanied by two letters of recommendation and a photograph. Try to apply 1 month in advance.

539 W. 54th St., between Tenth and Eleventh aves. (©) **212/757-6989.** Daily rate: $45 single, with shared bathroom; $40 per person double. Weekly rate (minimum stay 4 weeks): $150 single with shared bathroom; $135 per person double. Facilities: Shared bath; maid service; limited kitchen; TV room; recreational room; chapel; laundry. Subway: C/E to 50th St.; A/B/C/D/1 to 59th St.–Columbus Circle.

El Carmelo Residence   This small residence, located on the border of the West Village and Chelsea, offers its prime location to single women between the ages of 18 and 35. Established and operated by the Carmelite Sisters Teresas of St. Joseph, the residence's dormitory-style rooms each house two residents. You can expect the rules to be tight and the bathrooms to be shared, but rates include breakfast and supper Monday through Friday. As a bonus, residents have access to the property's garden and rec room. You must apply in person, but call at least 2 months in advance of your stay.

249 W. 14th St., between Seventh and Eighth aves. ℂ 212/242-8224. Daily rate (1-20 days): $60 per person double. Weekly rate (1-13 weeks): $160 per person double; $120 per person double for stays over 13 weeks. Facilities: Shared bathroom; garden, recreational room, laundry. Subway: A/C/E to 14th St.; L to Eighth Ave.

Markle Evangeline Residence Built by the Salvation Army in 1930, the Markle has been providing women with a viable alternative to the New York housing mire for 75 years. The rules are predictably strict—no alcohol, no smoking, no men under 55 inside—and the rooms will never be described as spacious, but for about $240 a week, a resident gets her own fully furnished bedroom with private bathroom, and two squares a day, 5 days a week. Access to a TV room, computer labs, a rooftop garden, and organized social activities help justify the somewhat higher rates. *Note:* More communal souls can save cash by opting for shared doubles, triples, and quads, all of which charge lower rates. Summer student residents under 16 must have a female parent or guardian reside with them. Nonstudent residents must be 18 or older. Two references, an application, and a security deposit equal to 1 month's rent are required for long-term stays.

123 W. 13th St., between Sixth and Seventh aves. ℂ 212/242-2400. www.salvation army-newyork.org/housing/Markle/index.htm. Long-term monthly (minimum 31 days): $1,136-$1,154 single (seniors $1,009); $802-$929 double; $775 triple; $699 quad. Short-term nightly: $85 single. Facilities: Private bathroom, in-room telephone, 24-hr. security, maid service (once a week), roof garden, computer lab, TV lounge, laundry. Subway: 1 to Christopher-Sheridan Sq.

4 Beauty & Massage

HAIR TODAY

NYC's hirsute astute take advantage of salon training sessions. Both students and pros need live heads to demonstrate on, and in exchange for your modeling they'll provide all kinds of services for little or no money. Though there's no guarantee you'll get an expert cut, a lot of salon students in New York have the scissor skills to eclipse the masters. In addition to cuts, coloring services are sometimes available.

Some salons want to look you over first (it helps if you've got a surplus of hair begging for a snipping), but generally it's pretty easy to get your grooming on the house. *Note:* Many salons need models, but not all like to advertise it. If you've got your eye on a prohibitively expensive spot, give them a call and see if they can use you.

SALON STYLINGS

Arté Salon   This lovely Nolita salon uses both men and women as hair models. Cuts are free, usually scheduled on Mondays. Hair coloring costs $25, to cover the materials. Call first to set up an appointment.

294 Elizabeth St., between E. Houston and Bleecker. ℂ 212/941-5932. www. artesalon.com. Subway: 6 to Bleecker St.; B/D/F/V to Broadway/Lafayette St.

Aveda Institute New York   The popular environmentally conscious spa Aveda offers up its many services at deep discounts if you go through the students at the institute. Haircuts, coloring, blowouts, perms, facials, and waxing are all available. The prices aren't dirt cheap, but they are relative bargains compared to the rest of the neighborhood. You can get work done for free by acting as a model during the Advanced Academy classes. Call for schedules. You must be at least 18 years old.

233 Spring St., between Sixth Ave. and Varick St. ℂ 212/807-1492. www.aveda. com. Subway: C/E to Spring St.

☆ **Bumble and bumble.University**   The old-school butchers would never have believed it, but the Meat-Packing District is now style central in Manhattan. The slick new Bumble and bumble salon is right in the thick of it, but you can partake of the services for no money down. Their stylist training program offers model calls every Monday from 5:30 to 6:30pm. You can register in advance or just walk in, where a screener will try and match you with a seminar. The appointments last between 1½ and 2 hours, and you'll have to wait between 1 and 4 weeks. Once you're in the program, however, you can stay tapped into the gravy train. Men can ask for a free cut every 8 weeks and women every 10 without going through the screening process. You must be willing to get more than a trim, though they'll consult with you first to figure out what works. Tips aren't even necessary.

415 W. 13th St., 6th floor, between Ninth Ave. and Washington St. ℂ 866/7-BUMBLE. www.bumbleandbumble.com. Subway: A/C/E or L to Eighth Ave./14th St.

Christine Valmy International School of Esthetics, Makeup and Nail Artistry What you give up in experience, you gain in price here. Facials are a great deal. Instructors do the supervising while students do the work. A full hour and a half facial is only $27. A similar procedure for your back is only $44. Call a week ahead for an appointment.

437 Fifth Ave., between 38th and 39th sts. ℂ 212/779-7800. www.christine valmy.com. Subway: 7 to Fifth Ave.; 6 to 33rd St.

Clairol Product Evaluation Salon Become a product testing guinea pig here and you'll receive free Clairol hair coloring from a professional stylist. The first step is to get an appointment for a half-hour interview. Appointments are available Monday through Thursday from 9:30 to 11am and again from 1:30 to 4pm. I recommend calling ahead to schedule. If you're accepted, you can come back once a month—some people have been taking advantage for years. Only the stylist will know for sure. Both men and women are accepted, but you have to be at least 18.

345 Park Ave., lobby level, between 51st and 52nd sts. ℂ 646/885-4200. Subway: 6 to 51st St.; E/V to 53rd St.-Lexington.

Face Station This casual second floor salon holds training sessions throughout the year. Both cuts and coloring are covered here, for men and women. Call to see what their model needs are.

855 Lexington Ave., 2nd floor, between 64th and 65th sts. ℂ 877/815-FACE. www.facestation.com. Subway: F to Lexington Ave./63rd St.; 6 to 68th St.

L'Oréal L'Oréal's Matrix Technical Salon tests out coloring and styling products. If you make it through an interview, you can join in the experiment. Appointments are scheduled Monday through Thursday from 8 to 11am and 1 to 3pm. Women should have middle-length hair, and men are used for some studies. If you're accepted, you'll get a free coloring and follow-up visits if the study requires them. You can also sign up for the Consumer Expressions Research Center, where you can test L'Oréal from home. Participants get free gift bags of products at the end of the trial, although the test products have to be returned lest they fall into enemy hands. You'll also score a guest pass to shop at the L'Oréal company store, where beauty products (including the ever-popular Kiehl's) are offered at a big discount. Downtown seekers can find a free testing facility at the L'Oréal Professional Soho

Dirt Cheap Cuts

Barber colleges offer cut-rate cuts. The level of experience varies, however, from student to student, so I don't recommend going for anything too tricky.

American Barber Institute   Haircuts are only $3.99 here. Cuts are available Monday through Friday, and for men only on Saturday. 252 W. 29th St., between Seventh and Eighth aves. ✆ **212/290-2289.** Subway: 1 to 28th St.

Atlas Barber School   Both men's and women's stylings are only $5 at the Third Avenue location. At 10th Street they're even cheaper—$4 for both men and women. 34 Third Ave., between 9th and 10th sts. ✆ **212/475-1360.** 80 E. 10th St., between Third and Fourth aves. ✆ **212/475-5699.** Subway: 6 to Astor Place; N/R/W to 8th St.

You can get cheap cuts from pros, too. The cuts will run you a bit more, but you can rest a little easier knowing the scissors are in experienced hands.

Chung Wah Barber Shop   This Chinatown cheap-chop shop offers $7 men's and $8 women's cuts. Note that those with straight hair may get the most reliable results. 19 Pell St., between Doyers and Mott sts. ✆ **212/267-4849.** Subway: J/M/N/R/Q/W/Z/6 to Canal St.

Lee Lee Beauty and Hair Salon   A regular cut is only $12, and you can augment for not much more at this Chinatown salon. The shampoo, style, and cut package is only $15. 12 Pell St., between the Bowery and Doyers St. ✆ **212/528-1381.** Subway: J/M/N/R/Q/W/Z/6 to Canal St.

Astor Place   The sprawling three-floor setup here has been consolidated to just a single basement, but you can still find a dizzying array of barbers and hairstylists. Cuts are professional, and more stylish than you might expect for $12. (Astor Place has had charge of my locks for years, and I look like a million bucks.) 2 Astor Place, between Broadway and Lafayette St. ✆ **212/475-9854.** Subway: N/R/W to 8th St.; 6 to Astor Place.

Academy. Hair models receive hair coloring, styling, cutting, and relaxer services. Call ahead for an appointment.

Matrix Technical Salon: 575 Fifth Ave., 3rd floor, at 47th St. ℂ **212/984-4926.** Subway: B/D/F/V to 47th-50th sts.-Rockefeller Center. *L'Oréal Professionnel Soho Academy:* 15 Mercer St., between Grand and Howard sts. ℂ **212/984-4735.** Subway: J/M/N/Q/R/W/Z/6.

New York International Beauty School The salon here will swap service for experience, as trainees learn best on live bodies. The price list starts at $4.50 for a wash and roller set. Simple haircuts begin at $5.50 and top out at a blow-dried $13. Highlighting, braiding, and facials are among the other services on offer.

500 Eighth Ave., between 35th and 36th sts. ℂ **212/868-7171.** www.nyibs.com. Subway: A/C/E to 34th St./Penn Station.

INSTANT MASSAGING

Swedish Institute College of Health Sciences Swedish massage has been around for a couple of centuries now, but you don't need to travel all the way to Stockholm to improve your circulation. Since its founding by a Swede in 1916, this institution has dedicated itself to natural approaches to health, which it makes available to the public at reduced rates. You'll be worked on by a student, but they're very well trained. Two clinical programs are offered, stress-reduction and therapeutic massage. The former program provides six 1-hour sessions for $150, and the latter is 12 hours in 12 weeks for $250. Both programs are very popular, so registration is by mail only. Call the P. H. Ling Clinic at ℂ **212/924-5900** (ext. 6208) and leave your name and address so information can be mailed to you.

226 W. 26th St., between Seventh and Eighth aves. ℂ **212/924-5900.** www. swedishinstitute.edu. Subway: 1 to 28th St.

Wu Lin Services Massages are yet another bargain that can be found in New York's cheap alternative universe of Chinatown. A bunch of places will work out your kinks, and a few of them can combine it with acupuncture, acupressure, and herbal medicine. One place I like is Wu Lin Services, which will knead away your cares while you keep your clothes on. Ten minutes are $7, 16 minutes are $11, 21 minutes are $31, and a full hour's massage is $42.

145 Grand St., between Crosby and Lafayette. ℂ **212/925-1276.** Daily 10am-10:30pm. Subway: J/M/N/R/Q/W/Z/6 to Canal St.

5 Recreation in the City

BIKE GANGS

Biking makes a virtue of New York's hard paved surfaces, turning our miles of roadway into recreational opportunities. One of the best ways to take advantage is by banding up with fellow riders. If you're not yet of the wheeled class, consider checking out **Recycle-A-Bicycle.** This nonprofit sells refurbished rides at low prices from two retail locations (p. 205).

Fast and Fabulous Cycling Club   Whether you're a fast rider or a fabulous rider, or both, this LGBT biking group will welcome you. Annual membership is $30 ($20 if you join after May 1st, and only $10 after September 1st), but it'll get you invites to a series of rides around the city and out of town (say, a day trip to DIA Beacon). Intermediate cyclists are the target group. Meals and socializing often follow the rides.

© **212/567-7160.** www.fastnfab.org.

Five Borough Bicycle Club `FREE`   This friendly club hosts a slew of day trips in and around the city. Beaches, Bronx greenways, and Woodlawn Cemetery are among the attractions. The club runs some great tune-ups (as long as 90 miles) leading up to the 100 miles of the annual Montauk Century ride in May. Registration isn't necessary; just show up with water, wheels, and lunch money. Day rides are free. A year's dues to join the club isn't particularly onerous at $20.

Departure locations vary. © **212/932-2300,** ext. 115. 5bbc.org.

Time's Up `FREE`   This environmental group sponsors several well-organized rides. The most well known is **Critical Mass,** held on the last Friday of every month and taking place simultaneously in over 300 cities worldwide. The ride is designed to raise consciousness about environmental alternatives and biker rights. It's fun for sidewalk spectators, too, who can watch every kind of bike and bike rider pedal past to a chorus of perversely gratifying taxi horns. The route varies, but the meeting place is always the same, 7pm at Union Square Park North. Time's Up also hosts rides on tri-state rural routes, but the best trip to the country comes on the first Friday of the month. The **Central Park Moonlight Ride** shows off the water and trees and general tranquility of the park at night. With guides riding point and taking up the rear, it's a safe and leisurely pedal. Rollerbladers with at least intermediate skills are welcome, too. The ride meets at 10pm at the southwest corner of Central Park, across from Columbus Circle. The trip is around 10 miles, and runs all 12 months of the year. Check the Time's Up website for more information on their programs. They also offer bike repair workshops (some geared to ladies), and Thursday nights at 8pm you can catch progressive films at the Time's Up HQ. All events are free, although as a volunteer-run organization, donations are cheerfully accepted.

Time's Up, 49 E. East Houston St., between Mott and Mulberry sts. ✆ 212/802-8222. www.times-up.org. Subway: F/V to Second Ave.

GYM NEIGHBORS

When hauling groceries and laundry up to your sixth-floor walk-up is no longer exercise regimen enough, it's time to hit a gym. The cheapest choice by far is signing up with the department of parks and recreation, though other options that don't much exceed $1 a day are available. If you want to shop around first, the website **www.gymsearch.net** has free coupons and guest passes for gyms around the region. It's free, but you have to register your contact info.

☆ **Department of Parks and Recreation**   On top of playing fields and courts, the city also runs 36 recreation centers. The amenity list is long and varied, including indoor and outdoor tracks, weight rooms, dance studios, and boxing rings. All of this can be yours for only $50 a year. If you want to join a center with a pool, it's an additional $25. (For seniors age 55 and over, it's only $10 a year with or without pools, and for under-18s it's all free.) Many centers also offer classes in Pilates, aerobics, karate, kickboxing, wrestling, swimming, and the like. Some centers even have personal trainers. Usually an extra fee applies for classes, say $5 for an hour of yoga instruction. The scene varies from rec center to rec center, but generally they're family-friendly and community-oriented. You won't find classic meat markets in most of these city-run facilities.

✆ 212/360-8222. www.nycgovparks.org.

OTOM Gym Physical Culture   In addition to the Y, Greenpoint residents can take advantage of this large, affordable gym. Monday, Wednesday, and Friday mornings feature classes in kickboxing, aerobics, and strength training. Classes are $5 for members and $10 for everyone else. A year's membership is $389. Night owls can take advantage of a late-night special: $269 per year for limited nighttime access Monday through Thursday and normal hours on the weekends.

169 Calyer St., between Lorimer St. and Manhattan Ave., Greenpoint, Brooklyn. ℃ 718/383-2800. www.otomgym.com. Open 24 hr., except closed from Fri midnight to Sat 7am and Sat midnight to Sun 7am. Subway: L to Bedford Ave.

24-7 Fitness Club   These round-the-clock clubs are a little rough around the edges, but they're hard to beat on both cost and convenience. There's a ton of machines, and they tend not to be overly crowded. The Chelsea gym (47 W. 14th St., between Fifth and Sixth aves.; F/V to 14th St., L/N/Q/R/W/4/5/6 to 14th St./Union Sq.; ℃ **212/206-1504**) is $30 per month plus a $48 initiation fee if you commit for a full year. The TriBeCa location (107 Chambers St., between West Broadway and Church St.; 1/2/3 or A/C to Chambers St.; ℃ **212/267-7949**) is a little more expensive. $399 buys you a full year (averaging out to $33.25 a month), or you can go month to month for $40 per, with no initiation fee.

YMCA of Greater New York   The Y (℃ **212/630-9600;** www.ymcanyc.org) runs 17 health and wellness centers in the city. The facilities vary from site to site, but the general roster includes gyms, pools, racquetball and handball courts, aerobics studios, exercise machines, steam rooms, and saunas. Fees vary. The state-of-the-art facility is the new McBurney location (125 W. 14th St., between Sixth and Seventh aves.; F/V or L to 6th Ave./14th St., or 1/2/3 to 14th St.; ℃ **212/741-9210**). A 1-year membership is $972, plus the $125 initiation fee. To get fit at a less central location is a much better deal— the Greenpoint YMCA (99 Meserole Ave., between Leonard St. and Manhattan Ave.; G to Nassau Ave. or Greenpoint Ave.; ℃ **718/389-3700**) is only $500 for a year, with a $75 initiation fee.

CHEAP SKATES

The Pond at Bryant Park `FREE`   The winter of 2005 marked the inaugural season of this ingenious use of the center of Bryant Park. Surrounded by the boutique stalls of the Holiday Shops, the ice-skating rink has a European small-town feel. Thanks to the bottomless pockets of Citibank, skating is free, though folks whose skates are hanging by their laces in their parents' garages will have to plunk

FREE NYC's All Skate

The Dead Road in Central Park is one of my favorite spots in the city for a workout (well, an eyeball workout to be completely accurate). Watching dozens of expert roller skaters and bladers dancing and spinning to a jamming disco beat is a hypnotic sight. Some of the regulars have been rolling together for more than 2 decades and the skill level is very high, but if you're halfway competent you shouldn't feel intimidated. The scene is friendly and inclusive, so strap on some wheels and jump in. Even for nonskaters, this event is a highlight of the park. The DJs are great, especially now that the city has relented on its antibeat campaign. (In 1995, music was temporarily banned from the park so skaters wore Walkmen all tuned to the same radio channel, creating a surreal silent choreography.) The outdoor roller disco is in session most Saturdays, Sundays, and national holidays in warm weather. For specifics about dates and DJs, check the Central Park Dance Skater's Association's website (**www.cpdsa.org**). The Dead Road is in the middle of the park, between 66th and 69th streets, just a little southwest of the Bethesda Fountain.

If skating in a boogielicious roller inferno is a little daunting to you, find safety in numbers with Wednesday Night Skate (www.weskateny.org), New York's biggest skating event, which wheels away from Union Square Park every Wednesday night. The routes vary from week to week, but generally you'll get to see a few miles' worth of NYC, say up Park Avenue, into Central Park, and back on over to Times Square. The event usually lasts 2 hours. The flock meets at the north end of Union Square Park between 7:30 and 8pm, from May to October. Helmets and wrist guards are required before you turn yourself into a vehicle.

down $7.50 per session for rentals. The rink is open from late October through mid-January.

Bryant Park, between W. 40th and 42nd sts., along Sixth Ave. ✆ **212/768-4242.** www.bryantpark.org. Open daily 8am–10:30pm. Subway: B/D/F/V to 42nd St.; 7 to Fifth Ave.

The Sky Rink at Chelsea Piers `FREE`   Frank J. Zamboni's brainchild smooths the ice for free weekend skate sessions inside this cavernous space. The rink is usually only open for a couple of afternoon hours, and the free ice time doesn't come around every month. Check the Chelsea Piers website for exact times and details. Skate rentals are $6; regular admission is $11.

23rd St. at the Hudson. ℂ **212/336-6100.** www.chelseapiers.com. Subway: C/E to 23rd St.

POOLING RESOURCES

It costs $75 a year to use the city's indoor pools (see "Gym Neighbors," above), but if you're a frequent crawler, the price turns out to be pretty reasonable. There are 51 outdoor pools scattered across the city, and they're free and open to the public (most keep hours of 11am to 7pm). The indoor pools stay open year-round (unless they're superseded by an on-site outdoor pool), but the tubs under the sun synch up with the school year. Late June to Labor Day is the usual season, and you will find many, many kids taking advantage. In addition to the city pools (**www.nycgovparks.org**), the state runs an Olympic-size natatorium in Manhattan. Local favorites include

Asser Levy   An indoor and outdoor pool make this a great year-round swimming destination.

E. 23rd St. and Asser Levy Place, near the FDR Dr. ℂ **212/447-2020.** Pool Mon-Fri 7am-9pm; Sat-Sun 8am-4:45pm. Subway: 6 to 23rd St.

Astoria Park Pool   This is one of largest (designed to hold some 2,000 swimmers) and most famous pools in the country. Built in 1936 through the WPA with stunning skyline and bridge views.

Astoria Park, 19th St. at 23rd Drive, Astoria, Queens. ℂ **718/626-8620.** Daily 11am-7pm. Subway: N/W to Astoria-Ditmars Boulevard

Hamilton Fish   Despite its enormous size, this Lower East Side outdoor pool fills up quickly. Kids from the neighborhood splash while parents relax in the large adjoining plaza.

128 Pitt St., between E. Houston and Stanton sts. ℂ **212/387-7687.** Pool Mon-Fri 7am-8:30pm; Sat-Sun 11am-7pm. Subway: F to Delancey; J/M/Z to Essex St.

Metropolitan Pool   Williamsburg is kept buoyant at the indoor Met Pool, which still gleams from a recent multi-million-dollar renovation.

261 Bedford Ave., at Metropolitan Ave. ℂ **718/599-5707.** Pool Mon-Fri 7am-9:30pm; Sat 7am-5:30pm. Subway: L to Bedford Ave.

Riverbank State Park This 28-acre park on the Hudson ably disguises its foundation, which is a wastewater treatment plant. The indoor pool here is run by the state, which charges $2 per visit.

679 Riverside Dr., at 145th St. ℂ 212/694-3600. www.nysparks.state.ny.us. Pool Mon-Fri 6:30am-8:15pm; Sat 2pm-6pm; Sun 9am-6pm. Subway: 1 to 145th St.

Tony Dapolito Recreation Center Another pool with both indoor and outdoor bases covered, this rec center is a longtime West Village fave.

1 Clarkson St., between Seventh Ave. S. and Hudson St. ℂ 212/242-5228. Outdoor pool (summer) Mon-Fri noon-3pm, 4pm-6:45pm; Sat-Sun 11am-3pm, 4pm-6:45pm. Indoor pool (Sept-June) Mon-Fri 7am-10pm; Sat-Sun 9am-5pm. Subway: A/B/C/D/E/F/V to W. 4th St.-Washington Sq.

OM MY GOODNESS: MEDITATION

In a town so loud it can be hard to hear one's own thoughts, the contrast of a quiet meditation space can be startling. Though just about any house of worship in the city will suffice, sometimes it's nice to get a little guidance for inner journeying.

Change Your Mind Day `FREE` 🖉 One extraordinary June day, the Buddhist magazine *Tricycle* sponsors a series of lectures and demonstrations. Music, chanting, and guided meditation are also part of the scene. I find this day totally inspiring. The speakers are fascinating and the crowd is responsive. If any 1-day experience in NYC can make a person more aware, this is the day. (At worst, you'll leave slightly relaxed and better informed.) The event, usually held the first Saturday of June, runs 11:30am to 4:30pm. If you're planning on watching a lot, a cushion or a blanket is probably a good idea.

The Great Hill in Central Park, 106th St. at midpark. ℂ 800/950-7008. www.tricycle.com. Subway: 6 or B/C to 103rd St.

Shambhala This Tibetan Buddhist group hosts open meditations in its two lovely meditation rooms. Beginners can learn more at weekly lessons, Wednesdays at 6pm and Sundays at noon. Every Tuesday night at 7pm is the weekly dharma gathering, which is a half-hour of group meditation followed by a talk, a discussion, and a reception. Suggested donations for most events are $5.

118 W. 22nd St., 6th floor, between Sixth and Seventh aves. ℂ 212/675-6544. www.ny.shambhala.org. Subway: 1 or F/V to 23rd St.

The Three Jewels Community Center `FREE` In order to further the teachings of the Buddha, this impressive organization offers much of its programming for free. In conjunction with the Asian Classics Institute, you can find a wide range of classes, many of which are suited to beginners. There are also meditation sessions, with on-hand instructors to help conduct them. The main loft in Astor Place houses a combination dharma, yoga, meditation, and outreach center. Check the calendar for the latest schedule (some offerings, like yoga, do come with a charge).

61 Fourth Ave., 3rd floor, between E. 9th and E.10th sts. © **212/475-6650.** www.threejewels.org. Subway: 6 to Astor Place; N/R/W to 8th St.

Transcendental Meditation `FREE` Howard Stern is just one of many New Yorkers who talk up the benefits of T.M. A way to learn more about the technique is at a lecture by one of His Holiness Maharishi Mahesh Yogi's acolytes. The follow-up course will set you back a not-quite-dirt-cheap $2,500, but the introductory lecture is free. Reservations are required, lectures usually on Wednesday nights at 7:30pm.

130 W. 42nd St., between Sixth Ave. and Broadway. © **212/779-9933.** www. tm.org. Subway: 1/2/3/N/Q/R/S/W to 42nd St./Times Square.

Zen Center of New York City Discover what one hand clapping sounds like at this Zen center in Brooklyn. Contributions are requested to participate in the meditation sessions (generally $3–$5), which are held almost every day. If you're new to zazen, you can attend an introductory session on a Sunday morning. Sessions start at 10am and last around 3 hours. Admission is by a suggested contribution of $5.

500 State St., between Nevins and Third Ave., Boerum Hill, Brooklyn. © **718/ 875-8229.** www.mro.org/firelotus. Subway: 2/3/4/5/B/Q to Atlantic Ave.; 4/5 to Nevins; D/M/N/R to Pacific; A/C/G to Hoyt-Schermerhorn.

WATERSPORTS

New York's waterways were once great recreational resources, but years of environmental laxity made much of the local liquid too toxic to touch. A handful of burgeoning groups are trying to speed along the rivers' rebounds with giveaways along the shore. The East River, Hudson, and Gowanus are all covered for seaworthy (or at least sea-curious) New Yorkers.

☆ **Downtown Boathouse** FREE   If you know how to swim, you're eligible for free Hudson paddling. Out of the goodness of their hearts (and a desire to promote the Hudson as a recreational outlet), this group loans out kayaks and equipment all summer long. Some 50,000 people get out on the river this way each year. The trips are limited to 20 minutes in protected areas near three west side piers, but if you show up a few times and get into shape, you'll be eligible for a long paddle from Pier 96 into New York Harbor. This spectacular field trip lasts 3 hours, with unbelievable views all the way. Potential paddlers gather before 8am and wait to have names picked from a hat. On a nice day you've got about a 50-50 chance of going, though you can increase your odds by arriving on a day with cloud cover. The long-trip season runs mid-June to mid-September. Pier 96 is open from 9am to 6pm on weekends and holidays, with kayaks available on select weeknights from mid-June until the end of August (call ✆ **646/613-0740** to check the daily status. In really lousy weather the kayaks stay docked). The Hudson is cleaner than it's been for decades, so getting splashed here and there no longer has any negative health consequences. FINE PRINT The boathouse's season runs from mid-May to mid-October.

Pier 96, Clinton Cove Park, West Side Highway, at 56th St. ✆ **646/613-0375.** www.downtownboathouse.org. Subway: A/B/C/D/1 to Columbus Circle. Pier 40, at Houston St. and the Hudson. Subway: 1 to Houston; A/C/E to Canal St. 10am–5pm weekends and holidays. 72nd St., at the Hudson. 10am–5pm weekends and holidays. Subway: 1/2/3 to 72nd St.

The Gowanus Dredgers Canoe Club FREE   The Gowanus Canal is in a transitional phase between being the butt of jokes and serving as a genteel Brooklyn natural resource. A canoe trip here still leans toward the former, providing a surreal float through what is mostly a forgotten industrial wasteland. Equipment is loaned out on select weekends and holidays. Guided tours that run down to the Gowanus Bay are available by appointment. The season lasts from late March through the end of October. Pick up is near 2nd Street and Bond Street in Brooklyn, but check the calendar for availability details first. There are also expanding trips around the waters of Red Hook. For landlubbers, the Dredgers also have a series of free bike tours. There's no charge for any of these programs, but as this is a grass-roots organization, every little bit helps.

Gowanus Dredgers, Carroll Gardens, Brooklyn. ✆ **718/243-0849.** www.gowanus
canal.org. Subway: F/G to Smith-9th St.

L.I.C. Community Boathouse FREE   The East River (it's not really
a river; it's a tidal strait) is also open to experienced and newbie paddlers alike. At least twice a week, this enthusiastic group runs free
paddle trips. The waterways are the Queens waterfront, with occasional forays to other boroughs. The kayak tours require an advance
appointment; you can get a walk-up canoe ride from the beach at
Socrates Sculpture Park. Check the website for a calendar. Though the
shore here is pretty industrial, as a tidal strait, the possibilities of por-
poise and whale sightings are significantly greater than they are on
the Hudson.

Kayak tours, L.I.C Community Boathouse at Anable Pier, Hunters Point, Queens.
44th Drive and the East River. ✆ **718/786-8388.** www.licboathouse.org. Subway: 7 to Vernon-Jackson; E/V to 23rd St.-Ely Ave.; G to 45th Rd.-Court Square.
Walk-up canoes, L.I.C Community Boathouse at Hallets Cove, Astoria, Queens.
31st Ave. and the East River. Subway: N/W to Broadway.

YOGA & TAI CHI
New York offers several free and dirt cheap classes in tai chi and yoga.
Tai chi has been slow to gather momentum as a trend, but yoga is
entrenched as the aerobics of the naughts. It's a good idea to wear
comfortable clothing for either type of class, and bring a mat or towel
for yoga in the parks.

Battery Park City FREE   From 8:30 to 9:30am on select Fridays
in summer you can get a master's guidance in tai chi at Battery Park's
Esplanade Plaza (at the end of Liberty St.) Another class is taught in
Rockefeller Park, but that one will set you back $70 for 7 meetings.

Battery Park City, along South End Ave., just west of West St. ✆ **212/267-9700.**
www.bpcparks.org. Subway: 1/2/3 or A/C to Chambers St.; 1 to Rector St. or South
Ferry; 4/5 to Bowling Green.

Bryant Park FREE   Bryant Park loans its central location to a host
of activities, most notably a Thursday morning tai chi class. The class
is taught from 7:30 to 8:30am, May to October, so you can focus your
energy before punching the clock. If you're new to the practice,
World Tai Chi Day might be the thing for you. On the last Saturday in
April, Bryant Park is the site of a day of classes and demonstrations.
Thursday evenings (6 to 7pm) are dedicated to yoga. From June until

late August, on the southwest corner of the lawn, you can salute the setting sun and improve your flexibility. (As an added bonus, you can also take a knitting class on Monday afternoons between April and October; call ☎ 212/387-0707 to register or get more information.)

Bryant Park, between 41st and 42nd sts., and Fifth and Sixth aves. ☎ 212/786-4242. www.bryantpark.org. Subway: B/D/F/V to 42nd St.; 7 to Fifth Ave.

Om Yoga   Om Yoga provides an introduction to yoga for beginners for only $5. This drop-in class explains the basics of alignment, breathing, and stretching. The class lasts about 90 minutes and is held on select weekends, usually from 2 to 3:30pm.

826 Broadway, 6th floor, between 12th and 13th sts. ☎ 212/254-YOGA. www.omyoga.com. Subway: L/N/Q/R/W/4/5/6 to Union Sq.

Riverside Park South `FREE`   Unwind after work in Riverside Park, where hatha yoga for beginners is taught every Wednesday from 6:30 to 7:30pm. The "Evening Salute to the Sun" class meets during summer months. In those same months, you'll also be able to tone up your muscles with a Pilates mat class. Hey, the art of contrology just might be the new yoga. Classes are Tuesdays from 6:30 to 7:30pm; please bring your own mat.

Riverside Park, the Plaza at 66th St., at the Hudson. ☎ 212/408-1209. www.riversideparkfund.org. Subway: 1 to 66th St.

Sivananda Yoga Vedanta Center `FREE`   Once a month this yoga center introduces the community to their practice via an open house. The day begins at 10:30am with a lecture and demonstration, followed by a trial class, a meditation introduction, and a vegetarian meal. If you can't bring your own mat, bring a towel to place over one of their mats. Usually the first Saturday of the month.

243 W. 24th St., between Seventh and Eighth aves. ☎ 212/255-4560. www.sivananda.org/ny. Subway: C/E or 1 to 23rd St.

6B Garden `FREE`   This community garden is best known for its tall rustic tower, made of wooden planks and discarded design elements (i.e., junk). The garden is a beautiful pocket of green on the Lower East Side, and it opens its gates to the public for a handful of events. One day a week from 7 to 8am, you can take advantage of a free yoga class (check online, usually a day early in the week.) Meditation, slide shows, and poetry readings are also part of the schedule. The garden is open for greenery appreciation on the weekends from 1 to 6pm, April through October.

Corner of E. 6th St. and Ave. B. www.6bgarden.org. Subway: F/V to Second Ave.

Socrates Sculpture Park FREE   Situated along the East River with Manhattan views, this park is a lovely setting for classes. Sessions run from late May to late August. Kilipalu yoga is taught Saturdays from 11am to noon, open to all levels. On Sundays from 11am to noon, tai chi is taught, also suitable for all levels. Kids get a chance to make some art during Saturday sculpture workshops, from noon to 3pm.

32-01 Vernon Blvd., at Broadway, Long Island City, Queens. (C) **718/956-1819.** www.socratessculpturepark.org. Daily 10am–sunset. Subway: N/W to Broadway. Walk 8 blocks along Broadway toward the East River.

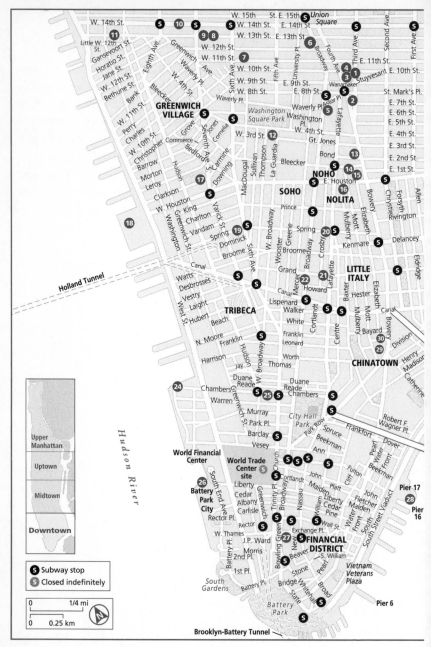

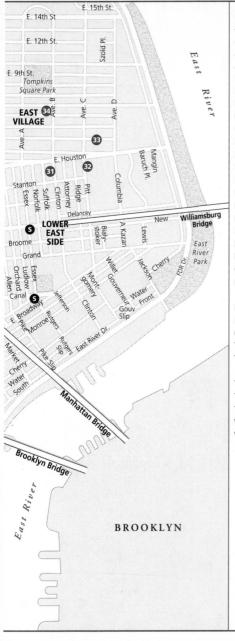

24-7 Fitness Club Tribeca **25**
Arté Salon **15**
Astor Place Hair **5**
Atlas Barber School **1, 4**
Aveda Institute **19**
Battery Park City, Esplanade Plaza **26**
Battery Park City, Rockefeller Park **24**
Bumble and bumble.University **11**
Chung Wah Barber Shop **29**
Cooper Union **2**
David Ores, M.D. **31**
Downtown Boathouse, Pier 40 **18**
El Carmelo Residence **10**
Hamilton Fish **32**
League for the Hard of Hearing **27**
Lee Lee Beauty and Hair Salon **30**
L'Oréal Professionnel Soho Academy **22**
Markle Evangeline Residence **8**
New School University **7**
New York University Kimmel Center **12**
Om Yoga **6**
Planned Parenthood Margaret
  Sanger Center **14**
Poets House **20**
Ryan-NENA Community Health Center **33**
6B Garden **34**
Tango Porteño, Pier 16 **28**
Theodore Reik Clinical Center
  for Psychotherapy **9**
The Three Jewels Community Center **3**
Time's Up **16**
Tony Dapolito Recreation Center **17**
Whitehouse Hotel of New York **13**
Wu Lin Services **21**

CHELSEA, THE FLATIRON DISTRICT, GRAMERCY & MIDTOWN LIVING

24-7 Fitness Club Chelsea **18**
The American Center for the
  Alexander Technique **19**
Asser Levy **23**
Big Apple Hostel **4**
Bryant Park **28**
Callen-Lorde Community
  Health Center **10**
Central Park Tango **34**
Centro Maria **2**
Chelsea Center Hostel **6**
Chelsea International Hostel **11**
Chelsea Market Milonga **9**
Christine Valmy International School of
  Esthetics, Makeup and Nail Artistry **27**
Clairol Product Evaluation Salon **31**
Dance Manhattan **17**
Downtown Boathouse, Clinton Cove
  Park, Pier 96 **1**
Eglise Français du St-Esprit **32**
Face Station **33**
Gay Men's Health Crisis **12**
Graduate Center at CUNY **26**
The Henry George School **25**
L'Oréal's Matrix Technical Salon **30**
New York City Free Clinic/Sidney
  Hillman Clinic **21**
New York International Beauty School **5**
New York University College
  of Dentistry **24**
Pacific College of Oriental Medicine
  Clinic and Acupuncture Center **20**
Ryan Chelsea-Clinton Community
  Health Center **3**
Shambhala **15**
Sivananda Yoga Vedanta Center **13**
Sky Rink at Chelsea Piers **8**
Swedish Institute College of Health
  Sciences **14**
Teachers and Writers Collaborative **22**
Transcendental Meditation **29**
YMCA of Greater New York
  (McBurney) **16**

UPPER WEST SIDE

Lincoln Center

CENTRAL

West End Ave.
Amsterdam Ave.
Columbus Ave.
Central Park W.
West Drive

W. 66th St.
W. 65th St.
65th St.
W. 64th St.
W. 63rd St.
W. 62nd St.
W. 61st St.
W. 60th St.
W. 59th St.
W. 58th St.
W. 57th St.
W. 56th St.
W. 55th St.
W. 54th St.
W. 53rd St.
W. 52nd St.
W. 51st St.
W. 50th St.
W. 49th St.
W. 48th St.
W. 47th St.
W. 46th St.
W. 45th St.
W. 44th St.
W. 43rd St.
W. 42nd St.
W. 41st St.
W. 40th St.
W. 39th St.
W. 38th St.
W. 37th St.
W. 36th St.
W. 35th St.
W. 34th St.
W. 33rd St.
W 32nd St.
W. 31st St.
W. 30th St.
W. 29th St.
W. 28th St.
W. 27th St.
W. 26th St.
W. 25th St.
W. 24th St.
W. 23rd St.
W. 22nd St.
W. 21st St.
W. 20th St.
W. 19th St.
W. 18th St.
W. 17th St.
W. 16th St.
W. 15th St.
W. 14th St.

Central Park S.
Columbus Circle

DeWitt Clinton Park

Tenth Ave.
Ninth Ave.
Eighth Ave.
Seventh Ave.
Broadway

THEATER DISTRICT

MIDTOWN WEST

Twelfth Ave.
Eleventh Ave.
Tenth Ave.

TIMES SQUARE

Port Authority

Lincoln Tunnel

Javits Convention Center

GARMENT DISTRICT

Penn Station/
Madison Square Garden

Tunnel Entrance

Chelsea Park

CHELSEA

West Side Hwy.
Eleventh Ave.
Tenth Ave.
Ninth Ave.
Eighth Ave.
Seventh Ave.

Hudson River

Chelsea Piers

MEAT-PACKING DISTRICT

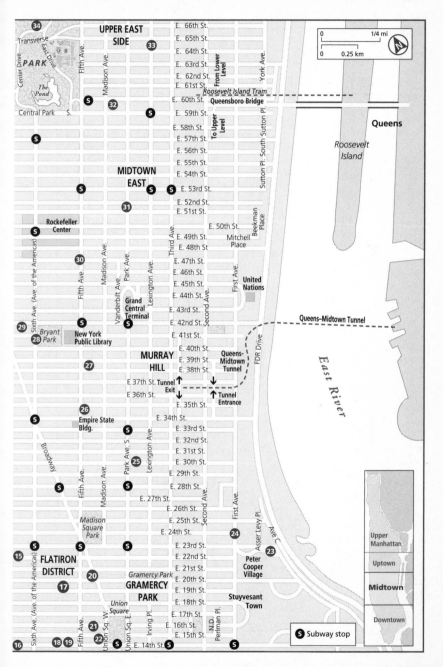

UPTOWN LIVING

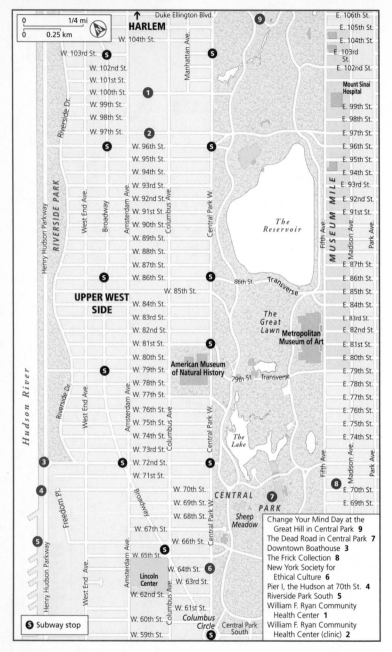

Duke Ellington Blvd.

HARLEM

W. 104th St.

Manhattan Ave.

9

E. 106th St.
E. 105th St.
E. 104th St.
E. 103rd St.
E. 102nd St.

W. 103rd St. **S**   **S**

W. 102nd St.
W. 101st St.
W. 100th St.   **1**
W. 99th St.
W. 98th St.
W. 97th St.   **2**
W. 96th St.   **S**   **S**
W. 95th St.
W. 94th St.
W. 93rd St.
W. 92nd St.
W. 91st St.
W. 90th St.
W. 89th St.
W. 88th St.
W. 87th St.
W. 86th St.   **S**   **S**

Mount Sinai Hospital

E. 99th St.
E. 98th St.
E. 97th St.
E. 96th St.
E. 95th St.
E. 94th St.
E. 93rd St.
E. 92nd St.
E. 91st St.

The Reservoir

MUSEUM MILE

E. 87th St.
E. 86th St.

86th St. Transverse

W. 85th St.

UPPER WEST SIDE

W. 84th St.
W. 83rd St.
W. 82nd St.
W. 81st St.   **S**
W. 80th St.
W. 79th St.   **S**
W. 78th St.
W. 77th St.
W. 76th St.
W. 75th St.
W. 74th St.
W. 73rd St.
W. 72nd St.   **S**   **S**
W. 71st St.

E. 85th St.
E. 84th St.
E. 83rd St.
E. 82nd St.
E. 81st St.
E. 80th St.
E. 79th St.
E. 78th St.
E. 77th St.
E. 76th St.
E. 75th St.
E. 74th St.

American Museum of Natural History

79th St. Transverse

The Great Lawn   **Metropolitan Museum of Art**

The Lake

3
4

5

W. 70th St.
W. 69th St.
W. 68th St.
W. 67th St.
W. 66th St.   **S**
W. 65th St.   **S**
Lincoln Center
W. 64th St.   **6**
W. 63rd St.
W. 62nd St.
W. 61st St.
W. 60th St.
W. 59th St.

CENTRAL   **7**
PARK

Sheep Meadow

8

E. 70th St.
E. 69th St.

S Subway stop

Columbus Circle   Central Park South   **S**

Riverside Dr.
Henry Hudson Parkway
RIVERSIDE PARK
West End Ave.
Broadway
Amsterdam Ave.
Columbus Ave.
Central Park W.
Hudson River
Freedom Pl.

Fifth Ave.
Madison Ave.
Park Ave.

0   1/4 mi
0   0.25 km

Change Your Mind Day at the Great Hill in Central Park **9**
The Dead Road in Central Park **7**
Downtown Boathouse **3**
The Frick Collection **8**
New York Society for Ethical Culture **6**
Pier I, the Hudson at 70th St. **4**
Riverside Park South **5**
William F. Ryan Community Health Center **1**
William F. Ryan Community Health Center (clinic) **2**

On Sundays, any kind of clothing can be found for bargain-basement prices in the Lower East Side's "Bargain District." See p. 189 for more information.

SHOPPING

T he last time my country friend came to visit I noticed him limping around the avenues of New York with a broken shoelace. I immediately tried to steer him into the nearest drugstore, but he demurred, telling me he didn't want to get slammed with those "big-city shoelace prices."

This memory still induces a chuckle whenever I'm scoring some crazy deal in the heart of NYC. The volume advantage that 8 million citizens provide can't be touched out in the sticks. Clothes, film, electronics, furniture, food, and, yes, even shoelaces, are available here for a fraction of their price in the hinterland. Plus Gotham's refined taste is great news for the cost-conscious when it comes time for gowns and coffee tables to begin their second and third lives. New York thrift stores, flea markets, and curbside trash piles are all treasure troves for the patient and sharp-eyed, meaning savvy New Yorkers can finish off their cheap shopping lists better than anybody else in the US of A. Which is helpful, when your rent bill ensures you're living on a shoestring.

1 Dirt Cheap Shopping Zones

Maybe I was dozing through my Capitalism 101 classes, but I don't understand why New York stores of similar stripe all jam themselves into the exact same neighborhood. The Bowery is clogged with restaurant supply shops, and then suddenly every storefront is dedicated to lighting. A series of lampshade shops gathers on a couple of nearby side streets. Whatever the initial cause, the effect of the single-product density is bargaining power galore for the consumer. Don't like the price? Walk next door and see if you can't do a little better.

DOWNTOWN
THE FINANCIAL DISTRICT
Come lunchtime downtown, the streets fill with office workers scurrying around the cheap shopping outlets. **Fulton, Nassau,** and **Chambers** streets are big destinations, although there isn't anything here that can't be found in other places in the city. The two exceptions to that rule are the city's best electronics and best clothes stores, both near City Hall (see "Shekels and Chains: Department Stores" and "Electronics," later in this chapter).

Subway: J/M/2/3/4/5 to Fulton St.; A/C to Broadway Nassau.; N/R/W to City Hall; 6 to Brooklyn Bridge/City Hall.

CHINATOWN
A trip to Chinatown can feel like a visit to a foreign country. What I like even better is the way it can feel like a visit to a foreign economy. A vibrant, but still developing, economy, where prices are only a fraction of what's charged across the border in the city's various America-towns. Dispersed around **Canal Street, between Lafayette and Mott streets,** you'll find a mind-numbing variety of knockoff versions of just about anything with a designer label, from Oakley sunglasses to Kate Spade bags. The area along **Allen Street between Division Street and**

East Broadway doesn't attract many tourists, but locals take advantage of the abundance of cheap apartment-ware shops, where good prices on appliances, furniture, knickknacks, and hardware can be found.

Subway: A/C/E/J/M/N/R/Q/W/Z/6 to Canal St.

THE BOWERY

Chinatown inflections can be found on nearby **Bowery.** The street is rapidly transforming from a district of missions to a nightlife destination, but its primary character in daylight derives from a profusion of restaurant- and kitchen-supply stores. Many are wholesalers, oriented toward the industry. Those that sell to the public often also have great deals on chairs, small tables, and stools. When you cross **Delancey Street** heading south, you'll be in the cheap-lighting district. Having so many dealers in one place gives the buyer a lot of leverage when it comes time to barter on the price.

Subway: J/M/Z to Bowery; F/V to Second Ave; 6 to Spring St.

NoLITA & THE EAST VILLAGE

NoLita and the East Village are stylish boutique playgrounds. As such, bargains can be hard to find. The good news is that low—if not dirt cheap—prices on haute couture can still be tracked down, if you put in the legwork. NoLita's **Elizabeth, Mott, and Mulberry streets** (between Houston and Spring) are dotted with an ever-increasing number of fashionable stops, including one of the city's best consignment stores (see "Designer Consignment Stores" later in this chapter). In the Village, **East 9th Street,** between Second Avenue and Avenue A, is home to a slew of up-and-coming local fashion designers—great for window-shopping, if nothing else—and loads of small gift shops.

Subway: N/R/W to Prince St.; 6 to Spring St.; F/V to Second Ave.; J/M/Z to Bowery.

THE LOWER EAST SIDE

Holdover street signs designate the chunk of Manhattan south of Houston and east of the Bowery as the "Bargain District." You can still find fabric, bedding, and some clothing, but expensive boutiques and trendy restaurants are crowding the bargains out. The state of flux makes it fun to visit, especially on Sundays. **Orchard Street** closes to traffic **between Delancey and Houston streets** and vendors lay out cheap goods on tabletops, in the spirit of the pushcarts that were once ubiquitous here. In the warmer months you may also get a free band, or a fashion show, usually on a stage at the corner of Orchard and

Stanton streets. On the weekdays, you're more likely to hear the hard sell of a barker. Many of the shopkeepers will bargain, if that's in your skill set. Little hipster shops have infiltrated Orchard and can also be found scattered around **Ludlow and Stanton** and other nearby streets. Much cheaper goods are available on **Delancey Street,** which has a good selection of 99¢ stores and bargain-bin housewares.

Subway: F to Delancey St.; J/M/Z to Essex St.

ON BROADWAY

The stretches of **Broadway between Bleecker and Canal streets** are a fashion runway for New York youth. With cheap stores abounding, the streets stay packed until nightfall. Though it's sometimes semi-derisively referred to as the "Cheap Sneaker District," lower Broadway has a great selection of hip and affordable jeans, sweats, jackets, and, yes, sneakers. The area's traffic flow has only increased with the open-ing of a Bloomingdale's satellite in the dearly departed Canal Jeans' space. Thus far, fortunately, the high-profile addition hasn't priced out its cut-rate neighbors.

Subway: B/D/F/V to Broadway/Lafayette; 6 to Spring St.; N/R/W to Prince St.

CHELSEA

Proximity to Fifth Avenue's deep purses helped propel Chelsea's stretches of **Sixth Avenue and Broadway** to the top of Manhattan's shopping heap in the late 19th century. The deep purses moved uptown and the department stores followed, but not before leaving behind some lovely cast-iron architecture. Big discount chains have moved in, including a popular Old Navy. There's great thrift shopping along **17th Street between Fifth and Sixth avenues,** and the neighbor-hood is also home to the photo district, the best place for photo-graphic supplies (soon to be digital-printing supplies, no doubt).

Subway: L to Sixth Ave.; F/V to 23rd St.

GRAMERCY

The residential enclave of Gramercy, sandwiched between hectic Midtown and East Village streets, is often overlooked as a shopping destination. That's great news for thrift aficionados, who can take advantage of less competition. Gramercy's almost total lack of hipster cred makes the cool clothing, furniture, and collectibles somewhat easier to come by than in picked-over East Village and NoLita stores.

The shops along **23rd street between Second and Third avenues** are well stocked and the goods are priced low enough that they're continually flowing. For my money, this is the best place in the city to bargain hunt for thrift threads.

Subway: 6 to 23rd St.

MIDTOWN
THE GARMENT DISTRICT

The huge old buildings in **the 30s between Madison and Eighth avenues** still bear faded advertisements for the furriers and milliners whose shops and factories filled the lofts here. Although much of the manufacturing has moved to cheaper zip codes, the garment trade is still active in ground-floor showrooms. Most are wholesale only, particularly the stretch on **Broadway that runs into the 20s.** A few places are open to the retail public, but the majority of plastic gewgaws they sell aren't very desirable, on the express track for a landfill eternity. Toward the west, Penn Station is a hub for light rail and subway trains, and the streets nearby are a natural mecca for shoppers. Several big discounters are stationed here, as is the largest store in the world, Macy's. For garment shopping, however, downtown is a better bet.

Subway: 1/2/3/B/D/F/N/Q/R/V/W to 34th St./Herald Sq.

UPTOWN

Clustered on the Upper West and Upper East sides are some of the highest per capita incomes in the world. The big chains and department stores that cater to those lofty budgets dominate the local retail trade, though a few exceptions exist for discerning shoppers. For high-end fashions at low-end prices, the consignment shops on **Madison and Amsterdam avenues** are some of the best in the city.

Subway: 1/2/3 to 72nd St.; B/C to 72nd St.; 4/5/6 to 86th St.

2 Dirt Cheap Threads & More

DIRT CHIC

Used clothing falls into two categories in New York, "thrift" and "vintage." In a thrift shop you'll have to sort through racks of junk to find that one perfect shirt, but it won't set you back more than a few bucks. A good vintage proprietor will do the editing for you, but you'll pay for access to her good taste. For the trendiest items—like a '70s rock

Easy Streets: 17th & 23rd Streets

Chelsea is home to a great series of thrift stores on 17th Street between Fifth and Seventh avenues. Each stop has its own dynamic shopping scene, and items are priced to sell. Stocks turn over frequently, rewarding close-proximity return visits.

My favorite block to thrift shop is 23rd Street between Second and Third avenues. The location in prosperous Gramercy ensures high quality levels for discarded goods.

concert T-shirt—a couple of holes in the sleeve may not lower the $60 price tag. Uptown consignment shops will sell you a Chanel suit at a fraction of the original cost, but that's still going to be a several-hundred-dollar commitment. My favorites are shops that split the difference between thrift and vintage, selling used stuff that's still got some life left in it, but not at budget-busting prices. Many of the city's thrift shops are charitable non-profits, so not only will you be getting a bargain, you'll also be helping out a worthy cause.

Note: Clothing isn't the only reason we tightwads love thrift stores. Most of the shops listed below also stock an impressive variety of used furniture, jewelry, electronics, books, records, and even art.

On 17th Street

Angel Street Thrift Shop   Angel Street does an impressive job of keeping its recycled goods au courant. The clothes are in good shape and most don't scream "just bought at a thrift shop." Some unused ringers like sealed sheets and electronics sneak into the bric-a-brac and bedding sections.

118 W. 17th St., between Sixth and Seventh aves. ℂ 212/229-0546. www.angel thriftshop.org. Subway: 1 to 18th St.; F/V to 14th St.; L to Sixth Ave.

☆ **Housing Works Thrift Shop**   Housing Works has the city's best thrift shops, with a constant stream of quality donations coming and going. Designer names pop up often on the clothes racks, and the jewelry racks are filled with intriguing items. The real draw, however, is the furniture. Although the premium pieces end up in the store windows (they're up for grabs in silent auctions), many a well-preserved table or chair finds its way to the sales floor.

143 W. 17th St., between Sixth and Seventh aves. ℂ 212/366-0820. www.housing works.org. Subway: 1 to 18th St.; F/V to 14th St.; L to Sixth Ave. Other locations:

202 E. 77th St., between Second and Third aves. ℭ **212/772-8461.** Subway: 6 to 77th St.; 306 Columbus Ave., between 74th and 75th sts. ℭ **212/579-7566.** Subway: B/C to 72nd St.; 157 E. 23rd St., between Third and Lexington aves. ℭ **212/529-5955.** Subway: 6 to 23rd St.; 1730 Second Ave., between 89th and 90th sts. ℭ **212/722-8306.** Subway: 4/5/6 to 86th St.; 245 W. 10th St., between Hudson and Bleecker sts. ℭ **212/352-1618.** Subway: 1 to Christopher St.

17@17   The UJA (United Jewish Appeal) runs a solid thrift shop, with great prices on groovy art and assorted bric-a-brac. Though the furniture can be dated (the '80s just haven't aged very well), the clothes stay current. Frequent sales knock already-low prices in half.

17 W. 17th St., between Fifth and Sixth aves. ℭ **212/727-7516.** www.ujafedny.org. Subway: F/V to 14th St.; L to Sixth Ave.

ON 23RD STREET

City Opera Thrift Shop   Locals sing the praises of this lovely shop, with its balconies full of deals on art, books, and bric-a-brac. Prices for furniture are excellent. Costumey looks dominate the clothing selection, including some pieces that look like they just left the stage.

222 E. 23rd St., between Second and Third aves. ℭ **212/684-5344.** www.nyc opera.com. Subway: 6 to 23rd St.

Goodwill   The fashion quota in these stores tends to be pretty low, with racks full of the fashion miscues of the last couple of decades. There's a lot to look at here, however, and when you do find your diamond in the rough you won't pay much for it. (And if it were easy all the time, the big scores wouldn't be nearly as thrilling.)

220 E. 23rd St., between Second and Third aves. ℭ **212/447-7270.** www.good willny.org. Subway: 6 to 23rd St. Other locations: 2196 Fifth Ave., at 135th St. ℭ **212/862-0020.** Subway: 2/3 to Lenox Ave; 217 W. 79th St., between Broadway and Amsterdam Ave. ℭ **212/874-5050.** Subway: 1 to 79th St.; 512 W. 181st St., at Audubon St. ℭ **212/923-7910.** Subway: 1 to 181st St.; 1704 Second Ave., between 88th and 89th sts. ℭ **212/831-1830.** Subway: 4/6 to 86th St.; 103 W. 25th St., near Sixth Ave. ℭ **646/638-1725.** Subway: F to 23rd St.

OFF 23RD STREET

The Vintage Thrift Shop   The selection here is very well chosen, with most items in good enough shape to make this feel more like a boutique than a thrift shop. Cheap glassware, scarves, and shirts can all be found. There isn't room for much furniture, but what's here is priced to sell.

A Sample Plan

New York's top fashion designers can't sell just everything they lay their scissors to. Sample outfits made specially for store buyers end up sitting on a rack, along with canceled orders, overstock, and items whose day in the fashion sun has come and gone. When it's time for these garments to leave the warehouse, they go to sample sales, NYC's cheapest way of nabbing haute couture. These websites can help you track down time and locations of sample sales throughout the city (you have to sign up for all of them, but membership is free):

● **www.clothingline.com** This site provides information on the SSS Sample Sale. Designers change every week but the location stays the same, 261 W. 36th St., 2nd floor, between Seventh and Eighth aves, ℰ **212/947-8748.** Days of the week and hours vary, usually opens 10am. Subway: 1/2/3 or A/C/E to 34th St.

● **www.dailycandy.com** The email newsletter generated by this site is hugely popular, meaning events advertised here can be crowded. The website is well organized, with whimsical graphics and listings of all manner of city events, including

286 Third Ave., between 22nd and 23rd sts. ℰ **212/871-0777.** www.the lowereastside.org/oldisnew. Subway: 6 to 23rd St.

In Brooklyn

Atlantis Basement Basement steps lead to a lost city of thrift. Huge selection means that with agile hanger shuffling you can come up with real finds. With Williamsburg's vintage-wearing population at a peak, however, you will also find plenty of hanger-shuffling competition. Prices here are good for the nabe, with plenty of items under $10.

57 Hope St., between Havemeyer St. and Rev. Dr. Gardner C. Taylor Blvd., Williamsburg, Brooklyn. ℰ **718/599-3737.** Subway: G/L Lorimer St.-Metropolitan Ave.

food and drink choices. The deals section is a great shopping facilitator.

- **www.nysale.com**   Store openings and bridal events augment the sale and sample sale information provided when you register here.

Note: Designers have to tiptoe around their retail buyers, who are getting bypassed in the sample system. Rather than flaunt customer-filching, they make their sales low-key. Few are advertised widely, and many of them subsist on word of mouth alone. Keep your eyes open in retail neighborhoods, especially the Garment District; many sample sales take place in vacant storefronts, rented out for only a single weekend's sale.

Tips: Wear elbow pads if you're going at peak hours, especially during weekday lunches. A lot of sales don't take credit cards. Even if they do, cash is still a good idea because sometimes they'll let the sales tax slide. Dressing rooms are few and far between at sample sales, so be prepared to try things on over your clothes. Also, don't expect a lot of latitude for sizes, it's all catch as catch can. Finally, items go "as is," so check carefully for stains and rips before you cash out.

Beacon's Closet   Hipsters delight in the well-stocked palaces of the two Beacon's Closet locations. As a clothing exchange, this store actively buys clothes off its customers, no appointment necessary. Clean out your closet and turn it into cash. Or you can pick up 20% more by taking store credit and putting all those newly empty hangers to immediate use. They're a little picky about what they'll take, but that just makes for better selection for shoppers. Both locations have extensive collections of stylish clothes and shoes.

Park Slope: 220 Fifth Ave., between President and Union sts. ✆ **718/230-1630.** www.beaconscloset.com. Subway: R to Pacific St., exit at Union St. Other location: *Williamsburg:* 88 N. 11th St., between Berry and Wythe sts. ✆ **718/486-0816.** Subway: L to Bedford Ave.

DESIGNER CONSIGNMENT STORES

It's not that hard to look like a million bucks in NYC, even if your clothes budget tops out at a substantially smaller number. New York's best consignment shops carry loads of pre-owned, vintage, and over-stock garments in near show-room condition. The clothes are by no means dirt cheap, but for the high end of design, the prices are as low as they come.

Allan & Suzi   From the window this looks like a shop targeting transvestites, but there's consignment for all tastes inside. Heavy hitters like Halston and Versace mix with one-off numbers and the rest of the best of 20th-century design.

416 Amsterdam Ave., at 80th St. ✆ **212/724-7445**. www.allanandsuzi.net. Subway: 1 to 79th St.; B/C to 81st St.–Museum of Natural History.

Encore   For resale women's wear, the Upper East Side is the place to be. Encore is the best of the best, chock-full of big, big names on two floors. A lot of it costs a fortune the first time around and it's still not cheap, but periodic sales can bring luxury into reach. Some of Jackie O.'s wardrobe made its curtain call here.

1132 Madison Ave., between 84th and 85th sts., 2nd floor. ✆ **212/879-2850**. www.encoreresale.com. Subway: 4/5/6 to 86th St.

Ina   When Sex and the City's wardrobe department sold off its left-overs, of course it turned to Ina. This designer consignment shop carries the height of style, including the likes of Halston, Prada, and Daryl K. The racks are filled with both vintage and current items, and they're always in excellent shape. Shoes and accessories are here as well, and everything is marked way, way down (though outside of the sales, it's still not cheap). A new men's store on Mott Street caters to the burgeoning metrosexual class.

NoLita: 21 Prince St., between Mott and Elizabeth sts. ✆ **212/334-9048**. www.inanyc.com. Subway: 6 to Spring St.; N/R/W to Prince St. *SoHo:* 101 Thompson St., between Prince and Spring sts. ✆ **212/941-4757**. Subway: C/E to Spring St. *Men's store:* 262 Mott, between Prince and Houston. ✆ **212/334-2210**. Subway: N/R/W to Prince St.; 6 to Spring St. *Uptown:* 208 E. 73rd St., between Second and Third aves. ✆ **212/249-0014**. Subway: 6 to 77th St.

Michael's   Designer wear for women is the focus of this much-loved two-story consignment boutique. The names are familiar—Chanel, YSL, Prada, and Gucci—but the prices are barely recognizable. As pickers, they're very careful, making sure no rips or stains make it onto the floor. The bridal salon is a great find, also specializing in top-shelf quality at rock-bottom prices.

1041 Madison Ave., 2nd floor, between 79th and 80th sts. 🕾 **212/737-7273.** www.michaelsconsignment.com. Subway: 6 to 77th St.

Tokyo Joe   When hipsters need the good stuff, they turn straight to this designer consignment shop. Cramped quarters can make for tough browsing, but the clothes themselves are in excellent shape. Don't miss the big section of lightly used and new shoes, going for a fraction of their cost Uptown.

334 E. 11th St., between First and Second aves. 🕾 **212/473-0724.** Subway: L to First Ave.

OTHER TRÉS CHEAP FASHIONS

Centricity   If accessories are your bag, this is your place. With brooches and bangles that span the twentieth century, you'll find retro aplenty. Clothes and hats round out the selection of womenswear, all at old school East Village prices.

63 E. 4th St., between Second Ave. and Bowery. 🕾 **212/979-7601.** Subway: F/V to Second Ave.; 6 to Bleecker St.

H&M   Swedish discounter Hennes & Mauritz knocks out the latest looks at low, low prices. They specialize in hip looks for women and men, and as such they're a big hit with the teens. Durability is not the greatest, though it is about what you'd expect for these prices.

1328 Broadway, at 34th St. 🕾 **646/489-8777.** www.hm.com. Subway: 1/2/3/B/D/F/N/Q/R/V/W to 34th St./Herald Sq. Other locations: 640 Fifth Ave., at 51st St. 🕾 **212/656-9305.** Subway: E/V to Fifth Ave.; 558 Broadway, between Prince and Spring sts. 🕾 **212/343-0220.** Subway: N/R/W to Prince St.; 6 to Spring St.; 515 Broadway, between Spring and Broom sts. 🕾 **212/965-8975.** Subway: 6 to Spring St.; N/R/W to Prince St.; 162-164 East 59th St., at Lexington Ave. 🕾 **212/935-6781.** Subway: 4/5/6 or N/R/W to 59th St./Lexington Ave.; 435 Seventh Ave., between 33rd and 34th sts. 🕾 **212/643-6955.** Subway: 1/2/3/A/B/C/D/E/F/N/Q/R/V/W to 34th St./Herald Sq.; 125 W. 125th St. 🕾 **212/665-8300.**

Loehmann's   When the original Barneys faltered, longtime discount fave Loehmann's was quick to fill much of the square footage. Casual wear comes in at one-third to two-thirds off the department store prices, and you can reel in even deeper discounts on the likes of Donna Karan and Versace inside the "Back Room." Great prices for women's shoes, too, and there's an underpublicized men's floor.

101 Seventh Ave., between 16th and 17th sts. ⓒ 212/352-0856. www.loehmanns. com. Subway: 1 to 18th St.

Rags-A-GoGo   It's a rare thrift/vintage shop that hits the trifecta of good selection, good condition, and good prices. This Chelsea charmer succeeds, however, with rack after rack of cool pants, T's, sweatshirts, and button-downs. Dusty stuffed animals survey the scene, increasing the atmosphere of quirkiness essential to a good thrifting trip.

218 W. 14th St., between Seventh and Eighth aves. ⓒ **646/486-4011.** Subway: 1/2/3 or A/C/E to 14th St.; L to Eighth Ave.

For Fashion DIYers

The fabric selection in **Harry Zarin Company**'s upstairs warehouse goes the whole nine yards, with an almost over-whelming selection of textures and styles. Deep discounts get even deeper for overruns and closeouts. Downstairs is a recently remodeled conven-tional furniture store. *Warehouse:* 72 Allen St., at Grand St. ⓒ 212/226-3492. www.zarin fabrics.com. *Storefront:* 318 Grand St., between Ludlow and Orchard sts. ⓒ **212/925-6112.** Subway for both locations: B/D to Grand St.; F to Delancey St.; J/M/Z to Essex St.

Rainbow Shops   When the new women's and girl's clothes lines come out, Rainbow wastes no time in coming up with afford-able copies. Urban styles predom-inate, with the target audience well under 25. Shoes and acces-sories, lots of plus sizes, and you won't have to part with a pot of gold.

110-114 Delancey St., between Essex and Ludlow sts. ⓒ **212/254-7058.** www. rainbowshops.com. Subway: F to Delancey St.; J/M/Z to Essex St. Other locations: 308 W. 125th St., between Man-hattan Ave. and Frederick Douglass Boulevard. ⓒ **212/864-5707.** Subway: A/B/C/D to 125th St.; 380 Fifth Ave., between 35th and 36th sts. ⓒ **212/947-0837.** Subway: B/D/F/NQ/R/V/W to 34th St./Herald Sq.; 320 W. 57th St., near Eighth Ave. ⓒ **212/333-5490.** Subway: A/B/C/D/1 to 59th St.-Columbus Circle. Several locations in Brooklyn, too.

Weiss & Mahoney   Camouflage patterns are still fashion attention-getters locally, since green-shaded organics are about the worst ways to camouflage oneself in NYC (if it's stealth you seek, a series of large gray and black squares would better do the trick). Weiss & Mahoney has been outfitting the city for decades in camouflage, not to mention peacoats and berets. Work clothes are just at normal prices, but surplus and camping goods are way below retail.

142 Fifth Ave., at 19th St. ℂ 212/675-1915. www.weissmahoney.com. Subway: N/R/W or 6 to 23rd St.

SHOE INS & OUTS

All the miles New Yorkers log as pedestrians help explain the occasional obsessive bent applied to our shoe shopping. My two favorite shoe-shopping clusters can be found downtown. **Lower Broadway beneath 4th St. and down to Canal** has some great street options. **West 8th Street between Fifth and Sixth avenues** is another excellent minidistrict, with the stylish and all-too-stylish intermixed. NYU undergrads haunt both areas, and prices often accommodate student budgets.

ON BROADWAY

DSW   This chain came all the way from Ohio to liberate New Yorkers from high shoe prices. Their warehouse-style mega-stores are packed with recent releases. Special sale areas have the best buys, with markdowns exceeding 75%. Ladies in particular will have to exhibit patience, as the selection goes on forever. (The Battery Park location seems large enough to house a floor of a neighborhood mulitplex, which is exactly what it did in its previous incarnation.)

40 E. 14th St., 3rd Floor, between University Place and Broadway. ℂ **212/674-2146.** www.dswshoe.com. Subway: L/N/Q/R/W/4/5/6 to 14th St./Union Sq. Other location: *Battery Park*, 102 North End Ave., near Vesey St. ℂ **212/945-7419.** Subway: E to World Trade Center; A/C/J/M/Z/2/3/4/5 to Fulton St./Broadway Nassau.

Juno   The regular prices here are no great shakes, but during the frequent half-off and two-for-one sales you can shod your hooves for $40 or $50. The designs are interesting and in step with the latest style, though durability can leave something to be desired.

543 Broadway, between Prince and Spring sts. ℂ **212/625-2560.** www.junoshoes.com. Subway: N/R/W to Prince St.; 6 to Spring St. Other location: 426 W. Broadway, between Prince and Spring sts. ℂ **212/219-8002.** Subway: C/E to Spring St.

Shoe Mania   This popular discount store has a wide-ranging selection, putting Kenneth Coles sole to sole with Doc Martens, Birkenstocks, and

Mephistos. Whether you go for style or comfort, you'll find a good price on it here.

853 Broadway, at 14th St. ✆ **212/245-5260.** Subway: 4/5/6/L/N/R/Q/W to 14th St./Union Sq. www.shoemania.com. Other locations: 331 Madison Ave., between 42nd and 43rd sts. ✆ **212/557-6627.** Subway: 4/5/6/7/S to 42nd St./Grand Central; 30 E. 14th St., between University Place and Fifth Ave. ✆ **212/627-0420.** Subway: 4/5/6/L/N/R/Q/W to 14th St./Union Sq.; 11 W. 34th St., between Fifth and Sixth aves. ✆ **212/564-7319.** Subway: F/N/R/V/W to 34th St./Herald Sq.

Tip Top Shoes This Uptown shop is tops for walking shoes, which are essential equipment in New York. Rockport, Mephisto, and Ecco are among the brands represented here, sold at reasonable prices. They also carry shoes of a less practical nature for those who prefer form to function. Staff is knowledgeable, if a little harried by the frenetic pace of business here.

155 W. 72nd St., between Broadway and Columbus Ave. ✆ **800/WALKING** or 212/787-4960. www.tiptopshoes.com. Subway: 1/2/3 to 72nd St.

On 8th Street

Da'Vinci On-the-spot discounts are part of the code here. With a little bargaining savvy, you can get great prices on styles fresh off the boat from Italy.

47 West 8th St., between Fifth and Sixth aves. ✆ **212/982-9879.** www.davinci shoesvillage.com. Subway: A/B/C/D/E/F/V to West 4th St.-Washington Sq.

Kinway Shoes A family-run friendliness permeates this ramshackle shop. Selection is surprisingly broad given the close quarters.

5 W. 8th St., between Fifth and Sixth aves. ✆ **212/777-3848.** www.villageshoes. com. Subway: A/B/C/D/E/F/V to West 4th St. -Washington Sq.

Village Shoe Revue Frequent clearance sales here make this store worth frequent visits. The stock is kept up-to-date, with the latest footware often on hand. The best bargains lurk in the back section, where $50 is often enough for a $100 pair of shoes.

29 W. 8th St., between Fifth and Sixth aves. ✆ **212/529-1800.** Subway: A/B/C/ D/E/F/V to West 4th St. -Washington Sq.

3 Flea New York

New Yorkers seeking free stimuli can certainly do worse than whiling away a few hours at a flea market. The rows of tables can function as touchable museums, and the sheer width and breadth of available stuff is stunning. Prices for goods are generally not as cheap as they should be given the low-overhead locales, but there are ways to tip the scales in your favor. Sunday, as closing time approaches, the last thing a dealer wants to do is reload that half-ton armoire back into the truck. Likewise, a sudden rain can make parting with a wooden antique or a suede jacket more sweetness than sorrow. Use the elements to your advantage when it's time to haggle.

The Garage   Imagine a series of yard sales jammed up right on top of each other and you'll have an idea of the scene at The Garage. Lots of art, loose photos, and other oddball junk, and the prices are in the same stratosphere as you'd find on a suburban lawn. Two floors, open Saturdays and Sundays from 6:30am to 5pm.

124 W. 19th St., between Sixth and Seventh aves. ☎ 212/243-5343. www.annex antiques.com. Subway: F/V or 1 to 23rd St.

Greenflea   This bustling indoor/outdoor fair is a favorite way to spend a Sunday afternoon on the Upper West Side. The antiques tend to be priced fairly, marginalized as they are by dealers offering less-inspired contemporary imports, crafts, and clothes. The latter also line the nearby strip of Columbus Ave. Open 10am to 5:30pm, until 6pm April to October.

W. 76th St., at Columbus Ave. ☎ 212/239-3025. www.greenfleamarkets.com. Subway: B/C to 72nd St.; 1 to 79th St.

Hell's Kitchen Flea Market   Though it hasn't quite caught up with its dearly departed predecessor in Chelsea, this is still the scene to beat in the city. Over 150 vendors bring vibrancy to a dingy strip behind Port Authority. Open weekends, 10am to 6pm.

39th St., between Ninth and Tenth aves. ☎ 212/243-5343. www.hellskitchen fleamarket.com. Subway: A/C/E to 42nd St./Port Authority.

4 Shekels and Chains: Department Stores

New York traditionally makes it hard for big franchises and chains to survive. The city is competitive to an extreme and there just isn't enough profit margin to pay a bunch of middle management salaries. Though there are a few chains sprinkled through these pages, for the most part we avoid the national retailers. They don't give enough bang for your buck.

Come Sale Away

When out-of-towners gawk and marvel that anyone would pay what's printed on a New York price tag, they aren't taking into account that most locals won't throw money away on the full retail price. The key to dirt cheap shopping in the Big Apple is timing the sales. Stores trumpet their markdowns in window displays, newspapers, and flyers, and sales fever is contagious. If one shoe store is doing two-for-one, the rest of the block often isn't far behind. Season ends, like just before back-to-school and just after Christmas, are routinely great for bargain hunters. Buy your sundresses and air conditioners in August, and wait until February to pick up that new winter coat. If your tastes run to vintage or barely used, try looking around in January, when a fresh crop of nonreturnable items get consigned. A good way to keep abreast of the action is in the "Sales and Bargains" section of *New York* magazine, or on the website at www.nymag.com. "Check Out" in *Time Out* is another good source, as is NYSale, www.nysale.com.

☆ **Century 21**   Nearly destroyed on 9/11, Century 21 has risen from the ashes to reclaim its place as the top clothes shopping destination in the city. Fancy labels are fully represented here, sans the fancy prices. Expect designer goods at less than half the prices they carry in other department stores. Great deals on sunglasses, linens, and housewares, too. Avoid peak hours at lunch and on the weekends if possible. Don't be intimidated by long lines for the women's dressing room; the queue moves quickly.

22 Cortlandt St., between Broadway and Church St. ℂ **212/227-9092.** www.c21stores.com. Subway: E to World Trade Center; A/C/J/M/Z/2/3/4/5 to Fulton St./Broadway Nassau; R/W or 1 to Rector St. Other location: 472 86th St., between Fourth and Fifth aves., Bay Ridge, Brooklyn. ℂ **718/748-3266.** Subway: R to 86th St.

Daffy's   Daffy's never seems as crowded as it should be, given how cheap the clothes are. The merchandise usually isn't big names, and you have to sort through some cheesy-looking Italian designs, but

FREE Take an Unböring Trip to Ikea

Ikea gives Manhattanites a free lift to the massive mothership furniture store in Elizabeth, New Jersey. Unfortunately, the bus only
runs on weekends, and weekends at Ikea are *insane*. The children
of a thousand scattered tribes stream through tasteful simulations
of living rooms and kitchens. Parents fondle vaguely cheap-looking
Swedish furniture. The checkout lines wind into infinity. Ikea's
labyrinth layout also means you can't just dash in, get want you
want, and get right back out. That said, the prices are pretty amazing. Nobody else in the tri-state can compete for decent-looking
post-dorm furniture. The big basket racks are often filled with
amazingly cheap items; I'm still using the complete kitchen knife
set I bought for $3 a few years back. There's an in-store cafeteria
should you need a break from the action, with affordable food
(including Swedish meatballs, of course). The views from the cafeteria of Newark Airport runways are spectacular, almost enough on
their own to make this interstate excursion worthwhile. Gate #5,
lower concourse, Port Authority, Eighth Avenue at 42nd Street.
Buses leave every half-hour between 10am and 2:30pm and return
from Jersey every half-hour between noon and 6pm. The trip takes
about 30 minutes each way (© **800/BUS-IKEA;** www.ikea-usa.
com). *Note:* The bus can accommodate your new possessions on
the ride back, as long as they're not too big to carry.

patient shopping always reveals gems. Excellent for staples for men,
and New Yorkers are just starting to discover the great kids' selection.
The Herald Square location is comprehensive.

1311 Broadway, at 34th St. © **212/736-4477.** www.daffys.com. Subway:
1/2/3/B/D/F/N/Q/R/V/W to 34th St./Herald Sq. Other locations: 462 Broadway,
at Grand St. © **212/334-7444.** Subway: N/Q/R/W to Canal St.; 335 Madison Ave.,
at 44th St. © **212/557-4422.** Subway: 4/5/6/7/S to 42nd St./Grand Central; 125
E. 57th St., between Park and Lexington aves. © **212/376-4477.** Subway: 4/5/6
or N/R/W to 59th St./Lexington Ave.; 50 Broadway, between Exchange Alley and
Morris St. © **212/422-4477.** Subway: R/W or 1 to Rector St.; 4/5 to Wall St.;
J/M/Z to Broad St.; 1775 Broadway, between 57th and 58th sts. © **212/294-
4477.** Subway: 1/A/B/C/D to 59th St./Columbus Circle.

Kmart The words Kmart and inspiring are rarely found in the same sentence, but for me every trip to Astor Place's K is a thrilling reminder of NYC's awesome cultural diversity. Students, yuppies, outer-borough homemakers, and Japanese hipsters all rub shoulders as they prowl the long aisles for cheap clothing, housewares, furniture, and even food. The hardware and paint departments have great deals, and there's an excellent plant section. Direct access to the subway makes it easy to drag your haul home.

770 Broadway, between 8th and 9th sts. ✆ **212/673-1540.** www.kmart. com. Subway: 6 to Astor Place; N/R/W to 8th St. Other location: 250 W. 34th St., between Sixth and Seventh aves. ✆ **212/760-1188.** Subway: 1/2/3/B/D/ F/N/Q/R/V/W to 34th St./Herald Sq.

Jack's 99-Cent Stores If you think a dollar doesn't get you far in the big city, you don't know Jack. With central locations and a loyal/rabid clientele, these stores bustle at all hours with bargain-hunters stocking up on housewares, gifts, appliances, and chocolate bars. The 40th Street and 32nd Street locations even have groceries, at unbeatable prices. Daily specials, unadvertised to appease suppliers, reward frequent visits.

16 E. 40th St., between Madison and Fifth aves. ✆ **212/696-5767.** Subway: B/D/F/V to 42nd St.; 7 to Fifth Ave. Other locations: 45 W. 45th St., between Fifth and Sixth aves. ✆ **212/354-6888.** Subway: B/D/F/V to 47th-50th sts.-Rockefeller Center; 7 to Fifth Ave. 110 W. 32nd St., between Sixth and Seventh aves. ✆ **212/268-9962.** Subway: 1/2/3/B/D/F/N/Q/R/V/W to 34th St./Herald Sq.

Macy's (One-Day Sales) Covering 10 stories and an entire city block, this megalith has just about everything, including at any given time a large chunk of the metropolitan shopping population. The key is to buy during the frequent sales. The famous One-Days are the best,

---

FREE 🏛 **Macy's Flower Show**

Outside of sales, the big department stores aren't much help for the budget-minded. For free entertainment, though, they hold their own. Window displays make great theater and floor after floor of regal goods makes for great browsing. The first 2 weeks of April bring some serious spectacle when Macy's goes nuts for flowers. The store is transformed by over a million blossoms in 18 gardens. Free tours run every half-hour from 11am to 4pm. www.macys.com. Flower hot line ✆ **212/494-4495.**

usually held on Wednesdays, with the occasional Saturday thrown in. Check the *New York Times* for Macy's full-page advertisements, which sometimes include clip-out coupons for additional 10% to 15% discounts.

Herald Sq., W. 34th St. and Broadway. ℰ **212/695-4400**. www.macys.com. Subway: 1/2/3/B/D/F/N/Q/R/V/W to 34th St./Herald Sq.

Pearl River   This mini–department store couples Chinatown prices with SoHo ambience. The inventory favors Asian classics like paper lanterns, silk pajamas, and sequined slippers. Glazed bowls and other housewares make for inexpensive kitchen outfitting. This is a great spot for cheap-gift hunting, too.

477 Broadway, between Broome and Grand sts. ℰ **212/431-4770**. www.pearl river.com. Subway: N/Q/R/W to Canal St.

5 Dirt Cheap Shopping: A to Z

ANTIQUES
See "Flea New York," earlier in this chapter.

BIKES
Recycle-A-Bicycle   The organization that runs these shops promotes biking in the city by selling rehabbed bikes at reasonable prices. Prices start at a kid's BMX model for $15. A top-of-the-line bike could set you back as much as $500 (a fraction of its cost new, however), but remember, you'd be helping out a worthy cause.

75 Ave. C, between 5th and 6th sts. ℰ **212/475-1655**. www.recycleabicycle.org. Subway: L to First Ave.; F to Second Ave. Other location: *DUMBO, Brooklyn*, 55 Washington St., between Front and Water sts. ℰ **718/858-2972**. Subway: F to York St.

BOOKS
See the readings section (p. 88) for other great sites for literary browsing.

The Strand   The Strand is as legendary for its 18 miles of books as it is for its 5 inches of aisle space to maneuver in. The big crowds are a testament to the great prices. Review copies of recent books share space with art books at 85% off list and used fiction hardbacks that go for under $5. Bibliophiles with small apartments beware—it's hard to leave empty-handed.

828 Broadway, at 12th St. ℭ **212/473-1452.** www.strandbooks.com. Subway: L/N/Q/R/W/4/5/6 to 14th St./Union Sq. There's also a smaller, less crowded Strand Annex at 95 Fulton St., between William and Gold sts. ℭ 212/732-6070. Subway: J/M/Z/2/3/4/5 to Fulton St.; A/C to Broadway–Nassau St.

12th Street Books   This is a great place to look for used and rare books. The selection runs especially strong in history, psychiatry, art, and theater. Most fiction comes in for under $10. In front of the store the sales racks have great prices (under $1), though it may take some serious scrounging to find something you really want to read.

11 E. 12th St., between Fifth Ave. and University Place. ℭ **212/645-4340.** Subway: 4/5/6/L/N/R/Q/W to 14th St./Union Sq.

Westsider Books   This tiny, charming shop has the best used books Uptown. Browsers delight in the broad selection of literary and historical works. The occasional reviewer's copy can also be found, at discounted prices.

2246 Broadway, between 80th and 81st sts. ℭ **212/362-0706.** www.westsider books.com. Subway: 1 to 79th St.

EDIBLES

Cooking at home is an obvious way of cutting costs, but a trip to the corner deli for necessities can feel like a shakedown by the time you step away from the cash register. Most NYC grocery stores aren't much better, but a couple of specialty shops offer accessible comestibles.

Deluxe Food Market, Inc.   Several buffets in Chinatown offer variations on the theme of four dishes over rice for $4. The best by far can be found inside this bustling grocery store. Three dishes are only $3, though you'll probably be communicating by pointing rather than in English. The selection changes every day, and the food is always fresh and delicious. In addition to the buffet line you can find supercheap savory take-aways, and a bakery section where pastries start at 60¢. The rest of the real estate here is dedicated to regular grocery store goods. Fish, meats, and greens are all rock bottom. You can also load up on frozen specialties, like big packs of dumplings, for amazingly low prices. There's limited seating for cafeteria food.

79 Elizabeth St., between Hester and Grand sts. ℭ **212/925-5766.** Subway: B/D to Grand St.; J/M/Z to Bowery.

Dowel Quality Products   Many shoppers only know this store for its unrivalled beer selection, conveniently located near the BYOB restaurants of Curry Row. There's a lot more to like here, however, including health and beauty items, incense, teas, and fruits and vegetables. The best savings come on Dowel's own packaged goods, with bulk rice, chutneys, lentils, and curries of every hue among the highlights.

91 First Ave., between 5th and 6th sts. ⓒ **212/979-6045.** Subway: F/V to Second Ave.

☆ **East Village Cheese Store**   For gourmet on the cheap, nothing else in the city comes even close to this East Village gem. You can get bread, crackers, pâtés, pickles, and other side items here, but the real jaw-dropping prices are on the cheeses. In the front refrigerators, goat cheese tubes and brie wedges go for $1, and boursin packages are $1.50. Behind the counter you can find tons of specials on fancy goudas and cheddars for $2.99 a pound. The give-away prices aren't indicative of quality, either. They're not second-rate goods, just items picked up when some importer added a mistaken zero to an order. This mom and pop store is uniquely equipped to get rid of it all in a hurry.

40 Third Ave., between Ninth and Tenth sts. ⓒ **212/477-2601.** Subway: 6 to Astor Place; N/R/W to 8th St.

Essex St. Market   When the city squeezed the pushcarts off the Lower East Side 50 years ago, it built a garagelike city market as a replacement. The market has evolved into a low-rent grocery store and shopping mall, frequented by Spanish and Chinese locals, who love the prices. **Best Farms** (ⓒ **212/533-5609**), a huge Korean deli, has taken over the north end of the market. They sell just about everything, but the best deals are on fresh fruit and vegetables. A huge container with a blend of gourmet lettuces is just $1.99, fruit salads are $1.50, and when the mangos are ripe they're two for $1. The middle of the market has butchers, fish sellers, and a botanica. In the back you'll find **Batista Grocery** (ⓒ **212/254-0796**), a shop with great prices on Goya and other dry goods. Cafe tables are available if you want to make a picnic (on nice days you can take your food down to the East River, assuming the city finally finishes fixing up the park). Since this is downtown, there's even an art gallery tucked away in the very back (**Cuchifritos;** ⓒ **212/598-4124;** www.artistsai.org/cuchifritos; Mon–Sat noon–5:30pm). On your way out, grab a $5 bottle of kosher wine from longtime neighborhood presence **Schapiro's,** or save $5 and just try a free sample (℮ **212/832-3176;** www.schapiro-wine.com; Mon–Thurs 10am–6pm, Fri 9:30am–4pm).

120 Essex St., between Rivington and Delancey sts. ℮ **212/312-3603.** www. essexstreetmarket.com. Subway: F to Delancey St.; J/M/Z to Essex St.

May Wah Healthy Vegetarian Food, Inc.   Sometimes a vegetarian needs a break from the bean sprout and tofu regimen. The Chinese are fake meat experts, and this little Chinatown shop has a massive selection. A big package of frozen unchicken nuggets is only $3.55, and the citrus spare ribs are an even better deal at $2.90.

213 Hester St., between Centre St. and Centre Market Place. ℮ **212/334-4428.** www.vegieworld.com. Subway: J/M/N/R/Q/W/Z/6 to Canal St.

Sahadi's   This brightly lit and perennially mobbed Brooklyn grocery store is a great source for Middle Eastern cooking staples. Dozens of varieties of olive oil are available, as are nuts, dried fruits, olives, lentils, chickpeas, and, of course, top quality *maleb* (the Lebanese seasoning made from the insides of cherry pits).

187-189 Atlantic Ave., between Court and Clinton sts., Boerum Hill, Brooklyn. ℮ **718/624-4550.** www.sahadis.com. Subway: M/R to Court St.; 2/3/4/5 to Borough Hall.

Trader Joe's   Few new arrivals in the city have been awaited as breathlessly, by Californians and non-Californians alike, as Trader's. This legendary grocery store sells its own brands, eliminating the middle man and his attendant price premiums. Beyond the great prices are great products, with fresh, often organic ingredients. Somehow the Hawaiian-shirt-wearing staff stays California-friendly, despite the ever-descending hordes of hardcore New York shoppers. The wine shop next door carries legendary and quite drinkable "Two-Buck Chuck," though in New York we pay $3.24 for Charles Shaw's finest.

142 E. 14th St., between Third Ave. and Irving Place (wine shop is next door at #138). ℮ **212/529-4612.** www.traderjoes.com. Subway: L to Third Ave.; N/Q/R/W/4/5/6 to 14th St./Union Sq.

SWEETS

Economy Candy   The Lower East Side of the '30s was littered with small specialty shops like this one, which remains a family business almost 70 years later. With the other shops gone, Economy Candy has taken on their responsibilities, selling everything from coffee to nuts to dried fruit. Oh yeah, they also sell a little candy. From floors to rafters the store is packed with lollipops, gum drops, halvah, gourmet candy bars, bulk chocolate, and pretty much anything else sweet you can think of. Prices are very reasonable, especially when you buy by the pound.

108 Rivington St., between Essex and Ludlow sts. ✆ 212/254-1531. www. economycandy.com. Subway: F to Delancey St.; J/M/Z to Essex St.

ELECTRONICS

J&R Music World/Computer World I'm constantly surprised how often an online search for discounted electronics brings up J&R as the cheapest supplier out there. Save the shipping cost by coming in to the bustling block-long series of stores. The staff is well informed and not too brusque (at least by New York standards). The prices on cameras, stereos, computers, and software are excellent, and there's good CD and DVD shopping as well. Closeout specials are at 33 Park Row. Guitars are upstairs, half-price refurbished flat-screen TV's are at ground level, and luggage is downstairs. Check the paper or the website for dates on the frequent sales.

Along Park Row, at Ann St., opposite City Hall Park. ✆ 800/426-6027 or 212/238-9000. www.jandr.com. Subway: 2/3 to Park Place; 4/5/6 to Brooklyn Bridge/City Hall.

Toys 'R' Them

Among the hideous chains that characterize the new Times Square, Toys "R" Us stands out for its free entertainment. The central Ferris wheel, which rises 60 feet in the center of the store, is beloved by the kiddies, who don't begrudge the sometimes long waits. A 5-ton animatronic T-Rex is another crowd pleaser, as is the pink-overload-zone of Barbie's envy-inducing duplex dollhouse. Prices here are good and made better by frequent in-store specials. Demonstrations are fun to watch and usually come with discounts on the product at hand. Even if you don't have a buying agenda, this is an easy place to fill time on a rainy day. 1514 Broadway, at 44th St. ✆ 646/366-8858. www.toys rus.com. Subway: 1/2/3/7/N/Q/ R/S/W to Times Sq./42nd St.

GIFTS & OTHER CURIOSITIES

Daily 235 For gift shopping, this tiny, creative shop has tiny, creative gifts for under $10. In one convenient stop, fill all your Japanese lamp, John Paul II paper doll, wind-up lederhosen, Bond-Aid brand bondage tape, and evil unicorn figurine needs.

235 Elizabeth St., between Prince and Houston sts. ℂ **212/334-9728.** www.daily235.com. Subway: F/V to Second Ave.; J/M/Z to Bowery.

Pageant Print Shop   Some 10,000 antique prints and maps are packed into this tiny storefront. You can find great New York City ephemera, as well as images of everything else humans have been interested in during the last century. The owners, who've been in the business their whole lives, pride themselves on having the lowest prices in the city. Don't miss the poster file, with images that run $4 each or three for $10.

69 E. 4th St., between Second Ave. and Bowery. ℂ **212/674-5296.** www.pageant books.com. Subway: F/V to Second Ave.; 6 to Bleecker St.

SKSK   Steve Keene is somewhere between the Henry Ford and the McDonald's of indie art. With his one-man assembly line, he's sold over 140,000 paintings. If you're looking to decorate on the cheap, you could do worse than S.K.'s factory outlet in Brooklyn. The cave-like space is packed with a vertiginous array of plywood cut-outs, furniture, and paintings. A $20 investment will bring you enough to decorate two or three rooms, with change left over.

85 Wythe Ave., between N. 10th and N. 11th sts. www.stevekeene.com. Subway: L to Bedford Ave.

HOUSEWARES

Broadway Panhandler   Pan reviews consistently put this place at the top. For restaurant-quality cookware and kitchen tools, you can't find a better combo of selection, price, and service.

477 Broome St., between Greene and Wooster sts. ℂ **212/966-3434.** www.broadwaypanhandler.com. Subway: C/E to Spring St.

Fishs Eddy   You can reel in remainders of custom china here. Prices are relatively low, certainly the best you'll do on a plate marked "Blue Plate Special." You can also find retro designs, including soda fountain glasses and vintage-looking flatware.

889 Broadway, at 19th St. ℂ **212/420-9020.** www.fishseddy.com. Subway: 4/5/6/L/N/R/Q/W to 14th St./Union Sq. Other location: *Brooklyn Heights*, 122 Montague St., between Henry and Hicks sts. ℂ **718/797-3990.** Subway: 2/3/M/R to Borough Hall.

Leader Restaurant Equipment & Supplies   Take us to Leader for great prices on kitchenware, especially Asian appointments like chopsticks, bowls, and plates.

191 Bowery, between Spring and Delancey sts. ℂ **800/666-6888** or 212/677-1982. Subway: J/M/Z to Bowery; F/V to Second Ave.

Lighting by Gregory   Great selection and good prices on lighting, plus a big collection of ceiling fans. The latest lighting trends can always be found.

158 Bowery, between Delancey and Broome sts. ℂ **888/811-FANS** or 212/226-1276. www.lightingbygregory.com. Subway: J/M/Z to Bowery; F/V to Second Ave.

National Wholesale Liquidators   Almost anything you would want inside a house—from batteries to cosmetics to water filters—can be found here at absurdly low prices. Cappuccino machines for under $20! The Mary Kate and Ashley Soft Touch Hair Dryer for under $10! Two hundred fifteen tall kitchen bags for under $5! The upstairs clothing section is often overlooked, though it's just as cheap. Hardware along with Manhattan-anomalous auto supplies pack the basement.

632 Broadway, between Bleecker and Houston sts. ℂ **212/979-2400**. www.nationalwholesaleliquidators.com. Subway: B/D/F/V to Broadway-Lafayette Ave.; 6 to Bleecker St.

Pearl Paint   Pearl Paint has the city's best art supply prices and selection, in a sprawling compound tinted by an air of genial

FREE Drop Stitch Drop Offs

Knitters and their ilk can widen their shopping options by trekking up to Westchester on the Yarn Bus. The bus connects New Yorkers with the Flying Fingers Yarn Shop, which carries those tofu and bamboo yarns you have so much trouble tracking down in Manhattan. The ride to charming Irvington, on the Hudson, takes about a half-hour and it's totally free. The bus runs twice a day on the weekends, leaving from various spots around mid- and Uptown. If those times and places aren't convenient, they'll make a custom arrangement for you. Call or email in advance to reserve your place. Look for the blue van. The blue van with the lamppost-sized needles piercing three jumbo yard balls on the roof. 19 Main St., Irvington, New York. ℂ **877/359-4648**. www.flyingfingers.com.

disarray. Specialty stores on the rear block (Lispenard) back up five floors of supplies in front (Canal). Frames, papers, canvas, and incidentals like day-planners and portfolios all carry the lowest prices in the city.

308 Canal St., between Broadway and Mercer St. ✆ **212/431-7932.** www.pearl paint.com. Subway: A/C/E or 1 to Canal St. Other location: *School of Visual Arts,* 209 E. 23rd St., at Third Ave. ✆ **212/592-2179.** Subway: 6 to 23rd St.

LUGGAGE, LEATHER & HANDBAGS

Altman Luggage   This old-time LES classic has wheeled luggage galore, in addition to businessperson sundries like pens, wallets, and watches. Already deep discounts get even deeper for closeouts and items that have been too long on the showroom floor.

135 Orchard St., between Rivington and Delancey sts. ✆ **212/254-7275.** www.altmanluggage.com. Subway: F to Delancey St.; J/M/Z to Essex St.

> ### Flower Power
>
> Two green thumbs go up for the selection of plant and flower stores on **28th Street between Sixth and Seventh avenues,** and overflowing onto Sixth Avenue. (For those with brown thumbs, a great selection of plastic plants awaits you.) The stores are a mix of wholesale and retail, with the best prices going to bulk buyers. Small purchasers can also reel in good buys, especially at **Starbright Floral Design** (150 W. 28th St., between Sixth and Seventh aves.; ✆ **800/520-8999;** www.starflor.com. Subway: 1 or N/R/W to 28th St.).

Jobson's   For 50-some years, Jobson's has been selling luggage and leather at only 10% above cost. Discount shoppers mingle with professional travelers here.

666 Lexington Ave., between 55th and 56th sts. ✆ **212/355-6846.** Subway: 6 to 51st St.

MUSIC

Between burning, shredding, and downloading, brick and mortar music stores are increasingly imperiled. It's hard for shops to match the prices of cut-rate Internet retailers like **www.alldirect. com,** and they definitely can't compete with free. If you still take your music in hard form, a broad selection of used CDs can be found on and around **St. Marks Place between Second and Third avenues** in the East Village. My favorite place, by far, is in the Flatiron District. At **Academy Records and CDs,** music junkies clog the aisles, sorting through secondhand shelves packed with classical, jazz, opera, and rock. Prices are excellent and the selection is forever in motion as Academy aggressively acquires collections.

Knock It Off

By lore, the first major New York swindle was Dutch settlers trading $24 worth of beads and baubles for the island of Manhattan. There's some question as to who was scamming whom in that arrangement (it's likely the natives didn't think the land could be bought or sold), but it set a karmic pattern that's still in place today. Tourists buy a Movado watch or a Chanel purse or Armani sunglasses, giggling as they leave $18 with some sucker of a vendor. It's not until the cheap knockoff disintegrates 3 days later that they realize which side of the con they were actually on. If the price seems too good to be true, it certainly is. **Orchard Street** on the Lower East Side has decent fakes, but the real action is in the stalls of **Chinatown.** The designer purses and bags are pretty convincing and they'll survive a little wear and tear. Along Canal Street between Lafayette and Mott you can also find decent wallets, scarves, perfume, and a surfeit of counterfeit Von Dutch. Vendors of the Vuittonesque and Burberryish keep to where the tourists are, and you'll also find knockoffs near Bloomie's in Midtown, and Broadway in the west 40's. Periodic police busts (of the sellers) keep proprietors on their toes, so expect the hot locations for the real fakes to be in a state of constant flux.

12 W. 18th St., between Fifth and Sixth aves. ℂ **212/242-3000.** www.academy-records.com. Subway: 4/5/6/L/N/R/Q/W to 14th St./Union Sq.; F/V to 14th St. **Vinyl:** *Academy LP's,* 77 E. 10th St., between Third and Fourth aves. ℂ **212/780-9166.** Subway: 6 to Astor Place.

PHOTO

Adorama   Photo pros flock to Adorama, which has unbelievably low prices for film, paper, and sundry items like blank cassettes. Also, there's a decent collection of used lenses and bodies in the back, though most of them are headed the way of the 8-track tape.

42 W. 18th St., between Fifth and Sixth aves. ℂ **212/675-6789.** www.adorama. com. Subway: 1 to 18th St.; F/V to 14th St.; L to Sixth Ave.

⬧ Vinyl Haven: The WFMU Record Fair

If you've got an issue with piracy, or album art is a must, old-fashioned vinyl is the way to go. Thrift stores top out at $2 per disk, though DJs assure there are slim pickings outside of classical. For record fanatics, the paramount weekend comes in early November, when the **WFMU Record Fair** comes to town. WFMU's free-form radio is one of New York's greatest cultural assets, and the record fair brings an incredible array of dealers. The show costs $5 to enter, but that fee includes free live bands, screenings in an AV room, and table after table of cheap CDs and vinyl. I ignore the $70 collector disks and head straight for the boxes under the table, where the two for $1 disks are most likely to be found. The fair is held at the **Metropolitan Pavilion** (125 W. 18th St., between Sixth and Seventh aves. Subway: 1 to 18th St.). For more information, call ✆ **201-521-1416**, ext. 243, or log on to www.wfmu.org/recfair. *Tip:* Sunday afternoon is the best bargain-hunter's time. Buyers are burned out and dealers are doing everything they can to keep from hauling all that obsolete technology back home.

B&H   A bustling 35,000-square-foot space holds B&H's massive inventory of film, digital equipment, lighting, DVD players, home theater systems, and a host of other photo-related products. Prices are very competitive, especially for used cameras and accessories. If you don't know exactly what you want, the pros here provide expert advice. *Note:* B&H is closed on Friday evenings, all day Saturday, and Jewish holidays.

420 Ninth Ave., between 33rd and 34th sts. ✆ **800/606-6969** or 212/444-6615. www.bhphotovideo.com. Subway: A/C/E to 34th St.

6 Free From New York

My apartment would be an exercise in minimalism if it weren't for the generosity of the sidewalks of New York. Lamps, chairs, end tables, and even the lovely beveled mirror in the kitchen have all been harvested from the bounty of the curbs. The key is to strike without hesitation because good stuff doesn't lay around the streets for long.

MANHATTAN SIDEWALK GIVE-AWAY/
TRASH PICKUP DAYS

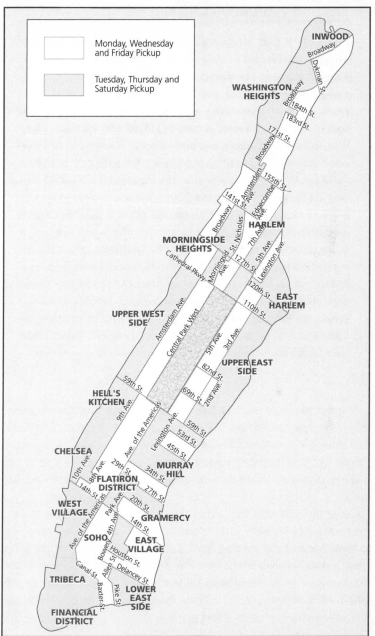

Monday, Wednesday and Friday Pickup

Tuesday, Thursday and Saturday Pickup

Getting Free & Dirt Cheap Furniture Online

It's no secret that bargains galore can be found in the ether. Collectibles, clothes, even subway maps end up on the online auction block. If you're in the market for furniture in New York City, you may have an advantage over your midwestern and West Coast rivals. Many of New York's eight million residents live in tiny spaces, and **ebay** (www.ebay.com) is loaded with our local treasures. But dressers, desks, and other pieces with heft can cost several hundred dollars to ship, doubling or tripling the cost of an ebay purchase. When you're doing your bidding keep an eye out for New York zip codes—you may be the only person who can get a Man with a Van to take it home for a reasonable price. In addition to ebay, **craigslist** (www.craigslist.org) is another site worth scoping. A whole section of postings is reserved for free items. Ugly furniture, moving boxes, pit bulls, boa constrictors, and computers are easy to come by, as well as less essential items like box turtles, hermit crab shelters, and 12-packs of nonalcoholic beer, purchased in error. Look for "Curb Alerts," which tip off the public to salvagable items about to be dumped unceremoniously on the street. Check back frequently because the free mosaic is constantly shifting.

A good place to start is the Department of Sanitation's website (www.nyc.gov/html/dsny), where you can find out the current collection schedule for any address in any of the boroughs. Unless you're a van owner, you'll probably want to target places that are within close hauling distance. (Trash-picking pros invest in small wheeled hand trucks.)

Generally, just after the first of the month is the best time to be on the prowl. People have just moved in or out, and they're more likely to have been of a disposing bent. Late May, at the end of the school year, is another excellent time. The streets around NYU and Columbia overflow with abandoned student goods. Though much of what you'll see is better suited to a dorm than your swanky digs, with careful culling you can always find gems.

Freecycle NYC `FREE` This new grass-roots organization is trying to do something about the inevitable waste that takes place in our megalopolis. They take three main tacks to hooking up discarders and consumers. The first is online, via a Yahoo Group (www.groups.yahoo. com/group/freecyclenewyorkcity) which generates almost a hundred leads a day. You can join for free. The main stipulation is that everything offered must be free—not even trading is allowed. Your second opportunity to clear out or stock up comes with **FreeMarts**. These fests allow reusable goods to change hands. Look for the Post-Holiday Re-Gifting event in January, and at least one other bazaar in the summer. The third option is the Reuse Center in Downtown Manhattan. Make an appointment to drop off a bag or two of goodies. While you're there, pick up free stuff to fill those new voids in your closet. Check the website, **www.recyclethisnyc.org**, to get the location and other information.

Swap-O-Matic `FREE` More art project than large-scale redistribution system, at least for now, this vending machine dispenses free items of marginal utility. To get swapping you first need to donate something to the machine. With that credit, you can select an item to take as your own. A computer and combination locks prevent gaming of the system. Giveaways tend to the shell necklace/used book/bottle opener end of things, but maybe the project will expand as the world's climate forces us to become more conscious of our consumption. Currently installed at Bluestockings on the Lower East Side.

172 Allen St., between Rivington and Stanton sts. ℭ **212/777-6028**. www.swap-o-matic.com. Subway: F/V to Second Ave.; J/M/Z to Essex St.

Swap-O-Rama-Rama Sort through 4,000 pounds of clothes, for free! That's the come-on to this community event, where you dump off some of your own fashion don'ts and then replenish your closet with whatever you find. A $10 donation is suggested, but that entitles you to much more than free clothing. There's film, comedy, and a host of workshops. "Shoppers" can get help with on-the-spot iron-ons, silk-screening, and tailoring. Successful projects are oohed and aahed over at the end of the day fashion show. Swaps are held seasonally; check the website for the location, **www.swaporamarama.org**.

7 Pet Project

Sure, your loyal, vicious Yorkie saves you thousands of dollars a month in bodyguards and private security services, but you don't want to turn around and sink all that cash into an expensive pet-care proposition. Fortunately, New York has a couple of places that provide veterinary support at pint-sized prices. Don't yet have that mouse-killing tabby in the house? NYC has pets available at low, low costs.

American Society for the Prevention of Cruelty to Animals Subsidized pet care is available at the Berg Memorial Animal Hospital & Clinic, run by this legendary group. An appointment for an exam with a vet costs $70, and an emergency visit is $100. They also provide shots, $20 for rabies and $25 for distemper, on top of the regular exam fee. If you need to get a pet before you can start worrying about pet care, the ASPCA also has adoption services. Cats and dogs start at $75, puppies and kittens at $125, and purebreds go up from there. The cost covers several necessities, including "pet Lojack"—a microchip should your new best friend make a break for freedom. If you want to microchip your current pet the cost is $25 with an exam, and $45 for walk-ins.

424 E. 92nd St., between First Ave. and York St. ℂ **212/876-7700.** www. aspca.org. Subway: 4/5/6 to 86th St.

Bide-A-Wee The name of this century-old charitable organization derives from the Scottish for stay awhile, though they'd prefer to put cats and dogs through the revolving door as quickly as possible. Adoptions here can be had for around $100, which covers a host of services. When it's time for follow-up, Bide-A-Wee's veterinary clinic is subsidized and among the most reasonable in the city.

410 E. 38th St., 2nd floor, between First Ave. and the FDR. ℂ **212/532-5884.** www.bideawee.org. Subway: 4/5/6/7/S to 42nd St./Grand Central Station.

The Brooklyn Animal Resource Coalition Love dogs, but not ready for the full-out commitment of daily walking and feeding? Billburg's BARC will let you test-drive a pooch. You'll be helping the shelter out by giving one of their minions some exercise, you'll have a handy conversation-starter, and who knows, maybe you'll form a bond. Allow a couple of hours if you want to walk or adopt.

253 Wythe Ave., at N. 1st St., Williamsburg, Brooklyn. ℂ **718/486-7489.** www. barcshelter.org. Subway: L to Bedford Ave.

Mayor's Alliance for NYC's Animals   Mayor Mike has ambitious plans to make us a no-kill city. To that end, his alliance connects low-income residents with low-cost spaying and neutering services. If you're in the pet market, the alliance puts on a series of adoption festivals. In addition to spontaneously falling for an unclaimed cur there, you can hook up your current pets with microchips at a special $25 rate. For citywide pet services, the alliance's website is a very helpful clearing house.

ⓒ **212/252-3250.** www.animalalliancenyc.org.

SHOPPING DOWNTOWN

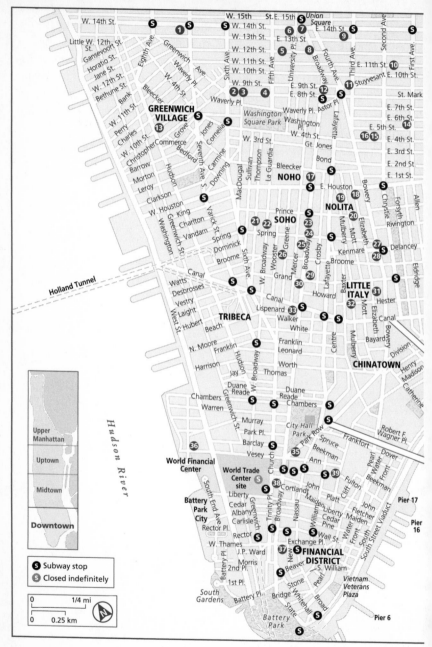

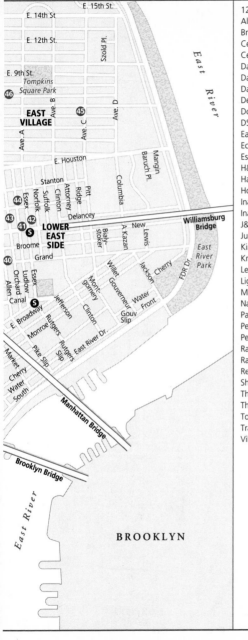

SHOPPING MIDTOWN

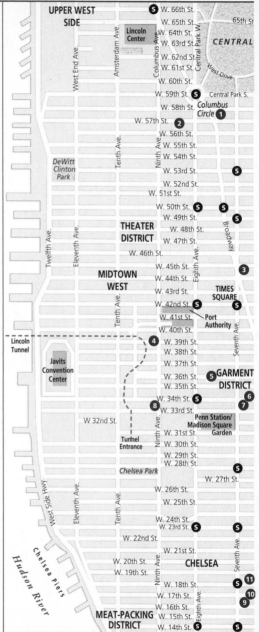

UPTOWN SHOPPING

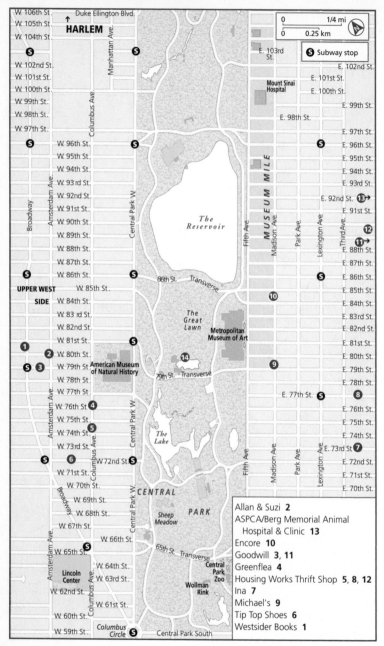

W. 106th St.
Duke Ellington Blvd.
W. 105th St.
HARLEM
W. 104th St.

Manhattan Ave.

E. 103rd St.

W. 102nd St.
E. 102nd St.
W. 101st St.
E. 101st St.
W. 100th St.
Mount Sinai Hospital
E. 100th St.
W. 99th St.
E. 99th St.
W. 98th St.
E. 98th St.
W. 97th St.

Columbus Ave.

E. 97th St.
W. 96th St.
E. 96th St.
W. 95th St.
E. 95th St.
W. 94th St.
E. 94th St.
W. 93rd St.
E. 93rd St.
W. 92nd St.
E. 92nd St.
W. 91st St.
E. 91st St.
W. 90th St.

Amsterdam Ave.

Central Park W.

The Reservoir

MUSEUM MILE

Fifth Ave.
Madison Ave.
Park Ave.
Lexington Ave.
Third Ave.

E. 89th St.
W. 89th St.
W. 88th St.
E. 88th St.
W. 87th St.
E. 87th St.
W. 86th St.
86th St. Transverse
E. 86th St.
UPPER WEST SIDE
W. 85th St.
E. 85th St.
W. 84th St.
E. 84th St.
W. 83rd St.
The Great Lawn
E. 83rd St.
W. 82nd St.
E. 82nd St.
W. 81st St.
Metropolitan Museum of Art
E. 81st St.
W. 80th St.
E. 80th St.
W. 79th St
American Museum of Natural History
79th St. Transverse
E. 79th St.
W. 78th St.
E. 78th St.
W. 77th St.
E. 77th St.
W. 76th St
W. 75th St.
E. 76th St.
W. 74th St.
E. 75th St.
W. 73rd St.
The Lake
E. 74th St.
E. 73rd St.
W.72nd St
Columbus Ave.
E. 72nd St.
W. 71st St.
E. 71st St.
W. 70th St.
E. 70th St.
W. 69th St.
CENTRAL
W. 68th St.
Sheep Meadow
PARK
W. 67th St.
W. 66th St.
W. 65th St.
65th St. Transverse
Central Park Zoo
W. 64th St.
W. 63rd St.
Wollman Rink
Lincoln Center
W. 62nd St.
W. 61st St.
Columbus Ave.
W. 60th St.
W. 59th St.
Columbus Circle
Central Park South

Broadway

0 | 1/4 mi
0 | 0.25 km

S Subway stop

Allan & Suzi **2**
ASPCA/Berg Memorial Animal Hospital & Clinic **13**
Encore **10**
Goodwill **3**, **11**
Greenflea **4**
Housing Works Thrift Shop **5**, **8**, **12**
Ina **7**
Michael's **9**
Tip Top Shoes **6**
Westsider Books **1**

A haven of elegant, Beaux Arts architecture, the Humanities and Social Sciences Library offers a wealth of free exhibits. *See p. 307 for more information.*

EXPLORING NEW YORK

W hen it comes to culture, New Yorkers have so many amazing options it's probably inevitable we start to take them a little for granted. We sometimes forget that many of the world's great treasures have found their way to our little island and its surrounding boroughs. New York is in a constant state of transformation, but miraculously a lot of history has survived, too, in houses, churches, and museums. Foundations and galleries protect New York's cutting-edge reputation, putting on thousands of risk-taking, avant-garde art shows every year. What's most amazing, given the out-of-control nature of New York rents, is how easy it is to access these jewels on the cheap. Many museums let the public in for free, and many more either have special pay-what-you-wish times or admission prices that are only suggestions. If it all seems a little overwhelming, you can get a professional to guide you through the cultural minefield. New York has a bushel of free tours as well. Just remember to get out there and take advantage—nothing lasts forever.

1 Museum Peace

Museum admission prices in New York are working their way skyward, with their inflation running higher than even our outrageous movie tickets. Fifteen bucks seems to be the going price for big institutions and the Guggenheim takes $18 (despite recent exhibitions like motorcycles and Armani that were closer to corporate promotions than art shows). It's a good thing that New York's cultural resources run deep. Below you'll find almost 40 places that never charge, 24 that have select times when the museum is free, and 7 museums that only suggest their admission prices. Even the Guggenheim and the MoMA will let you in for free if you time it right. Go and revel in NYC's embarrassment of cut-rate culture riches.

ALWAYS FREE

American Folk Art Museum Eva and Morris Feld Gallery `FREE`
The main Folk Art collection has moved to 53rd Street to rub shoulders with newly renovated MoMA, leaving not much beyond a gift shop in this original location. New acquisitions and a smattering of selections from the permanent collection fill the galleries. `FINE PRINT` A sign at the security desk notes that there's a $3 suggested donation, but nobody hits you up as you go in.

2 Lincoln Sq., Columbus Ave., between 65th and 66th sts., across from Lincoln Center. ✆ 212/595-9533. www.folkartmuseum.org. $3 suggested donation. Tues–Sat noon–7:30pm; Sun noon–5pm. Subway: 1 to 66th St.

Art Students League of New York Gallery `FREE` This independent art school, founded in 1875, is a New York legend. A host of big names started out here, including Norman Rockwell and Georgia O'Keeffe, who left behind work in the league's permanent collection. The galleries on the second floor exhibit portions of that collection along with art by current students, members, and other contemporaries.

215 West 57th St., between Broadway and Seventh Ave. ☎ 212/247-4510. www.
theartstudentsleague.org. Mon-Fri 9am-8:30pm; Sat-Sun 9:30am-5pm. Subway:
N/R/Q/W to 57th St.; B/D/E to Seventh Ave.

Audubon Terrace   Broadway, between 155th and 156th streets,
boasts a complex of educational and cultural institutions, housed
around a central courtyard with an odd, oversized statue of El Cid.
The sedate classical structures are highly unexpected in the middle of
a colorful Harlem neighborhood, so unexpected that few people
make the trek this far north. As a result, Audubon Terrace has been
hemorrhaging institutions at a rapid pace. All but two have flown
south.

The Hispanic Society of America `FREE`   Hispanic treasures ranging from Bronze Age tools to Goya portraits, seemingly assembled at
random, fill this musty but intriguing museum. Don't miss the intricate marble chapel sculptures on the first floor and the gorgeous
arabesque tiles upstairs. Audubon Terrace, Broadway, between 155th
and 156th sts. ☎ 212/926-2234. www.hispanicsociety.org. Tues–Sat
10am–4:30pm; Sun 1–4pm. Subway: 1 to 157th St.

American Academy of Arts and Letters `FREE`   This prestigious
century-old organization extends membership to the cream of the
nation's writers and artists. In the spring and fall exhibits highlight the
works of these artists, as well as the recipients of Academy prizes.
Three exhibits are mounted yearly. Audubon Terrace, Broadway,
between 155th and 156th streets. ☎ 212/368-5900. www.artsand
letters.org. Open when exhibitions are up, Tues–Sun 1–4pm. Subway:
1 to 157th St.

Austrian Cultural Forum `FREE`   The architecture of the new Austrian Cultural Forum has garnered more eyebrow raises than critical
praise. I find the exterior ominous, like a dagger looming over the
street. The interior is more attractive, with sleek touches compensat-
ing for a cold quality. The multilevel spaces accommodate several galleries. Austrian and European-themed shows rotate through. Films
and music programs round out the calendar. FINE PRINT Events are free,
but many require advance reservations.

11 E. 52nd St., between Fifth and Madison aves. ☎ 212/319-5300. www.acfny.org.
Mon-Sat 10am-6pm. Subway: E/V to 53rd St.

Carnegie Hall `FREE`   The Rose Museum recounts the practice, practice, practice it takes to get to this storied music hall. A chronology

and memorabilia are on view, in addition to occasional temporary exhibits on Carnegie legends like the Gershwins, Tchaikovsky, or Leonard Bernstein.

154 W. 57th St., 2nd floor, between 6th and 7th aves. ℰ **212/903-9629.** www. carnegiehall.org. Daily 11am–4:30pm and to ticket holders during concerts. Closed most of July and Aug. Subway: A/B/C/D/1 to 59th St.-Columbus Circle; N/Q/R/W to 57th St./Seventh Ave.

Center for Jewish History `FREE`   Beautiful new galleries document the Jewish experience. Photos, prints, and portraits are the primary mediums. See p. 301 in chapter 7 for a full review.

15 W. 16th St., between 5th and 6th aves. ℰ **212/294-8301.** www.cjh.org. *Reading Room and Genealogy Institute:* Mon–Thurs 9:30am–5pm; Fri by appt. *All other galleries:* Mon–Thurs 9:30am–5pm; Fri 9am–3pm. Subway: L/N/Q/R/W/4/5/6 to 14th St./Union Sq.

The Chancellor Robert R. Livingston Masonic Library of Grand Lodge `FREE`   The museum front room of the Masons' library is adorned with several display cases. Most artifacts are only of limited interest to non-Masons, although there is a grandfather clock that watched over George Washington's visits to a Yorktown, Virginia lodge. More interesting are the tours, which show off colorful meeting rooms and the ballroom whose design was lifted for the Titanic.

71 W. 23rd St., rear elevators to the 14th floor, between Fifth and Sixth aves. ℰ **212/337-6620.** www.nymasoniclibrary.org. Tours Mon–Fri 11am–3pm, call for Sat tours. Library open Mon, Wed–Fri 8:30am–4:30pm; Tues noon–8pm. Subway: F/V or N/R/W to 23rd St.

The City Reliquary `FREE`   This is the city's smallest museum, which packs its displays into a couple of windows fronting Williamsburg streets. Dedicated to NYC detritus, objects like subway tokens and false teeth washed up in Dead Horse Bay make the curatorial cut. Two locations, open 24-7, and guaranteed to hold your attention for at least a minute or two.

307 Grand St., at Havemeyer St., Williamsburg, Brooklyn. ℰ **718/782-4842.** www.cityreliquary.org. Other location: 370 Metropolitan Ave., between Havemeyer St. and Rev. Dr. Gardner C. Taylor Blvd., Williamsburg, Brooklyn. Subway to both locations: G/L Lorimer St.-Metropolitan Ave.

Fashion Institute of Technology Museum `FREE`   This museum on FIT's campus is long on historical fashion, specializing in the 20th century. Fashion showoffs complement surprisingly sophisticated student shows. Other exhibits display items from the special collections, like accessories or sketches.

The southwest corner of 7th Ave., at 27th St. ℭ **212/217-5970.** www.fitnyc.edu. Tues-Fri noon-8pm; Sat 10am-5pm. Subway: 1 to 28th St.

Federal Hall National Memorial FREE A former customs house, this columned Wall Street museum now recounts the long history of the site. After lengthy renovations, the grand reopening is set for the fall of 2006. See p. 312 in chapter 7 for a full review.

26 Wall St., at Nassau St. ℭ **212/825-6888.** www.nps.gov/feha. Mon-Fri 9am-5pm. Subway: 2/3/4/5 to Wall St.

Federal Reserve Bank FREE In addition to the gallery of the American Numismatic Society on the ground floor here, advance sign-up will give you the chance to glimpse a little of the building. It's basically a tour of a bank. A bank with the largest gold cache in the world, but still a bank. Along the way you'll see two short videos, one weirdly defensive about the employees of the currency-processing division, and one weirdly defensive about the employees who work with the gold. Five stories beneath the street you'll get to see the vault itself, which resembles a gym locker room, only with $90 billion in gold shimmering behind the bars. As a reward for your attention, they'll give you $1,000 in cash. Shredded cash. FINE PRINT Call 1 to 2 weeks in advance to reserve a space.

33 Liberty St., between William and Nassau sts. ℭ **212/720-6130.** www.newyork fed.org. Tours weekdays 9:30am, 10:30am, 11:30am, 1:30pm, and 2:30pm (they last about an hour). Subway: A/C/J/M/Z/2/3/4/5 to Fulton St./Broadway Nassau.

Fisher Landau Center for Art FREE Few New Yorkers know about the 25,000-square-foot exhibition and study center inside this converted Queens industrial space. The pristine galleries display painting, sculpture, and photography from 1960 to the present, including works by the likes of Agnes Martin, Robert Rauschenberg, and Cy Twombly. You'll find three floors of viewing pleasure. You'll also delight in the cultlike glazed eyes of security guards who relay your every move via walkie-talkies.

38-27 30th St., between 38th and 39th aves. ℭ **718/937-0727.** www.flcart.org. Thurs-Mon 10am-5pm; Fri 10am-7:45pm. Subway: N/W to 39th Ave.

☆ **Forbes Magazine Galleries** `FREE` Wind through well-maintained displays of Malcolm Forbes' idiosyncratic fancies in this whimsical boutique museum. See p. 300 in chapter 7 for a full review.

62 Fifth Ave., at 12th St. ✆ **212/206-5548**. www.forbesgalleries.com. Tues–Wed, Fri–Sat 10am–4pm. Subway: L/N/Q/R/W/4/5/6 to 14th St./Union Sq.

General Grant National Memorial `FREE` Manhattan is home to the nation's largest mausoleum, the graceful 1897 structure that houses the remains of General Ulysses S. Grant. For punch-line sticklers, Mrs. Julia Grant is interred here as well. The hushed interior conveys peaceful repose. There's a small on-site museum where you'll be surprised to discover what a big deal Grant's funeral was in New York. The tomb itself was once a huge attraction, but tourists have found more pressing enticements and the memorial feels secluded, nearly forgotten.

Riverside Dr., at 122nd St. ✆ **212/666-1640**. www.nps.gov/gegr. Daily 9am–5pm. Subway: 1 to 125th St.

Hall of Fame for Great Americans `FREE` You'd think a gigantic monument designed by Sanford White with tablets by Tiffany Studios, memorializing American heroes like Mark Twain, Abe Lincoln, and Susan B. Anthony, would be a major draw, but this oddball attraction is sadly overlooked. The distant location, on the Bronx Community College campus, might be part of the problem. If you're in the area don't miss out because the open colonnade with its 102 bronze busts and classical architecture is a wonderful surprise.

Hall of Fame Terrace, 181st St. and University Ave., the Bronx. ✆ **718/289-5161**. www.bcc.cuny.edu/halloffame. Daily 10am–5pm. Subway: 4 to 183rd St.

Hamilton Grange National Memorial `FREE` Federalist Paper author and first secretary of the treasury Alexander Hamilton started construction on his country home in 1800. Once part of a 32-acre estate, Hamilton Grange is now crowded by an undistinguished apartment building and an impudent church balcony. The National Park Service has well-maintained exhibits inside, including a scale model of the yellow Federal-style house as it looked when it was surrounded by the hills and trees of a vanished Harlem.

287 Convent Ave., between W. 141st and W. 142nd sts. ✆ **212/283-5154**. www. nps.gov/hagr. Wed–Sun 9am–5pm. Subway: 1 to 137th St.; A/B/C/D to 145th St.

Hebrew Union College–Jewish Institute of Religion, Brookdale Center FREE   Multiple galleries here display assorted Judaica and contemporary artwork of a Jewish bent. The curatorial team doesn't seem particularly discerning—clunkers and standouts are given equal prominence. Exhibitions change pretty regularly, with 8 to 10 moving through each year. FINE PRINT A photo ID is required to enter.

1 W. 4th St., between Broadway and Mercer St. ℂ **212/824-2205.** www.huc.edu/ museums/ny. Mon–Thurs 9am–5pm; Fri 9am–3pm; selected Sundays. Subway: N/R/W to 8th St.; 6 to Astor Place.

Irish Hunger Memorial FREE   This recent addition to the downtown Hudson waterfront memorializes the Irish famine of 1845–52. The center of the installation is a famine-era cottage moved stone by stone from the old country, resting on a field of blackthorn and heather. Take the path to the memorial's top and you'll be treated to sublime views of the Statue of Liberty and Ellis Island.

Vesey St. and North End Ave. www.batteryparkcityparks.org. Daily 6am–1am. Subway: 1/2/3/A/C to Chambers St.

The Italian American Museum FREE   The Italian-American presence in New York City goes back to the 1640s, but the bulk of the permanent exhibits here focus on the great migration around the turn of the last century. Artifacts illustrate immigrant life and the formation of the first Little Italys. Souvenirs of Caruso, Toscanini, and DiMaggio are among the items on display here. Temporary exhibits come through every couple of months.

28 W. 44th St., 17th floor, between Fifth and Sixth aves. ℂ **212/642-2020.** www. italianamericanmuseum.org. Mon–Thurs 10am–4pm. Subway: B/D/F/V to 42nd St.; 7 to Fifth Ave.

John M. Mossman Lock Collection FREE   When you first enter this room you think "well, it's just a bunch of old locks." Inevitably, though, as you learn more about the evolution of keys and vaults you get drawn in. The exhibit includes 4,000-year-old Egyptian devices, Renaissance locks with elaborate tracery, and spectacularly crafted 19th-century time locks. Sign in with the guard on the ground floor and you'll be taken to the exhibit, on a second-floor balcony overlooking the landmark General Society of Mechanics and Tradesmen library.

20 W. 44th St., between Fifth and Sixth aves. ℭ **212/921-1767.** www.general society.org. Sept-Mar Mon-Thurs 9am-7pm, Fri 9am-5pm; Apr-Aug Mon-Thurs 9am-6pm, Fri 9am-5pm. Closed July. Subway: 7 to 5th Ave.; B/D/F/V to 42nd St.

The Judaica Museum of the Hebrew Home for the Aged at Riverdale `FREE` This modest museum displays Judaica ranging from mezuzot to Persian ivory paintings to miniature folk-art arks. Stunning Hudson views provide additional incentive to make a jaunt to the Bronx.

5691 Palisade Ave., Riverdale, the Bronx. ℭ **718/581-1787.** www.hebrewhome. org/museum. Mon-Thurs 1-4:30pm; Sun 1-5pm. Subway: 1 to 242nd St.-Van Cortlandt Park.

Lesbian, Gay, Bisexual & Transgender Community Center Museum `FREE` This isn't really a museum per se, but a community center that puts up exhibits in its hallways. There's a lot of erotic art, along with the occasional historical perspective, like a recent encapsulation of a San Francisco public library archive. The real gem in this building is the Keith Haring Bathroom. Converted to a meeting room on the second floor, this space pulsates with life thanks to a spectacular, salacious mural created by Haring shortly before his death.

208 W. 13th St., between Seventh and Greenwich aves. ℭ **212/620-7310.** www. gaycenter.org. Lobby open daily, 9am-11pm. Subway: 1/2/3 or F/V to 14th St.; L to Sixth Ave.

Madame Alexander Heritage Gallery `FREE` Immigrant daughter and lifelong New Yorker Madame Beatrice Alexander Behrman pioneered dollmaking. Her version of *Gone With the Wind*'s Scarlett was the first doll to be based on a pop culture character. More on the story can be found in the Harlem headquarters, with its displays of photos, advertising, and, of course, dolls. Over 600 fill the display cases. You can also see dolls-under-construction in the factory, and dolls undergoing treatment at the doll hospital. Call ahead, as tours are by appointment only. Pediaphobics should steer clear.

615 W. 131st St., 6th floor, between Broadway and Twelfth Ave. ℭ **212/283-5900.** www.madamealexander.com. Tours Mon, Wed, Fri, and alternating Saturdays, 11am and 4pm, by appointment only. Subway: 1 to 125th St.

Museum of American Illustration `FREE` Illustrators never seem to get their proper respect as visual artists, constantly upstaged by showoff painters and photographers. The two galleries maintained by the Society of Illustrators strive to remedy that situation. Contest winners and works of society members can be found on the walls, along with classics from the permanent collection (the Society was formed in 1901, so there's a lot to fall back on). Exhibits change frequently.

28 E. 63rd St., between Park and Lexington aves. ✆ 212/838-2560. www.societyillustrators.org. Tues 10am–8pm; Wed–Fri 10am–5pm; Sat noon–4pm. Subway: N/R/W/4/5/6 to 59th St.

Museum of Biblical Art FREE
With its de rigueur acronym, MOBIA makes a game effort to fit in with its museum brethren in the heart of New Gomorrah. Recent subjects have ranged from oil lamps of the Holy Land to engravings by Fauvist Georges Rouault. Pagans and Satanists may tire quickly, as shows are limited to Judeo-Christian expressions. A range of sponsors, including the American Bible Society, bankrolls free admission for all. They also bankroll a changing roster of concerts, lectures, films, and tours. Event seating is limited, so you may want to reserve in advance.

1865 Broadway, at W. 61st St. ✆ 212/408-1500. www.mobia.org. Tues–Wed, Fri–Sun 10am–6pm; Thurs 10am–8pm. Subway: A/B/C/D/1 to 59th St./Columbus Circle.

FREE **Broadway Stars**

Given the city's light pollution, it would seem that whomever came up with the idea of building an observatory in Manhattan wasn't totally clear on the concept. Amazingly, however, some celestial sights do seep through our glowing night skies. On a Columbia University rooftop you can see for yourself. Select nights during the school year, professors and graduate students gloss the stars at the historic Rutherfurd Observatory. There are also family nights for kids ages 6 to 10, usually one Saturday a month. The price for all this isn't astronomical—it's totally free. **Pupin Physics Laboratories,** 550 West 120th St., between Broadway and Amsterdam Ave. Follow the signs to the roof. ✆ 212/854-1976. www.astro.columbia.edu. Subway: 1 to 116th St./Columbia University. After sunset and weather permitting, of course.

☆ **National Museum of the American Indian** FREE Housing Native American treasures in a former arm of the federal government seems a bit of a cruel irony, but the overall effect here is of reverence for endangered arts. This Smithsonian branch augments its exhibits with films and videos; check the schedule at www.nativenetworks.si.edu.

There's programming for kids, too, including storybook readings and workshops. Everything is free, though craft workshops can have material fees of up to $25. Some events require reservations. See also p. 316 in chapter 7.

1 Bowling Green, between State and Whitehall sts. ⓒ 212/514-3700. www.american indian.si.edu. Daily 10am-5pm; Thurs until 8pm. Subway: 4/5 to Bowling Green; 1 to South Ferry.

The National Museum of Catholic Art and History `FREE` Despite the intimidating name, this new institution isn't solely dedicated to wounds, gore, and thorns. Progressive contemporary Catholic art often lines these walls. With twelve galleries spread over three floors, there's a lot to look at, although the East Harlem location makes this an under-trafficked destination. FINE PRINT Admission is free, although there is a box in the foyer if you want to make a $5 suggested donation.

443 E. 115th St., between First and Pleasant aves. ⓒ 212/828-5209. www.nmcah.org. Open Wed-Sun 10am-4pm. Subway: 6 to 116th.

The New York City Police Museum `FREE` This museum borders on hagiography, but plenty of good little nuggets can be found here, including a 1933 letter from a private citizen suggesting police cars adopt sirens. See p. 311 in chapter 7 for a full review.

100 Old Slip, between Water and South sts., 2 blocks south of Wall St. ⓒ 212/ 480-3100. www.nycpolicemuseum.org. Suggested admission of $5 is not enforced. Tues-Sat 10am-5pm, Sun 11am-5pm. Subway: 2/3 to Wall St.; J/M/Z to Broad St.

Nicholas Roerich Museum `FREE` One of New York's least-known museums showcases the Russian scholar and painter Nicholas Roerich. A genteel Riverside Drive town house holds three floors of galleries, cluttered with Roerich's paintings. The images favor Russian icons and Himalayan landscapes. Although the bright colors and stylized lines border on the cartoonish, the overall effect is impressive. Objects gathered in Roerich's Asian explorations are scattered throughout the museum and a subtle spiritual air pervades. The museum's motto "Pax Cultura" (Peace Through Culture) gets expressed in a full schedule of free concerts and poetry readings. Music plays Sundays at 5pm; check online for additional dates and times.

319 W. 107th St., between Riverside Dr. and Broadway. ⓒ 212/864-7752. www. roerich.org. Tues-Sun 2-5pm. Subway: 1 to 110th St.

Onassis Cultural Center FREE Aristotle Onassis—or as most of us know him, Mr. Jackie O.—was the man behind this Midtown institution, which supports Hellenic art and culture. Winding stairs in the middle of the Olympic Tower atrium's south side lead to a warren of galleries with unexpected waterfall views. Samples from Byzantium show off the flat faces of a world before linear perspective was invented. Modern Greek efforts can often be found here as well. On the ground floor, a long-term display shows off rare casts of Parthenon marbles.

The Olympic Tower atrium, 641 Fifth Ave., entrance just east of Fifth on 51st or 52nd sts. (?) **212/486-4448.** www. onassisusa.org. Mon–Sat 10am–6pm. Subway: E/V to 53rd St.

Pratt Galleries FREE The fruits of Pratt Institute's prestigious arts and design programs can be found in the galleries the school runs. Current student shows are mixed in with alumni and faculty exhibitions, as well as those of other artistic innovators.

144 W. 14th St., between Sixth and Seventh aves. (?) **212/647-7778.** www. pratt.edu. Tues–Fri 10:30am–5:30pm; Sat noon–5pm. Subway: 1/2/3 and F/V to 14th St.; L to 6th Ave. Other location: *Schafler Gallery, Pratt campus:* 200 Willoughby Ave. Ft. Greene, Brooklyn. (?) **718/636-3517.** Mon–Fri 9am–5pm. Subway: G to Clinton-Washington aves.

FREE **Socrates Sculpture Park**

Among the most glamorous of New York's former industrial dumps, Socrates Sculpture Park brings large-scale modern art to the banks of the East River. The huge open field here encourages sculptors to spread out. The work, organic in feel and usually made by emerging artists, can make a visitor feel that a lot more than a river separates them from the chichi precincts of uptown Manhattan. Views back in that direction aren't too hard on the eyes, however. See p. 55 for their cinema series. 32-01 Vernon Blvd., at Broadway. Long Island City, Queens. (?) **718/956-1819.** www.socratessculpturepark.org. Daily 10am–sunset. Subway: N/W to Broadway. Walk 8 blocks along Broadway toward the East River.

☆ **SculptureCenter** FREE Though this institution has been supporting and showcasing modern sculpture since 1928, its new home in a former Queens trolley repair shop can make a visitor feel like she's come to a start-up. Maya Lin's industrial-chic design is of the moment, but many of the touches are timeless. Ceilings soar 40 feet in the main room, and the basement project spaces are like minimalist catacombs. The rough edges haven't been disguised, but the overall effect is still refined, a perfect backdrop for the contemporary sculptures and installation art exhibited here. I love this place—it's a miniature version of what the Tate Modern in London should have been.

44-19 Purves St., off Jackson Ave., Long Island City, Queens. © 718/361-1750. www.sculpture-center.org. Thurs-Mon 11am-6pm. Some shows have a $5 suggested donation, not enforced. Subway: E/V to 23rd St./Ely. G to Court St. 7 to Court House Sq.

Sony Wonder Technology Lab FREE Sony sucks in new generations of technology addicts with this four-level supermodern demonstration center. Kids can try their hands at robotics, medical imaging, and video game design, among other expensive toys. Free movies round out the stimuli; see p. 51 in chapter 2. FINE PRINT Reservations should be made in advance, up to 1 week ahead. Call on a weekday between 8am and 2pm. Otherwise, you may not get in, or you may get in at a less convenient hour later in the day.

550 Madison Ave., at 56th St. © 212/833-8100, or 212/833-5414 for reservations. www.sonywondertechlab.com. Tues-Sat 10am-5pm; Sun noon-5pm; last entrance 30 min. before closing. Subway: E/N/R/V/W to Fifth Ave.; 4/5/6 to 59th St.

Storefront for Art and Architecture FREE Designed with odd panels that expand into the street, this idiosyncratic institution does a lot with its very narrow space. Always intelligent exhibits explore architecture, art, and design.

97 Kenmare St., between Mulberry St. and Cleveland Place, near Lafayette St. © 212/431-5795. www.storefrontnews.org. Tues-Sat 11am-6pm. Subway: 6 to Spring St.; N/R/W to Prince St.

Tibet House U.S. FREE This institution presents Tibetan art through a small permanent collection and spacious temporary exhibits. See p. 300 in chapter 7 for a review.

22 W. 15th St., 2nd floor, between Fifth and Sixth aves. © 212/807-0563. www. tibethouse.org. Mon-Fri noon-5pm. Subway: L/N/Q/R/W/4/5/6 to 14th St./Union Sq.

Urban Center FREE The landmark 1882 Villard Houses on Madison Avenue have an exclusive look, but the north side is actually open to the public. Enter the central courtyard, designed like an Italian palazzo by McKim, Mead & White, and take the door on your left.

The Municipal Art Society and the Architectural League of New York both keep galleries here, with rotating exhibits detailing a love of the city. While you're here, check out the bookstore's huge selection of urban planning and architecture tomes.

The Municipal Art Society. ✆ **212/935-3960.** www.mas.org. Architectural League of New York: ✆ **212/753-1722.** www.archleague.org. Villard Houses: 451-455 Madison Ave. Galleries open Mon-Wed, Fri-Sat 11am-5pm. Urban Center Books: ✆ **212/935-3595.** www.urbancenterbooks.com. 457 Madison Ave. Mon-Fri 10am-6:30pm; Sat noon-5:30pm. Subway: 6 to 51st St.

Whitney Museum of American Art at Altria `FREE` This tiny Whitney outpost shows contemporary artists. The lobby is often adorned with large-scale modern sculpture. See p. 307 in chapter 7 for a full review.

120 Park Ave., southwest corner at 42nd St., opposite Grand Central Terminal. ✆ **917/663-2453.** www.whitney.org. Gallery Mon-Wed, Fri 11am-6pm; Thurs 11am-7:30pm. Sculpture Court Mon-Sat 7:30am-9:30pm; Sun and holidays 11am-7pm. Extended hours for performances and lectures. Subway: 4/5/6/7/S to Grand Central.

SOMETIMES FREE

Several museums that won't give up their goods for free full-time do set aside special hours and days where you can pay what you wish. If you're feeling energetic, you can link up multiple stops. Thursday nights are popular admission by donation nights in Manhattan. Although many of the Bronx's attractions are spread far afield, Wednesday is a clearinghouse day when many of them relax their entrance policies. Beware the last free day before an exhibition ends. More than a few procrastinators call New York home, and you can find what looks like all of them taking advantage of a final free window of opportunity.

American Folk Art Museum Recently relocated, the new folk art building has generated some serious architectural buzz for its slender modern design. Although the structure is fitting for a MoMA neighbor, its high-tech finishes are something less than harmonious with the rustic works on display. Rotating exhibitions complement the permanent collection, which includes some amazing oddball autodidacts.

45 W. 53rd St., between 5th and 6th aves. ✆ **212/265-1040.** www.folkartmuseum. org. Regular admission $9; free Fri after 5:30pm. Tues-Sun 10:30am-5:30pm; Fri 10:30am-7:30pm. Subway: E/V to Fifth Ave./53rd St.

Sometimes Free (or Pay-What-You-Wish) Museums

Tuesday	Wednesday	Thursday	Friday	Saturday	Sunday
China Institute (Tues 6-8pm)	Bronx Museum of the Arts (Wed noon-9pm)	Children's Museum of the Arts (Thurs 4-6pm)	Guggenheim Museum (Fri 6-8pm)	Brooklyn Museum of Art (First Sat 11am-11pm)	Frick Collection (Sun 11am-1pm)
	Museum of Jewish Heritage: A Living Memorial to the Holocaust (Wed 4-8pm)	China Institute (Thurs 6-8pm)	International Center of Photography (Fri 5-8pm)	The Studio Museum in Harlem (First Sat 10am-6pm)	Museum of the City of New York (Sun 10am-noon)
		Dahesh Museum of Art (First Thurs 6-9pm)	The Morgan Library & Museum (Fri 7-9pm)		New York Hall of Science (Sun 10-11am, Sept-June)
		The Jewish Museum (Thurs 5-8pm)	Museum of Modern Art (MoMA) (Fri 4-8pm)		
		Museum of Arts and Design (Thurs 6-8pm)	Museum of Chinese in the Americas (Fri noon-7pm)		
			The Museum of the Moving Image (Fri 4-8pm)		
			New York Hall of Science (Fri 2-5pm, Sept-June)		
			The Noguchi Museum (First Fri 10am-5pm)		
			The Rubin Museum of Art (Fri 7-10pm)		
			South Street Seaport Museum (Third Fri 5-9pm)		
			Whitney Museum of American Art (Fri 6pm-9pm)		

Asia Society   John D. Rockefeller III founded the Asia Society in the mid-fifties to encourage cultural exchanges and understanding between Asians and Americans. The newly renovated headquarters building has beautiful galleries, showing off parts of Rockefeller's collection in addition to rotating exhibits. The interior architecture is impressive, especially the sleek new staircase that looks like a snake's skeleton wandering up the floors.

725 Park Ave., at 70th St. ℂ 212/288-6400. www.asiasociety.org. Regular admission $10; free Fri 6-9pm, except July 4th-Labor Day. Tues-Sun 11am-6pm; Fri 11am-9pm, except July 4th-Labor Day. Subway: 6 to 68th St./Hunter College.

Bronx Museum of the Arts   This hulk of modernity plunked down amid the Art Deco restraint of the Grand Concourse puts on adventurous shows. Most of the artists who get exhibited here have logged time as Bronx residents. If not, they'll represent some aspect of New York's cultural diversity. Entrance is by a suggested admission, though the suggestion gets dropped all day Wednesdays, which are completely free.

1040 Grand Concourse, at 165th St., the Bronx. ℂ 718/681-6000. www.bxma. org. Suggested admission $5; free Wed all day. Wed noon-9pm; Thurs-Sun noon-6pm. Subway: B/D/4 to 161st St./Yankee Stadium.

Brooklyn Museum of Art   The second-largest art museum in the US of A, the Brooklyn Museum is as spruced up and thriving as the borough that hosts it. With a glorious new entryway, remodeled exhibitions, and a building with over half a million square feet, there are several days' worth of exploring to be done here. The Egyptian collection is world-class and beautifully displayed, with informative, well-written notes accompanying each object. The fourth floor's period rooms are definitely worth a peek. Don't miss the Jan Schenck House, a touch of Dutch in old Breuckelen that somehow survived on the edge of Jamaica Bay from 1675 to 1952.

200 Eastern Pkwy., at Washington Ave., Brooklyn. ℂ 718/638-5000. www. brooklynmuseum.org. Suggested admission $8; free 1st Sat of the month 11am-11pm. Wed-Fri 10am-5pm; 1st Sat of the month 11am-11pm; each Sat thereafter 11am-6pm; Sun 11am-6pm. Subway: 2/3 to Eastern Pkwy./Brooklyn Museum.

Children's Museum of the Arts   This institution, on an industrial stretch between SoHo and Chinatown, is dedicated to getting kids involved with art. Kids 12 and under and families roll up their sleeves for informative workshops, which cover everything from puppet making to computer drawing. On the walls you'll find selections from the museum's permanent collection, including some great WPA pieces, or rotating exhibits of kid-friendly artists like Keith Haring. Call or check the website for the current exhibition and activities schedule.

☆ FREE Date Night: First Saturdays at the Brooklyn Museum

One of New York's best cheap date opportunities comes once a month at the Brooklyn Museum. Every first Saturday the museum transforms itself into a house party on a massive scale. The crowd is more diverse than the U.N. General Assembly, with a dizzying range of ages, cultures, and castes represented. The museum keeps most of its galleries open for your perusal. When you run low on witty commentary, distractions like films and lectures beckon. Dance performances can be found, too, or if the date is going particularly well, you might let your feet work the floor yourself. The live music performances tend to be upbeat and very danceable. There's no charge for any of this and nobody hits you up for a donation. The night is so festive that your date may not even notice just how cheap it's been. See the Brooklyn Museum review above for address and subway directions. Some attractions require tickets which, although free, may require standing on line.

182 Lafayette St., between Broome and Grand sts. ℂ **212/941-9198.** www.cmany. org. Regular admission $8, but pay what you wish Thurs 4–6pm. Wed, Fri–Sun noon–5pm; Thurs noon–6pm. Subway: 6 to Spring St.

China Institute A scholarly approach informs the exhibits at this eighty-year-old culture and arts center. Narrowly focused shows present beautifully crafted versions of Chinese calligraphy, painting, architecture, and textile work. Through the spring of 2007, consecutive exhibitions will look at the influence of traditional Chinese books on contemporary Chinese artists.

125 E. 65th St., between Park and Lexington aves. ℂ **212/744-8181.** www.china institute.org. Mon–Sat 10am–5pm; Tues, Thurs 10am–8pm. Regular admission $5, free Tues and Thurs 6–8pm. Subway: 6 to 68th St.-Hunter College.

Dahesh Museum of Art This small museum presents the cream of classicist art, the academic school dedicated to European art before the academy was tainted by Impressionism. Renaissance, baroque, and rococo traditions play out on elaborate canvases documenting historical subjects and pastoral life. The Dahesh recently upgraded to three expansive floors in an office building and charges admission. The first Thursday of the month is free, however.

580 Madison Ave., at 57th St. ✆ 212/759-0606. www.daheshmuseum.org. Regular admission $10; free the first Thurs of every month 6-9pm. Tues-Sun 11am-6pm; until 9pm the first Thurs of every month. Subway: F to 57th St.; E/V to 53rd St./Fifth Ave.; N/R/W to 59th St./Fifth Ave.

Frick Collection Coke (the stuff for steel, not the soda or the stimulant) was very, very good to Henry Clay Frick, who was a Gilded Age plutocrat by the age of 30. When it came time to decorate the walls of his Upper East Side palace he looked to the likes of Titian, Vermeer, and Goya. Hank didn't skimp on the furniture or carpeting, either. Though there is a slightly musty quality to this place (it dates to 1914), the collection is undeniably impressive, and special exhibitions have lately garnered plenty of buzz.

1 E. 70th St., at Fifth Ave. ✆ 212/288-0700. www.frick.org. Regular admission $15; pay what you wish Sun 11am-1pm. Tues-Sat 10am-6pm; Sun 11am-5pm. Subway: 6 to 68th St.

Guggenheim Museum Artists complained bitterly about the curved walls that spiral up seven stories, but Frank Lloyd Wright knew what he was doing and flat art mounts on the walls of the Guggie just fine. You'll feel like you're climbing through a nautilus shell as you view the latest temporary installation in the central atrium, recently tending toward crowd-pleasers like Norman Rockwell. A tower alongside the spiral hosts a permanent collection stocked with Chagalls, Matisses, van Goghs, and Picassos. For a whole 120 minutes a week, on Friday nights, the Guggenheim lowers itself to letting regular folks poke around for free.

1071 Fifth Ave., at 88th St. ✆ 212/423-3500. www.guggenheim.org. Regular admission $18; pay what you wish Fri 5:45-7:45pm. Sat-Wed 10am-5:45pm; Fri 10am-7:45pm. Subway: 4/5/6 to 86th St.

International Center of Photography The ICP does a good job of balancing photography's past and future, with Daguerreotypes and digital receiving as much wall time as the classic b&w street photographers of the '50s and '60s. Usually three separate exhibitions are up at any given time, except when the museum's two floors are turned over to a larger survey like contemporary African work, or the ICP Triennial, which showcases the best new photography.

1133 6th Ave., at 43rd St. ✆ **212/857-0000**. www.icp.org. Regular admission $10, pay what you wish Fri 5-8pm. Tues-Thurs, Sat-Sun 10am-6pm; Fri 10am-8pm. Subway: B/D/F/V to 42nd St.

The Jewish Museum   Four thousand years of Jewish history for this? Absolutely. A French Gothic chateau on the Upper East Side holds these remarkable collections, which chronicle the twists and turns of the Jewish experience. Everything from ancient artifacts to Borscht Belt ruminations from television's Golden Age can be found under this roof.

1109 Fifth Ave., at 92nd St. ✆ **212/423-3200**. www.thejewishmuseum.org. Regular admission is $10 adults, but it's pay what you wish Thurs 5-8pm. Sun-Wed 11am-5:45pm; Thurs 11am-8pm; Fri 11am-3pm. Subway: 4/5 to 86th St.; 6 to 96th St.

The Morgan Library & Museum   J. P. Morgan's collection of manuscripts, books, drawings, and prints, has been housed in this McKim, Mead & White masterpiece since 1906. The building recently celebrated its centennial by doubling its public exhibition space with a glass and steel Renzo Piano expansion. Illuminated manuscripts, Rembrandt's etchings, and ancient cylinder seals, were among the first shows out of the chute.

225 Madison Ave., at 36th St. ✆ **212/685-0008**. www.themorgan.org. Regular admission is $12 adults, but free Fri 7-9pm. Mon-Thurs 10:30am-5pm; Fri 10:30am-9pm; Sat 10am-6pm; Sun 11am-6pm. Subway: 6 to 33rd St.

Museum of Arts and Design   Craft design gets its 15 minutes of fame at this small, stylish Midtown museum. Exhibits focus on emerging artists and new ideas of form, especially as the latter follows function. Clay, glass, wood, metal, and fiber are among the materials represented. For big spenders, the artisans on display often have their wares available in the shop. In 2008, MAD will upgrade to 2 Columbus Circle, where remodeled digs will allow the museum to triple its exhibition space.

40 W. 53rd St., between Fifth and Sixth aves. ✆ **212/956-3535**. www.american craftmuseum.org. Regular admission $9; pay what you wish Thurs 6-8pm. Daily 10am-6pm, Thurs 10am-8pm. Subway: E/V to 53rd St./Fifth Ave.

Museum of Chinese in the Americas   This small museum in an old public school building is dedicated to the Chinese immigrant experience. Oral history projects, photo shows, and art installations all have a place here, as do elaborate re-creations of Los Angeles Chinese restaurant banquet rooms.

70 Mulberry St., 2nd floor, at Bayard St. © **212/619-4785.** www.moca-nyc.org. Regular admission $3; free all day Fri. Tues-Thurs, Sat-Sun noon-6pm; Fri noon-7. Subway: J/M/N/Q/R/W/Z/6 to Canal St.

Museum of the City of New York   A gracious 1932 neo-Georgian mansion houses exhibits tracing NYC from the windmills of its Dutch colonial days up to its present status as the undisputed capital of the world. Lovely period rooms and a collection of theatrical memorabilia are highlights of the collection. The museum often throws in free music and film programs with the price of your admission.

Fifth Ave., at 103rd St. © **212/534-1672.** www.mcny.org. Suggested admission $9; free 10am-noon Sun. Free also if you work or live in East Harlem (tell the desk you're a neighbor). Tues-Sun 10am-5pm. Subway: 6 to 103rd St.

Museum of Jewish Heritage: A Living Memorial to the Holocaust   This institution's unwieldy name reflects its dual callings as museum and memorial. The six-sided original building has a permanent exhibit that puts a human face on the Holocaust. A recently completed new wing houses ambitious temporary exhibits. The renovation also brought an installation by Andy Goldsworthy. His *Garden of Stones* juts out towards the Hudson, creating a contemplative space enlivened by dwarf oaks growing inside 18 hollow boulders. Though most of the time there is an admission charge here, access to the garden is always free.

36 Battery Place, near Little West St. © **646/437-4200.** www.mjhnyc.org. Regular admission $10; free Wed 4-8pm. Sun-Tues, Thurs 10am-5:45pm; Wed 10am-8pm, Fri 10am-5pm (closed 3pm during Eastern Standard Time and on the eve of Jewish holidays). Subway: 4/5 to Bowling Green, R/W to Whitehall; 1 to South Ferry.

Museum of Modern Art (MoMA)   Van Gogh's *Starry Night,* Picasso's *Les Demoiselles d'Avignon,* and Mondrian's *Broadway Boogie-Woogie* have forsaken the relative charms of low-rise industrial Queens for the comfort of high-rise corporate Midtown. The nothing-left-to-chance makeover of MoMA has resulted in a structure with the overall feel of a nicely appointed Fortune 500 headquarters. Of course, for $650 million the finishes *should* look pretty damn nice. You'll pay through the nose for the privilege of wandering these manicured halls, except on Friday nights, which are free courtesy of corporate sponsorship. Is it just me, or could they have spent a bit less on top-grade marble, and allowed the art to be a little more accessible instead?

FREE No-Pressure Pier

The burnished public spaces at Chelsea Piers are attractive, but they lack the ramshackle charm of laid-back **Pier 63,** just to the north. The pier itself is actually a 1946 Erie Lackawanna Railroad barge, which plays host to historical ships and a 1946 E-L caboose, which is open for touring. Free music and dance performances pass through the stage at the back, and the cafe serves up reasonably priced snacks during the warmer months. There's even free ping-pong in front of the Lightship *Frying Pan,* a 1929 floating lighthouse raised from the bottom of the Chesapeake Bay. The most impressive boat on the pier is the *John J. Harvey* fireboat (www.fireboat.org). It's a spectacular scene when this retired fire department mainstay (it was in service between 1931 and 1994, and temporarily brought out of retirement on 9/11) shoots its high-pressure hoses. Free public tours of the boat run sporadically, often in concert with other riverfront-themed events, and occasional free excursions leave from the Pier 63 dock. Keep an eye open for the free fall foliage tour. The Harvey becomes the poor man's QEII, cruising up the Hudson to Cold Spring, with a return trip back the next day. Check the website for details and to sign up for a tour. Pier 63, the Hudson at 23rd St., accessible via a ramp at the back of the parking lot just north of Basketball City. ✆ **212/989-6363.** www.pier63maritime.com. Subway: C/E to 23rd St.

11 W. 53rd St., between Fifth and Sixth aves. ✆ **212/708-9400.** www.moma.org. Regular admission $20; free Fri 4–8pm. Wed–Mon 10:30am–5:30pm; Fri 10:30–8pm. Subway: E/V to Fifth Ave.

The Museum of the Moving Image   Adolph Zuckor opened Astoria Studios in 1920 and the lot soon became the biggest this side of Hollywood. The site still hosts television and film production, two activities that fuel this museum's obsession. Exhibits trace the moving image's evolution from 19th-century optical toys through film cameras and television sets. Interactive displays include a blue screen that lets visitors put themselves in fanciful environments. On free Friday evenings, demonstrations of editing and animation give additional insight into how all the magic happens.

35th Ave., at 36th St., Astoria, Queens. ℂ **718/784-0077.** www.movingimage.us. Regular admission $10; free Fri 4–8pm (film screenings not included.). Wed–Thurs 11am–5pm; Sat–Sun 11am–6:30pm; Fri 11am–8pm. Subway: G/R/V to Steinway St.

New York Hall of Science   Nominally a hall of science, this place is really a big playground. The exhibits are hands on, letting kids get engulfed by a giant soap bubble, float on air in an antigravity mirror, and retrieve astronomical images from the depths of outer space. In summer the huge Outdoor Science Playground provides jungle gyms, slides, seesaws, and spinners to help the physics medicine go down.

47-01 111th St., in Flushing Meadows–Corona Park, Queens. ℂ **718/699-0005.** www.nyhallsci.org. Regular admission $11; free Fri 2–5pm, Sun 10–11am (Sept 1– June 30 only). July–Aug Mon–Fri 9:30am–5pm; Sat–Sun 10am–6pm. Sept 1–June 30 Tues–Thurs 9:30am–2pm; Fri 9:30am–5pm; Sat–Sun 10am–6pm. Subway: 7 to 111th St.

The Noguchi Museum   Many New Yorkers have passed the Red Cube sculpture on lower Broadway, the stainless-steel plaque at the AP's headquarters in Rockefeller Center, and the sunken garden at the Chase Manhattan Bank Plaza, without realizing they're all by Japanese-American artist Isamu Noguchi. Noguchi's former home/studio shows off additional creativity in transforming a photo-engraving plant into a graceful oasis in the midst of industrial Queens. Overhauled in 2004, the museum features galleries of Noguchi's sculptural and architectural forms, and a tranquil birch-shaded sculpture garden.

9-01 33rd Road, at Vernon Boulevard, Long Island City, Queens. ℂ **718/204-7088.** www.noguchi.org. Regular admission $10; pay what you wish the first Friday of every month. Wed–Fri 10am–5pm; Sat–Sun 11am–6pm. Subway: N/W to Broadway. Walk 8 blocks along Broadway toward the East River.

The Rubin Museum of Art   Occidentals finally got a Himalayan art museum of their own when the Rubin opened up in 2004. A marble and steel spiral staircase, the focal point of the Barneys department store that was the previous tenant, winds through seven floors of painting, sculpture, and textiles. Though bodhisattvas and mandalas may be esoteric to some, the museum does a good job of glossing the nuances of its collection. On Friday nights, when entry to the museum is free, you can catch a tour with a contemporary artist and learn even more.

150 W. 17th St., between Sixth and Seventh aves. ✆ 212/620-5000. www.rmanyc. org. Regular admission $10; free Fri 7-10pm. Mon, Thurs 11am-5pm; Wed 11am-7pm; Fri 11am-10pm; Sat-Sun 11am-6pm. Subway: 1/2/3/F/L to 14th St.

South Street Seaport Museum   One of the city's lesser-known losses on 9/11 was the 799,982 artifacts this museum had collected from the old Five Points. The 18 objects that remain will go on display in the spring of '07, along with all matter of nautical ephemera, inside the revamped warehouses of Schermerhorn Row. Built as counting houses in 1812, the museum has artfully hollowed the warehouses out to better present its stores of ship paintings, Far East souvenirs, and scrimshaw. Three galleries are currently open and free to the public every third Friday of the month; stop in at the main visitor's center for a ticket, a calendar of that night's events (most geared toward kids), and directions to other free nearby galleries.

12 Fulton St., between Front and South sts. ✆ 212/748-8600. www.southst seaport.org. Regular admission $8; $5 on Mon; free every third Fri 5-9pm. Apr-Oct Tues-Sun 10am-6pm; Nov-Mar Fri-Sun 10am-5pm. Subway: 2/3/4/5/A/C/J/M/Z to Fulton St.

The Studio Museum in Harlem   Dedicated to the art of African Americans, with a sideline on the African Diaspora, this small museum has gathered together a terrific permanent collection. Exhibits rotate frequently and the calendar is packed with freebies. There are poetry readings, dance, forums, and open studios for the A-I-R program, which shows off the Artists in Residence that the Studio Museum helps support.

144 W. 125th St., between Lenox Ave. and Adam Clayton Powell Blvd. ✆ 212/864-4500. www.studiomuseuminharlem.org. Suggested admission $7; free first Sat of the month. Sun, Wed-Fri noon-6pm; Sat 10am-6pm. Subway: 2/3 to 125th St.

Whitney Museum of American Art   Behind somewhat imposing Bauhaus walls on Madison Avenue lies a spectacular collection of 20th-century art. The Whitney is rich in Edward Hopper, Louise Nevelson, and Georgia O'Keeffe, and they're good about rotating the permanent collection through their galleries. Shows of contemporary artists on other floors tend to be surprisingly cutting edge for a big Uptown institution.

945 Madison Ave., at 75th St. ✆ 212/570-3676. www.whitney.org. Regular admission $15; pay what you wish Fri after 6pm. Wed-Thurs, Sat-Sun 11am-6pm; Fri 1-9pm. Subway: 6 to 77th St.

SUGGESTED ADMISSIONS

Many New York institutions let in visitors on the basis of a "suggested admission." The price you have to pay isn't set in stone; it's set by the dictates of your own conscience. Before you decide how much to give remember that you're already giving if you pay local taxes. We working stiffs support the NYC Department of Cultural Affairs, the largest agency of its kind in the U.S. In 2006, the agency had $131 million set aside for expenses. It also had its largest capital budget yet, with another $803 million spread over 4 years. Cultural Affairs helps fund dozens of local institutions, many of which are owned by the city (and by extension, you and me). Sometimes $1 seems like the right amount to be spending on one's own museum. That's not to say if you're flush you should be stiffing these institutions. If you've got a spare couple of bucks, by all means toss them in the hat.

American Museum of Natural History   It's easy to lose yourself within the 4-square-block walls of this legendary museum. Low-profile sections still have the dingy lighting and old-fashioned lettering of a few decades ago, but the big players received radical upgrades. Dinosaurs have been brought into the 21st century and $210 million has space-aged the Planetarium. With that big an outlay, the museum likes to see its full $14 admission when you come, although technically it's only a suggestion and you can pay what you wish.

Central Park W., between 77th and 81st sts. 🕾 **212/769-5100** for information, or 🕾 212/769-5200 for tickets (tickets can also be ordered online). www.amnh.org. Suggested admission $14. Space Show and museum admission together are $22, plus additional charges for IMAX movies and some of the special exhibitions. Daily 10am–5:45pm; Rose Center open Fri 10am–8:45pm. Subway: B/C to 81st St., 1 to 79th St.

The Cloisters   This Met subsidiary is one of the city's most unlikely treasures. Situated on a Hudson cliff side, the Cloisters is a Frankenstein-esque amalgamation of medieval architecture: a Romanesque chapel, a 12th-century Spanish apse, and portions of cloisters from five different monasteries. The building is surrounded by tranquil gardens. If you've ever wondered why the Palisades in Jersey aren't more developed, it's because John D. Rockefeller, Jr., bought up the land there to preserve this view.

North end of Fort Tryon Park. 🕾 **212/923-3700.** www.metmuseum.org. Suggested admission $15. Nov–Feb Tues–Sun 9:30am–4:45pm; Mar–Oct Tues–Sun 9:30am–5:15pm. Subway: A to 190th St., then a 10 min. walk north along Margaret

Corbin Dr., or pick up the M4 bus at the station (1 stop to Cloisters). Or take the M4 Madison Ave. to Fort Tryon Park-The Cloisters.

El Museo del Barrio   A school classroom display was the genesis for this Museum Mile institution, the only U.S. museum dedicated to Puerto Rican, Caribbean, and Latin American art. The artistic history of the region, from pre-Columbian origins to the present, is recounted in a permanent installation. Changing exhibitions cover contemporary subjects and artists.

1230 Fifth Ave., at 104th St. ✆ 212/831-7272. www.elmuseo.org. Suggested admission $6. Wed–Sun 11am–5pm. Subway: 6 to 103rd St.

The Metropolitan Museum of Art   On the Upper East Side, tucked away just off Central Park, you can find this undiscovered little gem of a collection. Allow yourself a good 10 minutes to see everything they've got. Yeah, well, the Met is the 800-pound gorilla of New York's museum scene, and it's not hiding from anybody. If it's not the greatest museum in the world, it must be damn close, and it's all right there for the price of a suggested admission.

Fifth Ave., at 82nd St. ✆ **212/535-7710**. www.metmuseum.org. Suggested admission $20. Tues–Thurs 9:30am–5:30pm; Fri–Sat 9:30am–9pm; Mon 9:30am–5:30pm on select holidays. Subway: 4/5/6 to 86th St.

New York City Fire Museum   FDNY Engine Co. 30's former home holds an impressive collection of fire-service memorabilia. Exhibits range from the 18th century to the present, where the most poignant materials can be found. During the 9/11 attacks, 343 firefighters gave their lives just a few blocks to the south of the museum.

278 Spring St., between Varick and Hudson sts. ✆ **212/691-1303**. www.nycfire museum.org. Suggested admission $5. Tues–Sat 10am–5pm; Sun 10am–4pm. Subway: C/E to Spring St.

☆ **P.S. 1 Contemporary Art Center**   School is out, replaced by art that's in, inside this 19th-century former public school. The Renaissance Revival building has been beautifully converted, with avant-garde shows rotating through the former classrooms. Now affiliated with MoMA, P.S. 1 does a terrific job of bringing fresh, intriguing art to Queens. Don't miss James Turrell's *Meeting* on the top floor, which frames the dusk sky in an extraordinary way.

22-25 Jackson Ave., Long Island City, Queens. ✆ **718/784-2084**. www.ps1.org. Suggested admission $5. Thurs–Mon noon–6pm. Subway: E/V to 23rd St./Ely Ave.; G to 21st St./Van Alst; 7 to 45th Rd./Court House Sq.

Queens Museum of Art   This museum has reproductions of Greek marbles and some nice Tiffany glass, but the real draw is The Panorama of New York City, the world's largest scale model. Every single building in the five boroughs is represented, in addition to every street and bridge, and even airplanes that take off and land at a tiny LaGuardia. The Museum is located in Corona Park, on the site of the legendary 1964 World's Fair. Don't miss the nearby Unisphere, a highlight of the fair and the largest representation of Earth that we humans have cooked up yet. Twelve gleaming stories high, the Unisphere will give you a good idea of what the planet looks like from 6,000 miles in space.

Next to the Unisphere in Flushing Meadows-Corona Park, Queens. ℂ **718/592-9700.** www.queensmuseum.org. Suggested admission $5. Sep-Jun Wed-Fri 10am-5pm; Sat-Sun noon-5pm; Jul-Aug Wed-Sun noon-6pm, Fri noon-8pm. Subway: 7 to Willets Point/Shea Stadium, follow signs through the park.

DIRT CHEAP

Chelsea Art Museum   With the art gallery scene's near-complete assimilation of West Chelsea, the arrival of a new art museum in the area is something less than a surprise. The C.A.M. focuses on 20th-century and contemporary abstract art, with European artists dominating the permanent collection. Americans like Robert Motherwell can also be found inside the renovated galleries of this 1850 structure. The building is also playing temporary host to The New Museum of Contemporary Art, which will eventually eschew Chelsea for the aesthetic pleasures of the Bowery. Until the new headquarters are completed, this ground-floor space will host their rotating exhibits, which show off the work of contemporary artists from around the world. Regular admission is $6, but Thursday nights are half-off.

556 West 22nd St., at 11th Ave. Chelsea Art Museum ℂ **212/255-0719;** www.chelseaartmuseum.org. New Museum ℂ **212/219-1222;** www.newmuseum.org. Regular admission $6, $3 after 6pm on Thurs. Open Tues-Sat noon-6pm; Thurs noon-8pm. Subway: C/E to 23rd St.

Fraunces Tavern Museum   A small museum above the tavern and restaurant shows off the building's illustrious history along with scattered relics of colonial life. See p. 314 in chapter 7 for a full review.

54 Pearl St., near Broad St. ℂ **212/425-1778.** www.frauncestavernmuseum.org. Admission $4. Tues-Fri noon-5pm; Sat 10am-5pm. Subway: R/W to Whitehall; 1 to South Ferry; 4/5 to Bowling Green.

Museum of American Financial History   For now, this tiny basement space is more advertorial than enlightener. Photos, busts, and
numismatic matters make up most of the displays, but the gift shop
occupies nearly as much space as the museum proper. In early 2007,
however, the museum will change its name to the **Museum of American Finance** and expand into a spectacular historic bank building on
Wall Street. Expect admission prices to expand as well, up from the
current Scrooge-friendly $2.

28 Broadway, just north of Bowling Green Park. ℭ **212/908-4601.** www.
financialhistory.org. Admission $2. Tues-Sat 10am-4pm. Subway: 4/5 to Bowling
Green; J/M/Z to Broad St.

Scandinavia House   The Nordic Center in America has a stylish
new Midtown building. You can check out the cafeteria and gift shop
for free, but they ask for $3 for the third-floor gallery. The space isn't
very big, but the rotating exhibits are well presented, with a wealth of
informative notes. *Note:* There are occasional free gallery talks; check
the website.

58 Park Ave., between 37th and 38th sts. ℭ **212/879-9779.** www.scandinavia
house.org. Suggested donation $3. Tues-Sat noon-5pm. Sat usually closed in
summer, call ahead for other summer schedule changes. Subway: 4/5/6/7/S to
42nd St./Grand Central; 6 to 33rd St.

Theodore Roosevelt Birthplace   Though not the original birthplace, this historic site is a deft reproduction of the place where T. R.
spent his first 14 years. See p. 301 in chapter 7 for a full review.

28 E. 20th St., between Broadway and Park Ave. S. ℭ **212/260-1616.**
www.nps.gov/thrb. Admission $3. Tues-Sat 9am-5pm (tours hourly 9am-4pm).
Subway: N/R/W to Broadway/23rd St.; 6 to 23rd St.

FREE EXHIBITS AT THE LIBRARIES

Free books are just the beginning with New York's libraries. In addition to free classes (p. 149) and free films (p. 57), Gothamites also get
free exhibitions. The libraries really care about their material, which
comes through in the surprisingly well-crafted displays.

Brooklyn Public Library `FREE`   The galleries here present everything from painting to installation art to rare books. The works and the
artists often have a local connection.

Grand Army Plaza. ℭ **718/230-2100.** www.brooklynpubliclibrary.org. Tues-Thurs
9am-9pm; Fri 9am-6pm; Sat 10am-6pm; Sun 1-6pm. Subway: 2/3 to Grand Army
Plaza.

This Old House

I find it amazing than anything can survive for long in NYC, especially old houses that don't do anything except clog up prime real estate. The Historic House Trust of New York City has information on 21 surviving dwellings, spread across all five boroughs. Admissions are usually $2 or $3, which is not bad for the opportunity to travel a century or two. Recorded information from the Trust is available at 🕿 **212/360-3448,** or log on to www.historichouse trust.org. You can request a brochure at 🕿 212/360-8282; www. preserve.org/hht.

The Morris-Jumel Mansion   One of Manhattan's coolest surprises is coming upon the grounds of the Morris-Jumel Mansion in the midst of monolithic Harlem apartment buildings. This genteel Palladian wonder is the oldest house in Manhattan, built in 1765 as a summer getaway. There isn't much land left on the plot, but what remains is pleasant to stroll around. You have to pay to enter the house, which provides a fascinating snapshot of its era. *Tip:* Don't miss picturesque Sylvan Terrace across the street (just west of the mansion), one of the city's last blocks of wooden workers' row houses. 65 Jumel Terrace at 160th St., east of St. Nicholas Ave. 🕿 **212/923-8008.** www.morrisjumel.org. Admission $4. Wed-Sun 10am-4pm. Subway: C to 163rd St.

Edgar Allan Poe Cottage   Happy-go-lucky author E. A. P. moved to the Bronx in 1846, hoping that the country air would be good for his tubercular wife. She died the next year, and Poe himself checked out 2 years later. The cottage is now an anomaly among brick high-rises. The interior has period furnishings and Poe exhibits. 2460 Grand Concourse, at E. Kingsbridge Rd. 🕿 **718/881-8900.** www.bronxhistoricalsociety.org. Admission $3. Sat 10am-4pm; Sun 1-5pm. Subway: D/4 to Kingsbridge Rd.

☆ **Donnell Library Center** FREE   Many local fans of the writer A. A. Milne don't realize that Winnie-the-Pooh has been a fellow Manhattan resident for 50 years. Pooh and friends Piglet, Eeyore, Kanga, and Tigger are all on display in the Central Children's Room in

FREE Governors Island

Native Americans called it *Pagganck* ("Nut Island"), the Dutch called it *Noten Eylant*, and until 1995 3,500 Coast Guard members and their families called it home. Today, the former military base that is Governors Island has been set aside for public use. During the summer visitors can wander past abandoned mansions, forts, and parade grounds. Originally there was a $6 ferry fee to get here, but in 2006 the whole shebang went totally free (with live performances on Saturdays thrown in to boot). The breathtaking views make this New York's most ideal picnic spot. The ferry leaves from the Battery every hour on the hour from 10am to 3pm on Fridays and Saturdays in June, July, and August. During these same months, rangers give 90-minute tours (leaving Manhattan at 10am and 1pm) of the northern half of the island, on Tuesdays, Wednesdays, and Thursdays. Space on the ferries is limited, first-come, first-served; though the Friday and Saturday tours can take 400 people every hour. The island was only transferred to the public in 2003, so check the website, as policies may be no more permanent than a name. Battery Maritime Building, 10 South St., between Broad and Whitehall sts. ✆ 212/440-2202. www.govisland.com. Subway: R/W to Whitehall St.; 1 to South Ferry.

Midtown. These are Christopher's actual stuffed animals, instantly recognizable from their portrayals on the page. Though they look a little forlorn for being stuck behind glass, they've held up pretty well for 80-year-olds. Take the elevator to the third floor and you'll see the animals on your right. Nearby display cases show off children's books from the collection.

20 W. 53rd St., between Fifth and Sixth aves. ✆ 212/621-0618. www.nypl.org. Mon, Wed, Fri 10am–6pm; Tues, Thurs 10am–8pm; Sat 10am–5pm; Sun 1–5pm. Subway: E/V to 53rd St. B/D/F to Rockefeller Center.

☆ **Humanities and Social Sciences Library** FREE   The book- and manuscript-themed exhibits here are lovingly displayed and as well written as you'd expect from a library. See p. 307 in chapter 7 for a full review.

Fifth Ave., at 42nd St. ⓒ **212/869-8089** exhibits and events, or 212/661-7220 library hours. www.nypl.org. Thurs-Sat 10am-6pm; Tues-Wed 11am-7:30pm; Sun 1-5pm. Subway: B/D/F/V to 42nd St.; 7 to Fifth Ave.; 4/5/6/S to Grand Central.

New York Public Library for the Performing Arts FREE   This library branch is a performance clearinghouse, conveniently located near the arts central that is Lincoln Center. Performing arts exhibitions can be found in the Donald and Mary Oenslager Gallery.

40 Lincoln Center Plaza, between 64th and 65th sts. ⓒ **212/870-1630.** www. nypl.org. Tues-Wed, Fri-Sat noon-6pm; Thurs noon-8pm. Subway: 1 to 66th St.

Schomburg Center for Research in Black Culture FREE   The massive collection of books and art gathered by bibliophile Arturo Alfonso Schomburg is housed at this research branch of the New York Public Library. The Exhibition Hall, the Latimer/Edison Gallery, and the Reading Room all host exhibits related to black culture. Talks and performing arts are also part of the program here. Call or check online for scheduling details.

515 Malcolm X Blvd., at Lenox Ave., between 135th and 136th sts. ⓒ **212/491-2200.** www.nypl.org. Tues-Sat 10am-6pm; Sun 1-5pm. Subway: 2/3 to 135th St.

2 Gallery Scene

Art galleries may be Gotham's greatest free cultural resource. Not only do these minimuseums provide us with works of inspiration, they also give us free booze and snacks at their openings. Don't be shy about barging into a show with million-dollar pieces. Gallery owners are almost as happy raising the profiles of their artists as they are closing a sale; both are essential for upping the prices they charge. We should also take a moment to be thankful for the dot.com boom. Not only did we all make a killing on our stock options, the dot.com boom made it possible for scruffy people in jeans and sneakers to be stealth millionaires. Gallery owners and employees can no longer easily distinguish between the underemployed and walking gold mines, meaning that our presence in galleries is not merely tolerated, but actively sought and desired.

If you want invitations to openings, you have a couple of options. You can sign in whenever you visit a gallery and they'll keep you informed, or you can check online. Douglas Kelly keeps an amazingly comprehensive list of gallery openings at **http://dks.thing.net**. Most galleries are open Tuesday through Saturday from 10am to 6pm.

Moving Views

Straphangers get treated to a few spectacular scenes in exchange for their swipes. I love the 7 line as it approaches Manhattan from Queens. The track twists and turns like a slo-mo roller coaster with the Midtown skyline in the background. The J/M/Z ride across the Williamsburg has great views from windows north and south. The Manhattan Bridge is back to full train capacity and B/D/N/Q riders can enjoy dramatic East River vistas.

The most thrilling public transportation ride is the Roosevelt Island Tram (© **212/832-4543,** ext. 1). As you dangle in the air over the East River you get the East Side skyline, plus the U.N., plus great sightlines on the engineering marvels of the East River bridges. You also get the knowledge that one day in 2006 the tram stalled out for hours, stranding passengers without a viable evacuation plan. This frisson of actual danger comes free with the $2 one-way price (if you're on an unlimited Metrocard plan, you can get back via the F train's Roosevelt Island stop, just a few blocks away). The trip between 60th Street and Second Avenue and Roosevelt Island takes about 4 minutes. The Tram operates daily 6am to 2am; until 3:30am on weekends.

Many openings are on Thursday nights. Summers can be pretty dead in the art world, and many galleries keep shorter hours, often closing on Saturdays.

CHELSEA

New York's big money art scene has put most of its eggs in one basket by clustering galleries between Tenth and Eleventh avenues. For the gallery fan, this means you can visit hundreds of shows without ever leaving **the lower West 20s.** The geography also rewards the serendipitous, allowing for quick pop-ins at randomly selected spaces. Not interested in a bunch of paint splotches on a pile of brillo pads? Pop right back out. My favorite strategy is to write down some interesting-sounding shows from the listings in the *Voice* and then hit a few of their unlisted neighbors. With floor after floor of galleries in the old warehouse buildings here, you're bound to find something of interest.

Subway: C/E to 23rd St.

David Zwirner FREE One of many recent SoHo refugees, Zwirner shows a range of interesting, inventive art.

525 W. 19th St., between Tenth Ave. and West St. ℭ 212/727-2070. www.david zwirner.com.

Gagosian Gallery FREE Perhaps the heaviest hitter around, this gallery puts on major shows in a space large enough to accommodate sculptures by Richard Serra.

555 W. 24th St., between Tenth and Eleventh aves. ℭ 212/741-1111. www. gagosian.com.

> ### Sources
>
> The local papers provide rundowns on the higher profile shows. The *Village Voice* has good listings, which can also be perused online (www.village voice.com). Other sources include the "Art Guide" in the Friday "Weekend" section of the *New York Times* or the Sunday "Arts & Leisure" section; the "Cue" section of *New York* magazine; the "Art" section in *Time Out New York;* and the *New Yorker*'s "Goings on About Town."

Matthew Marks Gallery FREE Matthew Marks has built a mini-empire in west Chelsea. His three galleries show top-tier painting, photography, and sculpture.

523 W. 24th; 522 W. 22nd; 521 W. 21st, all between Tenth and Eleventh aves. ℭ 212/243-0200. www.matthewmarks.com.

Roebling Hall FREE One of the oldest and best NYC galleries. In it you'll find original takes on painting, photography, and sculpture.

606 W. 26th St., near Eleventh Ave. ℭ 212/929-8180. www.roeblinghall.com
Subway: C to 23rd St.

DOWNTOWN

In the early and mid-'80s, the headquarters of New York's avant-garde was the East Village. Tiny galleries dotted the landscape and helped break the era's big names. The stock market crash of '87 put an abrupt end to frivolous spending and most of the galleries withered away. It's taken more than a decade, but galleries are just now returning. Throughout the **East Village and Lower East Side,** and even into **Chinatown,** storefront operations are coming to life. **SoHo,** conversely,

FREE Watching the Auction Action

Sure, you know all about New York's auction scene, the way you follow a stranger in, take an inconspicuous seat off to the side, and try to suppress a sneeze just as a gavel comes down to announce you're the proud owner of a $50,000 Ming vase. But there's more to New York auction houses than expensive misunderstandings and antitrust violations. Viewings and sale previews are excellent chances to treat upcoming lots as museum exhibits. The current top house is **Christie's**, at 20 Rockefeller Plaza, 49th Street between Fifth and Sixth avenues (© **212/636-2000**; www. christies.com), and at 219 E. 67th St., between Second and Third avenues (© 212/606-0400). **Sotheby's** runs a close second on the Upper East Side, 1334 York Ave., at 72nd Street (© **212/606-7000**; www.sothebys.com). There are two often-overlooked smaller houses that sell equally intriguing artifacts. **Guernsey's,** 108½ E. 73rd St., between Park and Lexington avenues (© **212/794-2280**; www.guernseys.com), focuses on modern collections and memorabilia. The city's oldest privately owned house is **Tepper Galleries** at 110 E. 25th St., between Park and Lexington avenues (© **212/677-5300**; www.teppergalleries.com). Fine and decorative arts shows and estate sales are the specialties of the house.

Full calendars for all houses are available online.

continues to atrophy as an art scene. The galleries can't afford the rents and every year there are fewer and fewer hanging on. However, a few institutions are firmly embedded in the area, and they put on some of the best shows.

Subway: N/R/W to Prince; C/E to Spring.

Artists Space Young artists get exposure on the walls of this SoHo collective. Near year's end, cheapskate fine-art collectors take advantage of the space's "Night of 1,000 Drawings" benefit. Five dollars nets you an open bar and the chance to buy original one-of-a-kind drawings for $30–$50 a pop. Submit a drawing in advance and you can keep your $5.

38 Greene St., 3rd floor, between Broome and Grand sts. Ⓒ 212/226-3970. www.artistsspace.org.

Deitch Projects FREE SoHo standby Deitch puts up inventive shows, usually a lot more fun than anything else in the neighborhood. Two nearby locations.

76 Grand St., between Wooster and Greene sts.; 18 Wooster St., between Grand and Canal sts. Ⓒ 212/343-7300. www.deitch.com.

The Drawing Center FREE This downtown institution supports the often-overlooked discipline of drawing. Two spaces across the street from each other present simultaneous shows. Lectures and screenings, some of which are free, add to the "draw" here.

35 and 40 Wooster St., between Broome and Grand sts. Ⓒ 212/269-2166. www.drawingcenter.org.

Swiss Institute FREE The artists shown here usually have a Swiss connection. Innovative project ideas include the Institute's "Extension 17 project" featuring audio art (Sonic Youth's Kim Gordon contributed one)—just call the Institute and dial ext. 17.

495 Broadway, 3rd floor, between Broome and Spring sts. Ⓒ 212/925-2035. www.swissinstitute.net

FREE **Photo Ops**

Two of my favorite photo galleries can be found at 535 West 22nd Street, between Tenth and Eleventh avenues. This building has a bunch of interesting galleries for spontaneous pop-ins. **Julie Saul** (Ⓒ 212/627-2410; www.saulgallery.com) brings in up-and-coming contemporary photography, while **Yancey Richardson** (Ⓒ 646/230-9610; www.yanceyrichardson.com) represents an impressive stable of big names and new innovators.

Another photo scene worth checking out is at **Sepia**, which is a gallery and historical archive hybrid. A huge space far from Chelsea's beaten track brings in some great, overlooked international work (148 W. 24th St., 11th floor, between Sixth and Seventh aves., Ⓒ 212/645-9444; www.sepia.org).

MIDTOWN/UPTOWN

With the avant-garde ensconced downtown and in Brooklyn, the galleries that breathe the rarified air of the Upper East Side tend toward the staid side. Art here is of a classic bent, though the definition of classic is pretty elastic these days. Expect to see master works from the

FREE SoHo's Secret Installations

The **DIA Foundation for the Arts** maintains a pair of hidden galleries with eccentric conceptual works by Walter De Maria (© **212/ 989-5566;** www.diacenter.org).

☆ **New York Earth Room** As the name suggests, it's a room full of dirt. Really—140 tons of soil filling up a SoHo loft to a depth of almost 2 feet. It's an oddly compelling sight in the middle of the city, and the rich earthy scent is almost refreshing. 141 Wooster St., between Houston and Prince sts. www.earthroom.org.

The Broken Kilometer A few blocks away you can find a gallery floor covered with orderly rows of solid brass rods. Placed end to end, the 500 rods would stretch exactly—yup, 1 kilometer. (Its sister piece is in Germany, a sculpture with identical, unbroken brass rods buried vertically in the ground.) www.brokenkilometer. org. 393 West Broadway, between Spring and Broome sts.

Both galleries are open from Wednesday to Sunday, noon to 6pm (closed 3–3:30pm). Closed in summer.

Renaissance up to the last couple of decades. And if you thought the asking prices were wacky downtown, wait until you see these. . . .
Subway: 6 to 68th St.; F to 63rd St.; N/R/W or 4/5/6 to 59th St.

Americas Society Art Gallery FREE The Americas, from Canada all the way down to Patagonia, are the focus of art shows here.
680 Park Ave., at 68th St. © **212/249-8950.** www.americas-society.org. Tues–Sun noon–6pm.

Hirschl & Adler Galleries FREE Five floors of galleries display 18th- to 20th-century European and American painting and decorative arts in an exquisite landmark town house.
21 E. 70th St., between Fifth and Madison aves. © **212/535-8810.** www.hirschl andadler.com.

Pace Wildenstein FREE Modernism is now classicism, and this gallery specializes in the best of it.

32 E. 57th St., between Fifth and Madison aves. © 212/421-3292. www.pace
wildenstein.com. Other locations: *Chelsea*, 534 W. 25th St. and 545 W. 22nd St.,
between Tenth and Eleventh aves.

Richard L. Feigen & Co. FREE   Master works of the last few centuries are the focus here.

34 E. 69th St., between Park and Madison aves. © 212/628-0700. www.
rlfeigen.com.

Wildenstein FREE   This gallery has over a century's experience in
handling huge-ticket items. Renaissance and Impressionism treasures
are a specialty.

19 E. 64th St., between Fifth and Madison aves. © 212/879-0500. www.
wildenstein.com.

WILLIAMSBURG

Recently Williamsburg's orthodox Jewish population distributed peti-
tions asking for help from above to stem the "plague of the artists" that
encroaches on their community. There's been no immediate response
from G-d, but I'd bet that the plague continues to rage for the foresee-
able future, as artists flock to Brooklyn and overrun Bedford's hipster
boundaries. Though it's still more DIY and low-budget than Manhattan's galleries, the scene here is catching up quickly. The only draw-
back is that the spaces are spread far apart. To make a full tour here
be prepared to trek some blocks. *Note:* Brooklyn galleries keep different hours from the Manhattan side; many are open from Friday to
Monday, or weekends only.

Subway: L to Bedford Ave. or Lorimer St.; J/M/Z to Marcy Ave.; G to Metropolitan
Ave.

Dollhaus FREE   Welcome to one of Williamsburg's more eclectic
spaces, representing art from out in left field. Look for the occasional
free film screening on Sunday night, too.

37 Broadway, between Wythe St. and Dunham Place. © 718/384-6139. www.
dollhaus.org. Sat-Sun noon-6pm, or by appointment.

Pierogi 2000 FREE   This small, well-established gallery hangs
some of the best painting to be found in Brooklyn. Photo and installation work also go on display, often in the context of intriguing group
shows. If you're in need of further visual stimuli, some 750 artists are
browsable in the gallery's constantly evolving Flat Files collection.

177 N. 9th St., between Bedford and Driggs aves. © 718/599-2144. www.pierogi 2000.com. Fri–Mon noon–6pm.

31Grand FREE A solid crop of young artists shows their painting and photos here.

31 Grand St., at Kent Ave. © 718/388-2858. www.31grand.com.

Williamsburg Art and Historical Center FREE Housed in an amazing 1867 bank building, this community center is always good for an intriguing art exhibit or two.

135 Broadway, at Bedford St. © 718/486-7372. www.wahcenter.net. Sat–Sun noon–6pm.

3 Open Studios & Art Fests

Run-down industrial neighborhoods beget artist populations, as the creatively minded come in for cheap, raw studio space. In the old days a few neighbors would open their doors one weekend to show off their work to friends and their floormates' friends. With the explosion of New York's artist population, things have become more organized than the old flier-on-a-light-post invitation system. Several neighborhoods now offer full-blown arts festivals, with music, installations, theater, and gallery events supplementing open studios.

d.u.m.b.o. art under the bridge festival FREE The city's preeminent arts fest belongs to DUMBO, where yupster encrosions have yet to fully displace the hundreds of artists whose studios fill these broad-shouldered warehouses. This is probably the best art crop in town, which may or may not be related to the inspiring Manhattan views you'll find through many an artist's window. The festival also features music, dance, video, and gallery extravaganzas, and most of it is free.

DUMBO, Brooklyn. © 718/694-0831. www.dumboartscenter.org. Noon–6pm. Subway: F to York St.; A/C to High St.

EFA Studio Center FREE The Elizabeth Foundation for the Arts provides 110 artists with subsidized workspaces in Midtown. At least half the artists show off their work at the annual open studios over the third weekend in October. A new gallery space on the second floor provides additional art-viewing opportunities.

323 W. 39th St., between Eighth and Ninth aves. © 212/563-5855. www.efa1. org. Open studio hours vary year to year; gallery Wed–Sat noon–6pm. Subway: A/C/E/7 to 42nd St.–Port Authority.

Every Last Sunday on the Lower East Side `FREE` The "Bargain District" nickname has grown increasingly anachronistic as the influx of boutique shops and restaurants have upped the rents across my beloved LES. There are a few art gallery and studio spaces, however, and on select Sundays they open their doors for free. You can visit at your own pace or take a guided tour at 1pm.

Tour begins from Visitor Information Center at at 261 Broome St., between Orchard and Allen sts. ✆ **646/602-2338.** www.elsles.org. 1-7pm. Subway: J/M/Z to Essex St.; F to Delancey St.

Firstop: Williamsburg Design Weekend `FREE` If design is more your bag than arts of canvas and clay, this is an excellent weekend to check out. Dozens of studios, stores, and exhibition spaces burst with the creativity of Billyburg. You can catch free workshops among standout examples of fashion, architecture, and industrial design. Usually the first weekend in May.

Maps are available at the kiosk at North 7th St. and Bedford Ave. on the days of the event. ✆ **718/387-7927.** www.firstop.org. Subway: L to Bedford Ave.; J/M/Z to Marcy Ave.; G to Lorimer St.

Gowanus Artists Studio Tour `FREE` Gowanus Canal boosters claim the neighborhood is destined to be New York's answer to Venice. We're confident there's a few decades left to enjoy things just as they are now, with crumbling brick warehouses and factories and row house back streets, instead of marble palaces and singing gondoliers. The arts scene here leans toward the artsy-craftsy, but there's definitely some talent, and the spaces are great. The tour is held on the fourth weekend of October. The studio territory lies between Park Slope and Red Hook and Carroll Gardens, but the distances can be shortened by taking advantage of the free shuttle bus. The bus makes eight area stops starting at 1pm; check the map online.

Gowanas Canal and surrounding areas, in Brooklyn. ✆ **718/789-7243.** www. gowanusartists.com. 1-6pm. Subway: F/G to Carroll St.

Tribeca Open Artist Studio Tour `FREE` Tribeca certainly doesn't qualify as a run-down neighborhood, so the one-hundred artist studios that open up for T.O.A.S.T. are a bit of a surprise. You'll also find free music and slideshows amid the tony condos. Tribeca further strives for artistic cred with its Second Wednesdays program. Art galleries stay open until 8pm, to let the nabe's weary local commodity traders and corporate litigators take in a little nutrition for their souls.

FREE Mi Casa Es Su Casa: Open House New York

New Yorkers obsess about real estate. As much time as we kill poring over the property blog Curbed (www.curbed.com), there's no substitute for actually poking around someone else's space in person. Every weekend the *Times* provides hundreds of opportunities to impersonate solvent people and waste real estate agents' time by attending apartment sale open houses. Less ethically suspect is the program **Open House New York,** which opens the doors to some of the most mysterious spaces in the city. The second weekend in October brings New Yorkers access to envy-inducing private residences and awe-inspiring public structures. When else are you going to get a peek at JFK's abandoned Terminal Five, MoMA's conservation department, or the grounds of the Roosevelt Island Smallpox Hospital? Locales (an impressive 175 in 2006) are scattered across all five boroughs, and you'll have to come up with a schedule or limit your targets to a few spots. Obviously, intriguing spaces in central locations will have the longest lines. Certain venues limit the number of guests, so for personal must-sees sign up early on the website (www.ohny.org; ✆ **917/626-6869**).

From Canal south to Murray St., and Lafayette west to Washington St. ✆ **212/479-7317.** www.toastartwalk.com. Sat-Mon 1-6pm. Subway: 1 to Franklin St.; A/C/E to Canal St.

Washington Square Outdoor Art Exhibit FREE This Depression-era idea for helping artists get their work out there is now safely into its eighth decade. Streets near Washington Square Park become a gigantic open-air art gallery, where you can browse through the works of some 200 artists and artisans. The show is juried, so even the crafts have standards to meet. Pick up a free map at the intersection of 8th Street and University.

Show covers University Place between 3rd and 12th sts., and spills over to Washington Place between Green St. and Washington Sq., and LaGuardia between Bleecker and E. 4th. ✆ **212/982-6255.** Noon-7pm; Sat-Mon on Memorial Day weekend and Sat–Sun the following weekend, Sat–Mon on Labor Day weekend and Sat–Sun the following weekend. Subway: N/R/W to 8th St.; A/B/C/D/E/V to W. 4th St.

4 Free Tours

SPONSORED TOURS

New York's Business Improvement Districts (BIDs) started off as coalitions of local merchants who were mostly concerned with picking up trash and herding the homeless into neighborhoods without BIDs. Now fully established, BIDs have taken on cultural roles in their communities, sponsoring concerts and public art. Always eager to boost their 'hoods, a few now offer free summer tours, with some continuing throughout the year. Though there's always something new to learn about New York, don't expect to hear many critical words about the neighborhood or its friendly, hardworking BID.

The Alliance for Downtown New York FREE Manhattan's non–Native American history began at the island's tip and the area still holds a wealth of history. The Alliance runs two separate tours to show it all off. Every Thursday and Saturday at noon the Wall Street Walking Tour wanders past icons like the New York Stock Exchange, Trinity Church, and Federal Hall. Tours meet on the steps of the National Museum of the American Indian at 1 Bowling Green. Tuesdays at noon bring the Historic Downtown Walking Tour, which hits the north end of the nabe, past the Woolworth Building, City Hall, and the African Burial Ground. Tours begin from the NYC Heritage Tourism Center, on Broadway between Vesey and Barclay streets. Tours last about 1½ hours. Reservations not required.

© **212/606-4064.** www.downtownny.com. Tues, Thurs, Sat noon, rain or shine. Wall Street Walking Tour subway: 4/5 to Bowling Green, 1 to South Ferry. Historic Downtown Walking Tour subway: J/M/Z/2/3 to Fulton St.; 4/5/6 to Brooklyn Bridge-City Hall; R/W to City Hall; A/C to Broadway-Nassau.

8th Street Walking Tour FREE Eighth Street, and its East Village equivalent St. Marks Place, are among the city's most colorful commercial strips. Get the inside dirt on the area courtesy of The Village Alliance. Tours meet on the northwest corner of Second Avenue and St. Marks.

© **212/777-2173.** www.villagealliance.org. Select Sat 11:30am. Tours late May to early Oct.

Orchard Street Bargain District Tour FREE The Lower East Side is a bottomless well of history and lore. The neighborhood's current incarnation is marked by a revival of its commercial fortunes, which you will see in detail on this tour. Learn about stores old-fashioned and ultramodern as you wander the narrow streets between the tenements. Reservations not required.

Meet up with the guide in front of Katz's Delicatessen, 205 E. Houston St., at Ludlow St. ✆ 866/224-0206 or 212/226-9010. www.lowereastsideny.com. Apr–Dec 11am, rain or shine. Subway: F/V to 2nd Ave.

Sidewalk Surprises in Lincoln Square FREE Lincoln Square is on the cusp of major changes, with new buildings going up left and right and an overhaul of Lincoln Center in the offing. Learn more about the area and its overlooked history, courtesy of the Lincoln Square BID. Meet at the Maine Monument at Merchant's Gate in Columbus Circle, across from the fountain.

✆ 212/581-3774. www.lincolnbid.org. Sat 11am; usually June–Nov, rain or shine. Subway: A/B/C/D/1 to 59th St./Columbus Circle.

34th Street Tour/Penn Station Tour FREE The 34th Street Partnership presents two tours of their insanely crowded corner of the city. Every Thursday at 12:30pm, the Historic 34th Street tour meets at the Fifth Avenue entrance of the world's most famous building (the Empire State). (In case of rain call ✆ 917/438-5123 to make sure it's on.) New Yorkers still lament the murder of the old Penn Station. Tours of the new include many references to the old. The Late, Great Pennsylvania Station tours happen on the fourth Monday of each month from 12:30 to 2pm. Meet up in the rotunda of the main station, near the tourist information booth at Seventh Avenue between 32nd and 33rd streets.

✆ 212/719-3434. www.34thstreet.org. Subway: A/C/E or 1/2/3 to 34th St.-Penn Station, or B/D/F/V to 34th St.-Harold Square.

INDEPENDENT TOURS

Battery Park City FREE Battery Park is justifiably proud of its beautiful landscaped grounds. With the park restored to pre-9/11 showroom condition, the area is eager to show itself off. On select Mondays from 12:30 to 1:30pm you can get a 1-hour tour from a real live horticulturalist. Locations and times vary so check online. On select weekend days you can take a 2pm public art tour, surveying the mixed bag of public installations down here.

© **212/267-9700.** www.bpcparks.org. Subway: 1 to Rector St.; 4/5 to Bowling Green.

Big Apple Greeter FREE These New York boosters roll out the red carpet in an attempt to make their own enthusiasm for the city infectious to visitors. Visitors to our city can pick any neighborhood they like, and the greeters will find a knowledgeable volunteer to tour them around for 2 to 4 hours. FINE PRINT Reservations should be made at least a week ahead of time.

© **212/669-8159.** www.bigapplegreeter.org.

Brooklyn Brewery FREE More of a lecture than a tour, this popular Saturday event entails a visit to a room full of silver beer vats followed by a trip to the company store. Your attention is rewarded with two complimentary drink tickets, which will let you sample a couple of half-pints of Brooklyn's tasty brews. Tours run on the hour between 1 and 4pm. Doors open at noon and close at 5pm.

79 N. 11th St., between Wyeth and Levit sts. *©* **718/486-7422.** www.brooklyn brewery.com. Subway: L to Bedford Ave.

Central Park Conservancy Walking Tours FREE Central Park's rich history and hidden nuggets are explored in these 60- to 90-minute walks. Themes range from landscaping to Revolutionary War sites to the rugged Ramble. Check the website because times, dates, and locations vary. The tours run frequently, year-round. Also look out for the Conservatory Garden lunchtime tours, which take you through Manhattan's most beautiful garden.

© **212/794-6564.** www.centralparknyc.org.

☆ **City Hall and Tweed Courthouse** FREE When City Hall was finished in 1812, the builders didn't bother with marble and granite in the back, thinking cheaper sandstone would be good enough for a side that would forever face a bunch of hills and trees. Though the city expanded, this small-scale building still houses offices of the mayor and city council. The underpublicized guided tour here takes you through a graceful rotunda and up to the Governor's Room, which has a priceless collection of portraits as well as a desk that was used by George Washington. Next door Tweed Courthouse was used by Boss Tweed and his cohorts to fleece the city for millions. Recently renovated, the building is a fascinating melding of architectural styles, with elaborate arches and brickwork. An octagonal skylight lets sun pour on endless Board of Education conferences.

Broadway at Murray St. ℂ 212/788-2170. www.nyc.gov/html/artcom/html/tours/ tours.shtml. Reserve in advance for tours Tues 10am or Fri 2pm. Without reservations, meet Wednesdays at noon at the Heritage Tourism Center on the east side of Broadway at Barclay St. (tour limited to 20 people.) Subway: R/W to City Hall; 4/5/6 to Brooklyn Bridge-City Hall; J/M/Z to Chambers St.; 2/3 to Park Place.

Evergreens Cemetery Tour `FREE`

This boneyard on the Brooklyn/Queens border seems to stretch forever. As the final resting place for over half a million people, it's a good thing there's ample space (225 acres to be exact). Lovely rolling hills and vegetation galore make a lush contrast to the city. Guided walking tours of this historic site are held on select Saturdays at 11am. Call for a schedule.

1629 Bushwick Ave., at Conway St., Brooklyn. ℂ 718/455-5300. www.theevergreens cemetery.com. Tours assemble at the main entrance, Bushwick Ave. and Conway St. Subway: A/C/J/L/Z to Broadway Junction.

Privately Owned Public Space Walking Tour `FREE`

This tour comes with an agenda: to inform the public about city zoning laws, and to point out places where building owners come up short. If this is a topic of interest for you, you'll probably be able to handle the full 90 minutes of it. Tours are about once a month, on Saturdays at 3pm, usually leaving from One Worldwide Plaza, on 49th (between Eighth and Ninth aves.). Check the website for info.

www.walkingtoursnyc.com. Subway: C/E to 50th St.

Prospect Park Discover Nature Tours `FREE`

My favorite tour here leads into the wilds of Brooklyn, where you can see a newly rehabbed ravine, waterfalls, and Brooklyn's last forest. It's just like the Adirondacks—only less driving, and better proximity to ethnic food when it's over. Tours run on the weekends and Monday holidays at 3pm, March through November. Check the website for other destinations, like nearby Green-Wood Cemetery. Meet at the Audubon Center (at the Boathouse), just inside the Lincoln Road/Ocean Avenue entrance.

ℂ 718/287-3400. www.prospectpark.org. Subway: B/Q/S to Prospect Park.

Shorewalkers `FREE`

Shorewalkers sure know how to hoof it. This environmental walking group makes some huge treks around the city, usually keeping close to water. `FINE PRINT` A $3 donation is requested. Dates, times, and locations vary; call or check the website for specifics.

ℂ 212/330-7686. www.shorewalkers.org.

Dirt Cheap Tours Worth Checking Out

With so many free tours around, it seems silly to put down money, but **Adventure on a Shoestring** (© 212/265-2663) is worth every penny. Urban historian and general character Howard Goldberg has been providing the behind-the-scenes story on New York nabes for over 40 years, and you're guaranteed to learn something new. Tours follow themes like the "Haunted East Village," "Salute to Sinatra," or "Marilyn Monroe's Manhattan." At $5, they're an inexpensive way to load up on New York lore. Tours last 1½ hours and take place rain or shine. Call for more information.

Another set of $5 tours is run by Kevin Walsh of **Forgotten New York (www.forgotten-ny.com)**. From a website dedicated to vanishing elements of the city, like Bishop's Crook streetlamps and slate sidewalks, come tours of obscure haunts. See things like a 16th-century Queens cemetery in the shadow of a LIRR trestle, or the Bay Ridge church that once counted Robert E. Lee and Stonewall Jackson as members of its congregation. Tours tend to run in the warmer months; check the website for a schedule.

Surveillance Camera Outdoor Walking Tours `FREE`   Thousands of security cameras track New Yorkers' every move. The Surveillance Camera Players run weekly tours to make citizens a little more aware of this virtual police state, which has proliferated in dramatic fashion over the last couple of years. Free tours meet on Sundays at 2pm at varying spots around the city; no reservations necessary.
© **212/561-0106.** www.notbored.org/scowt.html.

Take a Walk, New York! `FREE`   The Listen to your Heart Campaign endeavors to slow the widening of New York waists through a series of guided urban walks. The walks are scheduled for weekends in all five boroughs and last 2 to 3 hours. Go fight the good fight against cardiovascular disease! Check online for current schedules.
© **212/379-8339.** www.walkny.org.

Urban Trail Conference `FREE`   A diverse selection of sites, from downtown Manhattan to the PepsiCo sculpture gardens in Purchase,

New York, are toured by these intrepid trekkers. They ask for a $3 donation from nonmembers (a few events cost a little more), although first-timers get to walk for free. Big spenders can shell out for a year's worth of activity by paying the club's $10 annual dues.

Phone numbers vary by tour guide; check the website **www.urban trail.org**.

5 Green Peace: Gardens

It's just not healthy for humans to spend too much consecutive time without a break from the concrete jungle. New York has some great parks, but the space tends to be pretty cultivated. Our community gardens are nice, too, but they're small and usually don't let the public in for more than a couple of hours a week. Botanical gardens are the best way to inhale fresh country air, and they're closer than you might think. Time your visit right, and they're also completely free.

Brooklyn Botanic Garden   Fifty-two acres of cherry trees, roses, formal gardens, and ponds in the heart of Brooklyn is nothing short of a miracle. This is the city's most popular botanic garden and it's spectacular almost year-round. May is particularly worth noting, with bright green leaves on the trees and the cherry blossoms rioting. Don't miss the Fragrance Garden, designed for the blind, and the world's oldest and largest collection of bonsai. The regular admission is $5, but Tuesdays are free, as are Saturday mornings from 10am to noon. In winter, you can add Wednesdays, Thursdays, and Fridays to the free list (mid-Nov to mid-Mar).

1000 Washington Ave., at Eastern Pkwy., Brooklyn. ℂ **718/623-7200.** www. bbg.org. Tues–Fri 8am–6pm; Sat–Sun 10am–6pm; closes at 4:30pm Oct–Mar. Open holiday Mondays, except Labor Day. Subway: 2/3 to Eastern Pkwy./Brooklyn Museum; B/Q to Prospect Park. S to Botanic Garden.

☆ **New York Botanical Garden**   Visions of the Bronx don't conjure up uncut forests, rhododendron valleys, waterfalls, ponds, and wetlands. As unlikely as it may seem, though, for over a century the Bronx has been home to one of America's premier public gardens. With over 250 acres of rolling hills and landscaped gardens, if it's flora you can probably find it. A combined admission to everything the garden offers is $13, but all day Wednesday and Saturday morning from 10am to noon you can get in to the grounds for free.

200th St. and Southern Blvd., the Bronx. © **718/817-8700.** www.nybg.org. Metro North (© 800/METRO-INFO or 212/532-4900; www.mta.nyc.ny.us/mnr) runs from Grand Central Terminal to the New York Botanical Garden station; it's a 20-min ride. Apr-Oct Tues-Sun and Mon holidays 10am-6pm; closes at 5pm Nov-Mar. Subway: B/D/4 to Bedford Park, walk southeast on Bedford Park Blvd. 8 blocks.

Queens Botanical Garden `FREE` This little-known park is an oasis in the heart of busy Flushing. Formal gardens are joined by a rose garden, a bee garden, a Victorian garden, and a 21-acre arboretum. A gorgeous new visitor's center, complete with environmentally friendly technology, will add to the attraction when it's completed in 2007. Spring is the natural time to visit here— the entire garden is awash with color.

43-50 Main St., at Dahlia St., Flushing, Queens. © **718/886-3800.** www. queensbotanical.org. Nov-Mar Tues-Sun 8am-4:30pm; Apr-Sept Tues-Fri 8am-6pm, Sat-Sun 8am-7pm. Subway: 7 to Main St. Flushing.

Staten Island Botanical Gardens `FREE` Staten Islanders have gardens galore nestled inside the Snug Harbor Cultural Center. The center is 2 miles from the ferry terminal, so getting here is a bit of a haul from the other boroughs. The grounds are open daily from dawn to dusk. They're free, but a couple of the gardens inside have fees ranging from $2 to $5. Connie Gretz's Secret Garden is well worth its $2 charge—

`FREE` **Close Encounters**

One of Manhattan's leafiest oases lies in Chelsea, on the campus of the **General Theological Seminary.** The Close, the campus's grounds, is a tranquil patch in the middle of an already-quaint stretch of 1850's row houses. The Seminary's buildings date to the late 19th century, constructed in the English collegiate-Gothic style. Wander the wisteria-choked grounds and you may feel like you've stepped through a wormhole straight onto the campus of a British university. Jack Kerouac and Allen Ginsberg used to stroll here; Kerouac lived across the street in 1951, where he typed his third draft of *On the Road.* Chelsea Square, enter at 175 Ninth Ave. between 20th and 21st sts. © **212/243-5150.** www.gts.edu. Mon-Sat, 11am-3pm; shorter hours when school is out of session. C/E to 23rd Street.

FREE Clang, Clang, Clang

When it comes to hyping NYC's attractions, the Bronx, Brooklyn, and Queens can understandably feel shorted by Manhattan. That's why God created cultural **trolleys.** Queens's version runs from the **Queens Museum** (© 718/592-9700, ext. 306; www.queensmuseum.org), connecting to great ethnic dining on Northern Boulevard and 74th Street., and the English Garden homes of Jackson Heights. The trolley runs from noon until 5pm on the weekends. For a loop around Prospect Park, look no further than the **Heart of Brooklyn Trolley** (© 718/638-7700; www.heartofbrooklyn.org). On weekends and holidays from noon to 6pm, the trolley will get you from the Brooklyn Museum all the way south around Prospect Lake, and back up again. The Bronx has no trolley envy, offering three ways for visitors to get around Jonas Bronck's old stomping grounds. On the first Wednesday night of every month (except Jan and Sept), the **Bronx Culture Trolley** (© 718/931-9500, ext. 33; www.bronxarts.org) whisks visitors around to free art, music, theater, and poetry readings. Free wine and snacks are even offered at the starting point, the Longwood Art Gallery at Hostos Community College, 450 Grand Concourse, at 149th Street. Advance reservations are recommended. On the first Friday night of every month, City Island shows itself off with its **Bronx Seaside Trolley Program** (© 718/885-3090; www.cityislandchamber.org), which connects the 6 train at Pelham Bay Park with local galleries, shops, and the Bartow-Pell Mansion Museum. The **Bronx Tour Trolley** (© 718/590-3518; www.ilovethe bronx.com) zips around New York's other Little Italy (where the food is better) on Arthur Avenue, the Bronx Zoo, and the botanical garden, with mass transit-friendly stops along the way. The trolley runs during the days on the weekends and holidays, with special evening hours for the Christmas season. Best of all, all these outer borough trolley rides are free. Take that, Manhattan.

it has a maze and a castle with a moat. They'll even waive the $2 if you've got a child in tow.

1000 Richmond Terrace, Staten Island. © 718/273-8200. www.sibg.org. Daily dawn–dusk. S40 bus from the ferry to Snug Harbor.

FREE Parking It

Parks are among the city's best freebies, and we're fortunate to be in an era of expansion. Some 550 acres (!) of new parkland have opened up along the **piers near Chelsea.** The city did a gorgeous job with these urban beaches, including planting some actual slender-leaved vegetation called "grass." Across town, restoration continues on the **East River Park.** When it's finally completed, epic Brooklyn views will complement benches, ball fields, and a wide jogging path. Everyone knows about the great Manhattan views from the **Brooklyn Promenade,** but Queens has an equally impressive skyline vantage that many New Yorkers have never seen. The **Gantry Plaza State Park** in Long Island City is fitted out with long piers that jut out over the East River, with the U.N. and Empire State Building standing tall among Midtown's architectural jumble. The park has been newly fixed up and expanded on its northern end, with a swath of grass and comfy seats for chilling out. 49th St. and East River Dr., Queens. ✆ **718/786-6385.** Subway: 7 to Vernon Jackson, walk west to the river.

Wave Hill   Some of the city's most gorgeous acreage can be found in Riverdale, in the Bronx, where Wave Hill's breathtaking views take in the panorama of the Hudson and the Palisades. Thousands of plant species are spread across the 28 acres here, originally the grounds of a private estate. The plant curious can educate themselves in the carefully labeled herb and flower gardens. Horticultural, environmental, and forestry programs provide further edification. Regular admission is $4, but the grounds are free in winter. In summer, Tuesdays are free, as are Saturday mornings from 9am to noon.

675 W. 252nd St., at Independence Ave., the Bronx. ✆ **718/549-3200.** www.wavehill.org. Mid-Apr–mid-Oct Tues–Sun 9am–5:30pm; Mid-Oct–mid-Apr closes at 4:30; Jun–Jul until 9pm on Wed. Subway: 1 to 231st St., then take the Bx7 or Bx10 bus to the 252nd St. stop; or A to 207th St. and pick up the Bx7 to 252nd St. From the 252nd St. stop, walk west across the parkway bridge and turn left; at 249th St., turn right. Metro North (✆ 212/532-4900) travel from Grand Central to the Riverdale station; from there, it's a pleasant 5-block walk to Wave Hill.

Winter Garden at the World Financial Center `FREE` This is the best spot in the city to get some perspective on Ground Zero. The Winter Garden was all but totaled by the collapsing towers on 9/11, but you'd never guess it to look at the towering Washingtonia robusta palm trees and gleaming marble inside the atrium. Beneath the stairs you'll find temporary exhibits outlining the plans for Ground Zero, which will hopefully someday include a worthy memorial in addition to the inevitable corporate skyscraper. Walk up the stairs to the panoramic windows and you'll have an elevated view of the former World Trade Center site. Turning around to face the pristine interior of the Winter Garden always helps me appreciate the incredible resilience of New York.

Between Vesey and Liberty sts., between the West Side Hwy. and the Hudson. Ⓒ 212/945-2600. www.worldfinancialcenter.com. Open 24 hours. A/C/J/M/Z/2/3/4/5 to Fulton St./Broadway Nassau; E to World Trade Center; R/W to City Hall; 1 to Rector St.

6 Zoo York

New York has plenty of fauna to go with its flora, though it isn't always cheap to check out. The minizoos in the major Brooklyn, Queens, and Manhattan parks charge $6 to $8 admission. The Bronx Zoo asks for $12 during the warmer months. Fortunately, there are alternatives. The Bronx has a pay-what-you-wish policy 1 day a week, and the city's parks are rich with other opportunities for getting close to critters.

Bronx Zoo Wildlife Conservation Park Yankee Stadium isn't the only place in the Bronx where you can find 4,000 wild animals running around in their natural habitat. The Bronx Zoo is the largest city zoo in the country, and one of New York's greatest assets. Gibbons, snow leopards, red pandas, Western lowland gorillas, okapi, and red river hogs are just a few of the famous residents. With 265 acres to explore, it's easy to wander away a full day here. For summer visits, try to get here early or late, as the midday heat often finds the animals sleepy in their enclosures. Admission is $12 ($8 from November through March), but Wednesdays are on a contribution basis (the suggested admission is the full price, but it's pay what you wish). Additional charges ($3 or so) will apply for some exhibits.

185th St. and Southern Blvd. Ⓒ 718/367-1010. www.bronxzoo.com. Nov-Mar daily 10am–4:30pm (extended hours for Holiday Lights late Nov to early

☆ FREE A Midnight Elephant Walk

When the pachyderms visit the big town, they're coming off their Nassau Coliseum stand. Their train only gets them as far as the Long Island City yards. They can't exactly get a lift to the gig from a town car, so they have to hoof it, through the Queens-Midtown Tunnel and down the streets of Manhattan. Watching the elephants emerge from the tunnel is an amazing spectacle. They walk in a file of trunks holding tails, with clown escorts all around. Often other hoofed beasts like zebras and camels come along for the stroll. The walk goes all the way to the elephants' five-story ramp at Madison Square Garden, but the best scene is at the tunnel entrance on 34th Street. The crowd is fun-loving, with the freaks that events in Manhattan invariably bring out well represented. The procession hits the Manhattan side of the tunnel around 11:30pm. Whether you come for the spectacle or just to hiss the exploitation of animals, be sure to be on time because the whole thing goes surprisingly quickly. The elephant walk takes place at the beginning of the circus' annual stand (usually late winter); check the weekly update on the website for the exact date and time. ✆ **212/465-6741**. www. ringling.com/weekly. Subway: 6 to 33rd. St.; A/C/E or 1/2/3 to 34th St.

Jan); Apr-Oct Mon-Fri 10am-5pm; Sat-Sun 10am-5:30pm. Subway: 2 to Pelham Pkwy., Metro North to Fordham Rd. (then Bx9 bus); BxM11 Liberty Line bus (✆ 212/652-8400).

FREE BIRDS

A dearth of rest stops on the Eastern Seaboard makes New York parks essential for avian travelers. Three New York parks loan out equipment for better boning up on our most welcome tourists.

Battery Park City FREE Eighty different bird species pass through the lush tip of Manhattan. At the Wagner Park pavilions binoculars and field guides are loaned out for free. Select Thursdays (usually 9:30 to 11am) and Saturdays (usually 11am to 1pm); check online as times vary.

✆ **212/267-9700**. www.bpcparks.org. Subway: 1 to Rector St.; 4/5 to Bowling Green.

Central Park `FREE` Birdsong fills the thickets of the Ramble, an unexpectedly rural stretch of the park. You can take a closer look at the warbling set with a kit available from the Belvedere Castle. The kit is a backpack with binoculars, reference materials, and a map. The Castle is open Tuesday to Sunday from 10am to 4:30pm. Two pieces of ID are required.

Midpark at 79th St. ✆ 212/772-0210. Subway: B/C to 81st St.

Falconry Extravaganza `FREE` The falcon has landed: One day a year the birds of prey uncloak in Central Park. All manner of raptors swoop through the air above the East Meadow under the close supervision of the Urban Park Rangers. Leave the Chihuahuas at home. Meet at the East Meadow on the east side of the park at 97th Street.

✆ 212/628-2345. Oct Sat noon–4pm. Subway: 6 to 96th St.

Prospect Park `FREE` During spring's annual northward migration, hundreds of different bird species pass through here. To get some expert assistance in figuring out what's what, hook up with an introductory bird-watching tour (times vary, usually mid-day). To catch the worm-getting birds, you'll have to get up earlier. On the first Sunday of every month join the Early Bird Walk as it ambles through the park from 8 to 10am. It's free, but you should call in advance to register. All tours leave from the boathouse, just inside the Lincoln Road/ Ocean Avenue entrance.

✆ 718/287-3400. www.prospectpark.org. Subway: B/Q/S to Prospect Park.

GO FISH

It's a fine line between standing along the shore like an idiot with a stick in your hands and going fishing, but kids love baiting up and casting in anyway. The city offers a few spots for gathering fodder for "the one that got away" tales.

Battery Park City `FREE` Drop a line in the Hudson and see if you can pull up any three-eyed specimens. (Actually, the river's been mending remarkably in recent years, thanks to antipollution measures.) Bait and equipment are loaned out in Wagner Park. Sessions run from 10am to 2pm on select Saturdays, and select Fridays at lunch 11:30am to 1:30pm.

✆ 212/267-9700. www.bpcparks.org. Subway: 1 to Rector St.; 4/5 to Bowling Green.

FREE **What Up, Dog?**

Being trapped in small, dark apartments is just as hard on dogs as it is on us. Fortunately for dogs, they have a release valve in the form of dog runs. The human and canine interactions make great free public theater. The **Tompkins Square** dog run is my favorite. Both the four-legged and two-legged regulars have a ton of character, and their friendships and rivalries are fascinating to observe. Don't miss the creative costumes of the **Dog Run Halloween Parade,** held at noon on the Sunday before Halloween. Tompkins Sq. Park, between 7th and 10th sts. and aves. A and B. © **917/797-7073.** www.dogster.org. Subway: 6 to Astor Place; F/V to Second Ave.

Central Park **FREE**   Like the good New Yorkers they are, some 50,000 fish pack uncomplainingly into the confines of the Harlem Meer. You can try your hand at catching a bass, catfish, or bluegill with equipment loaned by the Charles A. Dana Discovery Center. Bait, pole, and instructions are provided. Fish can be fondled, but they're not to be kept: It's catch and release. Open Tuesday to Sunday 10am to 4pm (last pole goes out at 3pm), mid-April to mid-October. Valid photo ID is required.

Inside Central Park at 110th St., between Fifth and Lenox aves. © **212/860-1370.** www.centralparknyc.org. Subway: 2/3 to Central Park North.

Hudson River Park **FREE**   There's no dilemma whether to fish or cut bait, as the Big City Fishing program takes care of the latter for you. Experienced anglers are on hand to offer advice, and the rods are free to borrow. Reel fun can be found at piers 46 (Greenwich Village), and 95 (Clinton). Don't get too attached to your oyster toadfishes, flukes, or cunners, however, because everything here is catch and release. Available on summer weekends; call ahead for exact hours.

Pier 46, the Hudson just north of Christopher St. © **212/533-PARK.** www.hudsonriverpark.org. Subway: 1 to Christopher St. Pier 95, the Hudson at W. 55th St.; A/B/C/D/1 to 59th St.-Columbus Circle.

EXPLORING DOWNTOWN

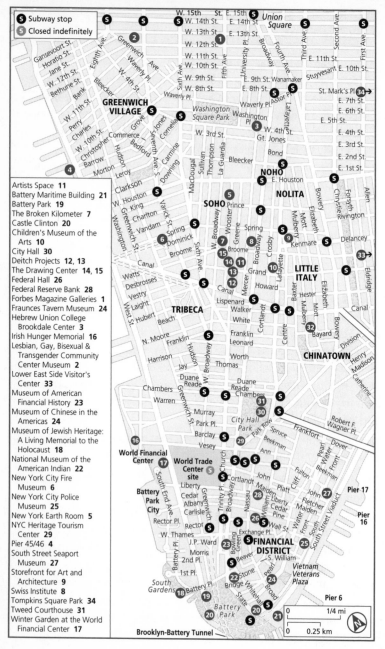

Subway stop ⑤
Closed indefinitely ⑤

Artists Space **11**
Battery Maritime Building **21**
Battery Park **19**
The Broken Kilometer **7**
Castle Clinton **20**
Children's Museum of the
 Arts **10**
City Hall **30**
Deitch Projects **12, 13**
The Drawing Center **14, 15**
Federal Hall **26**
Federal Reserve Bank **28**
Forbes Magazine Galleries **1**
Fraunces Tavern Museum **24**
Hebrew Union College
 Brookdale Center **3**
Irish Hunger Memorial **16**
Lesbian, Gay, Bisexual &
 Transgender Community
 Center Museum **2**
Lower East Side Visitor's
 Center **33**
Museum of American
 Financial History **23**
Museum of Chinese in the
 Americas **24**
Museum of Jewish Heritage:
 A Living Memorial to the
 Holocaust **18**
National Museum of the
 American Indian **22**
New York City Fire
 Museum **6**
New York City Police
 Museum **25**
New York Earth Room **5**
NYC Heritage Tourism
 Center **29**
Pier 45/46 **4**
South Street Seaport
 Museum **27**
Storefront for Art and
 Architecture **9**
Swiss Institute **8**
Tompkins Square Park **34**
Tweed Courthouse **31**
Winter Garden at the World
 Financial Center **17**

EXPLORING UPTOWN

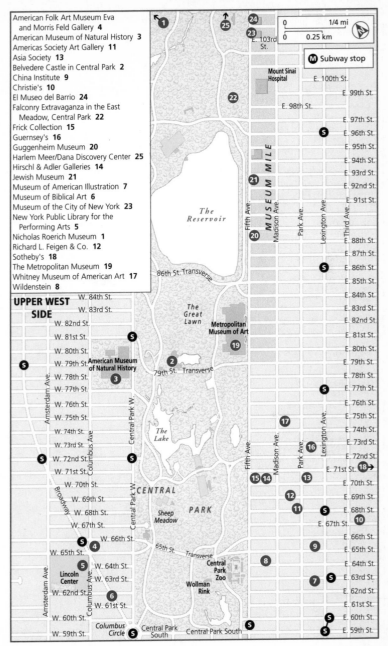

M Subway stop

Mount Sinai
Hospital

**UPPER WEST
   SIDE**

American Museum
of Natural History

*The
Great
Lawn*

Metropolitan
Museum of Art

*The
Lake*

CENTRAL

*Sheep
Meadow*

PARK

*The
Reservoir*

MUSEUM MILE

Central
Park
Zoo

Wollman
Rink

Lincoln
Center

*Columbus
Circle*

Central Park
South

Central Park South

EXPLORING MIDTOWN

EXPLORING BROOKLYN

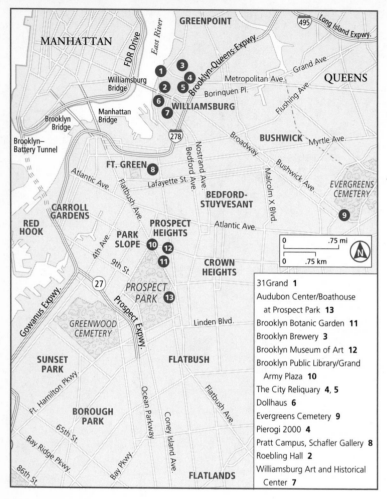

MANHATTAN

GREENPOINT

495 Long Island Expwy.

FDR Drive

East River

Williamsburg
Bridge

Brooklyn-Queens Expwy.

Metropolitan Ave.

Grand Ave.

QUEENS

Borinquen Pl.

WILLIAMSBURG

Manhattan
Bridge

Brooklyn
Bridge

Brooklyn–
Battery Tunnel

278

Broadway

BUSHWICK

Myrtle Ave.

FT. GREEN

Atlantic Ave.

Lafayette St.

Nostrand Ave.
Bedford Ave.

Flatbush Ave.

CARROLL
GARDENS

RED
HOOK

BEDFORD-
STUYVESANT

Malcolm X Blvd.

Bushwick Ave.

Flushing Ave.

EVERGREENS
CEMETERY

PROSPECT
HEIGHTS

Atlantic Ave.

4th Ave.

PARK
SLOPE

9th St.

27

Gowanus Expwy.

PROSPECT
PARK

Prospect Expwy.

GREENWOOD
CEMETERY

SUNSET
PARK

Ft. Hamilton Pkwy.

BOROUGH
PARK

65th St.

Bay Ridge Pkwy.

86th St.

Bay Pkwy.

Ocean Parkway

Coney Island Ave.

CROWN
HEIGHTS

Linden Blvd.

FLATBUSH

Flatbush Ave.

FLATLANDS

| 0 | .75 mi |
| 0 | .75 km |

N

31Grand **1**
Audubon Center/Boathouse
  at Prospect Park **13**
Brooklyn Botanic Garden **11**
Brooklyn Brewery **3**
Brooklyn Museum of Art **12**
Brooklyn Public Library/Grand
  Army Plaza **10**
The City Reliquary **4, 5**
Dollhaus **6**
Evergreens Cemetery **9**
Pierogi 2000 **4**
Pratt Campus, Schafler Gallery **8**
Roebling Hall **2**
Williamsburg Art and Historical
  Center **7**

EXPLORING QUEENS

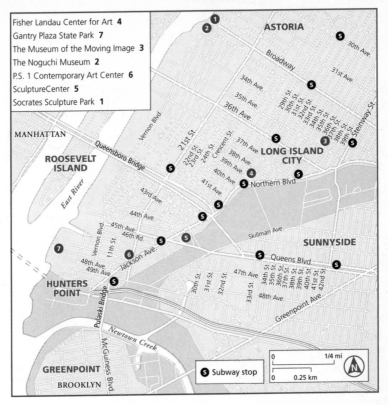

Fisher Landau Center for Art **4**
Gantry Plaza State Park **7**
The Museum of the Moving Image **3**
The Noguchi Museum **2**
P.S. 1 Contemporary Art Center **6**
SculptureCenter **5**
Socrates Sculpture Park **1**

ASTORIA

Broadway

30th Ave.

31st Ave.

34th Ave.

35th Ave.

36th Ave.

29th St.
30th St.
31st St.
32nd St.
33rd St.
34th St.
35th St.
36th St.
37th St.
38th St.
39th St.

Steinway St.

MANHATTAN

Queensboro Bridge

Vernon Blvd.

21st St.

22nd St.
23rd St.
24th St.

Crescent St.

37th Ave.

38th Ave.

39th Ave.

40th Ave.

41st Ave.

LONG ISLAND
CITY

ROOSEVELT
ISLAND

East River

43rd Ave.

44th Ave.

Northern Blvd.

Skillman Ave.

SUNNYSIDE

45th Ave.
46th Rd.

Jackson Ave.

Vernon Blvd.
11th St.

Queens Blvd.

30th St.
31st St.
32nd St.
33rd St.

34th St.
35th St.
36th St.
37th St.
38th St.
39th St.
40th St.
41st St.
42nd St.

47th Ave.

48th Ave.

48th Ave
49th Ave.

HUNTERS
POINT

Pulaski Bridge

Greenpoint Ave.

Newtown Creek

McGuiness Blvd.

GREENPOINT

BROOKLYN

0   1/4 mi
0   0.25 km

S Subway stop

N

283

Built in 1920, Coney Island's iconic Wonder Wheel spent decades as the tallest Ferris wheel in the world—and it's a pretty cool ride, too. See p. 289 for more information.

FREE & DIRT CHEAP DAYS

Though New York is happy to gouge visitors for $40 bus tours and boat cruises, a person can scope out a lot of city for no money at all. It's hard to swing a cat in NYC without banging into a free daylong adventure or cheap date. The city's close quarters means you can hit a huge range of sites without putting excessive mileage on your soles. You don't even need to pack—Gotham's corner stores are already storing your provisions for you.

Itinerary 1: A Day at Coney Island, Baby

Where	Coney Island, Brooklyn.
How to Get There	D/F/N/Q to Stillwell Avenue/Coney Island. The subway ride is about 40 minutes from downtown Manhattan. You can also use the B/Q at Brighton Beach.
How Long to Spend There	It's easy to amuse yourself along the boardwalk and environs for 2 or 3 hours. Anything longer probably requires a beach towel and a page-turner.
What to Bring	If you're planning on a dip, a bathing suit and towel are the obvious needs. There are public bathrooms, cabanas for changing, and showers for shedding saltwater. Even if you're going to keep to the streets, bring sunscreen because there's light aplenty reflecting off the sand and sea.
Best Times to Go	Morning's calm is nice. Midday summer days can be brutal and hectic. Late afternoons the crowds start to disperse and the light is lovely.
Related Tip	The big holiday weekends bring in special events, but they also bring the biggest crowds. If you're not in the mood for the big crush, go on a weekday, or keep to the fringes, which are less populated. In the nonsummer months the amusement parks are closed and the boardwalk is almost empty, but the experience can be peaceful and replenishing.

After a few weeks or months of city living, trapped in the concrete canyons, it's easy to forget that New York City grew so far and fast because of its access to water. New York Harbor stays close to the public consciousness, but too many of us overlook the Atlantic Ocean, which is just a subway ride away. When you feel like traveling to a distant place but don't want to invest more than a couple of Metrocard swipes, Coney Island is hard to beat. In summer the area becomes a blue-collar resort, with salsa bands and volleyball games and screaming kids on the rides. As with all of Brooklyn, it's the furthest thing from monolithic. Tourists, hipsters, and elderly immigrant residents all intermingle on the beachfront benches. Plans for a $1-billion makeover and the new $250-million subway terminal suggest impending gentrification, but chances are the island will stay low-budget and rustic for a long time to come.

① The Beach

The Atlantic up close is irresistible and the broad beaches here are a good spot to start a tour. Get good and hot in the sun and then go in for a dip. The water is not the cleanest, but just follow the lead of the other souls

ITINERARY 1: CONEY ISLAND, BABY

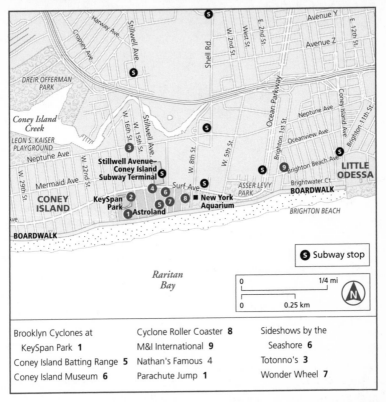

| Subway stop: **S** |

Brooklyn Cyclones at KeySpan Park 1
Coney Island Batting Range 5
Coney Island Museum 6

Cyclone Roller Coaster 8
M&I International 9
Nathan's Famous 4
Parachute Jump 1

Sideshows by the Seashore 6
Totonno's 3
Wonder Wheel 7

out there bobbing in the waves. On a hot day it's particularly refreshing. A few blocks to the east of Astroland and the subway station the bodies thin out quickly and you can even find open stretches. If you're unwilling to track sand back in your shoes, a stroll along the boardwalk offers endless people-watching entertainment.

② Mealtime

The options for cheap beach food in Coney Island are almost limitless. Fried clams, fried dough, French fries, and soft-serve ice cream are among the highlights.

- On July 4th at high noon, hefty Americans and rail-thin Japanese fight it out in the annual Coney Island Hot Dog eating contest. For $2.50 a pop you can hold your own minicontest at Nathan's Famous, which still sells some million dogs a year at their busy stand.

- As good as a meal on a picnic table just off the beach is, it's worth noting that one of New York's best pizzas is just a few

Coney Island Costs

Free	
Sun, sand, and sea	$0
Dirt Cheap	
A day at the beach + 1 museum	$1
Add-Ons for Spendthrift Millionaires	
Cyclone roller coaster or Wonder Wheel	$5-$6
+ Half a pizza	$8
+ 28 pitches	$4
+ Sideshow	$5

blocks away. Totonno's is a casual, family run operation that serves up fresh pies (no slices). The fresh mozzarella, tangy sauce, and delicious thin crust haven't lost a step through 80 years of operation. Large pies are about $16.

③ Astroland

Follow the sounds of electronic burbles and screaming kids up to this amusement park, where if you're feeling dirt cheap, the watching can be almost as much fun as participating. It's free to enter, and tickets for rides and games of chance range from $2.50 to $5.50.

④ The Batting Cages

The city's best mechanical pitchers hurl at the Coney Island Batting Range, a couple of blocks away. Swing away at deliveries that range from underhand to 95mph, $2 for 14 pitches. There's also mini-golf, bumper boats, go-karts, and a slick track.

⑤ The Legendary Cyclone

Technically part of Astroland but located across the street, the Cyclone Roller Coaster is the granddaddy of Coney Island amusements. Accelerating heart rates since 1927, it's the oldest and most-imitated roller coaster in the world. It's also a quota-starved insurance underwriter's nightmare, with engineering limited to a pulling chain and gravity, but still managing to get those rickety cars up to 60mph. The supporting rails and wooden boards look mighty untrustworthy, but of course that's the thrill (and in truth, the safety record here is excellent). Rides are $6 a pop ($5 for a reride) for 1 minute and 50 seconds of action, so it's not exactly dirt cheap, though it's definitely memorable.

⑥ The Coney Island Museum & Sideshows

The museum charge of 99¢ is just about right for a visit to this

The Coney Island Skyline

Parachute jumps were developed as military-training devices, but leave it to America to convert them to fun. Coney Island's parachute jump started out as a ride at the 1939 World's Fair in Queens before packing up for Brooklyn, where it served thrill-seekers until 1964. The skeletal form that remains has an unexpected elegance. A recent design contest was the first step in installing an architecturally ambitious new base, complete with a restaurant and visitor's center. The jump has been designated a historic landmark and it's the pride of the local skyline, so much so that it's sometimes called the Eiffel Tower of Brooklyn.

The Eiffel Tower of Paris was the motivator for George Washington Gale Ferris, an engineer who took up the challenge for America to respond to the Frenchies' innovations in steel. The famous wheels still bear his name and Coney Island's version, the 1920's Wonder Wheel, is one of the world's tallest at 150 feet. From the ground it looks like a gentle spin, but as the cars slide on lateral rails they create a somewhat stomach-churning effect. For panoramic views of the city and sea it's worth it. The $5 cost to ride, however, is a matter of individual budgetary discretion.

musty second-floor space. Funhouse mirrors, vintage bumper cars, and old signage form the bulk of the collection. A handful of small temporary exhibits reflect the love this organization has for Coney Island's vanished heyday. For one penny more you can watch a mutoscope reel of Thomas Edison's 1903 eletrocution of Topsy, a Coney Island elephant condemned for the deaths of three trainers.

Just around the corner you'll find **Sideshows by the Seashore,** run by the same people. It's the nation's last 10-in-1 freak show; step right up to see illustrated men and women, fire-eating, albino serpent handling, and even beds of nails. The theater is small and run-down, with no air-conditioning, but there's 45 minutes of entertainment for only $5 adults, $3 kids 12 and under. If you're patient, you may hear the barker hustle up some empty seats at a discount, usually $3 for all ages. Weekend shows from Memorial Day to Labor Day, Fridays from 2

Make a Date

Coney Island after hours is even seedier than the daylight spectacle, but that doesn't impede on the potential for a great cheap date. The sight of the dark swells of the Atlantic and the cleared-out beach is pretty grand. The only thing that could improve on it is free **fireworks,** which come around 9:30pm every Friday night from late June to late August. After the fireworks if you've got money to burn, check out Sideshows by the Seashore's **Burlesque by the Beach.** Troupes from around the city come down to shake various body parts. Campy costumes and fire-eating round out the experience. Friday nights at 10pm; tickets are usually $10.

On Saturday nights, the same Sideshow folk unfold chairs in the Coney Island Museum so they can project campy films (p. 48). Coney Island-themed fare and other B-movie obsessions are the norm, and it's only $5. 1208 Surf Ave., 2nd floor. ✆ **718/372-5159.** www. indiefilmpage.com. Sat 8:30pm.

to 8pm, Saturday and Sunday from 1 to 11pm. Partial cast on Wednesday and Thursday afternoons, weather permitting.

⑦ Keyspan Stadium

The return of baseball to Brooklyn certainly hasn't diminished local pride, and tickets to Mets farm-hands, the **Brooklyn Cyclones,** aren't that easy to come by. If the game you're aching to see sells out, keep in mind that some standby seats are made available on game day outside the board-walk stadium. Seats are pretty cheap, for professional sports, $6 to $14.

⑧ Bonus Round: Brighton Beach

If you want to leave America but have neglected to pack a passport, there is a close-by option. A quick trip east on the boardwalk will put you in the heart of **Little Odessa** in Brighton Beach. Between the strolling Russian émigrés, the cyrillic signs, and the clunky design on the side-walk cafes, you'll be forgiven for thinking you've walked into a Black Sea resort town. The cafes are surprisingly pricey, but there's plenty of cheap street fare 1 block inland. Take a left and walk toward the El, which runs above

Brighton Beach Avenue. This bustling street is dotted with caviar shops and street vendors.

For total immersion in a foreign land, check out the **M & I International supermarket.** You can stock up for the trip home, or enjoy Russian pastries or smoked fish in the upstairs cafe. Prices are all outer-borough low.

Special Events

● In mid-July, the *Village Voice* sponsors the **Siren Music Festival,** a massive rock concert. Some 100,000 indie fans show up to enjoy music on two stages from noon until 9pm. It's all free, no tickets necessary; just show up. Main stage: 10th Street at the boardwalk. Second stage: Stillwell Avenue at the boardwalk (© **212/475-3333;** www.villagevoice.com/siren).

● With body paint and beads, plus a few strategic scraps of fabric to keep things legal, the avatars of New York's retro-culture scene transform themselves into mermaids and Neptunes at the annual **Mermaid Parade.** Classic cars join the procession as it works its way up Surf Avenue, dispersing when the participants dash down the beach to the ageless Atlantic. First Saturday after the summer solstice. Surf Avenue from West 15th to West 10th streets. www.coneyisland.com/mermaid.shtml. See also June in the "Calendar of Events," p. 18.

Itinerary 1 Index

Astroland   1000 Surf Ave., at the Corner of W. 10th St. © 718/265-2100. www.astroland.com. Daily mid-June–early Sept noon–midnight, weather permitting. Weekends Apr–June 15, Sept–Oct noon–dusk, weather permitting.

Brooklyn Cylones at Keyspan Park   1904 Surf Ave., along the boardwalk. © 718/449-8497. www.brooklyncyclones.com. Check the website for game schedule.

Coney Island Batting Range   3049 Stillwell Ave., near the boardwalk. © 718/449-1200. www.coneyislandbattingrange.com. Daily 11am, noon for some rides.

Coney Island Museum   1208 Surf Ave., at W. 12th St. © 718/372-5159. www.coneyisland.com. Sat–Sun noon–5pm, with expanded hours in season.

Cyclone Roller Coaster 1000 Surf Ave., along W. 10th St. ✆ 718/372-0275. www.astroland.com. Daily noon–midnight.

Deno's Wonder Wheel W. 12th just south of the boardwalk. ✆ 718/372-2592. www.wonderwheel.com. Weekends and school holidays, April–May, Sept–Oct noon–9pm, weather permitting. Memorial Day–Labor Day daily 11am–midnight, weather permitting.

M&I International 249 Brighton Beach Ave., between Brighton 1st Road and Brighton 1st Place. ✆ 718/615-1011. Daily 8am–10pm.

Nathan's Famous 1310 Surf Ave., at Stillwell Ave. ✆ 718/946-2202. www.nathansfamous.com. Mon–Thurs, Sun 8am–2am; Fri–Sat 8am–3am.

Sideshows by the Seashore Surf Ave., at W. 12th St. ✆ 212/372-5159. www.coneyisland.com. Open most summer weekends Fri 2–8pm, Sat–Sun 1–11pm, and sometimes Wed and Thurs 2–8pm, All shows play depending on weather and crowd size.

Totonno's 1524 Neptune Ave., between 15th and 16th sts. ✆ 718/372-8606. Wed–Sun noon–8:30pm, and Cyclones home games.

Itinerary 2: From Brooklyn Bridge to DUMBO

How to Get There	To reach the Brooklyn Bridge, take the J/M/Z to Chambers Street or the 4/5/6 to Brooklyn Bridge-City Hall. Return from DUMBO on the F train at York Street, or walk about 15 minutes to Brooklyn Heights to catch the A/C train at High Street, or the 2/3 train at Clark Street.
How Long to Spend There	The walk across the bridge takes 30 minutes or so, and it's easy to spend an hour walking around on the Brooklyn side. Adding galleries, meals, and park time will stretch out the visit 2 or 3 hours.
Best Times to Go	A sunny afternoon is ideal, but it's all good. Late at night the bridge and DUMBO are close to deserted. It's more disconcerting than dangerous, but unless you're familiar with the area I recommend against it.
Tip	If you're interested in the galleries, check in advance to see which ones have exhibits up. Note that galleries in DUMBO keep different hours than those in Manhattan; many are closed mid-week, but open on Sundays.

ITINERARY 2: FROM BROOKLYN BRIDGE TO DUMBO

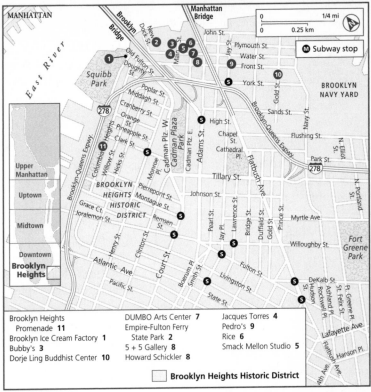

Brooklyn Heights Promenade **11**
Brooklyn Ice Cream Factory **1**
Bubby's **3**
Dorje Ling Buddhist Center **10**

DUMBO Arts Center **7**
Empire-Fulton Ferry State Park **2**
5 + 5 Gallery **8**
Howard Schickler **8**

Jacques Torres **4**
Pedro's **9**
Rice **6**
Smack Mellon Studio **5**

Brooklyn Heights Historic District

① The Bridge

The Brooklyn Bridge is one of New York's great treasures, and as such it's not a very well-kept secret. Tourists, joggers, and commuters flood the planks on sunny days. The dizzying rigging, stunning views, and towering Gothic charm leave a person feeling like they're within the sanctuary of an inside-out cathedral. The bridge's official romance with New York began in 1883, and from Walt Whitman through Hart Crane,

the love has only grown. When you reach the first tower, stop for a while so you can admire the Manhattan views. The assorted plaques here are a mix of the ceremonial and the informative.

② The Brooklyn Side: DUMBO & Its Galleries

On the far side of the bridge, the pathway slants downward and divides. Going to the right takes you to Downtown Brooklyn and Brooklyn Heights, and staying straight will put you beneath an

Brooklyn Bridge/DUMBO Costs

Free	
Historic walk, art galleries, afternoon in the park	$0
Dirt Cheap	
Walk, art, park, plus an ice cream cone or hot chocolate	$2.50–$3
Add-Ons for Spendthrift Millionaires	
Cuban sandwich at Pedro's	$4.50
Brunch at Bubby's or Rice	$6–$10

overpass. Walk down the stairs, take a left, and head toward the water. You'll find yourself among the cobblestones and broad-shouldered buildings that characterize **DUMBO.** DUMBO (Down Under the Manhattan Bridge Overpass) is a surprisingly well-preserved patch of old industrial New York. Artists have infiltrated the area, and their touches can be seen on and around many of the loft structures. For a closer look, check out some of the galleries. (Even if you hate the art, many of the galleries have killer views.)

● **Smack Mellon Studio** A DUMBO classic in a new home. 92 Plymouth St., between Washington and Main sts. Check the website for free outdoor film screenings. ✆ **718/834-8761.** www.smackmellon. org. Wed–Sun noon–6pm.

● **DUMBO Arts Center** A 3,000-square-foot gallery. 30 Washington St., between Water and Plymouth sts. ✆ **718/694-0831.**

www.dumboartscenter.org. Thurs–Mon noon–6pm.

● **Howard Schickler** Space and astronomy specialists. 111 Front St., #208, between Washington and Adams sts. ✆ **718/408-1220.** www.schicklerart. com. Tues noon–6pm; Wed–Fri 10am–6pm; Sat 11am–7pm.

● **5 + 5 Gallery** 111 Front St., #210, between Washington and Adams sts. ✆ **718/488-8383.** www.5plus5gallery.com. Sun–Fri 11am–6pm.

❸ A Moment of Zen & Vinegar Hill

When you've had your fill of art, walk up Front Street (keeping the water to your left). When you reach Gold Street, peek through the yellow cement blocks on the corner. The compound inside belongs to the **Dorje Ling Buddhist Center.** When Front Street dead-ends take a left and enter my favorite forgotten neighborhood in New York, Vinegar Hill. The well-preserved mid-19th-century buildings are oddly

Crossings Over

New York's two other East Village crossings are more utilitarian approaches to Brooklyn, but they're excellent alternatives if you've already done the Brooklyn Bridge to death. The **Williamsburg Bridge** is newly refurbished, with walk- and bikeways to connect Billyburg with the Lower East Side. The **Manhattan Bridge**'s pathway is narrow and the subway can be near deafening, but the views are unimpeachable. On the Manhattan end you get ancient tenements cutting razor-sharp lines through Chinatown, at midpoint you overlook the stunning full span of the Brooklyn Bridge, and on the far side you can spy on the parks of DUMBO.

juxtaposed with electric transformers. The neighborhood is only 4 square blocks, so it's a quick tour. Taking a right on Evans Street will bring you to a cul-de-sac, where you'll see an elegant white house behind a gate. Between 1806 and 1966 this is where the Navy Yard commandant hung his hat, while keeping watch over the outfitting of ships to fight everything from Barbary pirates to Nazis. The residence is now in private hands and the Navy Yard is closed to the public. If you're interested in checking out the vine-smothered ruins of old naval housing, walk up Navy Street and turn left onto Nassau Street (it becomes Flushing Ave.), and then retrace your steps. Otherwise, double back down to Plymouth Street and walk south to DUMBO.

Mealtime

Two popular Manhattan joints have opened satellite locations in DUMBO, and both have cheap brunches on the weekends.

- With huge ceilings and plenty of surplus space, this location of TriBeCa legend **Bubby's** seems like it belongs in a less space-starved city. Prices are not exactly dirt cheap, but quality is high, and you can get an omelet, pancakes, or sandwich for around $10.

- Asian fusion fave **Rice** has brought Brooklyn its exotic grains, from Thai black to Bhutanese red. Starches are accompanied by curries, salads, and satays. Prices at brunch are $5.50 to $8.50, and at dinner most every dish is under $10. There's a great side

Dim Sum Good Eats

The entrance to the Brooklyn Bridge is just behind City Hall, which is just behind Chinatown, which is the cheapest place around to fuel up for a hearty walk. At dim sum brunches, carts full of dumplings and other delights are wheeled around the big banquet halls of Chinatown restaurants. It's easy to pack away a lot of food for no more than $10. My favorite spot is Chinatown's Golden Unicorn, with a lobby that on weekends looks like an office building during a fire drill. With four banquet hall floors, the wait for dumplings, pork-filled noodle crepes, and balls of shrimp and eggplant usually isn't too long, and on weekdays you can waltz right in. 18 E. Broadway, at Catherine St. ⓒ 212/941-0911. Daily Mon-Fri 9am-11pm; Sat-Sun 8am-midnight; dim sum until 4pm. Subway: J/M/N/Q/R/W/Z/6 to Canal St.

garden, should the weather accommodate.

● My personal favorite is **Pedro's.** Gigantic, tasty burritos are only $7, and tacos are $2.50. Rustic seats in front allow for leisurely sidewalk dining.

⑤ Park It

DUMBO offers twin spots for the cooling of jets, the **Empire–Fulton Ferry State Park** and Brooklyn Bridge Park. The former was the point of departure for the Manhattan ferry, which ran until 1924 despite competition from the Brooklyn Bridge. The northern park was a parking lot until it was decided that billion-dollar views of the city, the water, and the bridges, might be better appreciated by human beings than panel trucks. The boat traffic and skyline are both hypnotizing, and this is my favorite place to chill in the entire city.

⑥ Bonus Round: Brooklyn Heights

Just up the hill on the other side of the Brooklyn Bridge lies Brooklyn Heights. The neighborhood is staid, but the historic building stock is astounding. The fruit streets (Pineapple St., Orange St., and Cranberry St., running east-west) are especially nice to stroll through. The **Brooklyn Promenade** along the Hudson has brilliant views of the Manhattan skyline.

Special Events

● Thursday nights in July and August walk over the Brooklyn Bridge and then reward yourself with a free flick. The **Brooklyn Bridge Park "Movies With a**

Make a Sweet Date

The Brooklyn Bridge at night is one of the most romantic spots in the city. You can take in the Manhattan skyline, plus the shimmering lights of Brooklyn, plus the mystery of the dark water below, plied by tugs and ferries. In the hours after dusk there's still plenty of foot traffic on the bridge so there's no menace, but it's much more secluded and sedate than at its rush hour and high noon peaks. If you've done a little planning, you can crank up the romance level a few notches by timing your visit with moonrise. The moon's exact westward rising varies throughout the year, but generally it can be found creeping up over the Brooklyn skyline to the northeast. Check the paper or a weather website for the exact time of moonrise, and allow an extra 20 minutes or so for the satellite to clear the rooflines. If you're really organized, make the date for the full moon—it's the best free show the city's got.

After strolling along the bridge, cool down at the **Brooklyn Ice Cream Factory.** The ice cream here is as pleasurable as the view, well worth the $3 per cone. A little more inland, chocolatier extraordinaire **Jacques Torres** operates a factory out of DUMBO. Though the chocolates themselves could never be confused with dirt cheap, once they take liquid form they become affordable. Drink the hot chocolate and you're basically drinking a candy bar. Order the "wicked" version, with its subtle hot pepper hints, and enjoy extra warmth. This rich treat is a relative bargain at $2.50.

View" Summer Film Series projects in the shadow of the anchorage. (See p. 54 in "Entertainment" for a full review.)

- One weekend in mid-October (Fri–Sun) you can get the entire DUMBO arts scene at once. During the **d.u.m.b.o. art under the bridge festival,** galleries and artists' studios open their doors. There's also live music and performances, as well as art installations adorning the streets. The DUMBO Art Center has a brochure with listings and a map (see p. 262 in "Exploring" for more info).

- Every August, the **Brooklyn Waterfront Artists Coalition** curates an **outdoor sculpture**

show at Empire–Fulton Ferry State Park. It's my favorite time to visit, as the modern works are routinely excellent. The placement is even better, complimenting the natural contours of the park and the man-made wonders in the distance. The installations stay up for a couple of months.

Itinerary 2 Index

Brooklyn Ice Cream Factory   Fulton Ferry Landing Pier, between Old Fulton and Water sts. ✆ 718/246-3963. Tues–Sun noon–10pm.

Brooklyn Waterfront Artists Coalition   ✆ 718/802-9254. www.bwac. org.

Bubby's   1 Main St., at Water St. ✆ 718/222-0666. www.bubbys.com. Kids (8 and under) eat free on Sun nights.

Dorje Ling Buddhist Center   98 Gold St., at Spruce St. ✆ 718/522-6253.

Jacques Torres   66 Water St., near Main St. ✆ 718/875-9772. www.mr chocolate.com. Mon–Sat 9am–7pm; Sun 9am–6pm.

Pedro's   73 Jay St., at Front St. ✆ 718/625-0031. Mon–Fri 7am–11pm, Sat 8am–11pm, sometimes open later on Fri and Sat nights, depending on the crowd. Sun noon–8pm. *Note:* All hours are approximate; exact open hours are determined daily.

Rice   81 Washington St., between Front and York sts. ✆ 718/222-9880. www.riceny.com. Mon–Fri noon–midnight; Sat–Sun 10am–midnight.

Itinerary 3: Square Deals, from Washington to Union

How to Get There	Take the A/B/C/D/E/F/V to W. 4th St.-Washington Sq.
How Long to Spend There	The walking distances here are short and can be covered on foot in just a few minutes, but if you stop to linger over the exhibits, it can take a couple of hours.
Best Times to Go	Traffic flow is pretty constant, both for the park (crowded) and the exhibits (underused). Some of the latter are closed by 4pm, as well as all day Sunday. If you want to take advantage of the Greenmarket, make sure you're here on a Monday, Wednesday, Friday, or Saturday.

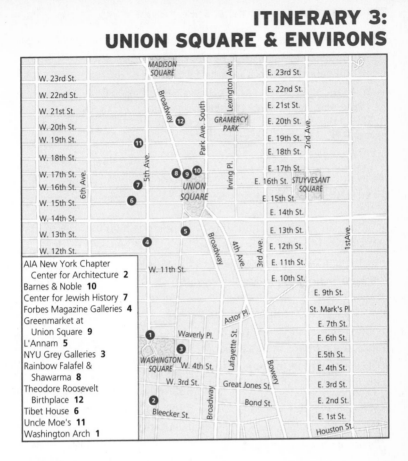

AIA New York Chapter
  Center for Architecture **2**
Barnes & Noble **10**
Center for Jewish History **7**
Forbes Magazine Galleries **4**
Greenmarket at
  Union Square **9**
L'Annam **5**
NYU Grey Galleries **3**
Rainbow Falafel &
  Shawarma **8**
Theodore Roosevelt
  Birthplace **12**
Tibet House **6**
Uncle Moe's **11**
Washington Arch **1**

① Washington Square

Nothing restores my faith in New York City quite like Washington Square Park. Functioning as a quad for both NYU students and Village locals, the juxtapositions of New York's various strata here make for peerless people-watching. Looking around at the circus atmosphere, it doesn't seem hard to believe that trout-fishing, burials, and public hangings are all part of this park's legacy. You can often find free entertainment courtesy of itinerant street performers at the central fountain. Along the fringes of the park neighborhood musicians are often noodling, or leading day-into-night singalongs. On the park's north end, **Stanford White's Washington Arch** is positively glowing. Soak up some atmosphere, and then peek into a couple of the interesting cultural attractions on the surrounding blocks.

② NYU Grey Galleries

NYU is one of the city's biggest landlords, and they own most

Square Deals Costs

Free	
5 museums/exhibits, a tour, and a literary reading	$0
Dirt Cheap	
The exhibits/ museums, tour, literary reading, plus a visit to a presidential birthplace	$3
Add-Ons for Spendthrift Millionaires	
Curry chicken and rice lunch	$5.25
Chicken burrito	$5.75
Chicken kabob sandwich	$4.75

of the surrounding buildings. Directly east of the park you'll find a nice NYU-run art space. The Grey Galleries, in the middle of the street on Washington Square East, show off every side of the visual arts, from painting to photo to sculpture. There's a lot of space, allowing shows to be fairly comprehensive. Afterwards, cut down to the bottom of the park and take a left on Washington Square South, followed by a quick left onto LaGuardia Place. A little ways down you'll find the:

③ AIA New York Chapter Center for Architecture

The exhibits here tend to be esoteric, geared more to the professional architect than the public at large. The space is interesting, however, with a nice layout. Beneath the ground floor is a side room that shows off the building's geothermal heating and cooling system: they drilled down deeper than the Empire State Building is high in order to make it work. When you're done, cut through Washington Square Park and walk 5 blocks up Fifth Avenue to #62.

④ Forbes Magazine Galleries

Magazine magnate Malcolm Forbes' galleries here approximate what a 10-year-old boy with unlimited financial means would think to collect. Fortunately, a 10-year-old boy's enthusiasms radiate off the exhibits as well. Every time I visit I find myself infected, caring more than I ever thought I could about model boats, toy soldiers, Monopoly boards, and trophies. For longer attention spans, the collection of presidential papers makes for engrossing reading. Walk 3 blocks up to 15th Street and take a left.

⑤ Tibet House U.S.

The faceless apartment house at 22 West 15th Street is an unlikely place to find inspiring Tibetan art, but the second floor is home to a small collection of beautiful paintings, sculptures, and artifacts. The art is intricate and vibrant, and the quiet rooms encourage lingering study. A large gallery space hosts rotating shows with a Tibetan angle. When you're done, double back to Fifth Avenue and walk up 1 block to 16th Street, where you'll take a left.

⑥ Center for Jewish History
The multifloor Center for Jewish History at 15 West 16th Street hosts several simultaneous exhibitions. Pass through the metal detector and get a badge at the front desk. Displays range from photo shows to manuscripts to paintings, most documenting Jewish contributions to American society. Artifacts are well lit and exhibit notes are informative without running on too long. Everything is free except for the **Yeshiva University Museum** galleries, which require a separate fee. For more American history, walk 4 blocks up to 20th Street and take a right, passing Broadway to 28 East 20th Street.

⑦ Theodore Roosevelt Birthplace
Theodore Roosevelt led an unlikely life. The asthmatic son of a prominent New York family, T. R. transformed himself into a symbol of fortitude, becoming a rancher, a soldier, a governor, and

eventually the only New York City native elected president. Along the way he managed to write some 33 books, and the exhibitions in his childhood home can inspire a visitor to think they don't get enough done in a day. The original town house was demolished in 1916, but 3 years later friends and family built a replica on the site. Period pieces, the majority of which belonged to the Roosevelts, fill the stately rooms. A pair of galleries cover Roosevelt's conservationist achievements and memorabilia from his fascinating life. Take one of the informative hourly tours and you'll learn Eleanor Roosevelt's maiden name (it was Roosevelt), the origins of the teddy bear, and that T. R. survived losing his wife and mother on the same day. Admission is $3.

⑧ Union Square
Three blocks south on Broadway will take you to Union Square. The park here opened in 1831, about the same time New York's wealthy reached this elevation on their inexorable climb uptown. The elegant neighborhood was soon steeped in culture, with an influx of theaters and concert halls. Over the next few decades, the moneyed set moved on, and by World War I the area was in decline. Union Square remained a popular location for labor

Make a Date

It's hard to make a full-out meal from the Greenmarket, but it's easy to snack, or assemble a serendipitous minipicnic. In my own delicacy hierarchy, the apples are at the top. Dozens of plump varieties—not just the three or four flavorless waxed models of a supermarket—fill upstate farmers' tables. Baked goods are another specialty here, with both sweets and gourmet breads represented. Buy some artisanal cheese and you're in business. Picnic tables are available at the north end of the park.

If you're a careful planner, you can go right from your picnic to a free reading. The Barnes & Noble opposite the north end of Union Square is one of the city's best bookstores. Their reading series routinely attracts big names.

rallies and protests, but the side streets got seedier and seedier. You can learn all about the neighborhood's history on a lively free walking tour given by the **Union Square BID** every Saturday afternoon at 2pm. Meet at the Lincoln Statue near the pavilion on the northern part of the park. When New York turned things around in the '80s, Union Square once again became the province of big spenders. Many of the city's trendiest and most expensive restaurants now fill the high-ceilinged spaces of cast-iron landmarks. The area is a popular shopping destination, which may contribute to general ignorance about the nearby cluster of cultural gems.

⑨ **Mealtime**

Besides the Greenmarket, you can find more substantial cheap eats all around Union Square. Three of my favorite spots in the city are nearby:

● At **Rainbow Falafel & Shawarma,** the crispy falafel sandwich with marinated onions is just about perfect, and a steal at $3. There's no room to sit, but picnic opportunities abound in Union Square. See also the review on p. 114 in "Eating & Drinking."

● Republic is Union Square's most famous noodle shop, but I find the place to be overrated. Vastly superior is the

Vietnamese cuisine at **L'Annam.** Monster bowls of *pho* and hot-and-sour soup are under $6, and the majority of entrees are $7.75 or $8.75. I especially love the rice vermicelli dishes. The luncheon special from 11:30am to 4:30pm is a mere $5.25, and dinner to go is only 70¢ more.

● New York seems destined to never have real Mission-style burritos, but **Uncle Moe's** serves up an array of California-Mexican standbys that are just as tasty. Burritos range from $5.75 to $7.75, depending on ingredients. A whole rotisserie chicken is only $10.75, and that comes with rice, beans, and corn tortillas. The ingredients are fresh, and you'll find plenty of tables to sit and enjoy.

Itinerary 3 Index

AIA New York Chapter Center for Architecture   536 LaGuardia Place, between Bleecker and W. 3rd sts. ℂ 212/683-0023. www.aiany.org. Mon-Fri 9am-8pm; Sat 11am-5pm.

Barnes & Noble   33 E. 17th St., between Broadway and Park Ave. S. ℂ 212/253-0810. www.bn.com. Daily 10am-10pm.

Center for Jewish History   15 W. 16th St., between Fifth and Sixth aves. ℂ 212/294-8301. www.cjh.org. Reading Room and Genealogy Institute Mon-Thurs 9:30am-4:30pm; Fri by appt. All other galleries Mon-Thurs 9am-5pm; Fri 9am-2pm; Sun 11am-5pm.

Forbes Magazine Galleries   62 Fifth Ave., at 12th St. ℂ 212/206-5548. www.forbesgalleries.com. Tues-Wed, Fri-Sat 10am-4pm.

Grey Art Gallery, New York University   100 Washington Sq. East, between Washington Sq. S. and N. ℂ 212/598-6780. www.nyu.edu/ greyart. Tues, Thurs-Fri 11am-6pm; Wed 11am-8pm; Sat 11am-5pm. Suggested admission $3; not enforced.

L'Annam   121 University Place, at 13th St. ℂ 212/420-1179. Daily 11:30am-midnight.

Rainbow Falafel & Shawarma   26 E. 17th St. ℂ 212/691-8641. Mon-Fri 11am-6pm.

Theodore Roosevelt Birthplace 28 E. 20th St., between Broadway and Park Ave. S. ℰ 212/260-1616. www.nps.gov/thrb. Admission $3 adults. Tues–Sat 9am–5pm (tours hourly 9am–4pm).

Tibet House 22 W. 15th St., 2nd floor, between Fifth and Sixth aves. ℰ 212/807-0563. www.tibethouse.org. Admission is free, although they do suggest a donation. Mon–Fri noon–5pm.

Uncle Moe's 14 W. 19th St., between Fifth and Sixth aves. ℰ 212/727-9400. Mon–Fri 11:30am–9:30pm; Sat noon–7pm.

Union Square BID ℰ 212/460-1200. www.unionsquarenyc.org.

Itinerary 4: Crosstown Through the Crossroads of the World—From the U.N. to the Hudson

How to Get There	The nearest trains to the east are the 4/5/6/7 and Shuttle trains at Grand Central Station. The west side is close to the A/C/E, 7, and 1/2/3 trains.
How Long to Spend There	Just under 2 miles, this walk can take an hour with quick stop-offs, or over 2 hours with longer deviations.
Best Times to Go	The middle stretch bustles at all hours, just as the fringes are generally pretty calm. One great time is late afternoon. Looking back east from Ninth Avenue at dusk is an amazing experience, with all the lights and the area's brand-new skyscrapers adorning an already-decadent skyline.
Tips	Consider timing your walk so you can take advantage of a free or cheap event. Availability of tours, movies, dance, theater, and music are outlined below.

New York is intimidatingly large and complex and few tourists are assuaged when you explain that Manhattan at its longest is only 13.5 miles long and 2.3 miles wide. Legendary 42nd Street is a perfect street for trying to come to terms with the city's range through a single, narrow slice. A walk along this schizophrenic cross-street (with a deviation here and there) brings you from the International Style idealism of the United Nations, through the classic New York icons of Grand Central Station and the Public Library, into the European-style repose of Bryant Park, the tourist/lunatic asylum of garish Times Square, the cultural magnet of Theater Row, and finally out to industrial fringes along the

Hudson. The whole trip is only 2 miles, but it spans the eras, cultures, and contrasts of New York City.

1 The United Nations

Walk due east from the Lexington subway line and you'll experience a dramatic shift, as the hustle of the avenues gives way to the genteel village of Tudor City. When you reach First Avenue head north along the United Nations Plaza. This is it—the capital of the world. At 46th Street you'll find the public entrance. After going through the security line, which moves with all the efficiency and enthusiasm of an American airport's, you'll enter the Visitors' Lobby. Built in 1950, it's a little dated but still impressive. Multiple U.N.-related art exhibits fill the space. For $12 you can take a full tour of the building, but if you're into cheaper thrills the Headquarters Park is a worthy diversion. The sculpture park is built on a sweeping scale unmatched in Manhattan. Wide vistas of Long Island City, Queens are across the river. When you're through, make your way south back toward 42nd. If you haven't eaten yet, you might consider a quick stop-off on Second Avenue and 43rd.

2 Looking for Mr. Goodburger

Goodburger is a new restaurant with an old formula: great burgers cooked to order in a friendly, malt shoppe-style atmosphere. Seats are hard to come by during business lunch hours, but the place is navigable off-peak. A juicy burger is only $5.25, and an extra 50¢ makes it a cheeseburger. Goodburger stands in the shadow of one of Manhattan's greatest icons, on 42nd between Third and Lexington aves.

3 Hop in my Chrysler

Though the Chrysler Building only got to enjoy its status as the world's tallest building for a few months (construction of the Empire State Building was hot on the Chrysler's heels), it holds a secure place in the hearts of architecture-loving New Yorkers. The stainless-steel Deco crown, with its jeweled notches, seems perpetually aglow, whether from sunlight or its own internal illumination. Designed by William Van Alen and completed in 1930, it's not much to look at up close, but you'll have some nice vistas when you get some distance. For a look at the lobby hang a right on 42nd, where you'll enter Art Deco overload (if this entrance is closed, there's a second one around the corner at 405 Lexington). The groovy ceiling mural and glossy marble veneers create a Deco-cavern effect.

ITINERARY 4: FROM THE U.N. TO THE HUDSON

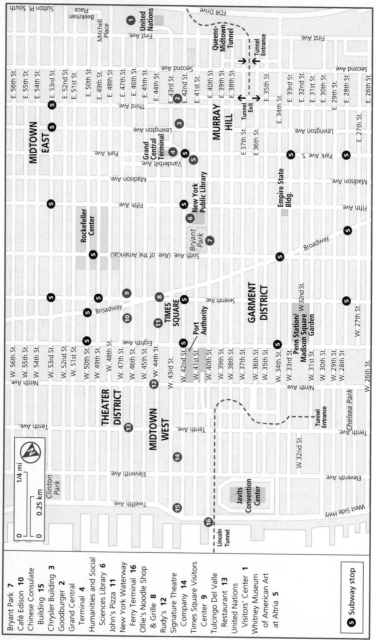

Bryant Park **7**
Café Edison **10**
Chinese Consulate Building **15**
Chrysler Building **3**
Goodburger **2**
Grand Central Terminal **4**
Humanities and Social Sciences Library **6**
John's Pizza **11**
New York Waterway Ferry Terminal **16**
Ollie's Noodle Shop & Grille **8**
Rudy's **12**
Signature Theatre Company **14**
Times Square Visitors Center **9**
Tulcingo Del Valle Restaurant **13**
United Nations Visitors' Center **1**
Whitney Museum of American Art at Altria **5**

S Subway stop

42nd Street Costs

Free	
Two parks, a mini-art museum, a walking tour, and three exhibitions	$0
Dirt Cheap	
Parks, a mini-art museum, a walking tour, two exhibitions, and two tacos	$4
Add-Ons for Spendthrift Millionaires	
A beer and two hot dogs	$3.50

④ Grand Central

Grand Central Terminal in its new restoration is as inspiring as public buildings get. It cost $175 million to get the 1913 Beaux Arts landmark in this shape, but you can enjoy it all for free. In the main concourse look down to admire half an acre of gleaming Tennessee marble. Look up and you'll see how the constellations of a New York winter sky would appear, were the roof and the light pollution gone. Free art exhibits are often mounted in adjacent Vanderbilt Hall.

⑤ Whitney Sampler

Philip Morris recently dropped its association-laden nom de smokes for the vaguely healthy-sounding and dot.commy "Altria," but the arts-friendly ground floor of its headquarters hasn't changed. There's a tiny branch of the Whitney Museum of Art off to the side of a sculpture court. Usually living contemporary artists are highlighted. There isn't much square footage to wander through here, but it's not much of a time commitment either, and it's free. Also, free lunchtime gallery tours are offered Wednesday and Friday at 1pm, in addition to irregularly scheduled gallery talks. The Whitney's Performance on 42nd Street series brings dance and performance art to the space. Check the schedule, but shows usually start at 8pm, often on Wednesday nights.

⑥ Reading Between the Lions: The Library

Officially called the Humanities and Social Sciences Library, this 1911 icon features elegant Beaux Arts architecture, discreet landscaping, and famous steps. I love to people-watch here; the constant bustle is hypnotizing. When you make it inside, you'll find the hushed interior just as impressive. Rotating exhibits show off rare editions from the collection. The thoughtful captions are a great reading experience on their own. As you leave, take a moment to admire the twin lion guards,

But I Digress

For some quickie edification, when you're through with your Whitney visit, cut down Park to 41st Street. Embedded in the sidewalks on both sides of 41st between Park and Fifth avenues are plaques reminiscent of the Hollywood Walk of Fame, only with elegantly illustrated literary quotations instead of handprints of washed-up celebrities. But hey, that's the difference between New York and L.A. The quotes lead you to a nice vantage of the classical triangular façade of the New York Public Library.

Fortitude and Patience. These two traits will serve you well when you reach the Times Square segment of 42nd Street.

⑦ Bryant Park

Looking at the flourishing vegetation around the pebbled paths and Parisian folding chairs, it's hard to imagine that until the early '90s Bryant Park carried the nickname "Manhattan's longest urinal." In its current fully gentrified form, this park is an oasis of European charm plunked right in the middle of harried Midtown. Further old-world touches include a free skating rink (in winter), and the elaborate sculpted animals of Le Carrousel ($1.75

per ride). Summer Mondays bring free films at dusk, and all through the warm months you'll find free music aplenty (see p. 53 and 40, respectively, for more information).

The Deuce

Once you cross over Sixth Avenue the crowds start to thicken. The intersections at Seventh Avenue and Broadway are among the most congested in the city. New York's refined theater scene thrived here in the early years of the 20th century. As the economy soured during the Depression, highbrow entertainment gave way to vaudeville. Vaudeville begat burlesque, and burlesque opened the door for garden-variety sleaze of every hue. The stretch toward Eighth became known as the "Forty Deuce," or just "The Deuce." Though there's still neon aplenty today, the peep shows have been replaced with sleaze of a corporate character. It doesn't seem to deter the tourist throngs, however.

⑧ A Play on Theater Row

As you get past the Port Authority Bus Terminal (7,200 buses and 200,000 passengers come through here on an average weekday), the streets calm down. Huge, newly cleared lots are signs of imminent, gargantuan condo construction.

Grand Tours

There are five, count 'em *five*, free tours waiting to edify you on and around 42nd Street. On Wednesdays at half past noon, the Municipal Art Society offers a walking tour of **Grand Central Terminal.** They ask for a $10 donation but there's no formal fee, just whatever you care to contribute. Meet at the information booth in the middle of the concourse, where you'll get great inside dope on America's commuter temple. The local BID, the Grand Central Partnership, runs a free tour on Fridays, also at half past noon. Meet in the Sculpture Court of the **Whitney Museum at Altria.** The **New York Public Library** shows itself off twice a day. Tours meet Tuesday through Saturday at 11am and again at 2pm beside the information desk in Astor Hall. When there's an exhibit mounted at Gottesman Hall, you can get a separate tour. Meet Tuesday through Saturday at 12:30 and 2:30pm, and also on Sunday at 3:30pm, at the entrance to the hall. If **Bryant Park's gardens** are more your speed, you can catch a free tour with a horticulturalist on selected Wednesdays at 12:30pm. Meet at the William Cullen Bryant statue on the east side in the park, between the cafe decks. Tours run from April through September. Fifth and finally, the **Times Square** BID leads tours from its visitors center on Seventh Avenue, between 46th and 47th streets. Tours go every Friday at noon. Of the five tours, this is the most bland, taking a mainstream approach to an overcommercialized stretch.

Along "Theater Row" most of the stages are well above the dirt cheap threshold, though the Signature Theatre Company recently used a grant to run $15 specials. Look for these incredible bargains to continue into 2007. Despite the industrial structures and clearings, as you reach the far west the area starts to feel a little like a village again, an alternative universe to 42nd's opposite end in Tudor City.

❾ The Hudson

Look up to the north and you'll see the *Intrepid* battleship, which is floating in the Hudson at the end of 46th Street. The 40,000-ton ***Intrepid*** was once a city itself, with some 3,000 sailors on board. Now it's a museum. (**Note:** The *Intrepid* will be closed through 2008 for repairs.) At press time, Pier 84 was undergoing complete reconstruction. Eventually there'll be a community garden and lawn space here. Two blocks south you can find an already-finished public space near the New York Waterway ferry terminal. (For $6 you can float away from Midtown altogether—boats connect to Hoboken from here, with dramatic views all the way.)

Before you move on, make sure to look back across Twelfth Avenue for views of the **Chinese Consulate Building.** At the end of 2 miles of attention-grabbing skyscrapers and neon signage, this building manages to be the oddest duck on the block.

⑩ **Mealtime & Libations**

If you passed on dining at Goodburger, you are not out of options. Ninth and Tenth avenues in Hell's Kitchen are loaded with cheap ethnic food. There's a burgeoning Mexican scene here, though my favorite by far is the:

● ☆ **Tulcingo Del Valle Restaurant** is tasty and totally authentic. A specials board (everything is under $10) lists fresh-made entrée platters, like chicken in a green pumpkin-seed sauce.

Tacos, including the delicious carne asada, are just $2 to $2.50 a pop.

A couple of favorites for the pretheater crowd can be found on 44th Street between Seventh and Eighth avenues:

● At **Ollie's Noodle Shop & Grille,** huge bowls of soup and noodle dishes come in under $7. Most dinner entrees are under $10, and at lunch they're all $2 cheaper.

● **John's Pizza** makes real New York pizza and they sell it by the pie—no slices here. A large runs from $12 to $16, depending on the toppings.

Between Broadway and Eighth you'll also find the:

● The mural-adorned **Café Edison** is a classic New York coffee shop lodged inside the Hotel Edison. Deli sandwiches come in under $6 and a huge bowl of soup will only set you back $3.50.

● But why pay for a meal when you can eat for free? **Rudy's** knows a person can work up an appetite over a few pints. As a public service, this neighborhood dive distributes **free hot dogs.** Order a drink first, though. After all that walking, you've earned it.

Itinerary 4 Index

Café Edison   228 W. 47th St., between Broadway and Eighth Ave.
℃ 212/840-5000. Mon-Sat 6am-9:30pm; Sun 6am-7:30pm

Goodburger   200 Second Ave., at 42nd. ℃ 212/922-1700. www.good
burgerny.com. Daily 10am-9pm.

Grand Central Partnership   ℃ 212/883-2420. www.grandcentral
partnership.org.

Humanities and Social Sciences Library   Fifth Ave. and 42nd St.
℃ 212/869-8089 exhibits and events, or 212/661-7220 library hours.
www.nypl.org. Thurs-Sat 10am-6pm; Tues-Wed 11am-7:30pm; Sun 1-5pm.

John's Pizza   260 W. 44th St., between Seventh and Eighth aves.
℃ 212/391-7560. Daily 11:30am-11:30pm.

Municipal Art Society   ℃ 212/935-3960. www.mas.org.

Ollie's Noodle Shop & Grille   200B W. 44th St., between Seventh and
Eighth aves. ℃ 212/921-5988. Mon-Thurs 11:30am-midnight; Fri-Sat
11:30am-1am; Sun 11:30am-11:30pm.

Rudy's   627 Ninth Ave., at W. 44th St. ℃ 212/974-9169. Free hot dogs
1-10pm.

Signature Theatre Company   555 W. 42nd St., between Tenth and
Eleventh aves. ℃ 212/244-7529. www.signaturetheatre.org.

Times Square Visitors Center   1560 Seventh Ave., between 46th and
47th sts. ℃ 212/768-1560. www.timessquarenyc.org.

Tulcingo Del Valle Restaurant   655 10th Ave., between 46th and 47th
sts. ℃ 212/262-5510. Daily 8am-midnight.

United Nations Visitors' Center   Free exhibits and sculpture park,
tours for $12. First Ave. at 46th St. ℃ 212/963-4475. www.un.org. Daily
9am-5pm; closed weekends Jan-Feb.

Whitney Museum of American Art at Altria   120 Park Ave., southwest
corner at 42nd St., opposite Grand Central Terminal. ℃ 917/663-2453.
www.whitney.org. Gallery Mon-Wed, Fri 11am-6pm; Thurs 11am-7:30pm.
Sculpture Court Mon-Sat 7:30am-9:30pm; Sun, holidays 11am-7pm.
Extended hours for performances and lectures.

Itinerary 5: The Secrets of Lower Manhattan

Where	Lower Manhattan, skirting the East River, Hudson, and New York Harbor.
How to Get There	The area is very well covered by trains; J/M/Z trains to Broad Street and 2/3/4/5 trains to Wall Street are good places to start.
How Long to Spend There	A straight walk can be done in an hour. To get your fill of museums add 2 more hours, and a round-trip on the ferry clocks in at another hour.
Best Times to Go	The ferry's views of downtown and the Statue of Liberty are great at night, and incomparable at dusk.
Tips	On the weekends Lower Manhattan feels deserted, with tourists the only signs of life. Quiet streets in New York are a great luxury, but many of the museums and almost all of the stores and restaurants are closed. To really get a feel for the area hit it on a weekday.

The combination of too many tourists and too many uptight money-grubbers never makes for an inviting scene, but the Financial District gets a bad rap. New York City's post–Native American life began here, and the oddly shaped streets attest to the patterns of ancient, organic urban planning. New York is notorious for paving over its own history, but Lower Manhattan has some unlikely survivors. The area is densely packed and even a short walk can put a person in easy reach of a host of historical sites. Ignore the $9 trillion that changes hands down here every year at the New York Stock Exchange; there are freebies aplenty for the discerning seeker.

① Federal Hall National Memorial

This is not an especially popular memorial, probably because the really interesting stuff happened in predecessor structures on this site. Federal Hall was built in 1842 to serve as a customhouse and it's now a Park Service museum. Exhibits cover Washington's inauguration, the drafting of the Bill of Rights, and the first stirring of rebellion against British authority, all of which occurred right here. The building itself is a preeminent example of Greek Revival architecture, with an impressive rotunda behind the metal detector in the lobby. After revamping the structure for a couple of years, the Park Service reopened the memorial in the fall of 2006. The vertiginously steep stairs outside the building are a popular spot to spy on the chaos that surrounds the New York Stock

ITINERARY 5: THE SECRETS OF LOWER MANHATTAN

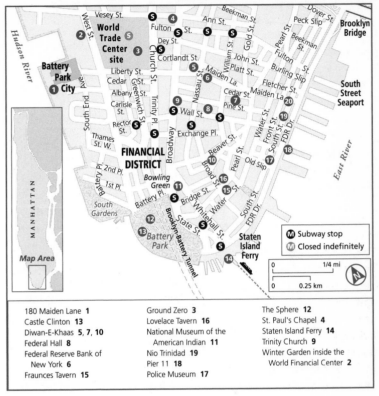

Vesey St.
World Trade Center site
Fulton St.
Ann St.
Beekman St.
Peck Slip
Dover St.
Brooklyn Bridge
West St.
Hudson River
Battery Park City
Dey St.
Church St.
Cortlandt St.
John St.
Gold St.
Beekman St.
Fulton St.
Burling Slip
Liberty St.
Greenwich St.
Cedar St.
Albany St.
Carlisle St.
Maiden La.
William St.
Platt St.
Nassau St.
Fletcher St.
Maiden La.
Cedar St.
Pine St.
South Street Seaport
Rector St.
Trinity Pl.
Wall St.
Exchange Pl.
Thames St. W.
FINANCIAL DISTRICT
Broadway
Beaver St.
Pearl St.
Water St.
Front St.
South St.
FDR Dr.
Old Slip
East River
2nd Pl.
Battery Pl.
1st Pl.
Bowling Green
Broad St.
Bridge St.
Water St.
South St.
FDR Dr.
South Gardens
Battery Pl.
State St.
Whitehall St.
MANHATTAN
Battery Park
Brooklyn-Battery Tunnel
Staten Island Ferry
Map Area

M Subway stop
M Closed indefinitely

0 ———— 1/4 mi
0 ———— 0.25 km

180 Maiden Lane **1**
Castle Clinton **13**
Diwan-E-Khaas **5, 7, 10**
Federal Hall **8**
Federal Reserve Bank of New York **6**
Fraunces Tavern **15**

Ground Zero **3**
Lovelace Tavern **16**
National Museum of the American Indian **11**
Nio Trinidad **19**
Pier 11 **18**
Police Museum **17**

The Sphere **12**
St. Paul's Chapel **4**
Staten Island Ferry **14**
Trinity Church **9**
Winter Garden inside the World Financial Center **2**

Exchange. Head east on Wall Street, hang a left on Front Street, and then a right onto Old Slip.

② The Police Museum

The Police Museum is a recent addition to the area, housed in an odd fortresslike structure at the end of Old Slip that for 6 decades was the First Precinct Station House. The exhibits can be a little uneven, and in places the museum is more of shrine than a source of information, but with three floors of galleries you're almost sure to find something of interest. I like the copper badges on the first floor (yes, that's where "cop" comes from), and the circa 1910–12 mug shots on the second floor. There is a suggested admission, but no one pays you much attention when you pass through the turnstile.

③ Meal Break

Nearby Front Street has several lunch vans to serve the worker bees from the adjoining financial and insurance offices.

Lower Manhattan Walk Costs

Free	
Five museums, exhibits at two churches, and a round-trip ferry ride	$0
Dirt Cheap	
The museums, exhibits, ferry, and lunchtime concert	$2 (suggested donation)
Add-Ons for Spendthrift Millionaires	
Fraunces Tavern Museum	$4
Lunch	$6

● The best of the bunch is the **Nio Trinidad** truck, which parks at the corner of Front and Pine. For $7.50 you can get a fish or oxtail dinner, but my favorite is the Caribbean pancake called "roti." A veggie roti, pollinated with a delicious chickpea paste, is only $5. Only the very daring should ask for hot sauce. The area is dotted by benches and small parks, perfect for picnicking.

● In bad weather, head over to **180 Maiden Lane,** an office building designed by I. M. Pei. The ground floor atrium is public space, and every Tuesday at 12:30pm, students from the Juilliard School present classical recitals. No food is available here; this is a good picnic spot for roti, however.

● On a nice day walk east to the river. Pier 11, at the end of Wall Street, has several spots for admiring the Brooklyn skyline as you nosh.

④ Lovelace Tavern

Make your way down Pearl Street. Just south of Coenties Alley, under the colonnade of the office building to your right, you'll see a brass railing over glass flooring. Peer through the glass and you'll be looking at stones laid in 1670. During construction of this skycraper, the foundations of an ancient tavern were discovered. You can also see the foundations of successor structures, and a support beam for the eyesore skyscraper overhead. A more famous historic tavern is across the street, just to the south at 54 Pearl.

⑤ Fraunces Tavern

This is definitely an optional stop because it comes with an admission charge. Fraunces Tavern has impressive historical credentials—the building's origins date from 1719 and George Washington gave his farewell speech to his officers in the Long Room upstairs—but multiple fires and remodelings have made the current version something less than authentic. Your $4 entry ticket buys you a grainy 20-minute video and two floors of exhibits, including a re-creation of the Long Room and a flag gallery. Among the more interesting relics under glass is a lock of George's hair, which will be absolutely essential when it comes time to clone the father of our country. History buffs should definitely cough up for the tariff, but everyone else has my permission to keep moving.

6 Staten Island Ferry

You're now very close to the poor man's Circle Line, the Staten Island Ferry (© **718/815-BOAT**). This is one of my all-time favorite NYC freebies. From Manhattan to St. George and back again takes a little more than an hour, with inspiring views all the way. The brand-new terminal rises exuberantly over the water at the end of Whitehall and State streets. Find a seat on the right-hand side of the boat as you enter. You'll have great vantages of the downtown skyline, including the somber gap marking Ground Zero. About halfway through the ride you'll spot Lady Liberty herself from the same western windows. Though there isn't all that much to do on the Staten Island side without a further bus or train ride, if you're really organized you can catch

an inexpensive minor league baseball game (p. 96), just a few steps from the terminal.

7 Castle Clinton

Back on the Manhattan side, a few steps west from the ferry is Battery Park. The park is anchored by Castle Clinton, a Napoleonic-era fort. Although this battery has undergone several renovations—from theater hall to aquarium—the original 1811 walls are intact. If you walk in and look up, the modern skyline of downtown makes an interesting contrast through the open roof. There's a small stage on the east side that hosts free concerts on Thursday nights in summer, usually popular indie-rock bands.

8 The Sphere

Exiting Castle Clinton into Battery Park, you'll enter an area that recently had its grounds turned over. The MTA was building a new subway tunnel, which was delayed by the surprising discovery of 45 surviving feet of a colonial wall. A lost halfpenny (dated 1744), pipe shards, and Delft pottery were also found. In January '06, workers struck a second wall. As Battery Park is reconstructed, look for the walls to reappear, although hopefully not right in the middle of the bike paths. Heading north past the Hope Garden you'll reach a small and moving 9/11 memorial. Fritz Koenig's sculpture, The Sphere, stands behind an eternal flame lit on the first anniversary of the terrorist attacks. Koenig designed The Sphere as a symbol of world peace and for 30 years it adorned the plaza at the World Trade Center. The sculpture was salvaged from the rubble and placed here, where the shoreline would have been in 1625 New Amsterdam. Though battered and abused, The Sphere is surprisingly intact. There's a metaphor in there someplace, I hope.

⑨ National Museum of the American Indian

On the far side of The Sphere you'll hit a busy intersection that marks the end of Broadway. The small park across the street is Bowling Green, Manhattan's oldest public park. It was here or very close by that Peter Minuit, director general of New Netherland, traded the legendary $24 in beads with the Native populations. Just a few feet away the Smithsonian maintains a museum dedicated to those Native populations. Most of the artifacts collected by New York banker George Gustav Heye are now on the Mall in D.C., but rotating exhibits remain in three galleries. The Native American craftsmanship is unparalleled and the exhibits here are well lit and lovingly curated. Even if the walls were bare, the building itself, the former U.S. Custom House, would be worthy of a visit. It was completed in 1907 to the specifications of Beaux Arts master Cass Gilbert (he also did the nearby Woolworth Building), and the central rotunda by Raphael Guastavino is a structural marvel. Make sure you see it before the Native Americans reclaim their title to Manhattan and the eviction notices begin.

⑩ Trinity Church

Head north on Broadway and at the intersection of Wall you'll see Trinity Church. Trinity has been ministering Episcopal-style on this spot since 1698. The current Gothic Revival church was built in 1846 and has a dark and somber interior. There's a small museum on-site. The churchyard is of more interest, with its ancient headstones somehow surviving in the shadow of Mammon. On Thursdays you can catch the **"Concerts at One"** program. (Mondays the series comes to St. Paul's Chapel; see below.) The suggested admission is $2, which in no way reflects the high caliber of the classical performers found here.

⑪ The Federal Reserve Bank of New York

Walk up 3 blocks on Broadway and you'll hit Liberty Street. A right turn and a 1-block walk will bring you to the Florentine Renaissance hulk of the Federal Reserve Bank (see p. 231 in chapter 6 for a full review). The American Numismatic Society keeps a gallery here, with a permanent exhibit on the history of money. You have to squint to see most of the coins, but the history behind them is fascinating. Among the cowrie shells and currency you'll find the only existing 1933 Double Eagle, a gold coin now worth some 400,000 times the value printed on its face.

⑫ Meal Break

Right around the corner is a small shop with fresh, delicious Indian food. **Diwan-E-Khaas** serves veggie entrees like rich palak paneer for only $5.30, and the chicken tikka masala is way undervalued at $6.25. Entrees include a choice of rice, nan, or roti.

⑬ St. Paul's Chapel

This satellite chapel of Trinity Church, completed in 1766, is the oldest continuously used public building in the city. The interior is cheerful and colorful. Even the 9/11 exhibits have an upbeat and healing tone, although the self-congratulatory tone wears thin. On the north side of the chapel you can see the pew used by George Washington when New York was the official seat of the U.S. government and not just the de facto capital. Over the pew is a 1795 painting of the Great Seal, in one of its earliest renditions. The small churchyard behind the chapel is visually tranquil, although often the traffic and bustle of Church Street around Ground Zero prevent auditory serenity. Behind the headstones the void of the former World Trade Center site appears as an eerie prairie. This might be the best spot in NYC to put the long thread of the city's history into some sort of context.

Bonus Round: Battery Park City

A recent invention, Battery Park City is a complex of offices, hotels, and apartment buildings built on fill created by the excavation of the World Trade Center's foundation in the '60s. The city has never done a better job of landscaping, and the walkways along the Hudson are ideal for strolling, or just sitting down to watch the river flow. **Vesey Street,** which runs along the north side of St. Paul's Chapel, will lead you past Ground Zero and straight down to the Hudson. The best perspective on Ground Zero can be found in the back of the Winter Garden inside the World Financial Center (see p. 274 for more info).

Itinerary 5 Index

American Numismatic Society gallery at the Federal Reserve Bank of New York   33 Liberty St., between William and Nassau sts. ℭ 212/234-3130. www.amnumsoc.org. Mon-Fri 10am-4pm.

Castle Clinton   In Battery Park. ℭ 212/344-7220. www.nps.gov/cacl. Daily 8:30am-5pm.

Diwan-E-Khaas   53 Nassau St., between Maiden Lane and Liberty St. ℭ 212/571-7676. Mon-Fri 11am-8:30pm. Other locations: 26 S. William St., between Broad and William sts. ℭ 212/248-2361; 26 Cedar St., between William and Pearl sts. ℭ 212/480-0697. (This location closes at 3:30pm.)

Federal Hall   26 Wall St., at Nassau St. ℭ 212/825-6888. www.nps. gov/feha. Mon-Fri 9am-5pm (check website to confirm new hours).

Fraunces Tavern   54 Pearl St., near Broad St. ℭ 212/425-1778. www. fraruncestavernmuseum.org. Admission $4. Tues-Fri noon-5pm; Sat 10am-5pm.

National Museum of the American Indian   1 Bowling Green, between State and Whitehall sts. ℭ 212/514-3700. www.americanindian.si.edu. Daily 10am-5pm; Thurs until 8pm.

The New York City Police Museum   100 Old Slip, between Water and South sts., 2 blocks south of Wall St. ℭ 212/480-3100. www.nycpolice museum.org. Suggested admission $5; not enforced. Tues-Sat 10am-5pm; Sun 11am-5pm.

Nio Trinidad   ℭ 718/287-9848. Mon-Fri lunch hour.

180 Maiden Lane   Between Front and South sts. ℭ 212/799-5000 for recital information.

St. Paul's Chapel   209 Broadway, at Fulton St. ℭ 212/233-4164. www. saintpaulschapel.org. Exhibit Mon-Sat 10am-6pm; Sun 10am-4pm. Churchyard 10am-4pm, extended to 5:30pm during daylight saving. Concerts Mon 1pm. Concert hot line ℭ 212/602-0747.

Trinity Church   74 Trinity Place, at Broadway and Wall St. ✆ 212/602-0800. www.trinitywallstreet.org. Church daily 7am–6pm. Churchyard daily 7am–4pm, extended to 5pm during daylight saving. Museum Mon–Fri 9am–11:45am, 1–3:45pm; Sat, holidays 10am–3:45pm; Sun 1–3:45pm. Free guided tours daily 2pm; also Sun following the 11:15am service. Concerts Thurs 1pm. Concert hot line ✆ 212/602-0747.

Get the skinny on destinations or events at information kiosks like this one, at the corner of Broadway and Park Row. See p. 321 for more information.

NYC BASICS

1 Information Centers

The city runs four information centers, with free maps and brochures as well as discount coupons for tourist-friendly fare.

New York City's Official Visitor Information Center   810 Seventh Ave., between 52nd and 53rd sts. ℂ **212/484-1222.** www.nyc visit.com. Mon–Fri 8:30am–6pm; Sat–Sun 9am–5pm; Thanksgiving, Christmas, New Year's Day 9am–3pm; other holidays 9am–5pm. Subway: B/D/E to Seventh Ave.; N/R/Q/W to 57th St.; 1 to 50th St.

Official Visitor Information Kiosk for Chinatown   At the triangle of Canal, Walker, and Baxter sts. Sun–Fri 10am–6pm; Sat 10am–7pm. Subway: J/M/N/Q/R/W/Z/6.

NYC Heritage Tourism Center   Broadway and Park Row. Mon–Fri 9am–6pm; Sat–Sun, holidays 10am–6pm. Subway: 2/3 to Park Place;

Current Events

The city does a decent job of providing the latest scoop on goings-on around town. The **New York Convention & Visitors Bureau** has a 24-hour information hot line (© **800/NYC-VISIT** or 212/397-8222). For updated listings of music, theater, museum, and other events, check online at www.nycvisit.com. **NYC On Stage** (© **212/768-1818**) also has info on theater, music, and dance performances. The **City Parks Special Events Hotline** (© **212/360-3456**) provides a rundown on outdoor concerts and performances, and New York Roadrunner Club events.

R/W to City Hall; 4/5/6 to Brooklyn Bridge/City Hall; A/C/J/M/Z to Fulton St./Broadway Nassau.

Harlem Visitor Information Kiosk   163 W. 125th St., between Adam Clayton Powell, Jr., Blvd. and Lenox Ave. Mon–Fri 9am–6pm; Sat–Sun 10am–6pm. Subway: 2/3 to 125th St.; A/C or B/D to 125th St.

Information at the Libraries   New York's public libraries are founts of information, and real live librarians are on hand to answer your brief *factual* questions (this service is of little utility for existential concerns). Bronx, Staten Island, and Manhattan residents can call © **212/340-0849** Mon–Sat 9am–6pm. In Brooklyn call © **718/230-2100,** option 5, Mon 10am–5pm, Tues–Thurs 10am–9pm, and Fri–Sat 10am–6pm. Queens InfoLine © **718/990-0714,** Mon–Fri 10am–8:45pm, Sat 10am–5:15pm.

2 Transportation

BY PLANE

New York City is served by three major airports: **LaGuardia Airport** (© **718/533-3400**), **John F. Kennedy** (JFK) International Airport (© **718/244-4444**), and **Newark International Airport** (© **973/961-6000**) in New Jersey. Newark often has the best cheap flight deals, and during high-traffic hours it can be the most accessible to and from Manhattan. For transportation information for all three airports call **Air-Ride** (© **800/247-7433**). The line is open 24 hours, with live operators

Monday through Friday from 8am to 6pm. Similar information is online at www.panynj.gov/airports.

GETTING TO THE AIRPORTS

Cheap LaGuardia Transportation The **M60 bus** ($2) serves all LaGuardia terminals, connecting to the Upper West Side of Manhattan. Bus rides from 106th Street average 1 hour, though traffic can cause that time to vary. The **Q33** and **Q48** also make LaGuardia runs. For the complete schedule call © **718/330-1234** or log on to www.mta.nyc.ny.us/nyct.

Cheap JFK Transportation The new **AirTrain JFK** is a little cumbersome if you have a lot of luggage, but it's a definite improvement over the old subway transfer system. The AirTrain costs $5 each way and connects terminals with the E/J/Z trains at Sutphin Boulevard/Archer Avenue, the LIRR at Jamaica Station, and the A train at Howard Beach. For the latter, make sure you catch an A to Far Rockaway, not to Lefferts Boulevard. The train runs 24/7. Allow an hour for the subway and monorail combined once you've left Manhattan. © **877/JFK-AIRTRAIN.** www.panynj.gov.

Cheap Newark Transportation The **AirTrain Newark** (© **888/EWR-INFO**) is a smooth ride, but it's a little pricey at $14 one-way. It takes 20 minutes to get from Penn Station in Manhattan to the airport monorail. The cheapest trip is to take the **Path train** from Manhattan to Newark ($1.50). At Newark Penn Station you can catch the **62 bus,** which makes several stops but will get you to the airport for only $1.25. On the down side, it's all but impossible to make that trip in under an hour. © **800/772-2222.** www.njtransit.com.

BY BUS

As symbols of cheap interstate travel, Greyhound buses will live on in country songs. In the hearts of Eastern Seaboard adventurers, however, the Greyhound has been displaced by **Chinatown buses.** A round-trip to Washington, D.C., is only $35, and the slightly longer trip to Boston is $30. The difference between any two companies isn't dramatic; I choose based on who's got the most convenient schedule for me on any given trip. You can buy a ticket online or you can just show up at the departure point and let eager touts jostle each other for your business. The buses are full size and every driver I've ever had has been a professional.

Fung Wah Bus Service   This bus line travels between Boston's Chinatown (68 Beach St.) and New York's Chinatown (139 Canal St., between Chrystie St. and the Bowery). A one-way ticket is $15. ☎ **212/925-8889.** www.fungwahbus.com.

New Century Travel, Inc.   For the DC to NY and NY to Philly routes, this company runs a full schedule. The run to DC's Chinatown (513 H St. NW) is $20 one-way and $35 round-trip, and Philly (55 N. 11th St.) is $12 each way, $20 round-trip. ☎ **917/443-3986.** www.2000coach.com.

Washington Deluxe   If DC and New York's Chinatowns aren't convenient for you, this bus company makes pickups in assorted NYC locations (Brooklyn, Lower East Side, and Penn Station), and drops off at 1015 15th Street NW and at 441 New Jersey Avenue NW in DC. $20 for one-way and $35 round-trip. ☎ **866/BUSNYDC.** www.washny.com.

GETTING AROUND TOWN

UNDERGROUND

The MTA cooked its books to put the screws to subway and bus riders—$2 is now the price of a single ride. Until straphangers are called upon for our next bloodletting, there are a couple of discounts. When you spend $15 or more on a **MetroCard,** you get a 10% bonus. For 24 hours of heavy commuting you can get a FunPass—all-you-can-ride for $7. Unlimited rides are also available in 7-day ($24) and 30-day ($76) formats. Children under 44 inches tall ride free. ☎ **718/330-1234.** www.mta.nyc.ny.us.

ON WATER

Ferries   Despite 2003's tragic accident, the **Staten Island Ferry** is as safe a mode of travel as you'll find in New York. It's also hard to beat for scenic satisfaction, with great views of the Statue of Liberty, Ellis Island, and Governor's Island (p. 315). The boat runs 24/7, leaving from the new terminal at Whitehall, on the southeastern tip of Manhattan. On the far side you can enjoy the scattered distractions of St. George, Staten Island, or you can follow the boat-loading sign and circle back across the harbor. Other ferry services and the New York Water Taxi also offer great views, but when you factor in ticket prices, they're not such great deals. ☎ **718/815-BOAT.** www.ci.nyc.ny.us/html/dot. Boats leave every 20 to 30 minutes on weekdays, less frequently during off-peak and weekend hours. Subway: R/W to Whitehall St.; 4/5 to Bowling Green; 1 to South Ferry (ride in one of the first five cars).

3 NYC's Free & Dirt Cheap Resources

Disability Services   The mayor maintains an office (© **212/788-2830**) that provides free advice to disabled visitors on how to get around the city. A few elevators aside, the subway system is largely inaccessible to the disabled, but 95% of the city's buses are equipped to carry wheelchairs.

Emergencies   © **911** is, of course, the number for emergency police, fire, and ambulance service. For nonemergencies and just about any city government function you can think of, call © **311.** Other emergency numbers include the **AIDS Hotline** (© 212/807-6655), **Animal Bites** (© 212/676-2483), **Poison Control** (© 800/222-1222), **Suicide Prevention** (© 212/673-3000), **Traveler's Aid** (© 718/656-4870), and **Victim Services Hotline** (© 212/577-7777).

Gay & Lesbian Resources   The **Lesbian, Gay, Bisexual & Transgender Community Center** (208 W. 13th St., between Seventh and Eighth aves.; © **212/620-7310;** www.gaycenter.org) is the meeting place for more than 400 organizations. The online calendar mostly lists events with charges, but there are a few freebies, in addition to the free lending library and archive. Other good places to look include the free weeklies *HX* (www.hx.com), *New York Blade* (www.nyblade.com), *Next* (www.nextmagazine.net), *Gay City News* (www.gaycitynews.com), and the *Village Voice* (www.villagevoice.com). You can find copies stacked up in bars, clubs, stores, and sidewalk boxes throughout town. If you don't want to risk getting a little ink on your fingertips, the websites are also good sources of information. **Gay and Lesbian National Hotline** (© **212/989-0999;** www.glnh.org), offers peer counseling and information on upcoming events. Open Monday through Friday 4 to midnight, Saturday noon to 5pm. **Gay Men's Health Crisis Hotline** (© **800-AIDSNYC**) provides information and support on HIV- and AIDS-related issues. The hot line is open Monday through Friday from 10am to 9pm, and Saturdays from noon until 3pm.

Moving   On city streetlamps, MAN WITH A VAN signs are ubiquitous. This is a good way to go for small moves. For the online version of

The Wi-Fi Wave: Wireless Access Across the City

The city is rapidly going wireless. Our Wi-Fi zones are constantly expanding, already enveloping Bryant Park, Union Square, City Hall Park, the South Street Seaport, and the Columbia campus, among other popular NYC destinations. By the time you read this, Central Park and Riverside Park will also be wireless. Several hotels have gotten on board, as have retailers like McDonalds and Starbucks. Check **www.nycwireless.net** for the latest sites.

Many public libraries are Wi-Fi friendly, in addition to providing free Internet. Check online for more information, or your nearest branch (www.nypl.org in the Bronx, Manhattan, and Staten Island; otherwise www.queenslibrary.org or www.brooklynpubliclibrary.org). Many cafes and fast-food establishments offer Internet access for cheap.

these streetlamp flyers, **www.citimove.com** is a great site. Movers bid against each other so you get decent prices, and movees critique the jobs so you know which companies to avoid.

Post Offices   The **Main Post Office,** at 8th Avenue and 33rd Street (© **212/967-8585**), is open 24 hours a day, 7 days a week. Call the **Postal Answer Line** (© 212/330-4000) for other information.

Telephone Service   Several small companies have come into the New York phone market, saving consumers hundreds of dollars a year versus the rates for AT&T and Verizon. Prices start low, but once the Man slaps on his $20 or so in monthly taxes and surcharges, it may not seem quite so cheap. If you're already paying for broadband, you can get around the gummint by signing up with a company like **Vonage** (www.vonage.com). Monthly rates start low: $14.99 for basic (500 free minutes of local and long distance), up to $24.99 for all-you-can-yak. With taxes et al, the two plans are $17.48 and $27.78 respectively. There are start-up fees and the bugs aren't out of this system yet, but the audio quality is improving. Usually you can keep your existing number, too. The next broadband telecommunications

No-Pay Restrooms Open to the Public

For comprehensive information, you can take advantage of the efforts of people with way too much time on their hands by logging on to www.thebathroomdiaries.com or www.addyourown.com and browsing the lists of public facilities.

Many city parks have comfort stations, though they're usually not the cleanest. **Bryant Park** is an exception, with neat facilities in the northeast corner of the park along 42nd, between Fifth and Sixth avenues.

Transit hubs are good bets. The downstairs **Dining Concourse at Grand Central** recently added a second set of facilities on the west end. Until everyone else figures it out, they're not nearly as crowded. **Penn Station** has public restrooms on the Main Concourse near the ticket windows. **Port Authority** is not nearly as scary as it used to be, and there are bathrooms all over the terminal. The main restrooms, on the Main Concourse of the South Wing and on the second floor between the North Wing and the South Wing, are clean enough and heavily trafficked by commuters.

Bookstores with cafes are almost always equipped with public restrooms. **Barnes & Noble** and **Borders** are good examples, with locations across the city. Other merchants worth noting are department stores and retailers like **Old Navy, Kmart,** and **Bed, Bath & Beyond.** Large, heavily trafficked tourist hotels are also great options. Times Square is a particularly unfriendly area for bathrooms, but the **New York Mariott Marquis** (1535 Broadway, at 46th St.) has nice facilities in its eighth-floor lobby.

wave is to turn your PC into a phone. **Skype** (www.skype.com) will let you talk free with other Skype users worldwide. You'll need a mic and headphones, but those are cheap enough, and the program downloads quickly. **Yahoo!** is another entrant into this field. Their rates start at nothing (PC to PC via Yahoo! Messenger), and vary widely for PC to phone. Long-distance starts around 1 or 2¢ per minute. Sixty cents per minute will let you catch up with your college buddies in Antarctica. Check www.voice.yahoo.com for the latest offer. If you're only interested in long-distance savings by traditional means, compare rates online at **www.lowermybills.com**. (The site also offers rate comparisons on everything from cellphones to insurance to mortgages.) When you're out on the street, **Popa Media** has the best deal around—free! They have some 50 pay phones scattered around the city, mostly in Brooklyn and the Bronx for now. You can pick up and dial anywhere in the country. In exchange, the company gets you to eye a billboard. The advertiser has an express dial code built into the phone, should you be inspired to want more information. If you're out on the Lower East Side with a juiceless cell, try the free phone at the **Municipal Parking Garage,** 107 Essex Street just below Rivington Street.

INDEX

Pick your Big Apple getaway guide.

You can do it all—or do nothing at all—in and around New York City with Frommer's guides. From car-free escapes to dirt-cheap adventures, Frommer's makes the going easy, with the best hotels, restaurants and attractions, plus exact prices, detailed maps, and more.

Don't miss these other New York City guides:

Frommer's New York City Free and Dirt Cheap
Frommer's Memorable Walks in New York

The best trips start here. ***Frommer's***

Available wherever books are sold. A Branded Imprint of ⊕**WILEY**
Now you know.

Frommer's Complete Guides

For those who value complete coverage, candid advice, and lots of choices in all price ranges.

Pauline Frommer's Guides

For those who want to experience a culture, meet locals, and save money along the way.

MTV Guides

For hip, youthful travelers who want a fresh perspective on today's hottest cities and destinations.

Day by Day Guides

For leisure or business travelers who want to organize their time to get the most out of a trip.

Frommer's With Kids Guides

For families traveling with children ages 2 to 14 seeking kid-friendly hotels, restaurants, and activities.

Unofficial Guides

For honeymooners, families, business travelers, and others who value no-nonsense, *Consumer Reports*–style advice.

For Dummies Travel Guides

For curious, independent travelers looking for a fun and easy way to plan a trip.

Visit Frommers.com

WILEY

Now you know.